ILLUSTRIOUS IMMIGRANTS

D1285668

E184
A1
F47
1971

ILLUSTRIOUS IMMIGRANTS

THE INTELLECTUAL MIGRATION FROM EUROPE
1930–41

Second Edition

LAURA FERMI

THE UNIVERSITY OF CHICAGO PRESS
CHICAGO & LONDON

SEP 1 8 1975

189273

⫸⫸⫸⫸⫸⫸⫸⫸⫸⫸⫸⫸⫸⫸⫸⫸⫸⫸⫸⫸⫸⫸⫸⫸⫸⫸

ISBN: 0-226-24376-1 (cloth); 0-226-24378-8 (paper)
Library of Congress Catalog Card Number: 67-25512

THE UNIVERSITY OF CHICAGO PRESS, CHICAGO 60637
THE UNIVERSITY OF CHICAGO PRESS, LTD., LONDON

© 1968, 1971 by the University of Chicago.
All rights reserved. Published 1968.
Revised edition 1971
Printed in the United States of America

⫸⫸⫸⫸⫸⫸⫸⫸⫸⫸⫸⫸⫸⫸⫸⫸⫸⫸⫸⫸⫸⫸⫸⫸⫸⫸

Photo Credits: Marc Chagall, from James Johnson Sweeney, *Marc Chagall* (New York: Museum of Modern Art, 1946); Franz Alexander (Harris & Ewing photo), Pierre Monteux (Weldon H. Wisler photo), Béla Bartók, Konrad Heiden (Arnold R. Morrison photo), Rudolf Flesch (Annie M. Graf photo), Thomas, Katja, and Erika Mann (Acme photo), all courtesy *Chicago Tribune*; Bruno Bettelheim, courtesy Office of Public Relations, University of Chicago; Max Delbrück, Leo Szilard and A. D. Hershey (photo by Dr. Karl Maramorosch), from *Phage and the Origins of Molecular Biology*, ed. John Cairns, Gunther S. Stent, and James D. Watson (Long Island, N.Y.: Cold Spring Harbor Laboratory of Quantitative Biology, 1966); George Szell, Marcel Duchamp, Igor Stravinsky, Hans Morgenthau, Albert Einstein, all from Brown Brothers; Rudolph Carnap and Max Rheinstein, courtesy Special Collections, Harper Library, University of Chicago; Rudolf and Irene Serkin, John Von Neumann, and Jacques Lipchitz, all from Wide World; Alvin Johnson, Felix and Helene Deutsch, Stan Ulam, Hannah Arendt, Maria Goeppert Mayer, George Gamow and Wolfgang Pauli, Felix Bloch, Enrico Fermi and Emilio Segrè, all supplied by Laura Fermi.

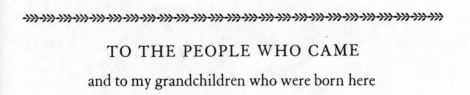

TO THE PEOPLE WHO CAME

and to my grandchildren who were born here

PREFATORY NOTE

The suggestion that I make a study of the cultural migration from Europe prior to World War II came from Anders Richter, now Director of the Smithsonian Press. Without his initial enthusiasm the book would not have been written. We believed it would be an easy book to write and at most might take one year; instead, it required over four years of work and the co-operation of a great number of persons. Members of the migration reminisced for my sake on their experiences in Europe and the United States and provided me with source material. American and European-born experts were generous of advice for the survey sections. Friends in specialized fields read parts of the manuscript and gave me the benefit of their criticism.

The names of some of the people who assisted me appear in the course of the narrative and those of others in the reference notes at the end of the book, but there are so many to whom I am indebted that I cannot mention them all. To each I express my deep gratitude. I owe special thanks to Drs. Hans Staudinger, Stanislaw M. Ulam, Gerhart and Maria Piers, Eugene P. Wigner, Hans A. Bethe, and Edward E. Lowinsky, who were all part of the wave of immigrating intellectuals; to George H. Pollock, M.D., Director of Research of the Chicago Institute for Psychoanalysis; to Mrs. Frances Stutzman of the Public Relations Office and to the staff of Harper Memorial Library of the University of Chicago. I am very grateful to Mrs. Morton Grodzins and Mrs. Hajo Holborn for reading the manuscript and suggesting improvements, and to Mrs. Gregor Wentzel, Mrs. Hans Morgenthau, and Miss Margaret Harris for their assistance at various stages of my work.

September, 1967   LAURA FERMI

NOTE TO THE SECOND EDITION

The publication of this book in 1968 aroused sufficient interest among illustrious immigrants and other persons to induce them to suggest corrections and to express their criticism. Criticism and suggestions did not affect the basic study, its premises and statistics, or the main conclusions drawn from it. Hence, this second, revised, edition is possibly more accurate than the first, more up to date where timed information is concerned, and, here and there, not as overly detailed. But fundamentally it is unchanged. In the three years since completion of the original work additional names of intellectual immigrants have come to my attention, but in percentage the number is too small to alter substantially the statistics and call for a complete recount. The study is still based on my original file of approximately 1,900 names.

Once more I am indebted to many persons for their advice and comments. Drs. Peter Gay, Karl Menger, Philipp Schwartz, and Alice K. Smith have been among the most helpful.

The card file of the immigrants and correspondence concerning them are deposited in the archives of the University of Chicago.

October, 1970

CONTENTS

LIST OF PLATES xii

⋙ PART I—ARRIVAL ⋘

I. The Great Wave 3

WHO WERE THE INTELLECTUAL IMMIGRANTS?   4
HOW MANY?   11
SOME DIFFICULTIES   13

II. The American Background 18

THE NATIONAL ORIGIN ACT   18
THE INTELLECTUAL AND THE LAW   25
THE INTELLECTUAL AND THE DEPRESSION   27

III. The Intellectual in His European Habitat 32

THE GOLDEN AGE OF SECURITY   32
THE END OF THE GOLDEN AGE   35
UNIVERSITIES AND CAFÉS   37
THE RISE OF THE DICTATORS   39
THE DICTATOR AND THE INTELLIGENTSIA   40
THE MYSTERY OF HUNGARIAN TALENT   53

IV. The Roads to America 60

SOME EUROPEAN ASSISTANCE AGENCIES   62
A SINGULAR HAVEN: TURKEY   66
THE LEAGUE OF NATIONS   71
ASSISTANCE IN THE UNITED STATES   71
THE INSTITUTE FOR ADVANCED STUDY   73
THE UNIVERSITY IN EXILE   74
THE EMERGENCY COMMITTEE IN AID
  OF FOREIGN DISPLACED SCHOLARS   76
ASSISTANCE TO PROFESSIONAL
  INTELLECTUALS   78
THE PERSONAL FACTOR   82
AFTER THE FALL OF FRANCE   84

CONTENTS

V. In America 93

DISTRIBUTION IN TIME   93
GEOGRAPHICAL DISTRIBUTION   95
GERMANS   99
AUSTRIANS   105
HUNGARIANS   111
ITALIANS   116
THE FRENCH   123
RUSSIANS   125
OTHER NATIONALITIES   129

⋙ PART II—ACHIEVEMENT ⋘

VI. European Psychoanalysts on the American Scene 139

PSYCHOANALYSIS TODAY   139
HISTORICAL PERSPECTIVES   141
PSYCHOANALYTIC ROADS TO AMERICA   145
THE BEGINNING OF THE WAVE   151
MORE ARRIVALS   156
MORE TRAINING CENTERS — MORE
 PSYCHOANALYSTS   159
CONTROVERSY   161
CONTRIBUTIONS   164
PSYCHOANALYSIS AND THE MELTING POT   172

VII. European-born Atomic Scientists 174

EARLY ARRIVALS   175
THEORETICAL MEETINGS IN WASHINGTON   181
SCIENCE AND GOVERNMENT   182
COLLABORATION AND CONFIDENCE   185
AFTER PEARL HARBOR   189
ARMY, INDUSTRY, AND EUROPEAN SCIENTISTS   191
PRODUCTION   194
A SECOND ROUND OF POLITICAL ACTIVITIES   198
THE DECISION TO USE THE BOMB   202
AFTER THE WAR   203
THE HYDROGEN BOMB   206
IN THE GOVERNMENT'S SERVICE   210
ATOMIC SCIENCE IN A LAND OF OPPORTUNITY   213

VIII. In the World of Art 215

MUSICIANS   215
CONDUCTORS   217

CONTENTS

COMPOSERS   221
INSTRUMENTALISTS   226
MUSICOLOGISTS   228
ARTISTS   233
ARCHITECTS AND DESIGNERS   233
PAINTERS AND SCULPTORS   241
ART HISTORIANS   247

IX. In the World of Books and Magazines   254

WRITERS   254
PUBLISHERS   270

X. More Natural Scientists   283

MATHEMATICIANS   283
ASTRONOMERS   295
IN THE FIELD OF MEDICINE   299
IN THE FIELD OF MOLECULAR BIOLOGY   308

XI. Social Scientists and Other Scholars   316

IN PSYCHOLOGICAL WARFARE   316
ECONOMISTS   320
SOCIOLOGISTS   331
POLITICAL SCIENTISTS   337
TEACHERS OF LAW   345
HISTORIANS   346
ORIENTALISTS   352
PHILOSOPHERS   357

XII. Notes Toward an Evaluation   365

YOUNGER EUROPEAN-BORN INTELLECTUALS   365
THE WIVES OF INTELLECTUALS   367
BRITISH INFLUENCE   368
EUROPEAN DEPLETION   370
EUROPEAN-BORN INTELLECTUALS
  AS TEACHERS   373
NEW INTERNATIONAL CULTURAL RELATIONS   376
RE-EMIGRATION   377
ANOTHER WAVE?   383
ONLY IN AMERICA   386

REFERENCE NOTES   389

INDEX OF PERSONS   407

PLATES

following page 148

Marc Chagall   Franz Alexander

Konrad Heiden   Pierre Monteux

Bruno Bettelheim   Rudolf Flesch

Béla Bartók

Stan Ulam   Maria Goeppert Mayer

Hannah Arendt   Felix and Helene Deutsch

George Gamow and Wolfgang Pauli   Felix Bloch

Max Delbrück   Leo Szilard and A. D. Hershey

Alvin Johnson

Rudolph Carnap   George Szell

Max Rheinstein   Marcel Duchamp

Albert Einstein

Hans Morgenthau   Igor Stravinsky

Paul Tillich   Thomas, Erika, and Katja Mann

Rudolf and Irene Serkin   Enrico Fermi and Emilio Segrè

Jacques Lipchitz   John Von Neumann

PART I
ARRIVAL

I

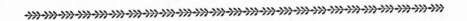

The Great Wave

America has always been peopled by immigrants, and among them have always been some intellectuals, men and women educated abroad, who enriched our culture with products of their own. But the wave of intellectuals from continental Europe arriving in the thirties and early forties, driven here by the forces of intolerance and oppression, was so large and of such high quality that it constituted a new phenomenon in the history of immigration. Thousands of Europeans scattered over our country, bringing with them their baggage of general and specialized knowledge, their traditions, and their personal abilities. They settled in large cities and small college towns, toured from coast to coast to give concerts and dramatic performances, exhibited their art in local shows, and sold the products of their pens in bookstores everywhere as they entered our cultural life.

Here it is my purpose to examine this wave, the circumstances under which it came and was received, and its performance in this country. The question of intellectual imports is still a lively one, and often debated. The migration of scientists has been called a world-wide phenomenon and problem. Figures have been published that indicate the financial loss to countries from which fully educated persons flee and the gain to countries where they settle. One estimate places the cost of a top education in the United States, from grade school through college and graduate school, as high as $45,000. The implication is that for each immigrant already educated before arriving on our shores the United States saves $45,000 (and now this figure should be adjusted upward, in line with higher costs). But the saving in education costs is only one of the many aspects of an intellectual immigration. A look into the great cultural wave of the thirties may reveal facts that are equally relevant today.

3

WHO WERE THE INTELLECTUAL IMMIGRANTS?

There is no single satisfactory definition of an intellectual, but I once heard an Arizona hotelkeeper refer to professors as "men who wouldn't be able to make a living if they didn't find someone willing to pay them for talking." Extended to include those who are paid, at least occasionally, for painting, writing, or producing music, this definition would be quite acceptable if it did not risk offense to those intellectuals who take pride in their manual abilities. Although Einstein's membership in the plumbers' union was not offered him because of his proficiency in the trade, others certainly would have been capable of making a living even by Arizonian standards. Enrico Fermi, for one, was once offered a job by a gas station operator somewhere in the Middle West after the two had worked together on Fermi's car; and he was flattered at the offer.

By intellectual immigrants I mean the men and women who came to America fully made, so to speak, with their Ph.D.'s or diplomas from art academies or music conservatories in their pockets, and who continued to engage in intellectual pursuits in this country. Their numbers and the high stature of many of them make them a unique phenomenon. Perhaps the only previous wave that may be comparable in the least was that of the Forty-eighters, the refugees of the revolutions and political upheaval that swept most of Europe in 1848. By far the largest and most influential group was the German. Among them were highly cultivated men and women who founded and ran schools, newspapers, and singing societies, but their immediate impact was felt more in American politics than in the learned fields. Many of the most prominent Forty-eighters were delegates to the 1860 Republican Convention which nominated Abraham Lincoln for the Presidency; and the best known of all, Carl Schurz, went on a 21,000-mile speaking tour to win the German vote for Lincoln. (Schurz later became a senator from Missouri and Secretary of State.) As a group, however, the Forty-eighters looked down on American culture and strove to remain German; the German language was used in their schools and newspapers; and they kept their own traditions, resisting assimilation. As a newspaper of the time put it, they came to Germanize America rather than to be Americanized. Their main cultural contribution to the United States was indirect; by founding singing societies they introduced music in many small communities where in those days long before radio and television

4

little music was heard; and thus they promoted music appreciation, the growth of taste, and a beginning to musical education.

The intellectual immigrants of the thirties were different from their predecessors, not only because of the greater concentration in their ranks of intellectual talent, artistic, scholarly, or scientific. They also became Americanized at a much faster pace than any previous group of immigrants. It is true that in the early period of adjustment they may have said too often *bei uns* or whatever was said in languages other than German to express the conviction that things were better in the old country and young America had much to learn. They may have insisted too long on wearing strangely tailed shirts or on staying away from cafeterias after a sad first trial. Their criticism of the schools their children attended may have been too precipitate, too harsh, and their opinions of the absurdities of English spelling too emphatically expressed. Undoubtedly a few evinced what Robert Maynard Hutchins called "refugee psychology"; after receiving in depression times appointments meant to save them from starvation they demanded "permanent tenure and a top salary." But as a group they set a remarkable record. They strove actively to become part of the American cultural scene; they sought and obtained American citizenship within a short time of arrival, often as soon as the law permitted; and they learned the English language so rapidly and through such a conscious process that hardly had they set foot on American soil than they were boasting to American friends of their skill in spelling. They recognized American qualities and imitated them, seeking to combine the best features of cultures old and new. European wives took eagerly to American roasts without giving up their favorite recipes for Hungarian goulash and Italian scaloppine. Teachers of physics, who deemed American students strong in solving problems but weak on theory, adjusted their courses to raise theoretical standards without lowering the practical.

I see two main reasons for this unpredecented speed of acclimation. On the one hand, the very traits and education that had shaped the intellectuals rendered them curious about their new environment and prepared them to explore it with open eyes. On the other, the sharp political, racial, and religious issues before World War II pushed them in a single direction: only America offered the possibility of rebuilding one's existence according to one's moral principles and convictions and of continuing work begun at home. America meant a clean break with the past and a hopeful future.

5

Because it gave a better perspective of the events in Europe than could be obtained where they took place, America, once reached, was a point of no return. Awareness of all this and gratitude to the country that offered asylum accelerated the process of Americanization among intellectuals from continental Europe.

The relatively few individuals who reacted antagonistically to the American environment, made no efforts to learn the language, or held that their mission in the United States was to preserve their own culture while converting Americans to its cult, created difficulties on the campus or in the communities in which they lived. There were often extenuating circumstances. As the early thirties turned into the middle and late thirties and then into the early forties, a larger proportion of the European intellectuals arriving in America were political refugees who had fled their countries under extreme duress. Most had left behind members of their families, either parents or children, and knew that for a long time they might be separated. Many came without money or other belongings, although at home they had been accustomed to every comfort. Under fascism, for instance, fifty dollars was all the money a person could take out of Italy, and at the peak of restrictions the Nazis allowed even less. Often there had been no possibility of arranging for the shipping of furnishings or clothing. A large number of refugees had been chased from country to country. The timetable of an intellectual's past may have been something like this: Germany until 1933, then Austria or Czechoslovakia (no change of language), or Italy (no anti-Semitism until the middle of 1938). After the *Anschluss* and Mussolini's sudden racial policies, the intellectuals fled to any European country that would let them in, even to Poland, still hoping against hope for the return of normal conditions. France was their last haven. But there they may have encountered a French concentration camp, and finally flight, after the German invasion. These were the lucky ones, for others were captured and exterminated by the Nazis.

Occasionally, the tensions under which the refugees lived involved them in humorous episodes. The Hungarian artist László Moholy-Nagy left Hungary in 1921 and settled in Germany where he taught for several years at the Bauhaus, the famous school of arts. When Hitler rose to power, Moholy-Nagy fled to England with his family. In June, 1937, the Association of

Arts and Industries of Chicago invited him to direct a new school similar to the Bauhaus. The cable read in part: MARSHALL FIELD OFFERS MANSION PRAIRIE AVENUE. STABLES TO BE CONVERTED INTO WORKSHOPS. Since at the time the cable arrived Moholy-Nagy was on a visit to Paris, his wife Sibyl dutifully forwarded the cable and with it sent one of her own urging him to decline. The reason? GERMAN EXAMPLE SHOWS FASCIST RESULTS WHEN FIELD MARSHALS TAKE OVER EDUCATION. STABLES AND PRAIRIE SOUND JUST LIKE IT. Unfortunately, amusing and soon corrected misunderstandings were rare.

A considerable number of refugees encountered great difficulties upon arrival. The strain and stress under which they had lived, the abrupt loss of home and family, and the exhausting adjustments to successive countries had undermined their physical and mental resistance. Many refugees had spent their entire time "inventing their lives," as one of them put it, and even after reaching America a few were faced with the problem of continuing to invent their lives. Tragedies were to be expected. In 1939 the German writer Ernst Toller was found hanging by a bathrobe cord in his hotel room in Manhattan. It is not clear what had driven him to suicide. He was a leftist, a rebel molded by the Nazi revolution, a fugitive from it, and had been in Switzerland and France before coming to America three years before. His death took place after the first intimations of the pact between Germany and Russia, and he was worried about the trend of events in Europe. He was poor. Not much more is known that might shed light on his end. The suicides continued in the early years of the war: Karl Duncker, a founder of Gestalt psychology who came in the twenties, killed himself in 1940; biochemist Rudolf Schoenheimer in 1941; and writer Stefan Zweig in 1942 (in Brazil).

Béla Bartók died in a New York hospital in 1945, a poor man, proud and sensitive, not appreciated in this country and not appreciating it. When he came from Hungary to the United States in the fall of 1940, a group of his friends in this country arranged an appointment for him at Columbia University as visiting professor; he was given $3,000 a year for two years, with no teaching obligations, through the grant of the Alice M. Ditson Fund. In comparison, Fermi's full professorship at the same university started at $8,500 in 1939 and was increased to $9,000 the next year. But

Bartók himself was partly to blame, for he would not teach at Columbia and declined an invitation to teach composition at the Curtis Institute of Music. Concerts were scarce, criticism too often harsh; the knowledge that the Columbia appointment would not last long kept him under constant strain. ". . . . never in my life since I earn my livelihood," he wrote in a letter, "have I been in such a dreadful situation as I will be probably very soon." And, "I do not know how long I can endure the insecurity of this gypsy life." It was not for long. But before his death he was to depend upon charity and experience the pains of a slowly killing illness and a lack of public recognition that eased only in the last months of his life.

Although the majority of European intellectuals came to the United States for political reasons or to escape religious and racial persecution, a number of them emigrated from their countries for less drastic causes, perhaps in a spirit of adventure or on a quest for better opportunities. But even in these instances, changing political conditions in Europe often affected their non-political decisions or induced them to settle in America, if they had meant to stay only briefly and then return home.

Conductor Arturo Toscanini is a case in point. He had conducted frequently in the United States (his first appearance was in 1908), but his home was in Italy where he spent long, uninterrupted periods. In the spring of 1936 he said good-bye to the New York Philharmonic and went back to Italy, for good he asserted: he was sixty-eight years old and felt his age. Possibly he had not taken into account that as he was a violent anti-Fascist, life in Italy would not be as peaceful as he expected. He had been in serious trouble with fascism before. Stubborn and undaunted, he always refused to have the national anthem and the Fascist hymn "Giovinezza" played at his concerts, for purely artistic reasons, he maintained. Over this issue, in 1929, he resigned from La Scala. Two years later the powerful Fascists of Bologna decided to force the issue: they invited Toscanini to conduct two concerts and, unknown to him, planned a great Fascist celebration on the day of the first concert. Mussolini's son-in-law, Count Galeazzo Ciano, was to be in Bologna and would attend the concert. The maestro was told that because Ciano would be present he would have to play the anthem. Toscanini refused. When he reached the theater he was roughly assaulted and beaten, until his chauffeur managed to rescue him. (The anti-Fascist story still told in Italy is that he suffered a broken arm;

the official version at the time was that only one man, on his own initiative, slapped Toscanini's face.)

Back in Italy in 1936, Toscanini resumed his old habit of shouting invectives against the Fascist regime and the Duce himself in public places, disregarding the most elementary precautions for self-preservation. When he began receiving cables and transatlantic telephone calls from David Sarnoff of the National Broadcasting Company who wanted him to accept a contract, he flatly refused and appeared adamant. But then the music critic Samuel Chotzinoff arrived in Milan with Sarnoff's proposal that Toscanini become the conductor of a radio orchestra to be created especially for him; and Toscanini capitulated without much resistance. He arrived in New York in the late fall of 1937. Almost a year later he returned to Italy on a visit and got into more trouble with the Fascist government, which suspended his passport for a time. After this incident, he settled for good in New York and bought a home in Riverdale where he lived until his death in 1957.

Was Toscanini a political refugee or a man taking advantage of a particularly attractive offer? The financial proposition was excellent: the salary was large and there were additional benefits. "You . . . pay . . . income tass," Toscanini's wife had told Chotzinoff when the contract was signed, and Chotzinoff, dazed by his sucess in winning Toscanini to Sarnoff's cause, had answered "Yes" without realizing what was at stake. But Toscanini's love of Italy was deep and enduring; without the danger that his sharp criticism created for him and his friends he might have remained in Italy; without the war and the European catastrophe he might have returned once again.

Other examples showing that political and non-political motives are often interlocked can be drawn from that astounding group, the Hungarian intellectuals. Three came to the United States in 1930: the mathematician John Von Neumann, the only Hungarian of his generation to be recognized as a genius by his countrymen (at least by all with whom I spoke): Eugene Wigner, who was later awarded the Nobel Prize and is considered a colossus in theoretical physics, the living physicist in the sixties whose over-all performance has been the greatest; and the psychoanalyst Franz Alexander, the one individual from abroad to whom American psychoanalysis owes the most. None of the three was under political pressure when he decided to come here. They were all living in Berlin, where Alexander was teaching and practicing psychoanalysis at the Psychoanalytic Institute and where Von Neumann and Wigner were docents at the university and the Technische Hochschule respectively.

They had different reasons for coming. Alexander had been in New York for an international congress of psychiatry and believed that in America there was a better climate for the growth of psychoanalysis than in Europe. Von Neumann and Wigner each received an invitation to spend six months at Princeton University. Von Neumann accepted because he had made some calculations about his chances of a career in Germany, the number of openings at German universities in the next few years and the number of docents aspiring to positions, and had come to the conclusion that he would do better elsewhere. Wigner, to whom the telegram from Princeton came out of the blue, decided to take this opportunity because he had always felt that America was "a country on paper" — on the maps only — and wanted to see if it really existed.

If their motives for coming to this country were non-political, their decision to leave home had been determined mainly by the political conditions prevailing in Hungary. Franz Alexander left Hungary after the rise to power in 1919 of the Béla Kun regime, which persecuted members of the intelligentsia and had discharged Alexander's father from his academic position. Wigner and Von Neumann left a few years later, when under the Fascist rule of Admiral Nicholas Horthy it became "unpleasant," as Wigner put it, to live in Hungary if one were either fully or partly Jewish. In Wigner's case the "unpleasantness" reached its apex when he was beaten by three university students. "But not badly, not badly at all," Wigner hastened to add — he is unmatched in understating.

Once in the United States, Alexander became so involved in activities to promote the expansion and organization of American psychoanalysis that I doubt he ever thought of going back to Europe. But Von Neumann and Wigner at first had only part-time positions. In fact, for five years after his arrival Wigner commuted between Berlin and Princeton. If the conditions had been different and the Nazis had not come to power, one or both of them might have settled eventually in Germany.

There is no need to stress the difficulty of separating political and non-political motives. What must be borne in mind is that the great majority of the intellectuals in the cultural wave of the thirties and early forties were

10

either driven to our shores by political forces or influenced in the decision to remain in America by worsening political conditions in Europe.

HOW MANY?

In trying to evaluate the size of the cultural migration, as in many questions about it, I was greatly aided by the book *Refugees in America*, by Maurice Davie, published in 1947. It is the report of a committee of which Davie was the director, appointed in 1944 to study "the recent immigration from Europe." The committee chose to consider the period between 1933 and 1944, and within this period the book is a mine of invaluable information. Interpreting data furnished by the United States Immigration and Naturalization Service, Davie and his committee grouped the immigrants by the occupations in which they had engaged in Europe. The estimated number of those who had been in professional occupations including teaching was 25,535 according to one method of computation and 22,842 according to another.

These are huge figures; and if similar ones were available for the period from 1930 to 1941, which is the range of my study, they would be even larger: the cultural migration was lively in the years 1930–32, not considered by Davie, and very slow after Pearl Harbor. (After 1941 it was limited mostly to persons who were already on their way to America, awaiting visas or transportation in Portugal, Africa, South America, Cuba, Mexico, and elsewhere.) It would be a mistake to believe, however, that the cultural wave was as large as even the smaller of Davie's two figures may seem to indicate, because many who had been professionals in Europe would not qualify if measured by my definition of an intellectual. First, there were those who in this country were not able to remain within the professions and were obliged to seek work outside them. Davie studied a sample group of men and women who had been in the professions in Europe and found that at the time of his study 66.9 per cent of the men and 51.7 per cent of the women were still, or again, in professional occupations. Even so, if the sample studied by Davie was representative — and I know no reason to believe it was not — the group of those who remained in the professions was huge: some 15,000 to 17,000. If all these professionals had been intellectuals, these figures would indicate the approximate size of the cultural wave (assuming that the immigration in the period 1930–41 was not very

different in numbers and characteristics from that in the period 1933–44).
But they were not. In such a group there were surely persons "endowed
with intellect to a high degree; fond of and given to learning and thinking,"
as Webster demands of intellectuals, and also some who were not. So the
above figures must be cut down further — to what extent, I frankly do not
know.

Davie, concerned mostly with statistics, published only a few, limited lists
of names, far from sufficient to form a picture of the cultural wave. So
for my study I compiled a file, adhering as closely as feasible to certain
rules of my own. It includes the names of men and women who had been
in intellectual pursuits abroad and continued to engage in intellectual pursuits in this country. It includes also a group of younger people who became
"intellectuals" only after their arrival here. They had not yet entered a career
or were at the beginning of a career when they left Europe, although they
had received a degree from a European institution of higher education: the
equivalent of an M.A., for instance, though not necessarily a Ph.D.; or the
equivalent of an M.D., though not necessarily followed by internship abroad.
I excluded younger people, feeling that they would bring a mixed outlook to
their work, a still European outlook in many cases, but much tempered by
American schooling and early exposure to the forces of the melting pot.
Since teaching is an intellectual pursuit almost by definition, I entered in my
file, without further screening, the names of university and college professors
who filled other requirements. Of the physicians, architects, and other professionals I chose those who brought new understanding or theoretical contributions to their disciplines. Similarly, I tried to select artists who influenced public taste to a great degree, and taught, lectured, or wrote extensively; but
I have not included dancers, singers, or actors who have only practiced their
art, nor have I considered writers who did not publish in English.

I started with the selected lists of refugees published by Davie, and entered
in my file twelve who had received the Nobel Prize before Davie's study;*
ninety-five of the 103 listed in *Who's Who in America* of 1944–45 (the other
eight I did not consider intellectuals); 197 of the 220 listed in the 1944 edition of *American Men of Science* (the other twenty-three were listed also in
Who's Who); and several dozen more who are mentioned throughout Davie's

* By 1969 the total number of Nobel laureates in the wave had risen to twenty-
four.

12

book because they are outstanding in their fields. I gathered additional names from books and articles about immigrants, autobiographical accounts, from friends, and from my own memory; but I entered only the names of persons about whom I found sufficient biographical data to be certain they should be included in the wave of European intellectuals. I felt that the number of those listed in *Who's Who* as early as 1944–45 was not an indication of the distinction of the intellectual wave, and I examined all sketches in the 1954–55 edition and found that in the intervening ten years the list had grown from the original 95 to over 400, despite several deaths and the return to Europe of a few more. (The list might have been longer had all the entrants given the year they came to the United States. Instead, many, especially the artists and musicians, neglected this information, and occasionally I was not able to establish whether a foreign-born notable had come to this country with the wave.) By these means, by consulting other editions of *Who's Who* and several biographical reference works, I compiled a list of about 1,900 names. This figure, I must stress, is not an estimate of the size of the intellectual wave, but the measure of the group I was able to study, which is much smaller and selected for the achievement of its components. The great majority are listed in current or past issues of biographical directories, a fact which, on the whole, is an indication of achievement (though not a few were not listed because they did not answer questionnaires).

SOME DIFFICULTIES

The more detailed a file, the better working tool it is and the sounder are the generalizations that may be drawn from it. But it is not easy to obtain minute and accurate information of the whereabouts and doings of such a large number of men and women who participated in a historical event that ended twenty-five years ago and who have dispersed in a country as large as the United States. Among the many difficulties I encountered not the least was that of determining the nationalities of the foreign-born. The map of Europe changed drastically in the intellectuals' lifetime, and most but not all accepted the political boundaries between the two wars when declaring their country of birth. Several intellectuals, for instance, claim Lwów, Poland, as their birthplace, and others claim Lemberg, Austria, but in fact there is only one city which has changed hands and name more than once and is called Lwiw in Ukranian. National pride often contributes to the confusion: there is the case of the scientist listed as a Czechoslovakian in *American Men of Science* but claimed as a countryman by my Hungarian friends because he was born in a part of old Hungary that the Versailles treaty assigned to Czechoslovakia. Once a Hungarian, always a Hungarian? But the equivalent truism does not always hold for other nationalities. Hungarian-born physicists and mathematicians are considered Hungarians by their colleagues even if they studied in Germany; but Polish-born mathematicians who spent time in France are regarded as French. In filing the names of intellectuals by nationality I took into consideration the place of birth rather than the country of longest residence, but in other contexts I occasionally deviated from this rule.

Establishing the year in which a European came to the United States presented even greater difficulties. Of the many biographical directories which I had occasion to examine, *Who's Who in America* gives this information with moderate consistency. But in talking with some of those listed in *Who's Who,* I discovered that they interpreted variously the phrase "came to the United States"; some indicated the year of their first visit (though at the time they might not have intended to stay), while others chose to state the year they came with an immigration visa. Other biographical directories do not indicate the year of arrival, but since they itemize professional careers, it is not difficult to deduce the year provided the biographee went directly from a position in Europe to a position here. In many cases, however, the intellectuals were forced to bide their time after losing positions under dictator's laws. They had to wait years for American visas, and once in America they had to engage in menial jobs, run elevators, help in factories, wash dishes, pack groceries, sell merchandise — or do all of these in succession. Understandably, in their biographical sketches they sometimes neglect to include these years of tribulation. Not infrequently, a man "disappears" from his last European position in the early thirties and reappears in this country many years later. Clearly he belongs to the intellectual wave, but unless more precise data about him are found, it is not possible to say just when he arrived in the United States. Of some it is not even possible to tell whether they belong to the wave at all, as in the case of the Russian who disappeared in Constantinople in 1922 and made his recorded entry as a scholar in the United States in 1932.

14

One of my failures was to find a term descriptive of the men and women in the wave. "Immigrant" denotes intention to settle in the country of immigration, but a minority in my file never intended to settle here for good. Yet they belong to the wave and cannot be excluded without risking a distortion of its character. I have in mind men such as Niels Bohr, who was in this country only a few years during the war and yet was tremendously important to the development of atomic energy and policies governing it. Or the former European statesmen who while living here influenced our plans for the reconstruction of Europe and prepared the reopening of postwar relations; and the many who added prestige to our culture by their temporary presence or assumed the important task of explaining America to their countrymen once they were back in Europe.

Maurice Davie was conscious of the problem, and wrote about "the refugee movement," thus avoiding the over-frequent use of the word "immigrant." But, as I've pointed out, not all in the cultural wave were refugees, and those who were resent the term if it is applied to themselves. The "most refugee" among my friends (if I am allowed this solecism) claimed that they left their homes of their own free will. And this is true. People were not forcibly expelled from their homelands, they were not pushed over national borders. There were always alternatives to emigration — though they might have meant imprisonment, suffering, torture, and death. The word "refugee" is out; "exile" and "expatriate" do not apply to those who intended to become American citizens; and "émigré" is awkward, though "émigré scholar" is used in scholarly books. The intellectual wave has been called "the cultural migration," and I have also done so, but "migrant" is not used in this context. There is, in conclusion, no single word descriptive of a group whose motivations and intentions were as varied as those of the European-born intellectuals who came here. Accordingly, I shall avail myself of the existing terms, selecting in each instance the most appropriate to the persons under consideration.

I avoided the difficulty of determining the incidence of religions or races in the wave by ignoring these categories. While the wave was in progress much was made of the fact that many in it were Jews, and fears were expressed that the Jews might flood America. The thirties and early forties were a time of peak racial awareness everywhere. If under European dictatorships the Jews were persecuted, in democratic America they were subjected to

15

a much subtler form of anti-Semitism, a form which can be summed up in the word "restricted." European Jews did not know this word and learned it with great shock. In Europe their lives had been in danger; America threatened their self-respect. In most European countries the blame for the excesses against the Jews could be put on a few. In America the majority was responsible, though for a much lesser sin.

The Jewish question was poignant when Davie wrote his book, and he discussed at some length the proportion of Jews among the refugees. He stated that if the immigration statistics of "Hebrews" were taken as a measurement of the number of Jews, these would compromise 33.6 per cent of the total immigration from all countries in the years 1933–44; 44.9 per cent of the total immigration from all European countries; and from 51.5 to 67.6 per cent of the estimated number of refugees. Among the intellectuals the proportion of Jews may have been slightly higher than in other groups. On the other hand, many refugees were Christians and came as a consequence of their political or ethical views, not because of race or religion — notable among them were Paul Tillich and Thomas Mann.

The building of a file was only one part of my study. I spent much time also writing letters and interviewing people in an effort to gather information about the wave from the European-born themselves and those who had been in close association with them. If I do not devote much space to this, it is because my task was made easy by the prompt and ready responses I received. One remark of an American-born friend was especially useful. When I mentioned the subject of this study, she asked: "Isn't there the danger of overdoing it?" I kept her question constantly in mind, for the danger is real.

Undoubtedly the Europeans made important contributions to American culture, but a good part of the credit for their achievements goes to America's willingness to accept and ability to assimilate foreign elements, and her generosity in offering opportunities to anyone, wherever born and speaking with whatever accent, provided he is prepared to take intelligent, unselfish advantage of them. The foreign-born themselves are astounded at how much they accomplished, and they are the first to assert that they would not have accomplished as much had they remained in their homelands. The cross-fertilization of ideas from different cultures and the mixing of backgrounds in such a rich, stimulating climate made possible the miracle.

16

The beginning and the end of the wave are not well defined in time. There is no day or year before which no European intellectuals came to America or after which they stopped arriving. Considering that the migration was, on the whole, due to the advent of European dictatorships, the choice of Pearl Harbor as the closing date appears logical; in the years when America was at war direct immigration from Europe was virtually impossible — only a trickle of persons who were already on the way managed to reach the United States — and after the war, conditions in Europe changed drastically, affecting also the character of later immigration.

The choice of 1930 as the beginning of the wave may be questioned and requires some comment. It might have been more logical to consider the whole period between the two wars, since it is a well-defined historical period characterized by unrest in most European countries and, from its very beginning, by the rise of dictators. But the intellectual immigration in the United States was slow in the twenties, when the early exiles could find asylum in almost any European country. The rise to power of Hitler in 1933 was also a possible starting date, and it was chosen by others, as by Davie for his *Refugees in America*. But that event, however dramatic, was not the first to encourage emigration. In Germany itself, it was in 1930 that the Nazis made their extraordinary gains in Parliament, from 12 to 107 seats, and in electoral votes, which increased 800 per cent. At any rate, the European scene was not the only factor in my choice. One reason for placing the beginning of the wave in 1930 is that in the two areas in which the impact of the Europeans was most felt, atomic science and psychoanalysis, the key men began arriving about 1930 and worked together with those who came later, in close collaboration and toward the same ends. In examining the final outcome of their presence in these fields, it would be extremely difficult and illogical to separate the participation of some from that of the rest. But the main reason for choosing 1930 is an event of great historical significance in this country: the slamming of the gates to mass immigration, which formally took place on July 1, 1929, when the National Origin provision of the Immigration Act of 1924 went into effect. Its consequences began to be felt in the months that followed, that is, at the beginning of 1930.

17

II

The American Background

The Europeans who were fully grown, as I was, when they came to the United States did not learn of the laws regulating immigration in history courses or in collections of American documents. They became aware — often painfully — of the provisions affecting them while going through the laborious process of getting visas and while sharing their anxieties with other prospective immigrants in consular offices abroad. Personal experience was a good teacher, and they learned their lesson well. Even before leaving Europe they were more familiar than most Americans with the machinery of the quota system and with the *4d* provision that saved the lives of a good number of scholars. After arrival in this country, they became better versed than the average citizen in all rules, regulations, and exceptions in matters of naturalization. But in general they had no idea of how and why America had sought to close the gates to immigration and had made it so difficult for foreigners to reach these shores.

THE NATIONAL ORIGIN ACT

Until World War I the United States had opened its gates to mass immigration — or so it was thought. In reality, though the gates were much too widely open to suit the taste of the restrictionists, not everyone was allowed to enter. Federal laws enacted at various times between 1882 and 1907 kept out the Chinese and a host of individuals, including professional beggars, polygamists, prostitutes, the mentally defective (labeled as idiots, imbeciles or the insane in different laws), persons suffering from loathsome and contagious diseases (of which tuberculosis was singled out in the most recent law), epileptics, persons who had committed crimes involving moral turpi-

18

tude, and those who believed in the violent overthrow of governments or in the assassination of public officials. This last provision, the so-called "anarchist clause," was an outcome of President McKinley's assassination. In addition to these legislative exclusions, the "gentlemen's agreement" of 1907 with Japan kept at home the bulk of would-be immigrants from that country.

Insofar as Europe was concerned, the little control on immigration that the law exerted before World War I acted through individual selection rather than by group discrimination. It so happened that the federal government sanctioned the early restrictions at about the time the Statue of Liberty was being erected, and Americans, who were to become proud of the symbolic significance of the statue, took no heed of the immigration laws and went on asserting and believing that their country offered asylum to all freedom-seekers. It is clear that "Orientals" were regarded as competitive labor to whom the freedom issue did not and never would apply.

In 1917, just as America was getting ready to enter the war, Congress passed an act that codified all previous legislation, considerably strengthened the anarchist clause, and added a few exclusions and the much debated "literacy test." The most striking of the newly added categories of aliens to be refused admittance was that of persons "of psychopathic constitutional inferiority," reflecting popular eugenic theories.

The literacy test, barring the admission of adults who could not read in some language, had a much greater import, not so much in its direct and immediate results as in the philosophy that it introduced into law. It was an ethnical or racial philosophy which had originated and evolved in the last two decades of the nineteenth century out of an aversion to the "new immigration," the Slavs, Italians, and Jews who were then pouring into America. They had the bad luck to arrive during the first revival of nativism after the Civil War, and upon them was pinned the hatred of the nativists.

The most stubborn attack came from a group of New England intellectuals who saw in the new immigration a threat to the purity of their Anglo-Saxon strain and to their privileged class. They spread the notion that the new immigration was intrinsically different from the old, inferior to it, and much more difficult to assimilate. (Intentionally or not they failed to take into consideration that the first immigrants had had a longer time in which to become Americanized.) As early as 1894, the New England group organized the Immigrant Restriction League, and at once the league initiated a campaign for the literacy test. Its avowed aim was to check the "illiterate and undesirable" new immigration without affecting the more acceptable immigration from northwestern Europe.

The battle for the literacy test was to last over twenty-three years. In the Senate it was led by the league's greatest ally, Henry Cabot Lodge. In 1907 Lodge was appointed one of nine members of the United States Immigration Commission, known also as the Dillingham Commission, which was to make an exhaustive study of the impact of immigration upon the nation. The findings of the commission were published in forty-one volumes in 1911, and though they were concerned in great part with economic questions, they were based on the assumption that there were, in fact, two types of immigration, that Anglo-Saxon "old comers" were hard-working pioneers who had made America what it had become, and more recent immigrants from southwestern Europe were opportunists seeking a share of American wealth but resisting the melting pot. Accordingly, the commission strongly recommended the literacy test as a means of restriction.

It is significant that only on the eve of America's entry in World War I, in the strained atmosphere of new fears and xenophobia, did the bill to introduce the literacy test in the law find sufficient support in Congress to pass over a presidential veto. The literacy test, though seemingly only a means to define an additional category of inadmissible individuals, introduced the principle that aliens being screened for admission to this country should be judged according to the ethnic or racial group to which they belonged. And it is not by chance that the literacy test and the exclusion of persons "of psychopathic constitutional inferiority" entered the law simultaneously. For some time eugenics and nativism had been allies; eugenic theories had been invoked by the New England restrictionists as scientific grounds for their claims when they first asserted that American racial purity was threatened by the new immigration.

The victory of the literacy test in 1917 proved of little practical value. Illiteracy was declining even among "undesirable" prospective immigrants, and the war in Europe had almost entirely stopped European immigration to the United States. Agitation for further restriction was stilled until the war was over, only to explode again with greater vigor and the new twists that it had acquired in the course of the war years.

Wartime patriotism, with its demand for total and unqualified loyalty and dedication, promoted the absurd concept of "100 per cent Americanism." Patriotic crusaders invaded minority neighborhoods to prompt the Americanization of the foreign-born — even among those who were already Americanized and participating in the war effort. The first acts of sabotage committed by German agents inevitably cast suspicion on the German-born and fed a campaign against "hyphenated Americans" whose loyalty was assumed to be divided. Theodore Roosevelt led the campaign and launched the slogan "America for Americans." By the time the war ended, America was thoroughly imbued with a new, patriotic nationalism, in the light of which the foreign-born constituted a danger and further admission of aliens seemed to many an unwarranted hazard.

Then the Red Scare began.

To learn that the United States too had been swept by the hysterical fear of bolshevism was a shock to me. I was a child when Italy was seized by the convulsions of the Red Scare, but I well remember the unrest, the demonstrations and strikes, the violence, the uneasiness of the middle classes, and in conclusion the rise of fascism. I grew up in the belief that these events were peculiar to Italy, that they were her own misfortune. Only later did I come to realize that most countries which had been involved in World War I had their Red Scare, that the same symptoms were to be seen everywhere, and that the only feature singular to Italy was the promptness of the reaction, the rapidity with which Mussolini attained power. (In fact, the reaction to communism came even sooner in Hungary, with the advent of Admiral Horthy's regency.)

But to most Europeans the America of 1919 and 1920 was the land of Wilson, and Wilson was the preacher of good-will and the rights of men. How could anything verging on the irrational take place in the United States? When, belatedly, I read of the American Red Scare, I wondered whether American democracy and institutions were the only reasons why totalitarianism had not followed, as it had in other countries. It occurred to me that there had been another safety valve: only in America was the number of foreign-born sufficiently large to pin on them a good part of the blame for the rise of bolshevism. Bolshevism, in other words, could be made to appear an entirely foreign import and no cause for civil strife.

Immigrants had been identified with radicalism for a long time, one reason being that many of the unskilled workers among them were members of the leftist labor union, the Industrial Workers of the World. The American Federation of Labor did not admit the unskilled in its fold and was a foe of the new immigration. In the decade between 1910 and 1920 the IWW was practically the only union open to unskilled immigrants, and it is likely that membership in it strengthened whatever leftist tendencies they may have had. The strikes that the IWW organized during World War I appeared as a breach of loyalty to the patriots and served to cast further suspicion on its foreign-born members.

During the Red Scare additional reasons were found for a tighter identification of immigrants with radicalism. The newly founded American Communist Party counted many foreign-born in its membership and recent comers played a prominent part in the sporadic acts of anarchism, the exploding of bombs and attempts on the lives of public officials. One unsuccessful attempt — it took place in the first months after the war — was directed at the chairman of the Immigration Committee of the Senate. In several of the great strikes of 1919 the majority of strikers were unskilled workers from southeastern Europe, and it must have seemed as if wherever violence exploded, recent immigrants had sparked it or added fuel to make it last. Thus the Red Scare created the impression that radicalism was a peculiar trait of the foreign-born, that all Slavs were Bolshevist agitators, all Italians anarchists.

Meanwhile racism was presented in scientific garb to the American people, helped by "eugenics" and poorly interpreted anthropology. In 1916 the distinguished anthropologist Madison Grant published *The Passing of the Great Race*, which was widely read after the war, when popular writers took up his views. Tinged with anti-Christian Nietzschean philosophy and purportedly based on Mendelian genetics, it proclaimed that the crossing of two races does not result in their blending but in the predominance of the "more ancient, generalized and lower type." Thus, preceding Hitler, Grant could not only assert the superiority of the Great Nordic race over the Alpine, Mediterranean, and Jewish races but could also state that the offspring of a non-Jew and a Jew is a Jew. He could plead for racial consciousness and pride to stop the influx of "hybrids."

Feeding on Madison Grant's sweeping views, nativist racism flared up and reached a new intensity in 1920. Anti-Catholicism revived, affecting especially Irish-, Italian-, and Polish-born immigrants. In May, 1920, Henry Ford launched a bitter anti-Semitic campaign in his *Dearborn Independent*, in which he fused the concept of the Bolshevist Jew created by the Red Scare with that of an international Jewry dominating world finance and plotting to control the world. In 1920 and 1921, Kenneth Roberts, the future author of *Lydia Bailey* and *Northwest Passage*, wrote a series of articles in *The Saturday Evening Post* in which he echoed the nativist and racist theories of the time, including the opinions expressed by the immigration commission in its report. In 1922 he republished nine revised articles in book form as *Why Europe Leaves Home*. With the efficacy of a top novelist and with a tremendous bias concealed under plain style and competent tone, he described the conditions and low standards of living that he had seen in a tour of countries formerly under the Austro-Hungarian Empire (in which he seemed to include southern Italy). He asserted that immigrants coming to the United States from those countries kept their own standards and "failed utterly to become Americans." Warning that Europe, or much of it, was on the move — toward the United States, of course — and under a cover of sympathy for the poor wretches he had seen in Europe, he indicted their brothers in America. In his articles he slipped in such sentences as "[These people] work all day by the side of other people of their own race. . . . Their first love is for their mother country. They have no hesitation in pursuing an emphatically un-American course. . . . [The Slavs] have been brought up to break the laws. . . . the Jews are most difficult to handle because of their ruthless concentration on self-interest. . . . [Recent immigrants] are paupers by circumstances, and parasites by training and inclination. . . . Races cannot be cross-bred without mongrelization. . . . Unrestricted immigration has made a mongrel race out of the south Italians . . . [and] out of the Greek. Unrestricted immigration will inevitably and absolutely do the same thing to Americans." So Roberts could conclude: "The future of America depends on the men she breeds. God has not given to America a special brand of ozone that enables her to ride triumphant over the laws of nature; and the hazy dreams of sentimentalists and the partisan desires of alien societies are poor substitutes for straight thinking and the inflexible rules of biology."

There was common sense in America's desire to regulate the influx of immigrants once pioneering times were over; and the attempt to preserve the existing ethnic composition was not altogether extravagant or senseless. But Roberts' articles were pure propaganda. Against this background of prejudice, postwar restrictive legislation was demanded in the light of economic factors: the first wave of immigration from Europe after the war coincided with a period of depression. The AFL lobbied, on economic grounds, in favor of total suspension of immigration until recovery set in. A suspension bill pending in Congress was favored as a measure to halt the "flood" of undesirables foreseen by Roberts and Madison Grant. The bill was defeated in the Senate, and instead Congress passed the first quota law in 1921. It limited immigration from Europe in any year to 3 per cent of the number of foreign-born of each nationality within the United States at the time of the 1910 census. Thus the quota system, based on the existing composition of the American population, was introduced into American immigration legislation.

The choice of the year 1910 displeased the nativists. They maintained that by that time too many Italians, Poles, and the like had come to America, that by assigning the same quota to them and to northwestern Europeans the law discriminated in fact against the old Anglo-Saxon stock. Agitation against the 1921 law resulted in the passage of the Immigration Act of 1924, known also as the National Origin Act or the Johnson-Reed Act. As a temporary measure, it reduced quotas to 2 per cent of the number of foreign-born of each nationality, as calculated on the 1890 rather than on the 1910 census. As a long-range solution to the restriction problem, it introduced a new concept: quotas ought to be apportioned, not according to the number of foreign-born, but according to the number of "inhabitants in continental United States in 1920 whose origin by birth or ancestry is attributable [to each nationality]." The law set at 150,000 the maximum number of immigrants from all countries except the Americas, which were exempt from quota restrictions. It provided that the "national origin" section of the act become effective on July 1, 1927. The time allowed was not too long for the difficult task of determining the national strain of each inhabitant on the basis of "statistics of immigration and emigration, together with rates of increase of population as shown by successive decennial United States censuses."

The principle of national origin produced heated debate, and the furor against it was so strong that twice Congress passed resolutions postponing enactment of the national origin provision — first until July, 1928, and then until July, 1929. The debated clause was a main issue in the electoral campaign of 1928. Early in 1929, President Hoover recommended to Congress that the provision be repealed, but his recommendation was voted down in the Senate and the House took no action. Thus the provision became effective on July 1, 1929.

Modified but retained by successive legislation until it was at last repealed in 1965, the national origin principle kept the camp of scholars sharply divided. As recently as 1957, Robert A. Divine wrote in *American Immigration Policy*: ". . . national origin quotas had been specifically designed to meet the goal of homogeneity, and they were as accurate as was humanly possible in view of the incompleteness of the available data . . . one must conclude that Congress made the better choice in retaining the national origins plan." From the other camp, J. P. Shalloo wrote in 1949: ". . . tracing the origin of the 1920 population from the founding of the Colonies . . . was a complicated, incomprehensible, and in many respects an occult and abstruse exercise in bias, speculation, statistical sleight of hand, and scientific nonsense."

THE INTELLECTUAL AND THE LAW

Right or wrong, the enactment of the national origin provision had immediate results and changed both the quantity and the quality of immigration. Some 1,468,296 persons immigrated to the United States in the five-year period 1926–30. In the next five-year period only 220,209 immigrated. The new provision effectively closed the gates to mass immigration and the small residual immigration was in great part of a different class.

The American immigration restrictions did not displease all the countries affected. In 1926, a spokesman for Mussolini's government commented: ". . . we wish the word 'emigrant' to disappear forever from official Italian . . . the shameful spectacle of hundreds of thousands of Italians wandering all over the world because they were starving at home no longer exists and will never return." That the closing of American gates played a part in the game of Mussolini's "demographic" policies is further suggested by Italian passport practices. Italian authorities would not issue a passport to the United States until the applicant had obtained an American visa. And American consular officials would not grant, or promise, a visa to a person who had not yet secured an Italian passport valid for travel in the

United States. Only occasionally was the impasse broken by Italian inventiveness, and then only after a long period of shuttling between Italian police headquarters and the American consulate.

The National Origin Act left a door open to intellectuals: the *4d* clause of section 4 of the act. It allowed the granting of non-quota, immigrant visas to ministers of any religious denomination, to bona fide teachers of higher education who would be teaching in this country, and to their families. These non-quota visas were to prove a blessing for many intellectuals even when the quota from their country had not been filled, because in general they could be obtained more easily than quota visas.

In achieving both the reduction and the change of quality of immigration the law was assisted by the instructions issued in 1930 by the State Department to its consuls abroad, in response to the new cry for restriction at the beginning of the depression. The consuls were to interpret very strictly the clause prohibiting admission of aliens "likely to become public charges" and to deny the visa to an applicant who in their opinion might become a public charge at any time. It created a paradoxical situation which worked in favor of the learned and against the unskilled. To play doubly safe, many consuls would have been willing to grant visas only to prospective immigrants who could prove that a job was waiting for them in the United States, and yet applicants who proved this to the consul were automatically excluded from admission, because another clause in current legislation excluded aliens "under contract." But artists, musicians, teachers, and members of learned professions (and domestic servants) were exceptions. If they could produce a written invitation from a theater, an orchestra, or a university, the consuls were satisfied that they would never be public charges. Thus, through the *4d* and the "public charge" provisions, the better educated among prospective immigrants were doubly privileged.

Other clauses were also applied rigidly in the thirties and worked in the same direction; for instance, those relating to physical and mental deficiency. I have seen with my own eyes visas refused to an entire peasant family, thus killing a dream that had seemed near attainment, because the youngest daughter who ought to have been in fourth grade showed the reading and arithmetic ability of a second-grader. But in our own case, the difficulties created by our seven-year-old daughter's unsuspected (and therefore uncorrected) eye defect were smoothed when a consular official whispered in the physician's ear that Fermi had received the Nobel Prize. American law had become a terrible snob.

It was inevitable that during the depression years the restrictionists should continue to agitate for the further reduction of quotas or the suspension of immigration. Conversely, from the very moment Hitler came to power and the mass exodus from Germany began, liberal groups invoking the traditional principle of asylum demanded relaxation of immigration restrictions in the case of refugees. Others were against this. In November, 1933, Al Smith wrote in the *New Outlook*, "We must uphold our traditions and indicate the principles on which this nation was established by making room here for our share of the refugees from Germany." A few months later, in March, 1934, Martin Dies declared in the *National Republic*, "We must ignore the tears of sobbing sentimentalists and internationalists, and we must permanently close, lock, and bar the gates of our country to new immigration waves and then throw the keys away."

Caught between opposed forces, Congress refused to act in either direction, and the law was not changed. But in 1934 President Roosevelt asked the State Department to instruct all consuls abroad to treat refugees with special consideration. This is as far as America could move officially to relieve the plight of refugees, but despite the legislative situation she succeeded in giving asylum to an untold number of exiles.

THE INTELLECTUAL AND THE DEPRESSION

One of my earliest recollections of America is of standing with Fermi in Times Square and watching unemployment statistics among the glowing headlines that appeared in rapid succession high on top of the *New York Times* Building. We were in the United States for the summer, on our first visit. The language of American headlines was unintelligible to us and that of newspapers was almost as difficult, for Fermi had learned English by reading scientific papers and I by reading British novels. But the lighted figures running into millions were perfectly clear and yet bewildering to us because the American level of prosperity was very high if measured against the standards of our own country. It was the year 1930, and we were witnessing, of course, the beginning of the great depression.

The market crash had occurred several months before, on October 24, 1929, but only in March, 1933, did the banking system come to a halt. On

March 6, Franklin Delano Roosevelt, President of the United States for exactly two days, declared a four-day national bank holiday, which marked a crisis of the first magnitude. (In Europe, Adolf Hitler had been Chancellor of Germany for one month and seven days.)

World-wide depression brought Hitler to power. Through him and his ruthless policies the depression acted on the cultural wave, pressing it out of Europe. At the same time the American crisis pushed in the opposite direction: scarcity of jobs and tightening of funds for institutions slowed admission of refugees and put a brake on the arriving wave. Without the depression in Europe and the rise of Hitler the intellectual wave would have been much smaller. But given the conditions in Europe, if there had been no depression in America the wave might have been of larger proportion.

Luckily for scholars and scientists, the higher ranks of American universities were not overcrowded before the thirties. In fact, to the European eye, accustomed to cluttered rooms in antiquated buildings which had not been meant to house laboratories at all, American scientific laboratories seemed vast, extremely well equipped, and understaffed. There also seemed to be a scarcity of scholars and teachers in the arts, musicology, Oriental studies, and German philology.

In the early thirties, many American universities were quite willing to hire top European men, usually on a temporary basis. But not all intellectuals were "top," and even many of those destined to attain honors and fame were obscure at the time they sought shelter in America. Some indeed were so little known to workers of assisting committees that they were told they would do much better if they sought an unskilled job. This experience was shared, for instance, by Hans Morgenthau, a most distinguished and authoritative teacher, long on the faculty of the University of Chicago (and an outspoken critic of some of our foreign policies). At the time of his arrival he was not well known. The girl who interviewed him at a New York agency designed to assist scholars was not impressed by his past achievements — a couple of published books and several years of teaching in Frankfurt, Geneva, and Madrid. There were too many like him, the girl said, and his chances would be much better if he were to look for a job as an elevator boy. His wife's experience was equally discouraging. A Jewish organization refused to try to place her as a saleswoman, claiming that she was too old, at thirty-one, to be employed in a store. But the Morgenthaus were stubborn and found work on their own, Irma at Macy's and Hans at Brooklyn College. He taught nights and was paid by the hour, which meant that on holidays and when he was ill he was not paid at all. Irma found time to write on economics (and published under the name Irma M. Thormann). Nevertheless their joint earnings were scant. In the rented room in which they lived at one time Irma was so badly bitten by bedbugs that her supervisor at Macy's asked her to stay home until her appearance improved. The only bright spot was that the students at Brooklyn College took it upon themselves to teach English to Hans. The Morgenthaus finally decided that they would not be able to survive in New York and moved to Kansas City, where Hans obtained an appointment at the university through an employment agency.

The depression hit the young in the academic world, both émigrés and natives, more than those already well established in their careers. In an article which appeared in the *Yale Review* in June, 1933, Alvin Johnson, head of the New School for Social Research, estimated that 5,000 American Ph.D.'s were unemployed. To them the foreigners seemed unfair competition, and they often strenuously opposed their appointment. Colleges and universities as well as relief agencies could not fully disregard these sentiments. Scientists, however, usually fared better than other intellectuals. Eugene Wigner told me that in his opinion the depression did not adversely affect the possibility of finding university positions for physicists. Good physicists never had difficulty, and some of his students received several offers upon obtaining their doctoral degrees. But Wigner's opinion requires some qualification: his students were not typical; among them were men as outstanding as Frederick Seitz, who became a leader in solid state physics, a chairman of the National Academy of Sciences, and later the president of Rockefeller University. For the average young European physicist hoping to emigrate to America the prospects may not have been so bright.

The situation was tighter in mathematics than in physics, according to Stan Ulam, a versatile mathematician who came to the United States from Poland in 1935 and in this country worked in several mathematical fields, both basic and applied, including the making of computers and hydrogen bombs. Reminiscing for my sake, Stan Ulam said that during the depression even his American friends had a hard time getting jobs. (He was twenty-six years old when he came to this country, and it is likely that his friends were also young.) He remembered in particular an American who had tried for two years to get a position and considered himself lucky when he finally was offered a lectureship at $1,500 a year. Positions for Europeans grew scarcer as more arrived. Even a man as famous and advanced in years as the French mathematician Jacques Hadamard obtained only a very small position. But the effects of the depression on European intellectuals were not all bad, according to Ulam. Periods without work or with manual jobs left more time for thinking.

The depression acted also in a less direct way on the intellectuals: it kept alive American xenophobia. When it became known in 1932 that Albert Einstein planned to come to the United States, the Woman Patriotic Corporation tried to prevent his entry, claiming that he was a member of Communist organizations. On December 4, 1932, the *New York Times* published testimony of the board of the National Patriotic Council calling Einstein a German Bolshevist and stating that his theory "was of no scientific value or purpose, not understandable because there was nothing there to understand." According to the same newspaper, Einstein remarked: "Wouldn't it be funny if they wouldn't let me in? Why, the whole world would laugh at America!"

American xenophobia was still noticeable, though often concealed by kindness, when I arrived in this country with my family in early 1939. A number of relatives and friends in Italy had asked us to look for positions for them. When I talked about this with friendly persons in the East, a frequent reply was: "There are not enough jobs for Americans. Why should we let more Europeans come over?" Occasionally I spotted an element of nativist racism, as when I went in quest of an affidavit for an Italian family. (It was not easy to secure affidavits — pledges of full financial support — to bring "more foreigners" to this country. In spite of Roosevelt's attempts to soften the law, without an affidavit or firm assurance of a position here, the "public charge" clause was an insurmountable obstacle for aliens.) I was directed to a wealthy woman, willing to help refugees. I found her to be kind, white-haired, and motherly. She told me politely but in no veiled terms that Italians had a bad reputation in this country and more of them would not be welcomed. She was right. The execution of Sacco and Vanzetti in 1927 may have left many Americans perplexed as to their guilt; but Al Capone was rightly regarded as the prototype of the gangster. Although as much a product of American prohibition as of Italian upbringing — prohibition provided the unscrupulous with an incredibly lucrative field of operation — Al Capone and his kind gave Italo-Americans the reputation of being potential criminals. In fact, Americans had formed strong stereotypes of each nationality. In the thirties at any rate racism and depression worked together.

For intellectual immigrants matters did not always improve after the depression. The easing of financial conditions was offset by the larger number of arrivals. After the fall of France, artists, writers, and scholars from all countries of Europe were crammed on our shores in such numbers that America could not provide adequately for all, and many endured great hardship. The Czech writer Hans Natonek has given a vivid account of his own calvary in an autobiography. He arrived in this country with $4.50 in his possession, an embittered man, broken by the experiences he had endured since 1933, looking old at forty-eight, proud and yet sometimes scornful. He was far removed from the well-meaning workers at the relief agency where he sought assistance. They lectured him on the advantages of manual labor and on his duty to learn the American way of life through manual labor. He listened, accepted financial help, and stubbornly isolated himself in a small room to pursue his writing. Later, driven by need and a sense of shame for the relief money that he was receiving, he tried all sorts of unskilled work, but always failed. He did not have what it takes, as a gas-station operator told him; he did not seem fit for anything — until a publisher accepted his manuscript. His first success in the America he had come to love was a victory in his own field. Similar experiences were shared by many Europeans.

III

➤➤➤➤➤➤➤➤➤➤➤➤➤➤➤➤➤➤➤➤➤➤➤➤➤➤➤➤➤➤➤

The Intellectual in His European Habitat

European intellectuals in the cultural wave belonged to more than one generation: a few, already old men when they arrived here early in the thirties, may have been born as early as 1860; a few of the youngest among those who left Europe in 1940 or 1941 were born close to the opening of the twenties. But despite the wide time-span, almost all were molded by a similar environment, the atmosphere of security which protected the European middle classes before World War I and which middle-class blindness protracted through the twenties. The sense of security sprang from the faith of the middle classes in the inherent worth of their moral principles and in the stability of the existing social and political order. Though this order collapsed in the uneasy peace after World War I, much of the European bourgeoisie refused to see the coming changes and hung on to the values and privileges of the old world. The effect of a middle-class philosophy of life was still recognizable in many European intellectuals when they landed in America and its ethical values were still important to them. The European background is relevant to an understanding of their performance in this country.

THE GOLDEN AGE OF SECURITY

The period between the Franco-Prussian war of 1870 and World War I was for Europe an interlude of quiet between turmoils. Armed conflict moved from the European theater to faraway colonial lands. European maps, which had changed so frequently and drastically in the past, now settled down and boundaries seemed permanent — at least until 1912, when the Balkan war changed the map of Turkey. The modicum of political liberty granted by recent constitutions satisfied the majority of the people. Almost all countries of Europe, with France the main exception, had their monarchs — kings, emperors, or czars — and the old ruling families were symbols of a continuity with the past which could be reassuringly projected into the future. They were also rallying points of the most extreme forms of nationalism; but few recognized the danger inherent in nationalism. All considered, the middle classes had no reasons for anxieties. In this period, it is true, socialism grew and socialist parties were formed all over Europe; but with the exception of the few intellectuals who were leaders of the socialist movement, the great majority of the bourgeoisie regarded socialist ideologies as Utopias and in no sense a threat to themselves. The political and social structure appeared sound and durable.

In these exceptionally calm decades, the European middle classes thrived. Thriftiness surged to the status of virtue, built up small savings and turned them into capital that could be tended, made to grow, and then passed on to children and grandchildren. In the spreading sense of financial security, increasing numbers of men and women delivered from other worries could dedicate themselves to the activities of the mind and the attainment of intellectual refinement. Literature, music, the arts, and the theater flourished, and the intellectual group that produced them was also the main consumer, for it had sufficient means, leisure, and taste to relish these pleasures. The recognition received by intellectual achievement and the social prestige that went with it fostered a certain trend to keep the intellectual trade in the family, as had always happened in other trades or businesses. There were families holding on to the tradition of literary and political salons; families of doctors, of literati, and of scientists; and families in which parents encouraged their children to develop the endowment of their minds in whatever direction it would lead.

After completing elementary school, children of "good families" were sent as a matter of course to the gymnasium or equivalent school which taught syntax and Latin to the ten-year-old. (The full curriculum included literature, the history of art, mathematics, history and geography, and later Greek, modern languages, and the sciences.) This type of school was no end in itself; its diploma opened no careers or special jobs, only the road to the university or other institution of higher education. A girl could easily drop out of school if she wished and take up the gentler arts of the "young lady." But a boy could not transfer to a more practical school and a shorter road to a trade or a profession without losing face and encountering parental resistance; for such a change of school meant to lose one's place on the social ladder. Young people who questioned the wisdom of so much classical education were told that dead languages were an excellent mental gymnastic which would prepare their minds for future tasks.

Schools were concerned with imparting knowledge and inculcating patriotism. The formation of character, the instilling of principles other than patriotism, the preparation for civic roles were left entirely to the influence of the family. And this influence was very strong. Family law derived from family traditions and parents' beliefs. It was not tempered, as it is in this country and in these days, by comparisons with other families' laws or attempts to subject whole groups of children to the same sets of rules. Thus, a frequent product of the upper middle class was a highly cultivated individual with an agile mind bent on theoretical speculations, leading a satisfactory spiritual life supported by a solidly built conscience, but aloof from practical matters and unfit for manual tasks.

One of the main mistakes of the European cultivated classes may well have been this detachment from the practical aspects of life. It led them to ignore too often some of their duties to society and shun participation in politics and government. It is undoubtedly a symptom of a common disease that in many European countries the majority of the people considered the government something entirely external to themselves, a sort of huge tax collector and imposer of restrictions. Co-operation with the state was inconceivable, and it was smart to cheat it. Perhaps a mistake of the middle classes as momentous as their aloofness was to cling tightly to their privileges and — in good faith — come to look on them as rights.

This presentation of the early background of future intellectual émigrés is a broad generalization from which there are necessarily many deviations. Not everywhere were the middle classes as modestly affluent and secure as I have described them. Nevertheless, almost everywhere the education received by those who could afford it had a common pattern. Pre-revolutionary Russia, for instance, did not enjoy the golden security of other countries. Differences in distribution of wealth were enormous, the separation between wealthy and poor was more pronounced than elsewhere, and in the gap between the two there was only a scant middle class, of recent origin and therefore with no strong traditions. As a result, the period from 1870 to

World War I was marked by social unrest, class strife, and the 1905 revolution. It is true that industrialization and westernization continued, but two wars, one against Turkey and the other against Japan, exhausted the country and kept her budget in constant deficit.

Education was to a large extent a privilege of the nobility and the landed gentry. But Russian intellectuals looked to the West for inspiration in the education of their children. I was amazed in reading of Vladimir Nabokov's childhood in his autobiographical *Speak, Memory* that his family gave him to read the celebrated books of the *Bibliothéque Rose* that generations of French children read and that I found on my shelves thumbed and earmarked by my elders in their childhood. Russian children were often kept out of school and their education entrusted to governesses and private tutors, but individual training was meant to prepare them for school at a later day or for school examinations that would open the way to the university. The westernizing trend of the Romanov dynasty had patterned Russian schools on curricula of western countries and produced the same type of humanistic, cultivated scholar.

The similarities in the cultural background of European countries are more striking than the differences, for Europe produced similar traditions and moral values, a similar atmosphere of cultural sophistication and refinement. And yet Europe was not one entity: it was divided into a large number of small nations, each speaking its own language, pursuing its own ideology, its commercial and political interests. Rival nations nursed petty or serious hatreds, had fought each other over centuries, and were going through what soon proved to be only a lull between clashes.

THE END OF THE GOLDEN AGE

World War I put an end to the long period of European peace. But in 1914 it was not evident that the war would also mark the end of the golden age of security for the middle classes; only a seer could have predicted then that the war would turn into a cataclysm and topple empires, destroy social structures and undermine those it left standing, wreck economies, and pave the way for the rise of dictators.

The future intellectuals of the cultural wave were affected by the war in different ways, depending on their age. A great majority of those who were to come to America in the prime of life were born in the two decades roughly between 1890 and 1910. In 1914 the oldest in the group were still attending the university or were at the very beginning of their careers. Their studies or their occupations were disrupted when they were called to serve in the armies of their countries. The youngest were in elementary school or preparing to enter it. They could not realize at first what was going on. But by the end of the war all had felt its impact.

The significance of World War I was a revelation even to people older than those born in the nineties. The Austrian writer Stefan Zweig, who was to become an émigré in the Americas, conveyed this sense of revelation in his autobiographical *The World of Yesterday.* It was the autumn of 1918. Germany and Austria-Hungary had collapsed, and the empire of the Habsburgs had been wiped off the map. Zweig, then in Switzerland, decided to go back home to Austria. When his train arrived at the station on the Austrian border, he noticed unusual activity, as in preparation for some extraordinary happening. The police piled up, people crowded on the platform, a train arrived and stopped. "Then I recognized behind the plate-glass window of the car the Emperor Charles, last emperor of Austria, standing with his black-clad wife, Empress Zita," Stefan Zweig wrote. "I was startled: the last emperor of Austria, heir of the Habsburg dynasty which had ruled for seven hundred years, was forsaking his realm! . . . The historic moment was doubly shocking to me who had grown up in the tradition of the Empire . . . and who had taken the military oath to obey . . . this serious and thoughtful-looking man . . . 'The Kaiser!' From earliest childhood we had learned to pronounce those words reverently, for they embodied all power and wealth and symbolized Austria's imperishability. . . . From century to century the glorious line of Habsburg had passed the Imperial globe and crown from hand to hand, and this was the minute of its end. . . . At last the conductor gave the signal . . . and slowly the train withdrew. . . . I knew it was a different Austria, a different world, to which I was returning."

It was indeed a different world. Gone were the empires and gone most security. The traditions and habits of the middle classes were sufficiently strong, or had a sufficient inertia, to survive World War I in many countries and remain outwardly unchanged for some years. But the new anxieties that took the place of security prepared the way for the tragedies to come.

European capitals lost their proverbial glamor, or whatever amount of it they had actually had. Literature went on stubbornly referring to "gay

Vienna," but when I incautiously used this term my Viennese friend Maria Piers commented in a letter to me: "None of us remember Vienna as gay. It may have had this appearance before World War I, but even that is doubtful. We suspect that the gaiety was strictly for export, or perhaps Vienna owes its reputation to the Strauss-operettas, which by definition were gay. . . . The steady economic decline and political unrest gave us rather a sort of '*Galgenhumor*' [the humor of the man en route to the gallows]. Ernst Gombrich [the Viennese art historian now living in England, who was on a visit to Chicago] feels quite seriously that 'there were so many intellectuals among us, because there were no jobs to be had. . . .' So, in a sense, the intellectuals owe their existence to the *absence* of gaiety. But . . . we may be extra gloomy."

UNIVERSITIES AND CAFÉS

After the war, the young future European émigrés resumed their studies and went on to one or another of the universities. German students usually moved from university to university within their country, until they found the professor with whom they wanted to work for their degree. Their moving about was a consequence of the freedom of learning which Wilhelm von Humboldt advocated for German universities, together with other freedoms, early in the nineteenth century. Through the territory that had been the Austro-Hungarian Empire students moved freely from city to city, crossing the newly set boundaries — from Hungary or Poland into Austria and Czechoslovakia — and the most ambitious young men sought the famous universities in Germany.

There were good reasons for this traveling even when it was· confined within the boundaries of the old Habsburg Empire, because the countries which emerged from the collapse of the Austro-Hungarian monarchy differed in their national traits, despite Habsburg attempts to unify them. Austria preserved her strong cultural traditions and the intellectual liveliness of her capital; Hungary still displayed light-heartedness and the heritage of her feudal system in which a lazy aristocracy looked down on culture, leaving it almost entirely in Jewish hands; Czechoslovakia retained 75 per cent of the industry of the old empire, was its most technically advanced heir, and under Masaryk and Beneš also its most democratic. Poland, her German, Russian, and Austrian parts reunited, kept her poverty, her traditionally minded intelligentsia, her crowded ghettos, and the stuffiness of her universities — a stuffiness that prevailed in most other countries and was Poland's characteristic only in its degree. In countries where the wandering instinct was less strong, as in Italy or France, students stayed at one university, often in the city where they were born.

The quality of education varied from university to university, from discipline to discipline, but at the best universities it was excellent. European training was in general more formal and more theoretical than the American; with few exceptions, at European universities there was little contact between professors and students. Enwrapped in their mantles of dignity, most professors avoided meeting the younger crowd at its own level. I am told of a European professor who refused a position at an American university because an American student in one of his classes had the cheek to speak up and say, "Professor, I agree with you."

Students were bound together by an *esprit de corps* unknown in this country and deriving from medieval traditions. In Italy this *esprit de corps* had a frolicsome quality and was expressed in pranks and absurd ceremonies, especially in the first year or two of student life. In Germany and Austria it had somewhat gruesome aspects: many of the young men joined student groups or associations with strict militaristic codes and spent much time in learning to drink heavily, according to ritual, in marching and singing in the streets, and especially in mastering the art of fencing. Then, to prove their manhood and honor their groups they would insult and provoke each other as well as peaceful youths who did not share their passion for aggression. They would fight as many duels as they could arrange and reach the time for their degrees with faces criss-crossed with scars.

In the Austro-Hungarian Empire and later in the states that were its successors, students, especially those with literary or political inclinations, complemented what they learned at school with what they absorbed in long hours in cafés. There, for the price of a cup of coffee, they could buy the right to a table top on which to study, the comfort of a heated room in winter, and a place to meet their friends. Of this café life I got in turn a romantic idea or a more matter-of-fact impression according to the person I talked to or the book I read. Of the cafés in Budapest, the Hungarian journalist and author Paul Ignotus (son of the writer Hugo, who was a refugee in this country during the war) wrote in *Political Prisoner* that they "were the fountain of illicit trading, adultery, puns, gossip and poetry . . . the meeting places for the intellectuals and those opposed to oppression. . . ." And Stefan Zweig stated somewhat chauvinistically in *The World of Yesterday* that "the Viennese café is a particular institution which is not comparable to any other in the world . . . every guest can sit for hours on end, discuss, write, play cards, receive his mail, and above all, can go through an unlimited number of newspapers and magazines. . . . Perhaps nothing has contributed as much to . . . the international orientation of the Austrian as that he could keep abreast of all world events in the café, and at the same time discuss them in the circle of his friends."

The appraisal of café life in Poland is varied. The Polish physicist Leopold Infeld wrote in his autobiography *Quest*: "Most of my colleagues slept in their apartments, worked at the University and lived in the cafés." But another Pole, the well-known mathematician Antoni Zygmund, told me that whatever a café could offer was not as good as the space assigned to a graduate student in American universities. Stan Ulam was a patron of the Scottish Coffee House in the Polish city of Lwów, one of the places where he and his friends discussed mathematical problems among themselves and with visitors from other countries. To keep track of the problems, the mathematicians used to write them in a big notebook which they left in the custody of the headwaiter of the coffee house, who kept it safe and produced it on demand. Translated into English by Stan Ulam, the *Scottish Book* has been privately published and distributed. Among the contributors of problems, several were to come to this country: Ulam himself, John Von Neumann, Zygmund, Mark Kac, and Samuel Eilenberg.

THE RISE OF THE DICTATORS

While the more urbane future exiles sat in cafés and the bellicose slashed each other's faces with fencing swords, while others were quietly immersed in studies or had already embarked on a career, a novel product of mankind, the modern dictator, began to appear here and there in Europe. The timetable of this weird blossoming is worth recalling.

The first of the modern dictatorships was proclaimed in Russia in January, 1918, in the wake of the Bolshevik revolution while the war was still raging. Lenin called it a "dictatorship of the proletariat," and most historians concede that the Soviet dictatorship did not become "personal" until the advent of Stalin. Yet Lenin was not only its leading spirit but its driving force, and as the head of the council of people's commissars he exerted virtually dictatorial powers, making his will prevail even if it went against the opinion of the majority of his associates. At any rate, the second European dictatorship, an offshoot of the Russian, was unquestionably personal: Lenin's disciple and emissary Béla Kun became dictator of Hungary in March, 1919. Though his Bolshevik regime lasted only 133 days, it proved fateful to Hungary, for it provoked a rightist reaction. Led by Admiral Nicholas Horthy, the reaction replaced the Red terror with a White terror, and soon evolved into a Fascist dictatorship.

October, 1922, saw the March on Rome and the ascent to power of a man who was unquestionably a full-fledged dictator, Benito Mussolini. Victor Emmanuel III of Italy yielded to the shouts of the Fascists and called Mussolini to form his cabinet. About a year later King Alphonso of Spain followed suit and submitted to the military *pronunciamento* of Miguel Primo de Rivera. Under this general Spain experienced her first dictatorship that was to last for seven years. In 1926, Marshall Józef Pilsudski initiated his more veiled but no less real dictatorship in Poland. The year 1928 is generally regarded as marking the beginning of Stalin's personal dictatorship, though he had gained ascendancy even before Lenin's death in 1924. A university professor of law, Antonio de Oliveira Salazar, obtained full powers in 1932 in Portugal and ruled there until 1968.

In retrospect and in view of the place that nazism had taken in history it seems unbelievable that Adolf Hitler, coming to power in 1933, was not the initiator of the dictatorial system but only the ninth in the series of European dictators, a pupil following the example of many teachers. He stands out not for his priority but for his viciousness. After him and before the onset of World War II, one more dictator appeared on the European scene: in 1936 Generalissimo Francisco Franco's mutiny brought in the second and more lasting Spanish dictatorship. (Other strong men like Chancellor Engelbert Dollfuss of Austria and General Antonio Carmona of Portugal are not included in this list because history has not pinned on them so clear a label.)

THE DICTATOR AND THE INTELLIGENTSIA

The rise of the dictators did not equally affect intellectuals in all countries, but some general considerations can be made and may help to explain why dictatorial methods were so effective when turned against the intelligentsia.

Dictators, modern and ancient, dread spiritual and ideological dissent more than open action, for revolt may be easily quashed, but ideas tend to spread insidiously. Hence dictators are especially wary of the behavior of intellectuals and persecute them at the first signs of non-conformity. On the other hand, non-conformity is a trait widespread among intellectuals, who tend to be individualists because they are preoccupied with the product of their own minds and trained to be critical of the opinions of others. Organized political opposition to dictators usually springs from intellectual quarters.

To a point, it is a question of definition: the word "intellectual" is given varied meanings at different times and by different people, but almost always it implies not merely thinking power but a critical attitude of mind. And the word "intelligentsia," which now simply denotes intellectuals collectively, was coined in Russia around 1860 to indicate a particular group of ideological intellectuals who opposed the regime of the czars. Consequently, if by intellectuals is meant the critics of existing social and political orders, then the intellectuals are by definition those who inspire opposition and revolt. As a group, they are the worst potential foes of dictators and a target of authoritarianism.

The main weapon of modern dictators against the intelligentsia was anti-Semitism. The European intelligentsia was especially vulnerable because a large part of it was Jewish. Through the centuries in which the Jews had lived as oppressed minorities they had developed ambitions to improve their lot, but unlike the ambitions of other oppressed minorities, theirs were peculiarly intellectual. This is a fact on which many authors have written. Leopold Infeld, who was raised in the Polish ghettos and throughout his years in Poland experienced the Polish resistance to admission of Jews in the universities, remarked that "every Jew, even before he is born, longs to be a *dozent* in a university." And Stefan Zweig analyzed Jewish intellectualism at length in *The World of Yesterday*:

"The real determination of the Jew is to rise to a higher cultural plane in the intellectual world. Even in the case of Eastern orthodox Jewry, where the weaknesses as well as the merits of the whole race are more intensely manifested, this supremacy of the will to the spiritual over the mere material finds plastic expression. The holy man, the Bible student, is a thousand times more esteemed within the community than the rich man . . . this elevation of the intellectual to the highest rank is common to all classes; the poorest

41

beggar who drags his pack through wind and rain will try to single out at least one son to study, no matter at how great a sacrifice, and it is counted a title of honor for the entire family to have someone . . . who plays a role in the intellectual world. Subconsciously something in the Jew seeks to escape the morally dubious, the distasteful, the petty, the unspiritual, which is attached to all trade, and all that is purely business, and to lift himself up to the moneyless sphere of the intellectual, as if — in the Wagnerian sense — he wished to redeem himself and his entire race from the curse of money."

In most European countries, the fulfilment of these aspirations raised the proportion of Jews among the intellectuals above that in the rest of the population. In Germany, for instance, the Jews constituted less than 1 per cent (0.9 per cent) of the total population, but among university professors over 12 per cent were Jewish.

The oppression of the intelligentsia was facilitated by the fact that in most countries of continental Europe the universities were state institutions. They usually had some autonomy and in questions of learning were governed by the rector and faculty committees. Nevertheless, they were under the central control of the state. All salaries and allocations were paid by the Ministry of Education, and all business was transacted through it; the minister ratified the appointments of professors, changes of policy, constitution of certain faculty boards, and other activities. A similar governmental control was exerted over art academies and music conservatories, and also, though perhaps to a lesser degree, over the theater and opera. This system worked well under democratic governments and constitutional monarchies, relieving the universities and other cultural institutions of much administrative drudgery and the need to raise funds. But it was open to dictatorial abuse. When a dictator arrogated all powers of government, he automatically came to hold in his hands the strings that controlled the universities and he could pull them at his whim.

Generalizations cannot be pushed further, and a rapid glance at some of the dictator-dominated countries is in order. The circumstances of the intellectuals in Russia differed substantially from those in western European countries, and though before the revolution anti-Semitism had frequently and violently recurred, it was not the main weapon in the almost complete destruction of the Russian intelligentsia. The very constitution of the intellectual class was singular. It originated among the nobility and gentry, the numerically insignificant section of the Russian population owning most of the land. From the land they derived cheap food and servants, and much leisure to devote to intellectual pursuits. Very often they were educated by tutors from western countries and absorbed ideologies that were important forces in the westernization of Russia. Their numbers were reinforced by the clergy, who were a second, smaller source of intellectuals. By the turn of the century many elements from other strata had joined the intelligentsia. They were the product of the universities which were introduced together with a system of elementary schools and gymnasia, all according to the western pattern. After various vicissitudes and setbacks, the universities were opened to those who could afford them or could find a protector who would pay the cost of schooling — a means by which some peasants and commoners were able to rise to intellectual status.

What Richard Pipes, in *The Russian Intelligentsia*, called "the splendid cultured class in pre-Revolutionary Russia" towered high above the illiterate masses — approximately 90 per cent of the Russian population were illiterate throughout the nineteenth century (and 70 per cent were so in 1920). Its greatest achievement was Russian classical literature, but the greatest role it played was to breed opposition to the old Russian social structure and to rear the leaders of the revolution. There were Jews among the intellectuals and consequently there were Jews among the Bolshevik organizers — Leon Trotsky, Leo Kamenev, Grigory Zinoviev, and others. This fact alone was of the greatest importance because it brought about the identification of the Jews with bolshevism (although Lenin was not a Jew) and provided anti-Semites all over the world with a new reason and new justification for their sentiments. But within Russia itself the racial issues did not belong among the ideologies of the revolution and had a part only in the counter-revolution.

More relevant than anti-Semitism to the history of intellectual emigration from Russia is the class warfare that the revolution relentlessly urged, turning against the cultured class in which the revolution had its ideological roots. Large numbers of intellectuals perished in the early struggle and the Red terror that ensued, and many more were forced to take the road to exile. When the White reaction set in, the old endemic anti-Semitism flared up, and wherever the White armies went they were followed by waves of violence against the Jews. Though Lenin outlawed anti-Semitism, he could not stop it, and an additional force came to work toward the destruction of the intellectual class, a force which was directed specifically against the Jewish section of that class. After the civil war, Lenin's government and later Stalin's continued to regard anti-Semitism as a counter-revolutionary activity and a criminal offense. The Russian intellectuals did not suffer principally because of anti-Semitism and were driven to emigrate by ideological conflict, not racial persecution.

Most of the once wealthy intellectuals lost their fortunes in the revolution and were penniless when they went into exile. But a few succeeded in salvaging enough to fill at least their first needs in new lands. The sudden fall from extreme wealth to poverty was not as great a disaster as it might have been for Vladimir Nabokov and his family. In *Speak, Memory*, the author of *Lolita* and *Ada* tells the story of his family, which owned a city house and an immense country estate; traveled each year to fashionable foreign resorts in reserved compartments of luxury trains; was waited upon by "a permanent staff of about fifty servants" whose petty thefts made house bills soar to a stupendous figure; and had their children educated by a succession of French and English governesses and Russian tutors. All this vanished in the revolution, and the family fled first to Crimea, then to England, where they faced poverty. But the immediate strictures of poverty were relieved by "a handful of jewels that a farsighted chambermaid . . . had swept off a dresser" and into a suitcase when the family left their Saint Petersburg home.

Some of the White Russians who fled the Red terror were violently anti-Semitic and brought their hatred along with them to other countries. Of historical interest is the group that took refuge in Germany and even in the early twenties waged strong anti-Semitic and anti-Bolshevik propaganda in Hitler's own paper. The chief figure among them and their link with Hitler was Alfred Rosenberg, a Baltic German by birth who had been educated in Moscow. Later Rosenberg became the intellectual leader and racial theorist of national socialism. Though Hitler had developed his racial madness well before the Russian revolution, it is fascinating to speculate on this injection of Russian reactionism into Nazi brutality.

The conditions of the intelligentsia did not improve under Stalin. It is true that for a few years Stalin's Russia opened its doors to intellectuals from other countries and gave many of them positions at Russian universities, but most of these appointments ended in early dismissal or even imprisonment. The few men who did leave their posts and the country of their own free will did so under great hardship. A vivid impression of the strain and anxieties at a Russian university can be obtained from a letter that a non-Russian scientist sent to a friend and colleague outside the Soviet Union. The writer of the letter spent almost three years in Russia with his family and then managed to reach a free country from which he could write without restraint about his experiences. His letter, dated September 21, 1937, is in German. Freely translated, it runs in part as follows:

"The heaviest pressure of the last three years which wrecked my nervous system is now relieved. I recovered quite well in the last few weeks and I believe that I have regained my capability for work. . . .

"Now I would like to tell you briefly what happened to us . . . all experiences would take volumes. All foreigners were suspected in the highest measure and were always under supervision. This was done by the political police NKVD (formally the GPU or *Tscheka*), which reads all letters going abroad. In addition, housemaids and janitors, etc., must report on foreigners from time to time. . . .

"The first impression was depressing. The dehumanized faces of innocent people, all carrying an immense sorrow, were altogether heartrending. The sufferings of these men were chiseled in the flesh of their faces, and all wore an impenetrable mask that manifested itself in a dull, animal indifference. And so it was everywhere. Wherever one looked, there was a crowd of sad people. It was not much better in the Institute, where people in rags talked of forthcoming reforms which would bring the culture and civilization of this country to unsurpassed heights. Nobody listened with interest to these tales. . . . This was in 1934.

"Now came 1935 which brought some relief. The first stores were opened in which it was possible to buy freely. Young people considered this an unprecedented achievement of Soviet culture. I was asked whether I had ever seen similar stores abroad.

"In 1935 I picked up a little more courage and I built a series of new laboratories. What difficulties were involved, nobody in the rest of Europe can imagine. For each piece of iron or rubber hose I had to fight hard. But the hardest fights were with the people; they showed no inclination to do the enormous work for their starving salaries. . . . At the beginning of 1936 I was the unhappy director of eight large laboratories and . . . responsible for the well-being of thirty-five Soviet human beings.

"The worst came in the middle of 1936. In the Party Trotskyism allegedly

45

spread with enormous speed. . . . A nonsensical furor to destroy gripped the leadership of Stalin's party. The most valuable and intelligent elements were radically destroyed. In [our city] a large number of outstanding party men committed suicide. . . .

"From the party the bloody wave took hold of the army . . . almost all officers [here] were either killed or deported to Siberia. . . .

"Finally the terrible terror wave spread from the army to the big mass of the people and the foreigners. In each foreigner Stalin saw a dangerous spy who damaged the country systematically . . . the papers had long accounts of their ominous doings . . . Soviet people were urged . . . to report them to the NKVD on the least occasion. Only those who accepted Soviet citizenship could live in a reasonable way.

"For me too a rather uncomfortable time began. I was given work in a nonsensical way, sixteen hours a day. In 1937 I had almost entirely given up the habit of eating. . . . I was accused of the most impossible things. . . . At a big meeting of the whole Institute I was again the target of numerous perfidious attacks. . . . I lost patience . . . became furious . . . left the meeting ostentatiously. Naturally, there was a terrible scandal and the Party cell of the Institute held special deliberations. . . . I had also committed the greatest of Soviet crimes; I had left the meeting. . . . The atmosphere at the Institute became very tense . . . the same things that a year ago were great achievements now had become criminal actions. . . . My friends warned me that I should disappear from Soviet Russia as soon as possible. . . . An infinitely offensive article against me appeared in the papers, full of lies. Usually after such an article one could expect to be arrested. But the Soviets had to be more cautious with us foreigners especially since we were innocent. . . . An arrest would have led to complications with foreign countries. . . .

"[After having resigned from my Institute first, then from the university] I had to organize our departure. Nobody could help me anymore, because individuals who leave the country of their free will are most suspicious elements. . . . At this time there was mad terror in the country. Mass arrests took place every night. Among those arrested were a large number of university professors, also from [our] Institute. . . . And the worst of it is that nobody knows what happens to these unfortunate men. They are usually fetched late at night . . . and secretly taken to the crammed prisons of the

NKVD. Not even the wife knows where her husband is. . . . The terror wave now spread in an instant to the leading circles of the intelligentsia, which was now sacrificed for the second time. . . .

"My case is not even remotely the worst . . . and I hope that my experiences will open the eyes of the young people. . . . After three years in that country, many things are still an enigma to me. A European cannot understand everything that happens at the boundary of Asia. . . ."

Hungary was the second country to come under a dictatorial regime in the wake of World War I. As in most other European countries, in Hungary also anti-Semitism played an important role in driving out of the country the intelligentsia, which was in great part Jewish. The Hungarian intellectuals were less affected by the first, short-lived, Communist dictatorship than by the White reaction that followed it: Béla Kun and many of his associates were Jewish, and it was natural that Admiral Horthy's counter-revolution should direct its reprisals not only against the workers' organizers but also against the Jews. For the first time after World War I anti-Semitism became legal in a European country when Horthy became regent of Hungary in 1920. Despite his title, Horthy did not rule on behalf of any king; on the contrary, he twice thwarted the attempts of Charles of Habsburg to regain the crown of Saint Stephen.

The anti-Semitism of Horthy's regime was aimed less at Jewish capitalists and businessmen than at "the poor, hard-working, genuinely cultured Jewish intelligentsia," in the opinion of the Hungarian Oscar Jászi (who came to this country in the twenties) in his book *Revolution and Counter-Revolution in Hungary*. Horthy purged the public services and the school and university staffs of all Jews, and to prevent a later crop of Jewish intellectuals, he introduced the *numerus clausus* in the universities: since the Jews were 5 per cent of the Hungarian population, the number of Jewish students to be admitted to the universities was not to exceed 5 per cent of all students. Horthy was the first of the modern dictators to introduce the racial principle into anti-Semitism. In the past to be a Jew had been a question of religion, and a Jew converted to Catholicism had enjoyed all the privileges of other Catholics; several Jewish families, as those of Theodore von Karman and John Von Neumann, had received a title of nobility for special merit. Horthy, instead, declared that the Jews belonged to a separate race and nationality.

(It was at this time that the ideas of Madison Grant were becoming popular in America, assisted by Kenneth Roberts' skilful writings.)

As a consequence of Horthy's laws, and for other reasons, Hungarian intellectuals began emigrating in the early twenties. Bright students went to study in Berlin, Vienna, or Prague — including some who had been accepted for admission to Hungarian universities; and eventually many members of the Hungarian intelligentsia landed in America. As a group they were so outstanding, the total talent appeared so much out of proportion to the small size of their country, that the phenomenon puzzled and continues to puzzle their American friends. I was so intrigued that I looked into it in some detail and shall relate my limited findings later in this chapter.

The case of Italy is again different. Mussolini's attacks on the Italian intelligentsia remained strictly political during the first fifteen years of his rule, and only in 1938 did he indorse anti-Semitism as an element in the process of Prussianizing Italy. When fascism assumed power in 1922, the Italian intellectuals held different opinions about it. Some recognized at once that it constituted a threat to intellectual freedom and accordingly took a prompt stand against it. If they were in politics or if they belonged to the journalistic world, they expressed their opposition publicly, becoming early targets of Fascist aggressiveness. Their fate was either that of the martyr or that of the exile, and in some cases it was both. The young liberal Piero Gobetti, for one, having persistently criticized Mussolini's government in his political journal, was severely beaten and fled to Paris in 1925, where he died shortly afterward at the age of twenty-four. In 1937 the Socialist Carlo Rosselli, a fighter in the Spanish War on the Republican side, was killed in France at the instigation of the Fascist government, together with his brother Nello, a distinguished historian visiting from Italy

Other Italian intellectuals were originally pro-Fascist and some of them even participated in the March on Rome, though they may have become anti-Fascists later. It may be said in general that early fascism enjoyed the favor of the middle classes, which it claimed to have saved from bolshevism, and appeared especially attractive to the young. Many students and young intellectuals who had seen the debacle of the old institutions, the inefficiency of the old generation in government, and the pompousness of many university professors, placed their hope in the Fascist "experiment in youth." (Mussolini was thirty-nine when he rose to power and was surrounded by much younger men.)

The opposition, though significant in its quality, was small in number. To a Fascist "manifesto of intellectuals" drawn by philosopher Giovanni Gentile and bearing hundreds of signatures, philosopher Benedetto Croce answered with an anti-Fascist manifesto signed by about forty persons. When in the fall of 1931 Mussolini passed a decree requiring university professors to take an oath of loyalty pledging themselves to perform their teaching duties in order to produce "industrious, upright citizens, devoted to their *patria* and the Fascist regime," only eleven out of some twelve hundred refused to take the oath. With some justification, many must have thought that teaching chemistry, ancient history, or comparative anatomy had nothing to do with politics, and others may have asked themselves whether it was better to follow their beliefs and personal pride and quit teaching, thus acting against the interest of their students, or compromise with their conscience and continue their mission as educators.

As years went by and the Fascist screw gradually tightened, intellectuals kept leaving Italy. Until 1938 very few came directly to America; most went to France, Switzerland, or England, and some of them reached the United States only after the fall of France. But few stayed here for long: many pre-1938 exiles, the most politically active intellectual refugees, returned to Italy after the fall of Mussolini in 1943 or at the end of the war. They included men like former foreign minister Count Carlo Sforza, who acted as a spokesman of Italian anti-fascism in the United States and returned to Italy in 1943 to become a minister in the new republic; Alberto Tarchiani, who also returned to Italy in 1943, only to be sent back to the United States as the first ambassador of liberated Italy; and the well-known Catholic priest Don Luigi Sturzo, who had founded and led the Italian Popular Party until 1924 and had been in exile ever since.

The intellectuals who left Italy in late 1938 and after, in much larger numbers than at any other time since the rise of fascism, belong in a different class. Their flight was caused by the sudden, unexpected outbreak of official anti-Semitism in July, 1938, and the realization that after the *Anschluss* in March, 1938, Mussolini had become entirely subservient to Hitler. The Jews were an insignificant minority — about one per thousand of the population — and there had been no popular or official anti-Semitism in modern Italy, except

49

a dumb resistance in certain careers. Mussolini repeatedly declared that there never was and never would be official anti-Semitism in Italy. This statement, published in Germany in 1933 in Emil Ludwig's book *Talks with Mussolini*, may have been a reason why many German Jews settled in Italy after the rise of Hitler. At first the older German Jews resumed their occupations undisturbed while the younger continued their education in Italian schools.

But then Mussolini changed his mind. He launched his racial campaign in July, 1938, with the publication of the absurd *Manifesto della Razza* and followed it up with racial legislation. First to flee were the German refugees, already trained in the art of escaping. Among many Jewish and a few "Aryan" Italian intellectuals there were hushed consultations and an exchange of what meager information they had on possible ways to obtain foreign visas and get help from abroad, and on the valuables that might be smuggled out of Italy in place of the money that had to be left behind. All discussions were held far away from telephones, to which even the most levelheaded physicists attributed fantastic powers of interception and transmission. Many consultations were held at summer resorts in the Alps or on the beaches, for this was vacation time for the intellectuals connected with the universities.

The promulgation of the first racial laws in Italy early in September, 1938, coincided with the Munich crisis that kept Europe under the threat of war for several weeks. The Italian intellectuals who planned to leave realized by then that no country in Europe would be a haven and turned their eyes to the United States, but only the most fortunate could go there. Others scattered over Europe, despite the hazards of this course, or to more distant countries in Latin America and the Far East.

This last, larger wave of intellectual emigration from Italy may be regarded as one of Hitler's feats; Mussolini created his own Fascist anti-Semitism in a spirit of emulation of his German ally, as part of a campaign to Prussianize Italy. He initiated it upon his return in late 1937 from a visit to Germany where he had been dazzled by the show of efficiency organized in his honor and frustrated by the realization that his own Fascists were not as tough as Hitler's Nazis. Italian anti-Semitism was an accidental phenomenon born of Hitler's passion and Mussolini's mood of dependence upon Hitler.

In Italy, as in other countries, the two principal causes of the intellectual emigration were political oppression and racial persecution. But Italy's example is singular in that the political and racial motives remained almost entirely separate and belonged to two periods of time sharply divided by the year 1938. The Italian racial period is an illustration of one mechanism by which Hitler became the main force responsible for driving from Europe the intelligentsia of many countries: his policies were adopted by admirers like Mussolini and by frightened allies like Admiral Horthy: the official anti-Semitism that Horthy had promoted in the twenties was abating in the early thirties but was revived in 1938. The other, and chief, mechanism was imposition of German laws on the countries that Hitler occupied.

Within Germany itself, the Nazis laws simultaneously struck at the intellectuals on political, religious, and racial grounds. Victims of the Nazi were both Jews and Aryans, though the Jews were more numerous. In contrast with Mussolini, Hitler was a single-minded fanatic, set on a course at the end of which was the attainment of Nordic supremacy and extermination of the Jews. His hatred of the Jews fed upon itself, for he attributed to them all the traits he loathed. In a speech delivered on May 10, 1933, Hitler said: "The Jew has never founded any civilization, though he has destroyed hundreds. He possesses nothing of his own creation. . . . Everything he has is stolen. . . . He has no art of his own; bit by bit he has stolen it all from other peoples. He does not even know how to preserve the precious things others have created. . . . The Aryan alone can form states . . . the Jew cannot . . . all his revolutions must be international. They must spread as a pestilence spreads. Already he has destroyed Russia; now . . . he seeks to disintegrate the national spirit of the Germans and to pollute their blood."

Hitler's purge of the civil service in April, 1933, removed from office all persons of part or full Jewish descent and all those who had shown leftist, liberal, or strongly Republican tendencies. Civic service laws applied automatically to the universities, which were ultimately governed by the Ministry of Education in each of the eight federal states. Many professors and lecturers lost their positions. In the spring of 1933 Bernard Rust, then Minister of Education of Prussia, said: "It is less important that a professor make discoveries than that he train assistants and students in the proper views of the world." At about the same time, a newly established Ministry of Propaganda assumed control over intellectual activities outside the universities, and many persons in the press, theater, and the arts lost their positions. In the spring of 1934 all universities came under one central Minister of Education of the

Reich at the head of which Hitler placed Bernard Rust. Rust had direct control over faculty and student body, and was responsible exclusively to Hitler. Rules were tightened, civic merit was no longer recognized, and more university men were dismissed. As a consequence of Hitler's laws, 1,678 lecturers and professors lost their jobs and the number of students fell from approximately 150,000 in 1933 to about 60,000 in 1938.

The German universities have been criticized for having done nothing to check the rise of nazism or to organize resistance to its interference in the cultural field. Critics point out that the universities were attended almost exclusively by students from the upper, prosperous classes. Nationalism was strong among them and facilitated the spread of Nazi propaganda. Several years before Hitler came to power, nationalist student organizations in smaller universities staged classroom demonstrations and insulted their professors. The faculties did not recognize the threat, absorbed as they were in the scholarly pursuits that had made them famous throughout the world. Too many of them were optimists who waved away the thought of danger in the belief that nazism could not take hold in Germany. Even after the rise of Hitler, many believed that the country would return to normality within a few weeks, that the Nazi rage would soon die out. Not a few of the optimists who stubbornly refused to leave Germany eventually paid with their lives.

The blindness of the intellectuals is not sufficient to explain how a country of so high a cultural level and so proud of intellectual achievement could turn ruthlessly against culture and come within a hair's-breadth of destroying it altogether. The entire German population was aloof. It did not react to Hitler's blows to the universities or otherwise try to stop the cultural debacle. Significant in this respect was the lack of any strong public expression of indignation when on May 10, 1933, enthusiastic students in many university towns burned the "un-German spirit." That day, in Berlin alone, 5,000 students paraded along five miles of streets bearing swastikas and singing Nazi songs, behind trucks and private cars loaded with books. They had erected a pyre of logs on the square before the Opera House and there they burned 2,000 books — books by Jews like Einstein and Freud as well as by Aryans like Thomas Mann; by pacifists like the Austrian Nobel Prize winner Bertha von Suttner, and by foreigners like the Americans Helen Keller and Upton Sinclair; by political thinkers like Marx and Engels, and novelists like

Erich Maria Remarque and Stefan Zweig. Forty thousand Berliners witnessed the bonfire, cheered at first, then watched in silence. Similar ceremonies took place at the same time all over Germany.

A passage from *Arrow in the Blue*, an autobiography by the cosmopolitan
writer and journalist Arthur Koestler, may be a fitting concluding comment
to this tragic period in European history. "At a conservative estimate," he
wrote, "three out of every four people I knew before I was thirty were
subsequently killed in Spain or hounded to death at Dachau, or gassed at
Belsen, or deported to Russia; some jumped from windows in Vienna or
Budapest; others were wrecked by the misery and aimlessness of permanent
exile."

THE MYSTERY OF HUNGARIAN TALENT

One question is often asked in this country: Hungary is a tiny country, with
a population in 1930 of only 8,683,700, and yet she sent to America an
amazing number of outstanding men in all intellectual fields, scientific,
scholarly, literary, and artistic: how did she do it? At least one person told
me that there is no point to a study of European intellectuals in this country
unless it provides a solution to the Hungarian mystery. I took my clue and
posed the question to as many Hungarians as I could easily talk to, and while
none gave me a single satisfactory explanation, some of their views are
worth relating.

Physicist Edward Teller offered me his own case as an example. He
always knew, he said, that Hungary was foundering and if he wanted to
survive he would have to be better, much better, than anyone else. No one
had explicitly told him so, but his environment made him constantly aware
of this necessity. He was six when World War I broke out, and from then
on he saw conditions in Hungary growing steadily worse. Defeat, revolution,
and counter-revolution came in rapid succession. He felt strongly that if he
was to have a satisfactory career he should not remain in Hungary, and
in fact in 1926, when he was eighteen, he went to study in Germany. In
other words, it was his will to overcome the difficulties hampering his normal
wish for self-fulfilment which developed his mental abilities.

To Eugene Wigner I must have asked the question too emphatically and
mentioned genius rather than talent, for he answered that the question did
not make sense. In his generation, he said, Hungary had not produced

53

more geniuses than other countries; actually, she had produced only one: John Von Neumann. (But Hungarian-born physician Imre Horner admitted another Hungarian of genius, Béla Bartók.) Unlike Teller, Wigner never had the feeling that Hungary was foundering. But, he said, Hungarians had a tradition of emigration and knew that once they were outside their country they would make good only if they were decidedly better than the average. Among the main reasons for emigrating was the heavy bureaucracy. One out of every eight employees was in government service, and this huge number of white-collar workers in the Hungarian government arrogantly exerted political pressure. The deadening influence of this system was keenly felt in the universities: while Hungarian high-schools were excellent, in Wigner's opinion, the universities were very poor. The faculties were under the thumb of the Minister of Education who had appointed them, and there was a widespread resistance to the appointment of persons of Jewish ancestry, who in the Hungary of that time constituted a good portion of the intellectual class. It was symbolic of the bureaucratic influence, Wigner said, that professors at universities kept their libraries locked up and a student who needed to consult a book was often obliged to borrow the key from his professor. These dreary conditions pushed many young intellectuals out of Hungary and accounted, at least in part, for the concentration of Hungarian talent outside Hungary.

A different opinion reached me from Jerusalem, where the migratory wave carried the Hungarian scientist D. K. Szekely. In the Hungary of the twenties, he explained, talented boys were "pampered" by teachers and admired by school friends. There was also in Budapest a group of enthusiasts, called the "Society for the Study of the Child," who scouted the schools for talent and gave long years of guidance and moral support to the deserving. The society had no money, but occasionally a member managed to conjure up financial help by pulling the right strings. Szekely himself was one of the "protected talented children" from the time he was eleven until way past his boyhood. His protector took a real interest in him, steered him from art to science, gave him lessons in the philosophy of science, and managed to obtain for him a "very considerable stipendium" from a masonic brotherhood. At one time the protector put in jeopardy his own position and falsified some information in order to assist his young Jewish friend. This great encouragement given to promising children helps explain the "mystery of Hungarian talent," according to Szekely.

Psychoanalyst Franz Alexander, whose father was Bernard Alexander, well-known philosopher, university professor, and art critic, wrote in his autobiographical *The Western Mind in Transition*: "Father's generation and the next one grew up in an atmosphere in which creativity and intellectual and artistic accomplishments were publicly and officially held in the highest esteem. Young people were not aiming primarily at a prescribed routine career or social role, but at a development of their unique endowments. . . . My father's generation could . . . devote their lives to the realization of a progressive enlightened national culture dedicated to fostering the spiritual qualities of the citizen, the Platonic Utopia of a society led by the intellectual elite."

"Father's generation and the next one," the period considered by Franz Alexander, roughly coincided with the "golden age of security" which was so good to the European middle classes in general. But in Hungary it had some peculiar features: for centuries Hungary had been a feudal country in which a limited number of noblemen living in opulence owned the largest part of the land. The landed aristocracy administered the country, participated in its government, and insured the continuity of its own inherited privileges. The mass of the people was an immense, poor agricultural proletariat, owning no land at all or "dwarf properties," below the minimum size to provide a livelihood. (These conditions persisted until the dissolution of the Habsburg monarchy. In Hungary proper, just before World War I, the 324 largest *latifundia* occupied 14.3 per cent of the whole land and averaged about 41,000 acres each. All latifundia *together* covered 40 per cent of the land, while the agricultural proletariat accounted for 80 per cent of the agricultural population.)

Between these two groups, noble landowners and proletarian masses, a true bourgeoisie was lacking. Its role was assumed by an exiguous "historical middle class" or gentry of lesser or impoverished nobility, which furnished the leaders of the 1848 revolution, including Louis Kossuth himself. The revolution was repressed, but it was due to it, and therefore to the "historical middle class," that in 1867 Hungary attained partial independence: the Compromise of 1867 established the dual monarchy. Under the new national government, Hungary experienced great economic growth and many social changes. Roads and railroads were built, agricultural methods were greatly improved, and a tardy process of industrialization began, accompanied by urban development.

Commenting on this period, the Hungarian-born metallurgist Paul Beck remarked that many previously accepted taboos and inhibitions were abandoned, "the serfs were freed, Jews were given equal citizenship rights, opportunities for learning and entering the professions were gradually extended to large segments of the population, with the development in the cities of a middle class of professional people and businessmen." The salient feature of this new middle class, the feature that helps to explain the blooming of Hungarian talent, is that it was mostly Jewish. The Hungarian Jews were originally serfs without civil rights, not even the right to own a name, who lived on the property of the nobility or on imperial estates. Emperor Joseph's patent of toleration of 1781 somewhat improved their conditions — they could have names, provided they were German names, because the emperor was attempting the Germanization of his empire — but their rights were still very limited, and only a few attained middle-class status. The compromise changed their situation substantially: many of the barriers restricting their activities were lifted, and the new system of free enterprise introduced by the national government created opportunities for men in the professions and trades, in commerce and finance. But the nobility and the historical middle class despised any work that had nothing to do with exploiting their land holdings, participating in the public administration, or serving in the army; the masses were too poor and ignorant to either care or be able to take advantage of the situation. In this vacuum, new needs were filled mainly by the Jews.

After the Compromise of 1867, according to Paul Beck, the Hungarian Jews found themselves in a position similar to that in which the American Negroes are now; in both cases, the abolishing or the lowering of racial barriers and the economic growth of the country created a wealth of new opportunities for the rising group; and the long-repressed desire of the group to better its status gave it a strong motivation. To the Hungarian Jews, the smallness of the middle class was an additional favorable circumstance. Once the old restrictions against them were lifted, their activities underwent an enormous expansion. From peasants and peddlers they turned into merchants, bankers, and financiers; they moved into independent businesses and the professions; and soon they invaded all cultural fields, giving themselves at last to the intellectual pursuits that are the highest aim of the Jewish people.

Physician Imre Horner, who had given much thought to the "mystery of Hungarian talent," stressed the cultural importance of the Hungarian Jews. By the beginning of the century, he told me, they were exerting an intellectual influence out of proportion to their number. He estimated that at least half of the Hungarian newspapers were in Jewish hands (but the Jews were only 5 per cent of the population). They were excellent papers, sometimes cynical, sometimes irreverent, always thought-provoking, and had a considerable influence in creating the intellectual atmosphere of Hungary. Imre Horner also remarked that in the generation of the future immigrants to the United States, practically all scientists and mathematicians were of Jewish extraction, and so were many musicians, writers, and philosophers.

"These Jewish intellectuals had to excel, whether they intended to stay in Hungary or had emigration in mind," Horner wrote me. "If they stayed they had to overcome a government-instigated and institutionalized anti-Semitism. If they emigrated, it was the initial handicap of being a newcomer that they had to overcome. . . . In order to understand how it came about that so many outstanding scientists and artists of Hungarian origin have been recently active in America, one has to realize that the overwhelming majority of Hungarian intellectuals who emigrated to America after World War I and in the 1930s were Jews. (Bartók was one of the notable exceptions, and so was Albert Szent-Györgyi who came after World War II.) Many of these Jews were converts to Christianity, but that did not make any difference in the [Horthy] era of Hungarian racism. They left Hungary because of the then prevailing anti-Semitism. And speaking of 'disproportionately large number of Hungarians' one has to remember that, since the Jews of Hungary comprised 5 per cent of the total population of about ten millions (of which more than one million lived outside the Trianon borders of Hungary), their absolute number roughly equaled that of the German Jews, which made only 0.9 per cent of the total population of 60 millions. And while the German mass-emigration began in the 1930's with the advent of nazism, the exodus of Hungarian Jews began in 1919. Thus they had a much longer period of time to accumulate in the United States. Their number and accomplishments might be disproportionate to the small country they came from, but they are probably not out of proportion to the size of the group they belonged to. The comparison should not be between the size of Hungary and Germany, but between the relative size of the Jewish populations in Germany and Hungary."

On the whole, my Hungarian-born friends seemed to agree that the emergence of a Jewish middle class with high intellectual ambitions had much to do with the blossoming of Hungarian talent. Several, however, indicated a possible additional reason: the very quality of intellectual life in Budapest. Physicist Leo Szilard, who was considered the most unpredictable Hungarian in this country, once explained to Alice K. Smith that the high concentration of Hungarian talent in physics grew "out of a special environment in Budapest at the turn of the century — a society where economic security was taken for granted, a high value was placed on intellectual achievement, and physics was taught so badly that serious students were thrown upon their own resources."

Budapest was "a modern city," in Paul Beck's words, "largely free of the oppressive traditions of past ages and of the social restrictions of older communities. It became the natural home and breeding ground of the new middle class." Culture concentrated there at the expense of the rest of the country, and nowhere else did it reach so high a level. The Hungarian capital was situated halfway between East and West, but the intelligentsia ruled in favor of the West. Artistically it became Parisian; politically it admired the British and erected its Parliament on the pattern of Westminster. Budapest intellectuals, most of them individualists with no desire to conform, threw ideas at each other in cafés, expounded progressive or eccentric theories in the newspapers, turned their thumbs down in theaters at artists acclaimed in other countries, or made stars of unknown artists — of Isadora Duncan, for one, according to violinist Joseph Szigeti.

Even before becoming fully developed intellectuals, young Hungarians in Budapest were exposed to the ferment of liberal and radical ideas. Many students belonged to the Galileo Club of progressive undergraduates founded in 1908 by philosopher Julius Pikler and the future sociologist Karl Polanyi, who was to come to this country and teach at Columbia University. In the mind of its founders, this club was to be an alliance of future scientists against the pressures of religion, politics, and social conditions, but its interests rapidly spread from science to all current ideologies, which its members discussed with mystic fervor and often with blindness.

Most future émigrés lived in Budapest or went there for their education. Most met each other as students in the Galileo Club and participated in its ebullient discussions. Virtually all breathed at some time or other the hyper-intellectualism and hyper-estheticism of the capital and did not escape its influence. In Budapest they had to keep mentally alert, to emulate and compete, and in order not to be submerged they had to develop their capabilities to the full.

It seems reasonable to conclude that the flowering of Hungarian talent in the generation of the cultural wave was due to the special social and cultural circumstances obtaining in Hungary at the turn of the century. A strong middle class by then had emerged and asserted itself. Having risen in response to needs that the nobility did not feel inclined to fill and the peasants could not fill, it was largely Jewish and was animated by the intellectual ambitions of the Jews. The intellectual portion of this middle class converged upon the capital where it created a peculiarly sophisticated atmosphere and kept its members under continuous stimulation. The political anti-Semitism of the early twenties hit this segment of the population with great vehemence and gave the intellectuals a further reason for striving to excel and stay afloat. Under these circumstances talent could not remain latent. It flourished.

IV

The Roads to America

Until Hitler's ascent to power in 1933, the exiles from dictator-dominated countries — Russia, Hungary, and Italy — were able to find refuge in other European countries. In the early thirties, political, religious, and racial persecution was not the direct cause of the intellectual immigration to the United States. For the intellectuals, as for other classes of immigrants, the main motive was opportunity. After the end of World War I, the poor state of many European economies and the rigidity of educational systems that allowed for little expansion contributed to create a great shortage of positions for intellectual workers. In America before the depression, on the other hand, the demands of education were rapidly increasing, and there were more openings for intellectuals under better financial conditions than in Europe. The large immigration of scientists from north European countries is an excellent illustration of this migratory mechanism.

According to figures published in the *Enciclopedia Italiana* in 1932, Norway had a single university, in Oslo, with an enrolment of 3,734 students; one institute of technology, and one academy of art. In Sweden there were two universities proper, one in Lund and the other in Uppsala, and a group of faculties in Stockholm; in Stockholm there were also one technical institute and one academy of art. Denmark had one university, one institute of technology, and one academy of art. William Zachariasen, a Norwegian-born physicist who has been at the University of Chicago since coming to this country in 1930, told me that at the University of Oslo there were two professorships in each of the main scientific areas, and the time gaps between openings for young scientists were very large. This is why he emigrated after teaching only two years in Oslo. According to statutes, Scandinavian institutions of higher education should have been staffed with teachers and researchers from any of the three Scandinavian countries; in practice, this interchange occurred only on a limited scale and did not increase appreciably the academic opportunities for young Norwegian scientists. Even in Holland, with three state universities, one city university, and a number of private universities and other private institutions of higher education, openings were few and the emigration of scientists had been considerable ever since the twenties.

These early intellectuals, as well as many of those who came in the later, more difficult period, made their own arrangements for visas and travel, and for life and work in this country. Yet, after Hitler's rise to power, an increasingly large number of intellectual exiles needed assistance, and numerous agencies promptly sprang up in the free world to aid them. The problem was spectacular: the Comité International pour le Placement des Intellectuels Réfugiés (assisting artists, writers, and professionals, but not academics) reported that in its first year of operation alone almost 3,000 persons sought assistance.

As time went by and what had seemed an emergency of the moment turned into a stubborn, spreading phenomenon, the agencies multiplied, broadened their scope, merged together, or split into specialized branches. Not a few that had set to work enthusiastically were compelled to disband within a short time for lack of adequate funds. On the other hand, some of those groups organized for work in one country established channels of communications with organizations of similar aim in other countries and eventually acted as clearinghouses through which refugees were helped to resettle in the free world. So a web of routes was spun, over which European intellectuals were able to escape in larger and larger numbers as Hitler invaded one country after another.

As remarkable as the extent of the rescue operations is the scarcity of the publicity they received. Not even the European intellectuals themselves realize how much was done for them. They may remember the committee from which they received assistance or to which they made financial contributions, but most of those I talked to had no further knowledge. As for myself, I was very ignorant and was set on the path of discovery while reading Maurice Davie's *Refugees in America*. I learned more facts from books and articles than from conversations with the persons involved, though personal accounts occasionally opened new vistas and always added vivid details.

SOME EUROPEAN ASSISTANCE AGENCIES

The burning of the Reichstag occurred on February 27, 1933, and was the signal for the beginning of Nazi persecutions. In March came the elections confirming Nazi rule; the appointment of Dr. Josef Goebbels to the Ministry of Public Enlightenment and Propaganda; the first dismissals from universities, the theater, and the opera; and the first massive flight of leftists and Jews. The first law for the "cleansing of the civil service" was promulgated on April 9, and brought a large number of dismissals from the staffs of educational institutions. By May many agencies had already been organized outside Germany to help refugees and self-exiles.

A group of German refugee scholars formed a self-help organization in Switzerland and named it *Notgemeinschaft deutscher Wissenschaftler im Ausland* (Emergency Society of German Scholars Abroad). A Hungarian-born intellectual, Philipp Schwartz, was behind the creation of the *Notgemeinschaft*, a fact which is not surprising as bright Hungarians are likely to appear suddenly anywhere. "Professor Philipp Schwartz," Lord Beveridge wrote in his *A Defence of Free Learning*, "Hungarian by birth but holding a Chair of General Pathology and Pathological Anatomy at Frankfurt-am-Main in Germany, was an immediate victim of Hitler's racial persecution and went in March, 1933, to Zurich in Switzerland. There he founded at once the *Notgemeinschaft* and directed it for six months. . . . For money it had to depend almost wholly on contributions from displaced scholars whom it had helped to re-establish. But by its personal knowledge of the scholars themselves and by using its contacts with universities everywhere, it rendered invaluable service." A part of this "invaluable service" was the preparation of a detailed list of nearly 1,500 names of Germans dismissed from their academic posts. It was published in 1936, with the assistance of the Rockefeller Foundation.

The Comité International pour le Placement des Intellectuels Réfugiés was established in Geneva. Its council was formed of representatives of many western nations, including the United States. Persons who have been assisted by it call it "Marie Ginsberg's committee" after its honorary secretary and active director, whom Norman Bentwich described as "a woman of inexhaustible energy and resolution." The committee did not assist academic intellectuals as such, but through one of its executive members, Professor Rappard, rector of the University of Geneva, several refugee professors from Austria, Germany, and Italy were given positions at a postgraduate school for international studies created *ad hoc*. In the years 1940–43 the committee was forced to close its offices in Paris, Brussels, and Amsterdam and direct its efforts to the assistance of academics and professionals who managed to get into Switzerland.

England, France, Belgium, Holland, Denmark, and Sweden also formed committees, mostly to help academics and other intellectuals who had found temporary refuge in these countries. These agencies lasted shorter or longer periods according to the availability of funds and the vicissitudes of war. One of the early agencies, the Academic Assistance Council, remained in existence in England until 1966, under the name Society for the Protection of Science and Learning. It was formed by heads of English universities and learned societies at the initiative of Sir William, now Lord Beveridge, the director of the London School of Economics and Political Science. Its aim was "to assist those university teachers and investigators who, on grounds of religion, political opinion or race, were unable to carry on their work in their own country." Sir William himself was its first honorary secretary, and Lord Rutherford of Nelson, one of the most brilliant physicists of modern times, was its first president. Walter Adams, a lecturer at the University of London, carried the work load until 1939. He was succeeded by Esther Simpson who had been his assistant and stayed in office until the organization terminated its work. For the extent and the broadness of operations, the Academic Assistance Council was the most prominent organization in its field. By November, 1938, it had placed 524 persons in presumably permanent positions in 36 different countries — 161 in the United States alone — and 306 in temporary positions.

Working behind the scenes of the Academic Assistance Council in its early years was the second Hungarian to take a lead in rescue operations, Leo Szilard. In *A Defence of Free Learning*, Lord Beveridge does not record Szilard's unofficial part in promoting the British committee. Since Szilard was to become one of the most prominent European intellectuals in the United States and will be mentioned often in these pages, his activities in aid of fellow refugees are worth recording briefly. Until early 1933 Szilard was on the teaching staff of the university in Berlin, but being endowed with a great deal of political foresight, he kept a packed suitcase in his room. Thus it was easy for him to leave Berlin and go to Vienna shortly after the burning of the Reichstag. When he learned of the first dismissals from German universities, he thought that something should be done. Through a chain of Germans and Austrians, some of whom he met accidentally and others by arrangement, he learned that Sir William was in Vienna at his own hotel. Szilard approached him at once and put the problem to him. Norman Bentwich relates that Sir William had already heard of the dismissals while "passing an evening with fellow economists in a Vienna café," and had thought of appointing one of the dismissed economists to the London School of Economics. At a subsequent tea with Szilard, "Beveridge agreed that as soon as he got back to England and got through the most important things on his agenda, he would try to form a committee . . . and he suggested that Szilard should come to London and occasionally prod him. If he prodded him long enough and frequently enough, he would probably be able to do something." Szilard did go to London, and once the council was established he helped in several ways, not least by arranging to recruit Esther Simpson, who had been working for an international cause in Geneva. In the early summer of 1933 Szilard was reported traveling to foreign countries and in the later part of summer he was constantly in the office of the Academic Assistance Council. Esther Simpson felt that the information and advice he then gave were invaluable.

The Academic Assistance Council acted as a specialized employment agency, with a detailed file on every scholar and academic worker who had been dismissed from his position. It also paid small living allowances to refugees until work could be found for them. The substantial funds that were needed for allowances and other operations were raised both among the general public and the academic world. Many members of British universities taxed themselves a percentage of their salaries. When the council was founded, the faculty of the London School of Economics pledged 3 per cent on larger salaries and 2 per cent on smaller salaries. Intellectual émigrés who in 1933 already had a position in England or elsewhere also taxed themselves to support the council. A group of academics in Princeton, New Jersey, of whom Eugene Wigner was one, contributed 5 per cent of their salaries to the Academic Assistance Council. This organization collected £30,000 from all sources in its first two years of operation.

Although it was created to meet the German emergency, the council soon extended its help to displaced academics from many countries including Austria, Hungary, Czechoslovakia, Italy, Poland, and Spain. British univerties did all they could to create new positions, but they could not make room for so many newcomers. To place at least some of them in the United States, the council kept in close contact with its American counterpart, the Emergency Committee in Aid of Displaced Foreign Scholars. But in 1937 the American committee urged the council not to send more refugee scholars to the States: American colleges and universities were crowded and the younger staff members opposed the hiring of foreigners. The council shrugged its shoulders — it could not impose its will on the emergency committee nor could it give up its faith in the land of opportunity. It decided to by-pass official America, advance its protégés enough money for travel expenses, and let them scout on their own the maze of American educational institutions. One of the men sent out in this way was Marcel Schein, a Hungarian physicist who had not had much luck in his attempts to get a stable position in Europe. He had taught in Switzerland and Russia, but at the end of 1937 he was in Prague with no position and a wife and a son. He left his family and, with the help of the council, reached the United States. There he went to see a friend from Switzerland who had immigrated three years before, the future Nobel Prize winner Felix Bloch, and in Bloch's car the two made the rounds of many institutions. Finally, Schein was offered a position at the University of Chicago, where he remained until his death in 1960. His family remained in Prague a few months. But in September, 1938, Schein cabled his wife to leave Czechoslovakia at once with their son and go to Zurich. She obeyed, though she did not know the reason for the hurry, and left Czechoslovakia just before the Munich agreement gave part of it to Germany. In those troubled times it was often easier to recognize the trend of events from the United States than in the very place where the events were to occur.

Several heads of university departments in England took initiative independently of the Academic Assistance Council (which afterward co-operated with them) to help displaced scholars until they found their own feet. Notable among them was the biochemist Frederick George Donnan, who soon after Hitler's rise to power persuaded the Imperial Chemical Industries to provide funds for scientist refugees, on the ground that this was a unique chance to hire theoretical chemists. Having obtained the pledge, Donnan went to scout Germany but interpreted the definition of "theoretical chemists" broadly enough to include theoretical physicists like Edward Teller. Once in England, the rescued scientists did not work mainly for the company that provided their livelihood but carried on their research in Donnan's laboratory. This may be the reason why a few years later, after a change of director and policies, the Imperial Chemical Industries decided to discontinue the plan and gave a year's notice to the refugee scientists on its payroll. Some of them began to think of the United States.

The Russian-born chemist and biologist Eugene Rabinowitch, one of the men whom Donnan helped to escape from Germany, believes that Leo Szilard was behind this operation too. In the *Bulletin of the Atomic Scientists* of October, 1964, Rabinowitch wrote that Szilard "persuaded British scientists, in particular F. G. Donnan, to start a rescue action for German-Jewish scientists who were rapidly losing their jobs. After a hundred or so were brought to Britain and given a chance to work, Donnan wondered about Szilard himself. 'We thought,' he reminisced, 'that Szilard was a rich Hungarian aristocrat, but he turned out to be as much in need of assistance as all those he had helped to leave Germany — only he did not mention it.'"

A SINGULAR HAVEN: TURKEY

In the spring of 1933, Mustafa Kemal Pasha (Atatürk), who was then carrying out an ambitious program of reforms to westernize Turkey, announced his intention to reorganize the University of Istanbul. Because of long-standing ties between Turkey and Germany, the Turkish government looked favorably upon the possibility of hiring some of the eminent German scholars made suddenly available by Hitler's policies. The *Notgemeinschaft* seized this opportunity. Philipp Schwartz, assisted by the Swiss Professor Albert Malche, expert adviser on the reorganization of the university in Istanbul, negotiated with members of the Turkish government in Ankara and received full power to enter into contracts with German professors. Only after some thirty Germans had signed their contracts was the Turkish parliament in a position to dissolve the old school in Istanbul and establish in its stead a modern university with five faculties. When it opened on November 1, 1933, some fifty Germans were on its faculty. Most of them were appointed for five years and had to accept the condition that they learn the Turkish language and lecture in it within a specified time. Schwartz himself was one of the fifty. He was to spend twenty years in Istanbul as head of the Pathological Institute before coming to the United States, to continue his life work on the cerebral birth lesions of the newborn at Warren State Hospital in Pennsylvania. After his arrival in Turkey, the Turkish government sought his advice in the hiring of more university teachers and government experts. At his suggestion, mathematician Richard Courant and physicists James Frank and Max Born visited Turkey as scientific advisers under Turkey's protection. The university was housed in old government buildings hastily renovated and in ancient palaces.

In 1935 a full university was established in Ankara around an existing school of law which had been created when Turkey had secularized its law system. The University of Ankara absorbed another group of German teachers, and more found positions in other institutions throughout Turkey. In all, over one hundred men and women were thus placed in academic positions in Turkey. One of the best known was composer Paul Hindemith, who helped the government reorganize Turkish musical education, then came to live in America in 1939. Another was Carl Ebert, the very popular opera director. He was called to Ankara in 1933 and founded and directed the Turkish State School of Opera and Drama and the Turkish State Theater. Later, he spent six years in California and became an American citizen before returning to Germany in 1954.

Early appointments to the University of Istanbul in 1933 were negotiated directly by the *Notgemeinschaft* with the Turkish government, but later appointments had to be approved by the Nazi government, although the government had been responsible for the dismissal of all the candidates. The Nazis had come to regard the Turkish project as an operation of *Kultur* propaganda abroad. In fact, they kept a close eye on Germans in Turkey; when the war broke out the German embassy summoned all men who still had a German passport to report for military service — "full" Jews had lost their passports, but "half" or "quarter" Jews retained them. The German summons could not be avoided: one day Hittitologist Hans Güterbock (who in 1949 joined the University of Chicago) was driving home in Ankara and found his street blocked by a German embassy car parked with doors sprawled open. He received his summons. At the embassy, however, he was told that university teachers were excused from military service because they were doing an important job of culture propaganda. Güterbock, who joined the University of Ankara in 1935, later married Frances Hellman, the daughter of one of the first German professors to be appointed to the University of Istanbul.

The German academic community in Turkey kept very much together. In Ankara alone there were some fifty German families, Güterbock said — but according to his wife, the "height" of social life, German of course, was in Istanbul. One joint effort of German professors from various fields of learning was the publication of a journal. They could not publish in German or Austrian journals; and American journals were completely out of reach during the war. The only possibility left to German teachers was to publish in Turkish journals. To do this the authors were often required to write one version of their work in Turkish. It did not make much difference. No one read Turkish journals outside Turkey. So German academics set up their own publication for scholarly work in any subject, from dermatology to Oriental history and Sanskrit. The journal, which lasted through some eighteen issues, was brought out by a private printing house in Turkey which had some experience of the German language, but the selling had to be done by the German scholars themselves.

It was hard to teach in Turkish even for those who studied the language seriously. For the first few years the German professors were allowed to use interpreters in the classrooms. Friedrich Dessauer, in Ankara from 1934 to 1937, told an interviewer from Radio-Bremen that a Turkish instructor who had been trained in Germany translated his lectures sentence by sentence. "This lengthened the lectures, but compelled us European professors to concise and clear expression." Hans Güterbock took about five years to learn enough Turkish to lecture informally to his students and about eight years before he felt sufficiently assured to give a formal talk. "But," his wife remarked, "he is a linguist by profession." Others took longer or never learned the language.

Students came from all parts of Turkey. Many were the children of peasants or soldiers, the two largest population groups at that time, and a number of them had never before seen electric lights. But now they came to study biophysics with Dessauer or the history of the Hittites with Güterbock or the modern techniques of medicine with Philipp Schwartz, and they did very well.

There were in Turkey other classes of German intellectuals beside those with official positions at universities or other schools. The Turkish government hired a considerable number of scientific and government experts, and other intellectuals came as assistants or relatives of persons holding positions. Turkey did not have free immigration and in general admitted only persons under government contracts (university positions were in this category). Professors with regular immigrant status could obtain entry permits for a few research assistants — but the prospect of advancement for the assistants was almost nil. Relatives of immigrants also could enter Turkey with special permits. Oskar and Susanne Schulze were among them. Later they came to the United States, where Susanne was for many years a professor at the School of Social Service Administration of the University of Chicago. In Germany they had both been active Social Democrats and therefore in danger from the Nazis. And Susanne was Jewish. Oskar was one of the mayors of Leipzig (German cities had several mayors) in charge of the Department of Welfare, until Hitler deposed him for his political stand. Susanne had studied languages and had obtained a doctor's degree in education; when the Nazis came to power, she was teaching at a school of social work founded in Berlin by the Workers Welfare Association. The school was closed in May, 1933, and Susanne took up the teaching of French and English to persons who wanted to emigrate. Oskar and Susanne had met while he was in office and her school provided social workers to his department. At the time of the advent of nazism they were not yet married, and they could not marry while the Nazis were in power because an Aryan could no longer marry a Jew. But both were optimists: nazism would blow over in a matter of weeks. It was a question of patience.

After being patient for a year, Susanne gave in to her sister's insistence that she visit her in Turkey. Her sister was the wife of astrophysicist Erwin Freundlich and had been in Turkey since 1933. Susanne arrived in Istanbul in August, 1934, with ten marks and a few summer clothes, on a short visit, just to see how things in Germany looked from outside. They looked very bad, and she did not go back. Within three months she had a position at a branch of the YWCA. (The YWCA was established in Istanbul after the Armenian massacre but was called the "American Social Service Center" because the epithet "Christian" was anathema in Muslim Turkey.) She taught English, German, and French to people of all nationalities, Greek, Armenian, Levantine, and, unlike university faculty members from Germany, she mingled with the Turks. Thus she was at an advantage and in two and a half years she learned the language well enough to carry on a conversation with the Turks.

In Berlin, Oskar was very angry at first: he could not see why she did not come back. But then his eyes were opened, and in the summer of 1935 he left for Turkey and an immediate marriage. He was not eligible for a government appointment and it was more difficult for a man than for a woman to find a position outside the government. Oskar privately tutored three children, Frances Güterbock's youngest sister, Erwin Freundlich's son, and a nephew of Kemal Pasha, a nice if not too bright boy who had been raised by a German nurse and could not speak Turkish. Oskar and Susanne Schulze enjoyed Turkey, their Turkish friends, and the beautiful view they had from their apartment, but to them as to many other Germans, Turkish culture and habits remained alien.

Most Germans did not become adjusted and left Turkey when their contracts expired or as soon as they could secure a Turkish passport with which to apply for an American visa. Occasionally the decision was made for them. Young Turks at the beginning of their academic careers resented German professors whom they thought were occupying posts that by rights belonged to them. In 1948 five Orientalists at Ankara, one of them Güterbock, were given three months' notice and dismissed. Güterbock estimated that almost half of the German intellectuals in Turkey eventually came to the United States. (The Schulzes came in 1937, the Güterbocks in 1949.) Others went to different European countries or back to Germany after the war was over. But some stayed on and were happy to be able to carry out their work uncompromisingly and, in Philipp Schwartz's words,, "to remain loyal to the spirit which is the foundation of modern civilization and humane feeling, and to impart this spirit, even in these dark days of history, to thousands of gifted young persons."

THE LEAGUE OF NATIONS

In the crisis created by the German refugees, the League of Nations could not remain aloof, but its work was hampered by several circumstances: the very nature of the League, a general concern about diplomatic propriety, and the objections from the German delegate. At a meeting on October 26, 1933, the Council of the League decided to create a High Commission for Refugees from Germany, but in order to circumvent the possibility of a German veto the League gave it autonomous status. Before this new body could begin to function, Germany withdrew from the League, thus removing at least one reason for the unfortunate separation of the commission from the League. And yet matters did not change. The high commission remained autonomous, and the high commissioner, the American James G. McDonald, was hampered by the fact that his organization lacked the moral authority invested in true bodies of the League.

In its first two years of operations, the high commission spent its efforts in attempts to mitigate the plight of the refugees by diplomatic negotiations with Germany. More successful was its work to provide documents for those who needed them: residence and work permits, and identity and travel documents for persons without passports. These activities were in behalf of all classes of refugees, not intellectuals alone, but in the spring of 1934 the high commission established the Committee of Experts for Academic and Kindred Refugees from Germany, headed by Walter Kotschnig (later an immigrant to the United States), to promote international co-ordination of the national academic committees and the pooling of their funds. Unfortunately, after the resignation of the first high commissioner, the whole work of the high commission was greatly curtailed and lost its importance. In his letter of resignation, McDonald showed unmistakable dissatisfaction with the League for its failure "to remove or mitigate the causes which create German refugees," as distinguished from its assistance to "those who flee from the Reich" which "could not have been any part of the work of the high commissioner's office."

ASSISTANCE IN THE UNITED STATES

The United States was no less prompt than European countries in setting up agencies to aid refugees. The early news of dismissals in Germany caused a great stir in academic circles. Many universities recognized at once their double opportunity: they could come out strongly for academic freedom and at the same time enlarge their staffs with the most eminent men from Europe. At a very brisk pace, university heads began consulting each other, exchanged copies of letters from Europe with requests or suggestions, and knocked on the doors of wealthy individuals and foundations to find ways of financing their hopes. I recently came to share some of this excitement in going through the special files, for the year 1933, of Robert M. Hutchins, then chancellor of the University of Chicago.

Hutchins' file, which is probably typical of files at many institutions, contained a large number of letters written in the spring of 1933. I read in them the names of dismissed scholars whose whereabouts were sometimes unknown: ". . . Kelsen is probably there [in Vienna], Palyi in London, Feiler I've heard is in Prague." "You will have undoubtedly heard about the firing of Born, Courant, Heitler, London and other Jewish physicists, and of Franck's praiseworthy resignation in protest. . . . If you should ever hear of an academic opening . . ." I read also the letters of dismissed professors who because of the "well-known changes in Germany felt it advisable to look for another job" and sent their qualifications in the hope that there might be an opening for them in the United States. I ran across, in that file, a list of names and qualifications, probably prepared for discussion at a faculty meeting, and learned of plans at the University of Chicago: ". . . we should bring at least four distinguished German scholars to the University of Chicago for no less than three years," Hutchins wrote to a wealthy attorney; the financial requirement was to be $100,000. But the resources of the university were restricted, and there was not much hope of future improvement.

This was the hard reality. Excitement, good-will, and awareness of the unprecedented opportunity were dampened by the depression, and not only at Chicago. At institutions throughout the United States the economic crisis limited the availability of funds and created a certain amount of xenophobia in certain quarters, not least among young American Ph.D.'s, so many of whom were unemployed in the spring of 1933. The duality between the wish to help colleagues in distress and the concern for struggling young Americans is evident in all planning of rescue operations. It is amazing that despite the financial difficulties and appreciable sentiment against foreigners, American organizations rose to the emergency and managed to assist countless European intellectuals in distress.

THE INSTITUTE FOR ADVANCED STUDY

As a result of the foresight of its director, the Institute for Advanced Study at Princeton had already recruited several outstanding Europeans when the dismissals from universities began in Germany. Director and founder of the institute was the well-known educator Abraham Flexner. For years Flexner had entertained the idea of an institute "of general scholarship and science . . . where everyone — faculty and members — in their individual ways endeavored to advance the frontiers of knowledge . . . ," as he wrote in his *I Remember*. An institute "afraid of no issue . . . under no pressure from any side which might tend to force its scholars to be prejudiced either for or against any particular solution of the problems under study . . . Its scholars should enjoy complete intellectual liberty, and be absolutely free from administrative responsibilities or concerns." In the past this role had been played by German universities, academies, and institutes, but all these "had declined in importance and were likely to decline still further." Flexner was an expert on German universities and had written the book *Universities — American, English, German*, comparing systems.

Flexner's idea materialized in 1930, when Louis Bamberger and his sister Mrs. Felix Fuld made funds available. The first meeting to discuss the organization of the institute was held in October, 1930, and others followed in 1931. "The year 1932," Flexner wrote, "was devoted to the selection of the initial personnel," both American and European. Flexner envisaged at that time several schools, but decided to start with mathematics, to which he soon added economics; at first he did not think beyond these two schools. He went abroad to initiate his recruiting in Europe, and it was due to this trip that Albert Einstein was offered a position in America before he lost his place in Germany soon after Hitler came to power. It was an act of Fate that the institute, which stressed intellectual liberty, should be ready to function at a time when Nazi oppression began to force the intelligentsia out of Germany.

As a response to the Nazis' "insane course," Flexner added a school of humanistic studies to the institute and hired Erwin Panofsky and Ernst Herzfeld as well as many younger scholars. For decades the institute was a haven for scores of Europeans. Its policy was to balance foreigners and Americans, in order not to create resentment among the latter. Of the foreign scholars who were given temporary positions at the institute, Flexner wrote: "We have tried to scatter them far and wide through Canada and the United States, so that they might infuse new life into struggling institutions and yet not block the path of young Americans bent on scholarly careers."

THE UNIVERSITY IN EXILE

If Abraham Flexner found himself almost accidentally with an institute to be staffed at the moment when many Europeans had to be rescued, another man, Alvin Johnson, created a smaller institution on the spur of the moment, to meet the emergency. Alvin Johnson, a liberal man of wide vision, was a founder of the New School for Social Research, in New York City, and its director from 1921 until his retirement in 1945. Like Abraham Flexner, he had traveled extensively in Germany and was personally acquainted with many academics. In the course of his work for the *Encyclopedia of the Social Sciences*, of which he was a founder and editor, he had corresponded with most of the social and political scientists who were later dismissed by Hitler. Like Flexner, he was in Germany in 1932 and was deeply disturbed by what he saw and heard there.

In the first two lists of dismissed professors in the early spring of 1933 Johnson read "the names of nearly all the social scientists who had any creative spirit in them." His immediate idea was to make a position at the New School for the victim of nazism whom he held in the highest esteem, the Austrian-born economist Emil Lederer, a man "with a subtly and extraordinarily enterprising mind." But there was no money available. In New York, as in the rest of America, it is easier to arouse people for a big cause than a small cause and to raise a lot of money rather than a few hundred dollars. Alvin Johnson felt that he had better chances to finance a whole faculty than a single professor. Thus the idea of the University in Exile was born. It would be the graduate faculty of political and social sciences of the New School, which until then had been for undergraduates only. The University in Exile would be a means to preserve some of the German scholarship, to assert the principle of academic freedom, and to present German scholarship to American students.

Johnson's plan was to hire fifteen men for a two-year period and pay them the modest stipend of $4,000 a year, on which it was then possible to live. On April 24, 1933 (only two weeks after the passage of the law for the cleansing of the civil service in Germany), Johnson wrote a one-page letter to his friend Edwin Seligman at Columbia University, and sent copies to influential friends. "I want to make what return I can for liberties I have enjoyed," he wrote; and "The project must be big enough to stand out from obscurity, or there is nothing in it." On May 13 the *New York Times* announced the foundation of the University in Exile and the opening of the fund-raising campaign.

Modest contributions began to arrive; then Johnson received a telephone call from a benefactor whom he had not yet met. Hiram Halle declared himself ready to guarantee the needed $60,000 a year for two years. After this offer, things moved fast. A trip that Emil Lederer made to New York and one that Alvin Johnson made to London, where many Germans had taken refuge, served to assemble the faculty. By summer "they were arriving ship by ship," Alvin Johnson wrote in his *Pioneer's Progress*. "It was exciting to wait for them at the foot of the gangplank." Two were already in New York: the Italian Max Ascoli, later publisher and editor of *The Reporter*, who had come to the United States as a Rockefeller fellow and had no intention of returning to Mussolini's Italy; and Horace Kallen who had been with the New School for many years. The graduate faculty, no longer called the University in Exile, is still in existence as an integral part of the New School.

Alvin Johnson's problems with refugee intellectuals were not over with the creation of the University in Exile. After the fall of France, Johnson set up within the New School the École Libre des Hautes Études for refugees from French and Belgian universities, and "a handful of Poles" — about seventy in all. Gustave Cohen hoped that the new institution would be a complete university, conducted entirely in the French language and giving certificates according to French civil service requirements for positions in the African areas controlled by General Charles de Gaulle. While the school never became a university, since it did not obtain the minimum endowment of half a million dollars called for by state law, it did give out diplomas that were recognized by De Gaulle's wartime government. Johnson saw it as a permanent French university in the United States that would link French and Latin scholarship with the American university world and train thousands of young Americans to teach French in high schools. Although some members of the original faculty rushed to join De Gaulle in Africa while the war was still on, and many went back to France after the war, several remained to provide the nucleus of a stable institution.

Alvin Johnson created the University in Exile and the École Libre des Hautes Études to aid the displaced teachers from Europe, but he did not limit his assistance to teachers alone. Over the years the New School made room for an incredible number of refugees and hired them to lecture in regular or special programs, sometimes on a permanent basis, more often on a temporary appointment. Thus countless scholars, scientists, artists, and musicians went through the doors of the New School in their early contacts with American education. Many Europeans owe their lives to Alvin Johnson. On the occasion of Johnson's ninetieth birthday, on December 17, 1964, the president of the Federal Republic of Germany, Heinrich Luebke, sent him a congratulatory message to express the gratitude of the German people for his "devoted help and support . . . to the German scientists and artists persecuted under Nazi terrorism."

THE EMERGENCY COMMITTEE IN AID OF
FOREIGN DISPLACED SCHOLARS

When Alvin Johnson conceived the idea of a University in Exile, he thought that its graduate faculty of political and social science would be at the New School and that friendly institutions would set up other faculties in the physical sciences, engineering, medicine, and arts and letters. "I thought," he wrote me, "that a University in Exile, thus distributed among the universities, would dramatize American faith in academic freedom. And my experience in raising money for my own faculty convinced me I could raise money for one of the constituent faculties after another."

In Alvin Johnson's plan, the faculty of science of the University in Exile would be established at the University of Chicago, and to this effect he initiated a correspondence with Robert M. Hutchins. (Copies of the few letters exchanged are in Hutchins' files.) In May, 1933, Hutchins wrote to Johnson that Beardsley Ruml of the Chicago faculty would arrive in New York to discuss the proposal with Johnson. Here matters rested, and no science faculty was established in Chicago. But there is an explanation: Alvin Johnson's friend Stephen Duggan, director of the Institute of International

Education in New York, was organizing a large committee to assist refugee teachers, and this changed Johnson's plans.

The Emergency Committee in Aid of German (later Foreign) Displaced Scholars began work in May, 1933. It was formed of presidents of universities and similar institutions, one of them Robert Hutchins, and eventually came to co-ordinate the activities of the American academic world on behalf of their persecuted European colleagues. Its director throughout the twelve years of its existence was Stephen Duggan. Edward R. Murrow was the first assistant director, and when he joined the Columbia Broadcasting System in 1935 Betty Drury succeeded him. The committee felt that foreign scholars and researchers should scatter to many American institutions and did not favor the formation of groups like the University in Exile, which inevitably would tend to keep the refugees separate and apart. Other policies of the committee reflected its concern with the American economic crisis: American universities and colleges were to provide positions for refugees but were not to bear the financial burden; the positions were to be temporary, from one to three years; and they were to be offered only to men of professorial standing or to eminent scholars, in order to avoid competition with young Americans.

In practice, the emergency committee took the responsibility for raising funds, mostly from the large foundations. A college or a university willing to make room for a qualified European could invite directly the man of its choice, either a man already in the United States or a man still in Germany; if it had no particular person in mind, the emergency committee would provide a list of names and qualifications. The committee would pay the institution a grant toward the stipend of the appointed man, or, in certain instances, a fellowship.

In the beginning, the emergency committee paid grants of $2,000 for one year, renewable for a second year if the institution was not able to put the scholar on its own budget. As the number of scholars increased, the committee found itself compelled to decrease the amount of the grants. In their history of the committee, Duggan and Drury reported that by the time the committee terminated its work in June, 1945, over 6,000 persons had appealed to them. They had helped 335 individuals for periods ranging from one to seven years. Of the persons assisted, 288 were scholars between the age of thirty and sixty years according to rules originally set by the committee; the others were younger men and women in academic and artistic fields for whom the Rosenwald Foundation had made money available in the form of fellowships for special projects. The balance were a few older men of a group called research associates, organized in 1939 by the Harvard astronomer Harlow Shapley.

The emergency committee worked in very close collaboration with other institutions assisting foreign scholars, like the Institute for Advanced Study and the University in Exile.

Alvin Johnson wrote me that he had dropped his project of a complete University in Exile both because "Duggan's committee had access to the great foundations," which he, Johnson, did not have, and because it seemed to him "even better to have the displaced scholars distributed through the universities." Of the other institutions with which the emergency committee collaborated I shall mention only the Institute of Fine Arts of New York University. Its director was the outstanding American art historian Walter W. S. Cook, who was as great a friend of refugees as Alvin Johnson. He said: "Hitler is my best friend. He shakes the tree and I collect the apples," according to an early member of the institute, Erwin Panofsky. Panofsky said also that a group of refugee scholars had a constructive role in the spectacular rise of the Institute of Fine Arts from the small department that it had originally been. Cook himself prepared a written statement, at Duggan's request, when the emergency committee terminated its work. It read in part:

"The history of art and archeology is a relatively recent field of study in this country, and there were relatively few Americans sufficiently equipped to teach graduate students in this field. But as a result of the addition of so many able scholars from Europe, numerous American students have been, and are now, receiving a training rarely received in this country before. The great contribution made at our Institute of Fine Arts is that these scholars have trained and are still training, a new generation of American students. . . ."

ASSISTANCE TO PROFESSIONAL INTELLECTUALS

The operations to rescue professionals met with greater difficulties than those to rescue scholars. The numbers of immigrants in the professions was much greater, and in all but liberal quarters American resistance to their competition was much harsher. But the liberal-minded in the American professions grew as indignant as the academic world over Hitler's methods and practices, and soon they moved to help the victims of nazism in their own fields. By the time the United States entered the war, almost all professional groups had set up, and a few had already terminated, emergency committees in aid of their European counterparts, lawyers, physicians, ministers, artists, writers, musicians. Some were formal, strong organizations, often related to each other through a broader committee; others were very informal.

Émigré lawyers claim that their group was the one to suffer the greatest hardships. Law is not a commodity easy to export, they point out. Physicians find the same human material to work with all over the world; artists and musicians may be appreciated anywhere; economists strive for similar goals in all countries; and the languages of scientists and mathematicians are universal. Lawyers from continental Europe instead found little resemblance between American legal practices and their own. They were used to rigid and unequivocal penal and civil codes and felt at sea when faced with common law and the courts' rulings by precedent rather than by the dictates of code-makers. Many had practiced in narrow, specialized fields such as corporation insurance and taxation law, for which each country had different legislation. Very few European lawyers in America could hope to remain in legal practice.

According to official immigration figures as quoted by Maurice Davie in *Refugees in America*, between 1,800 and 2,000 immigrant lawyers came to the United States from Europe in the period 1933–44, but Davie implies that the figures may be somewhat high. As in other cases, the question is one of definition: who were the lawyers? All persons with a law degree? But if I am to judge from what I have seen in Italy, a law degree was often regarded as a means to achieve professional and academic status without the expense of great intellectual effort — not as great as in medicine, engineering, mathematics, or the sciences. It was a master key to many positions in business and related activities. As a result, there are differences of opinion on who was in fact a lawyer, and in counting heads different persons may have reached different figures.

Little organized help was given to immigrant lawyers as such. Open to them were the large relief organizations like the Joint Distribution Committee, the National Council of Jewish Women, the American Committee for Christian-German Refugees, the American Friends Service Committee, the Hebrew Sheltering and Immigrant Aid Society (HIAS), and others that assisted refugees in general. In 1938 the American Committee for the Guidance of Professional Personnel came into existence and soon changed its name to the Committee for the Re-education of Refugee Lawyers. It was also known as the Riesman committee after one of its moving spirits, David Riesman, who later became the celebrated senior author of *The Lonely Crowd*. The committee sought to discover young, energetic, adaptable men and women who had something special to contribute to the practice of law in the United States. But this enterprise had little appeal for the public, and not much money could be raised; only twenty-eight men, thirty-five years old or younger, took retraining courses under the Riesman committee plan. Other lawyers applied directly to universities, but non-specialized service agencies would not assist them, feeling powerless before the resistance of American student groups in law schools.

There were a number of smaller aid groups of the self-help type, for the different nationalities of immigrant lawyers; and after the establishment of the École Libre des Hautes Études, courses were offered to acquaint Europeans with American legal terminology. One class, conducted by Ernst Fraenkel, was attended by students who did not intend to practice law but felt that an understanding of American legal questions would help them secure jobs in which knowledge of law was essential. The bulk of the lawyers did not receive assistance and were sometimes bitter because less was done for lawyers than for physicians.

Indeed, physicians were luckier than lawyers. One of the founders and inspirers of the Emergency Committee in Aid of Foreign Displaced Scholars was a medical man himself, and in the fall of 1933 he formed a splinter group on behalf of European physicians. Dr. Alfred Cohn of the Rockefeller Institute of Medical Research established the Emergency Committee in Aid of Foreign Physicians (later Medical Scientists); the National Committee for Resettlement of Foreign Physicians was established some time later, and the earlier committee worked closely with the second.

In an article in the *American Scholar* in the summer of 1943, Dr. Cohn estimated that more than 6,000 physicians, practitioners, specialists, and medical scientists had come to the United States since 1933. (The figures quoted by

Maurice Davie are appreciably lower, since he considers 5,000 the outside number of European refugee physicians for the longer period 1933–44.) According to Dr. Cohn, of 5,000 physicians who arrived between 1933 and the end of 1940, over 3,000 were Jews; 44 per cent of the total were from Germany; 35 per cent from Austria; 18 per cent from Italy, Switzerland, Hungary, and France; and the remaining 3 per cent from other countries.

The problem of assimilating foreign physicians in this country was minor at first, but soon it grew and transformed the initial kindliness of American doctors into irritation and occasional hostility. As time went on, citizenship was demanded in an increasing number of states as a prerequisite to taking the examination for a medical license; and by 1943 all states except New York and Massachusetts had, in effect, barred aliens from taking the examination. The feeling in the profession, as recorded by Dr. Cohn, was that immigrants should not be allowed to profit from the fact that American doctors were called away from their jobs to fight in the war; that one good way was open to foreign physicians, to join the American army, for then they would be eligible for citizenship within three months, according to special wartime immigration laws.

The Emergency Committee in Aid of Foreign Physicians gathered and supplied information about immigrant physicians in need of assistance as well as about opportunities in medical research and teaching. It also made grants, at the request of hospitals or universities, to some 125 among the best qualified foreign physicians. The National Committee for Resettlement of Foreign Physicians, formed by a group of American doctors, placed over 1,700 physicians in laboratories, in hospitals as interns or residents, in private practice, or in research and teaching. It made special efforts to send refugee doctors to sections of the United States where medical care was inadequate or completely lacking and away from big cities where competition was most keenly felt.

Most agencies assisting immigrants were co-ordinated and, to various degrees, financed by the National Co-ordinating Committee which came into being in 1936. In 1939 it changed its name to the National Refugee Service. This, the largest refugee-service organization in the United States, was supported by Jewish funds, though it was non-sectarian in the distribution of its aid. In 1946 it merged with the Service to Foreign-Born of the National Council of Jewish Women and operated until 1954 as the United Service for New Americans.

A few committees sent limited financial help to Europeans who were in Europe and might or might not have been planning to come to the United States. An example is the American Guild for German Cultural Freedom which existed for four precarious years. The driving spirit was an Austrian exile, Prince Hubertus zu Loewenstein, the secretary of the organization, a self-appointed representative of writers in the German language, and a sort of non-official diplomat. The guild sent scholarships (some as small as five dollars a month for three months) to German artists, scientists, scholars, and writers in exile in Europe so that they could continue to express their views.

A few organizations operated in Europe: the Jewish Labor Committee rescued more than 800 political refugees from Nazi concentration camps, and the Emergency Rescue Committee (described later in some detail) carried forward successful underground operations in Pétain's France.

THE PERSONAL FACTOR

The impressive record of organized assistance to displaced intelligentsia should not be allowed to overshadow the role of personal relations. The organizations themselves did not mete out their aid at random but were guided by the advice of experts who knew the European cultural scene or some of its sectors through their professional activities. Accordingly, the General Committee of the Emergency Committee in Aid of Displaced Foreign Scholars consisted of university presidents, college deans, and heads of similar institutions of learning. These men, in their turn, often relied on the judgment of colleagues abroad or recently arrived foreign scholars and scientists who could recommend colleagues whom they knew or with whose work they were thoroughly acquainted. Thus, personal relations were of great importance in the selection of Europeans to be rescued. They were even more essential in the case of those who by-passed organized assistance. There is little doubt that of all the intellectuals in Europe who hoped to obtain a position here, those who had been in America on visits had the best chances. For one thing, the decision-makers were spared the character investigation, so baffling to the European, tending to determine whether the prospective appointee was likely to be "happy in America." A case in point, though perhaps not entirely representative, is that of Fermi. He decided to emigrate to America in the fall of 1938, when the American universities were already swamped by European physicists, the lingering results of the depression were still felt, and the wave of refugees from Europe was reaching a peak. Fortunately for him, he had spent several summers at American universities and his fondness for them and for America in general was well known. When in cautious terms, for fear of Italian censorship, Fermi informed four American institutions that he would welcome an invitation he was offered five positions.

Personal relations account for several instances of cluster formation. When a European was appointed director of a university department and entrusted with the task of strengthening it, the end result was the Europeanization of the department, especially if it dealt with a field in which Europe was more advanced, or produced more experts, than America. Examples of such clusters — of art historians and mathematicians at New York University, of astronomers at Chicago, and so on — will be found in this book.

As long as the personal relations were operative within the policies and framework of American institutions, they acted in general as selective forces, helping the best available to come from Europe to America, with or without organized assistance. But friendship and family relations were much less selective. In time of emergency in Europe, the lucky intellectuals on the point of sailing to America were showered with requests, on the part of friends and relatives, that once on American soil they seek affidavits of support, visas, and assurances of positions. They were entrusted with sheets of biographical data, letters of recommendation, and other products of the hopes and despair of those they were leaving behind. Once in this country, their prime concern was to bring over their closest friends and relatives rather than those who might be most useful to America — but a small measure of selection took place in these cases, through the greater difficulties encountered by those who tried to sponsor persons not as highly qualified as others.

I have often wondered whether this particular mechanism in the migration, the immigrants bringing over their relatives and friends, could account for a puzzling observation I made while compiling my file of intellectuals. As I passed from the most obvious émigrés, men like Toscanini, Einstein, and Von Neumann, to the less obvious, and from searching *Who's Who* to searching biographical directories, the proportion of Germans in my file increased. For the Germans, the emergency started as early as 1933, while for the nationals of most other European countries it began only in 1938, after Hitler became openly aggressive. (For the Russians and Hungarians who did not come here directly in the twenties, the emergency that drove them to America coincided with that of the country in which they had settled.) The Germans had a longer time to settle and find themselves in a position to help relatives and friends to immigrate to America, in a process that must have snowballed, at least to a certain extent. The German intellectuals arriving as friends or relatives rather than as colleagues may not have been able to go at once into intellectual occupations, but the postwar expansion of American education opened many positions and in filling these they also filled the biographical directories. Other nationals had little time to initiate a sizable friend-and-relative-saving process before Hitler's invasion of Europe brought chaos in planned procedures. Among the German-born in this country there must be therefore many who were not subjected to as strict a selective process as were other Germans and most non-German European-born.

AFTER THE FALL OF FRANCE

In 1940 many exiled intellectuals were still in Europe. Some had been unable to find a way to the United States or other non-European countries; some had not even tried, for it was easier to stay than to cross the ocean. Of their neighboring countries they had studied the history and geography in school and learned the cultural achievements through the press, personal relationships, and visits. Divided as it was, Europe remained a unit. Their travels from one European country to another did not have the uncertainty and finality of emigration, but America was worlds away, unknown. While they were still in Europe they could lull themselves into the belief that they were only biding time and soon would return home to resume their lives unchanged.

As they were driven out of one country after the other in larger and larger numbers, they gathered in France, whose tradition it was to leave the door open to the persecuted and oppressed. Artists and musicians had always wished to go to Paris and now they settled there. Political exiles had long had headquarters in Paris where they could keep in touch with one another and continue their friendships and feuds. Most creative writers preferred the small towns and villages of southern France, which offered quiet, beauty of landscape, and easier relationships with the locals. They could write in their mother tongue and have their works published by the several publishing houses especially created in various European cities to handle exile literature. The "phony war" gave them, as it gave almost everyone else, the feeling that some balance had been attained and nothing more would happen. Then Hitler's armies began moving, reached Paris, and France fell. The intellectuals in danger from the Nazis fled to the south, into Vichy France.

On June 22, 1940, France signed an armistice with Germany. One of its clauses required that the French government "surrender upon demand all Germans named by the German government in France, as well as in French possessions." The term "German" meant anyone from the "Greater Reich," German, Austrian, Czechoslovakian, or Pole, and so in practice the Nazis could lay their hands on anyone they wanted, anti-Fascists and Jews of any nationality, including the French. The intellectual refugees in Pétain's France were suddenly in great danger.

The Emergency Rescue Committee was formed in response to this new threat. Its chairman was Frank Kingdon, and among its national members were Alvin Johnson, Raymond Gram Swing, and Dorothy Thompson. The man who organized and directed the underground operations in France was Varian Fry. In 1945 he described the rescue operations in France in his book *Surrender on Demand*. The circumstances under which the committee came into being are not well known. "One of the attributes of an emergency operation is that it makes light of the concerns of the future historian," Charles Sternberg, acting executive director of the International Rescue Committee, the successor organization of the Emergency Rescue Committee, wrote me in 1965. He had worked with Fry in France, but clearly the workers had not been concerned with organization: Fry himself, who died in 1967, did not comment on the American committee in his book and had little to add about its origins when I talked to him twenty years later.

As I gathered from various sources, the inspirers of the committee were intellectual émigrés who knew the European situation. Thomas Mann was one of them. For years, he and his family had been on Goebbels' notorious list of persons wanted by the Nazis. At the time of the fall of France he and several of his children were in the United States, but his historian son

Golo was in France and so was his venerable older brother Heinrich whose name was on the first of Goebbels' black lists. Another behind-the-scenes founder of the rescue committee was Paul Hagen, whose real name was Karl B. Frank, an influential member of the American Friends of German Freedom. This Socialist organization managed to keep in touch with German anti-Nazis in Europe, especially through underground workers who traveled between the United States and Europe as long as this was feasible. According to Frank's wife Anna, the Emergency Rescue Committee was formed on the spur of the moment at a meeting of the American Friends of German Freedom. Whatever its origins, the new committee needed a volunteer to work in France and was extremely lucky in enlisting Varian Fry.

A scholar of Latin and Greek with a reading knowledge of several modern languages including French and a penchant for business, Fry had traveled in Germany, where he had witnessed Nazi excesses and become acquainted with the work of the German and Austrian Socialist parties. Out of sympathy with some of their work, he joined the American Friends of German Freedom and became Karl Frank's friend. When the Emergency Rescue Committee was formed in the summer of 1940, Fry was an editor on the staff of the Foreign Policy Association and a month's vacation was coming to him. Although not a member of the Emergency Rescue Committee, he offered to spend his month working in France. He thought, Fry told me, that his offer would stimulate a search for a better qualified man with a knowledge of refugee and underground work. Instead he was taken at his word and sent to France — where he stayed not one but thirteen months.

Alfred Barr, director of the Museum of Modern Art, helped raise funds and provided the names of artists to be rescued; thanks to him, artists were saved in large numbers, including Marc Chagall, Max Ernst, Jacques Lipchitz, and a host of others. Thomas Mann and author Hermann Kesten knew which writers were in danger; they feared not only for Heinrich Mann, but for Franz Werfel, Lion Feuchtwanger, and for those who had been outspoken against the Nazis, especially Konrad Heiden whose book *Der Fuehrer* had revealed the true Hitler to the world. Karl Frank gave Fry the names of Socialist labor leaders; and others furnished other lists.

On August 15, 1940, the *New York Times* reported that the newly formed Emergency Rescue Committee had held a first, fund-raising luncheon at which several prominent refugees spoke (the former Russian Premier Aleksandr Kerenski was among the guests), and that a representative of the Committee in France had already established contact with several hundred leaders of European culture and freedom. The representative was, of course, Varian Fry, but his name could not be revealed at that time because he was engaged in underground operations. When the next fund-raising affair took place in the following October, Heinrich Mann, Franz Werfel, and Konrad Heiden attended. Varian Fry had managed to rescue them and send them to New York, living testimony to his skill.

The operations in France would not have been so successful, Fry told me, without the co-operation of the State Department and the aid of Eleanor Roosevelt. After the fall of France, President Roosevelt ordered the State Department to issue visitor's visas to "those of superior intellectual attainment, of indomitable spirit, experienced in vigorous support of the principles of liberal government and who are in danger of persecution or death at the hands of autocracy." The State Department agreed to do this, but it was Eleanor Roosevelt who made sure that the promise was not forgotten. She went daily to prod officials and to speed up the more difficult cases; she obtained visas for some men and women in peril with little to go by but the assurance of émigrés (for instance, of Thomas Mann) that the person in question was all right. As long as the Emergency Rescue Committee functioned in France, she never tired of her self-imposed task, nor did her efforts slacken.

Varian Fry established his headquarters in Marseilles, the principal seaport of Vichy France, where many refugees were assembling. "Fry's innocence was his great advantage. A more sophisticated man would not have dared to undertake the tasks he carried out so successfully," said one of his associates in France years later. The situation was chaotic and dangerous. Several American organizations had representatives in France and Portugal working legally or illegally to help Europeans escape from France. At the official end of the gamut were the American consulates, hampered by diplomatic protocol and the need to avoid antagonizing French officialdom, but doing all they could within the law. Some of their staff, acting individually, went further. Harry Bingham, the vice-consul in charge of visas in Marseilles, for instance, smuggled Lion Feuchtwanger out of a French concentration camp. At the other end were Varian Fry and the staff that he was able to put together in

Marseilles, who worked decidedly underground. In between were such organizations as the Unitarian Service Committee in Lisbon and the American Friends Society in Marseilles, who pretended not to see illegality and gave a hand to underground workers.

Frank Bohn, a representative of the American Joint Labor Committee, preceded Fry to Marseilles. Bohn, a student of European labor movements in which he had participated before World War I, was especially interested in rescuing labor leaders and democratic political leaders. With some practical advice from Bohn and a plan to collaborate with him, Varian Fry went to work. He organized an escape route to Lisbon across the Pyrenees. It was by this route, with its steep climb, that the seventy-year-old Heinrich Mann got to Lisbon and finally to America with his nephew Golo Mann, Franz Werfel, and Werfel's wife, Alma Mahler Gropius Werfel. But a route was of no use if the escapees were not provided with the proper papers, passports or equivalent documents, exit visas from France, and entry or transit visas for Spain and Portugal. Fry plunged into the black market of documents, which he illegally purchased or arranged to have forged, with the help of his "specialist on illegal questions," a young political refugee from Germany whom Fry called "Beamish" because of his impish eyes. (Beamish's identity is no longer a secret: he is economist Albert O. Hirschman, a professor at Columbia and later at Harvard.) As a cover for these operations, Fry organized the Centre Américain de Sécours, ostensibly a relief agency for distributing food to the needy. "The American flag will cover a multitude of sins," said Beamish cynically.

A relief agency was a natural cover. Marseilles was overflowing with refugees from occupied France and people who had escaped from French concentration camps. Food became scarcer every day, and the *misère noire* set in. Mrs. Helmut Hirsch, who was among the refugees in Marseilles, once recalled the terrible black market and the stealing among the refugees, and it was evident that the memory still hurt her. According to Varian Fry, not even American money could buy adequate food, and though he may have been fifty pounds heavier in recent years, he was down to one hundred and twenty pounds when he returned from France. "We were always hungry," he told me. "And the worst of it was that because we were hungry we were constantly thinking of food. At night we dreamt of it."

Fry got in touch with as many of the refugees on his lists as he possibly could, and as word of his presence spread, many came of their own accord. He sent many of them off to safety, by the Pyrenees route as long as it was safe to use, and with the assistance when necessary of underworld characters. Later he arranged for boat passage to North Africa or Martinique from which, somehow, it was possible to reach America. Some of the refugees who came to Fry's office in Marseilles had not known that they were on the Gestapo lists and learned it from him, as was the case of Hans Natonek, the Czech writer. Many were reluctant to leave, either because they thought that their personal prestige made them immune to arrest or because they could not believe that the Nazis were as dangerous as they were said to be. Those who hesitated too long paid with their lives, as did the well known Socialist writer and former German Minister of Finance Rudolf Hilferding: the long arms of the Gestapo reached him as he prepared to board a ship in Marseilles.

Many of the refugees whom Fry helped out of France had been in French concentration camps and a few of the most distinguished people on his lists were still interned at the time he arrived in Marseilles: the physicist Peter Pringsheim (Thomas Mann's brother-in-law) and the pianist Erich Itor Kahn, among others. Fry managed to obtain their release. Of the French camps Fry wrote: "The conditions . . . could, with difficulty, have been worse. There was no deliberate torture . . . but there was everything else: cold, hunger, parasites and disease." These conditions were described in much greater detail by Joseph Weill in *Contribution a l'histoire des camps d'internement dans l'Anti-France* and in personal accounts by inmates, such as Lion Feuchtwanger's *The Devil in France.* The French had been sending enemy aliens to concentration camps since the beginning of the war, first the men, and not long afterward the women, keeping the two sexes in separate camps.

When the German invasion began, camps of internees were moved south. The French guards were often compassionate, and on the trek southward some internees were offered the choice between freedom and what protection against the Germans the camps under French jurisdiction could offer. Those who chose freedom were released. After the French surrender, kind souls among French officialdom helped reunite some husbands and wives. Besides, French authorities were usually willing to release a man if it was known that a position awaited him in the United States. They released, for instance, the French philosopher Jean Wahl whose name was on the Paris list of persons to be shot on sight. He was in a camp in occupied France, when he learned by chance of his appointment to the New School for Social Research. He was released, found his way to the free zone, and eventually came to the United States. As German pressures increased, the Vichy government extended its practice of interning aliens. According to a French report of November 20, 1940, which Weill published in his book, there were at that time 53,610 inmates in French camps, not including those in eight camps for which data were lacking.

An episode that seems amusing in retrospect to those who were involved in it was the brief life of the *311ᵉ Compagnie de Travailleurs Étrangers*. This corps was composed of some seventy men, most of them scientists and a smattering of scholars, who were transferred from internment camps to the university city of Montpellier. The idea was to let them work in their own fields with the facilities of the university, under the supervision of a French professor. It was said at the time that the initiative came from Madame la Baronne Édouard de Rothschild; but it was also said that the special treatment given to these few intellectuals was a show put on by the French to offset the bad impression made abroad, especially in America, by the internment of refugee scholars. At any rate, for reasons that members of the corps were at a loss to explain, they were all put into the uniform of the *Chasseurs Alpins* with huge berets and placed under the command of a French *capitaine*. At some distance from the men's quarters, their wives lived the tough life of single women in army camps, and since they were not allowed to reveal their identity, they were accused of loose morals when their husbands visited them. The *capitaine* did not know what to do with his charges, nor was he given much time to find out. The corps which had assembled in April, 1940, had been in existence two months when the Nazis arrived. Then the members were taken to the Pyrenees and told that they would be transported to North Africa. Fortunately, after much patience and some intrigue and assistance from various persons including Varian Fry, at least three men reached the United States with their wives: the chemist Alexander Gero, who became a teacher at Hahnemann Medical College; the physicist Hans

Ekstein, who has been at the Illinois Institute of Technology and at Argonne National Laboratory; and Assyriologist Leo Oppenheim, who had found his way into the group as a translator and has long been on the staff of the Oriental Institute in Chicago.

For the first few months Varian Fry collaborated with Frank Bohn and shared with him the risks of underground activities. Soon these activities began to embarrass the American embassy and its consulates. Both France and the United States tried to force Fry and Bohn to return home. Bohn complied and left in October, 1940; Fry stayed on, with the added burden of Bohn's political proteges. His office was periodically raided by the French police. Under pressure from Vichy, the American consulate became impatient and again asked Fry to leave. But he stayed until, in September, 1941, thirteen months after his arrival, the French police escorted him to the border.

In talking of these events twenty-five years later, Varian Fry was not critical of the French police. He seemed to have forgotten the difficulties created by some officials, the failures and frustrations they caused him. "Without the collaboration of French officials," he told me, "we would not have been able to save so many men." For example, the painter Max Ernst was to leave France but was not aware that his exit visa had expired. The French official who examined his documents at the railroad station cautioned him not to try to leave France and pointed out the train to Toulouse: "It's not the one in front, which goes to Spain. It's the one behind it." Having done his duty the official left, and Ernst promptly boarded the train to Spain. He was certain that the French official had deliberately given him this tip.

Indeed, French authorities often closed one eye and occasionally both eyes; without them, not even the most experienced underground workers would have been able to rescue as many persons as the inexperienced Fry and company sent to safety through Marseilles. True, there were also tragedies: betrayal by local people who had seemed trustworthy; escapes that ended in imprisonment or disappearance from the world; ships that never sailed; and ships that after a brief stretch at sea were obliged to return to Marseilles, exposing their human cargo to the risk of police inspection. But the figures are an unquestionable proof of success. Fry and his staff rescued almost 1,500 refugees, and his successor saved another 300 before the police raided the office and closed it for good in June, 1942. By then the United States had been at war for six months, and the rescue operations could not be continued.

Not all the refugees assisted by the Emergency Rescue Committee in their flight from France came to the United States. Not all could be admitted, for nothing could change American law, neither President Roosevelt's good will nor Eleanor Roosevelt's incessant pleas to the State Department. No visas could be obtained for persons with Communist affiliations or those who fell into other categories to be excluded. Most of those who were barred from entry went to South America, Mexico, or Cuba.

A vivid account of Fry and his activities is given by the refugee writer Hans Sahl in *The Few and the Many*. Sahl had experienced French concentration camps, the killing march from Paris to the south of France, and imprisonment in Marseilles. After being released, he was sitting in a café when a friend walked up to his table and said in a low voice that a man was stopping at the Hotel Splendide, a certain Mr. Fry, an American who had heaps of dollars and a list of people who were supposed to be rescued. "Your name is on the list. Call him up at once. . . ." Sahl went to the hotel and was welcomed by a friendly young man in shirt sleeves. Wrote Sahl: "Imagine the situation: the borders closed; you are caught in a trap, might be arrested again at any moment; life is as good as over — and suddenly a young American in shirt sleeves is stuffing your pockets full of money, putting his arm around your shoulders, and whispering with the conspiratorial expression of a ham actor: 'Oh there are ways to get you out of here,' while, damn it all, the tears were streaming down my face, actual tears, big, round, and wet; and that pleasant fellow . . . takes a silk handkerchief from his jacket and says: 'Here, have this. Sorry it isn't cleaner.' You know, since that day I have loved America."

Eventually Sahl left Marseilles "with a brand new Danish passport that had been forged for us by one of the foremost specialists in that field; and in my suitcase were a great many slips of paper with news from Occupied France — I hid them in toothpaste tubes and cans of shoe polish."

V

In America

By one road or another the intellectuals from continental Europe kept streaming to America from 1930 through 1941, until the war put a virtual end to their coming. A closer look at the migration will show how its flow varied in time, how it scattered in this country, and what was its composition by nationality. Since my considerations in this chapter are based on the analysis of the approximately 1,900 names in my file, my description of the wave will be only a projection of this smaller group with no claim to finality or precision in all details. It is likely, in particular, that if the analysis were conducted using a more exhaustive list of names, most statistics would have to be revised. Yet it is my feeling that the group I studied is sufficiently representative to furnish a general idea of the salient traits of the cultural migration.

DISTRIBUTION IN TIME

The flow of European intellectuals to America was at some times swifter than at others. Though its pace was determined by the events in Europe — with the depression in the United States acting as a brake — its response to the events was not always prompt. The fluctuations in the flow and the relations between them and their causes can be seen more easily if the time span of the migration is divided into several periods, corresponding to changes in European conditions.

The earliest, pre-Hitler period, from 1930 to 1932, was marked by a relative calm in Europe, although several dictators had already made their appearance. The stream of intellectuals coming to the United States was small. In the years 1933–34 thousands were dismissed from German universities and other cultural positions, and Europe received a strong warning. The increase in arrivals was sizable but, surprisingly enough, it did not constitute the true crest of the wave. From 1935 to 1937 the European intelligentsia did not receive further direct blows, but it witnessed the rapid deterioration of the political scene, the rearmament of Germany, and the wars in Abyssinia and Spain. The flow of intellectuals to America continued to increase at a moderate rate. Then came 1938 and 1939, the years that saw Hitler's prewar conquests and consequent expansion of political and racial persecution, bitter pogroms in Germany, the promulgation of racial laws in Italy, and the outbreak of the war in Poland. These were also the years in which those who had been waiting for the Nazi storm to spend itself realized that fascism was not a passing phenomenon and nothing short of a major cataclysm would stop its advance. The yearly influx of intellectuals in this country more than doubled that of the previous period and formed the crest of the wave. Finally, in 1940 and 1941 the largest part of Europe fell into the hands of dictators. Refugees from many countries and from the occupied French regions gathered in southern France, Spain, or Portugal, and America became their last hope. The yearly figures of arrivals here from 1940 to the early part of 1942 were higher than those for the period 1935–37 but did not match those of 1938–39.

The actual distribution in time is presented in the following table:

Date of Arrival	Total Arrivals	Arrivals per Year
1930–32	117	39
1933–34	208	104
1935–37	378	126
1938–39	582	291
1940–42	453	151
later*	18	. . .
uncertain	174	. . .

*Under this heading I have included a few persons who were out of Europe (in Turkey, South America, Cuba, and so on) in the period in question but did not arrive in the United States until later. Their names came to my attention for special reasons and not because of any systematic search, hence the figure of late arrivals in this table is not representative of their actual numbers.

94

The national composition of the wave varied in time. The Germans, who were the largest national group, representing about 44 per cent of the total, reached the highest percentage in the years 1933–34, when they constituted almost two-thirds of the intellectuals of all nationalities. This fact mirrors both the sudden outburst of widespread persecutions in Germany and the deafness of other countries to the warning. The ratio of Germans remained nearly as high in the period from 1935–37, before the great expansion of Hitler's sphere of influence, but it began to fall after the Nazis moved to the conquest of Europe and refugees from many countries left for America. The German percentage was at its lowest in the years 1940–41, when the Germans were only about one-third of the intellectuals coming here.

The Austrians were the second largest national group in the cultural migration, representing about 20 per cent of the total. Almost one-half of all Austrians in the wave came to this country in the period 1938–39, driven out of their homes by the *Anschluss* and Nazi rule in Austria. In those two years they formed about 29 per cent of all nationalities, the highest percentage they reached. The lowest was in 1933–34, when they were only a little over 11 per cent of the total.

Like the Austrian wave, the waves of Hungarians, Czechoslovakians, and Italians reached their peaks in the period 1938–39; the French, Polish and Russians showed their highest percentage in 1940–41. (Other national groups seem too small for statistical consideration.)

GEOGRAPHICAL DISTRIBUTION

Inertia, which causes immigrants everywhere to cluster together near their point of arrival, affected many of those who came in the new wave. Pleased by the highly satisfactory intellectual climate of New York, they remained near the port of entry. New York had much to offer beside the enticements of a large metropolis: some means of livelihood, boundless hope, and the reassurance that each individual draws from seeing legions in the same predicament. In New York were many outstanding art schools and concert halls, the best foreign-language publications, and the largest number of publishing houses, equipped to handle many languages or to patch up the lamest English. New York institutions such as the New School for Social Research and the Museum of Modern Art seemed willing to invent activities in order to accommodate scores — hundreds over the years — of European-born intellectuals, artists, and musicians. And last, but terribly important, the central offices of most organizations assisting immigrants were in New York.

To many writers, artists, and professionals, and to teachers with no positions awaiting them, it seemed absurd to go elsewhere. If New York could not absorb and support them, what other city would? Besides, who had the money for traveling in this immense country of exorbitant distances? So New York had the highest concentration of European-born intellectuals, and insofar as I can judge, it still has. Unfortunately, inertia fed more often on dreams and hopes than on reasonable expectations, and as one result it encouraged nationals to band together. This stubborn isolation furnished grounds for many legends, including one in the late twenties that all Brooklyn gravediggers and all Park Avenue doormen were Russian aristocrats.

If inertia had been the only force acting on the newcomers, all those who arrived in New York would have remained there. Instead, individual initiative and the spirit of adventure, and the efforts of organized assistance, pushed many from New York and resulted in a wide geographical distribution. Many places come to mind as I quickly review where I have met European intellectuals in the United States or where those of whom I know have been. Most are large universities and colleges that over the years have hired many émigrés, but others are smaller institutions. At Sweet Briar, in Virginia, a German woman, Hilde Stücklen, was the chairman of the physics department for thirteen years; in Winston-Salem, North Carolina, the distinguished Italian biologist Camillo Artom has engaged in research since 1939; the Austrian composer Ernst Kanitz taught at Winthrop College at Rock Hill, and Erskine College at Due West, both in South Carolina; the German psychiatrist Rudolph Kieve has practiced for many years in Santa Fe, New Mexico; and Los Alamos saw in wartime the highest density of European talent ever assembled in the United States. No state of the Union has been entirely without intellectual immigrants.

By and large, this pattern of distribution of European intellectuals is similar to that of American culture in general. It shows the highest concentration on a strip along the central part of the East Coast, the second highest on the West Coast, and the lowest in the vast spaces in between, with denser islands in such cities as Chicago. Some features in the pattern peculiar to the intellectual wave are worth pointing out here: most explanatory comments will be postponed to later chapters. Until recently, the department of astronomy at the University of Chicago was one of the most "European" departments of astronomy in the United States. Also at the University of Chicago, the Oriental Institute has been much favored by Assyriologists from Europe and other experts in civilizations of the Near East. Art historians flocked to New York University, and so did an outstanding group of mathematicians; other mathematical talent gathered in Princeton, New Jersey, and at Brown University in Providence, Rhode Island. Composer Darius Milhaud wrote about Mills College, whose faculty he joined in 1940: "I believe that Mills College is the only school in the United States to engage a French writer for the summer session every year . . . the 1941 summer school was placed resolutely under the sign of French culture, through the engagement of Fernand Léger, André Maurois, and me." And Black Mountain College in North Carolina was remarkable in so many respects that it deserves some comment.

I had never heard of Black Mountain College until I started to examine the biographical data of European-born intellectuals and noticed that many teachers, artists, and musicians had spent considerable time there. Not believing in coincidence, I sought an explanation, and to my confusion found that a coincidence was indeed at the heart of the matter. Black Mountain College was opened in the fall of 1933, just a few months after the first victims of Hitler's policies had begun to arrive in the United States. It was founded as an educational experiment by a splinter group of teachers and students from Rollins College, Florida. "Without the Europeans it could not have functioned," said the German-born musicologist Edward Lowinsky, who was a member of its music department from 1942 until 1947. Set at an altitude of 2,400 feet among green, wooded hills cut by swiftly running brooks and with its own little lake, the college strongly resembled many summer resorts on the slopes of the Alps. "I felt as if I were on a vacation," said Anna Moellenhoff, who after arrival from Germany organized the department of biology and taught biology and German. "In the four years I was there, I never wore a hat." But the Europeans were attracted also, I dare say mainly, by other features: the great stress that Black Mountain College placed on the arts, its communal life, self-government, and student-teacher relations. When the college opened in the fall of 1933, the painter Josef Albers and his wife Anni, a weaver, lecturer, and writer, were on the faculty. Josef Albers had been a member of the German Bauhaus until a few months earlier, when Hitler dissolved it. At Black Mountain he established a similar school, on a smaller scale but with the same emphasis on the reconciliation of the fine arts and the applied arts, of the medieval type of instruction in the crafts and the need for industrial design in the machine age.

Albers and his wife stayed at Black Mountain College from 1933 until 1949, at which time its rapid decline had begun. The Dutch painter Willem de Kooning, who came to the United States in 1926, joined its faculty in 1948, and several other European artists were invited to teach at special summer institutes, among them the famous German architect Walter Gropius, founder of the original Bauhaus in Weimar; sculptors José de Creeft and Ossip Zadkine, one from Spain, the other from Russia; the Spanish architect José Luis Sert; the French painter Amedée Ozenfant; and Lyonel Feininger, who was born in the United States but lived in Germany from the age of sixteen until Hitler drove him out.

The music department was also European. Several Germans besides Lowinsky were on its faculty at various times: conductors Heinrich Jalowetz and Fred Cohen (with their wives, singer and voice teacher Johanna Jalowetz and dancer and choreographer Elsa Cohen); composer Stefan Wolpe; harpsichordist Erwin Bodky; and violist and violinist Gretel Lowinsky. Among the musical celebrities teaching or performing at the college during summer institutes were German musicologist Alfred Einstein; Hungarian violist Marcel Dick; Russian cellist Nikolai Graudan; and three Austrians: Hugo Kauder, composer, Ernst Krenek, musicologist and composer, and Yella Pessl, harpsichordist. Although the largest number of European-born were in the arts and music, there were some in other departments. I've mentioned Anna Moellenhoff, who taught biology. Her husband Fritz taught psychology for two years and was succeeded by another German psychiatrist, Erwin Straus (whose wife is a violinist). Physicist Peter Bergmann, mathematician Max Dehn, and anthropologist Paul Leser were also German. Frances de Graaff, an expert in Russian literature, came from Holland. The Czech economist Karl Niebyl joined the faculty for one year, and another Czech, the eminent scholar and writer Erich Kahler, visited the college for long periods.

As an example of the advanced ideas prevailing at Black Mountain College, Edward Lowinsky recalled that it had attempted integration ten years before the decision of the Supreme Court. Lowinsky, charged with the execution of the plan, succeeded in recruiting Negro students and faculty. He persuaded the Negro tenor Roland Hayes to visit the college with his wife and daughter Africa for three weeks during the summer institute of 1945. And in the summer, the music department gave weekly concerts attended by the people of Asheville. Hayes sang for an overflow audience with perhaps 10 per cent Negroes, who were not seated separately by decision of the college. "The times have changed, haven't they?" an old woman in the audience reportedly commented to a neighbor. And that was all; there were no disturbances. At the height of the integration program the small college, with its ratio of twenty teachers to sixty to eighty students, had six Negro students and one Negro faculty member (the latter changing every semester).

Black Mountain College was held together by its spirit rather than by its finances or any benefits to its faculty. After the war it could not stand the competition of institutions of larger means and lost many faculty members. Their later careers are an indication of its excellence. Albers and de Kooning went to Yale and Bodky to Brandeis. Lowinsky was first at Queens College, then at the University of California at Berkeley, and finally at Chicago. Cohen went to the Juilliard School of Music; Erwin Straus became head of psychiatry at the Veterans' Hospital in Lexington, Kentucky, and Fritz Moellenhoff, after some wandering, became a member of the staff of the Chicago Institute for Psychoanalysis. Others scattered to various colleges, universities, and related institutions.

GERMANS

The Germans were by far the largest national group in the cultural wave, and account for about 44 per cent of the names in my file. Although they present wide variations in character traits and modes of adjustment to a changed environment, a few generalizations about them are possible. German-born intellectuals, prone by tradition to cultural introspection and minute verbalization of their findings, have left an impressive record of their lives, unlike that of any previous immigrant group. Going through some of their autobiographies and articles, and some published interviews, one sees that certain patterns are often repeated, that certain features are common to most.

While they still lived in Germany, many of the future émigrés, especially those outside the field of the natural sciences, did not think much of American culture. It was not that they actively despised it or believed America to be a cultural desert, but rather that the very positive opinion in which they held their *Kultur* and its ancient roots prevented them from paying attention to an intellectual society as young as the American, which committed the sin of still being preoccupied with practical matters. German scholars were then convinced, as some openly admitted much later, that there was only one humanism, one Protestant theology, one philosophy, and one way to look at social questions — the German. This attitude, shared by most learned Germans, and not only by those that were to emigrate, was awesome and impressive to American scholars. What struck me when reading Alvin Johnson's recollections of the founding of the University in Exile in 1933 was his repeated question: "Do you think we might be able to get So-and-so?" — that is, a man dismissed by Hitler. And what struck me next was that often So-and-so *was* unwilling to come, at least at that time; several of those who first refused American invitations were in the United States within a few years.

The well-known mathematician Richard Courant provides a typical example. Born in Poland, he is by education and loyalty a German. When Hitler rose to power, Courant was forty-five years old, and a professor at the University of Göttingen. He thought that the storm would quickly abate. Soon after being forced to take a leave of absence, despite laws that ought to have protected him, he received an invitation from the University of California. He declined, feeling that he should stay near at hand and able to return to Germany when the situation would again be normal. He went to England and only a year later did he accept an invitation from New York University. Courant's reluctance to accept a position in the United States appears groundless when viewed in the light of his American career. The trust placed in him by his American colleagues and the support he received from our government enabled him to build the largest department of applied mathematics in this country, make substantial contributions to the war effort, and earn many honors.

The social and political scientist Franz Neumann had experiences similar to Courant's and was very explicit in relating them in *The Cultural Migration*. Having lost his position in 1933, Neumann spent the first three years of exile in England "in order to be close to Germany and not to lose contact with her." In England he participated actively in refugee politics, and soon became aware "that one had to bury the expectation of an overthrow of the régime from within. . . . Thus a clean break — psychological, social, and economic — had to be made, and a new life started. But England was not the country where to do it . . . her society was too homogeneous and solid, her opportunities . . . too narrow. . . . Thus the United States appeared as the sole country where, perhaps, an attempt would be successful to carry out the threefold transition: as a human being, an intellectual, and a political scholar."

Once in this country, the Germans were surprised at the high academic level of their American colleagues. Most Germans were swiftly won over by the friendliness, benevolence, and tolerance of those with whom they came in contact, teachers and students alike. At the same time, they could not help missing the high status and distinction granted professors in Germany. Even as spiritual a man as Paul Tillich once remarked that in the change from a German to an American university he had, so to speak, "come down seven steps on the social ladder." But in the end they accepted this demotion with good grace. They had one common mission: to fight Nazi propaganda in the United States, urge Americans to make a distinction between Germany and the Nazi regime, and persuade Americans that there was popular opposition to Hitler in Germany. Each also had an individual mission: theoretical physicists felt they had to bring theory into American laboratories and explain its role; applied mathematicians devoted themselves to the task of removing American mathematics from the isolation of its abstractness and promoting interdisciplinary contacts with physics, mechanics, and technology; lawyers considered it their duty to acquaint Americans with European law; historians offered the solid background of experience that Germany had acquired during its process of maturation to help America strengthen itself. In general, the Germans rapidly recognized the good features of the American cultural patrimony and did not try to supplant American methods and ideas with their own but strove to fuse them, promoting understanding between the two traditions.

At the end of the war a good many Germans went back to Europe. In the ranks of those returning were chiefly, although not exclusively, persons who had lost their positions in Hitler's time because of political rather than racial discrimination, generally holding leftist views, and authors who found it difficult to write in English or to go on writing in German while living in an English-speaking country. (But one German author who did not go back,

Hans Sahl, asserted that from a distance he could better observe the people he wanted to describe, and that a writer cannot write well in the language in which he has to order a cup of coffee.)

A few went back because they were so basically and uncompromisingly German that they could not become Americanized. They were not the youngest in the wave. At the time of emigrating they had already reached an age at which the exigencies of well-set patterns of behavior and habits increase the difficulties of adjustment to a new mode of life. In America they remained tied to their old traditions, drawing strength from them, and could accept their exile because, like Arnold Bergsträsser, one of the major figures of this group, they could say "Germany is where I am." These profoundly nationalistic feelings did not prevent them from entering into fruitful relationships with American colleagues and maintaining these relationships throughout their stay. Bergsträsser's American activities are proof enough.

A versatile man with a powerful personality, Bergsträsser came from Germany in 1937. Although his formal training was in the social and political sciences, during his first years in America he taught history, cultural sociology, and German literature to large numbers of students at Claremont College in California. In 1944 he was called to the University of Chicago to teach in the Army Specialized Training Program for soldiers who were to be sent to Germany to become members of the military government. After the completion of this program he was invited to remain in the German department. Not only did he greatly strengthen the department but, enlisting the collaboration of German-born colleagues in other departments, he strove and succeeded in raising the level of German culture in the community. He improved the quality of the existing German Literary Society of Chicago and became a founder and editor of the *Deutsche Beiträge zur geistigen Ueberlieferung*, for which he secured the contributions of eminent scholars. (The first issue was published in 1947 by the University of Chicago Press. Among the collaborators belonging to the migration wave were historian Fritz Caspari, Germanist Otto Jolles, art historian Ulrich Middledorf, philosophers Werner Richter and Eugen Rosenstock-Huessy, historian Hans Rothfels, and historian of art Otto von Simson. The publication of *Deutsche Beiträge* proved too expensive for the University of Chicago, and the next four issues were published abroad. The fifth volume was published in 1964 under the general editorship of Otto Jolles and Stefan Schultz, another member of the cultural wave and professor of German at the University of Chicago. Wolfgang Liepe, who taught at the University of Chicago from 1947 until his retirement in 1954, has also been a contributor to this publication.)

Among Bergsträsser's achievements was the Goethe Festival at Aspen, Colorado, in 1949, which he organized with his Italian-born colleague G. A. Borgese. This international convocation, planned and worked out in detail by Bergsträsser, became the first of a long series of Aspen summer programs. In 1950 Bergsträsser returned to Germany to pick up the threads of his interrupted career and died there in 1964. Several years before his death, in an interview for Radio-Bremen, he said that in America he had considered himself an interpreter of German culture; that in a sense he had been a piece of Germany abroad. He also asserted that reconciling political and ideological differences between American and German-born colleagues had not always been easy. Indeed, his words recall the commotion that broke out when he was invited to teach in the Army program and his political fitness for this task was debated. They also betray his awareness of the resentment he had created in some German-born émigrés by assuming leadership of the intellectual life of the German community.

Most Germans, however, remained in this country and the majority became fully Americanized. They are found in all areas of American cultural life; the visual arts, music, and most branches of learning have Germans in their fold; and humanistic and scholarly fields have especially benefited from the influx of German scholars. Perhaps their most prominent attributes are a bent toward speculation and a theoretical approach to the investigation of issues and the solution of problems.

But not all Germans went into conventional cultural fields. One who did not is Frank Auerbach, whose American career led him into a singular role as a leading expert in immigration law and policy in the State Department. Auerbach held a degree of Doctor of Jurisprudence from the University of Heidelberg, but after 1935 the laws against the Jews in Germany prevented him from practicing and he became active in German organizations aiding Jews to emigrate. Social work to assist Jews, which he continued for several years after his arrival in the United States in 1938, and dealing with refugee problems kept him in touch with American immigration legislation. His contacts with government agencies administering immigration legislation were reinforced after 1946, when he became the editor of *Interpreter Releases*, a publication of the Common Council for American Unity (now the American Council for Nationalities Service). *Interpreter Releases* is an information service on immigration, naturalization, and related issues, and Auerbach collected material from first-hand sources; he also represented the council at government meetings and hearings. From 1951 he had an appointment in the visa division of the State Department, where one of his first assignments was to prepare visa regulations, especially in the implementation of the Displaced Persons Act of 1948. In 1955 he published *The Immigration Laws of the United States*, a standard text containing all the laws, regulations, and administrative decisions in the field of immigration. That same year he became assistant director of the visa office and deputy director for visa policies and special programs. Simultaneously, he was special adviser for immigration affairs to the administrator of the Bureau of Security and Consular Affairs and chairman of the Policy Committee on Immigration and Naturalization of the State Department.

The brightest star in the German-born constellation was undoubtedly Albert Einstein. When I met him at a dinner party in Princeton, New Jersey, he was still a vigorous man with small jet-black eyes, a big halo of white hair, and no socks. He filled the room with his presence. That evening he outshone his compatriot Thomas Mann, who, as I recall, slumped gray and withdrawn in his chair, allowing his wife to answer most of the questions addressed to him. It was a few months before Pearl Harbor, and our hostess, the wife of a British physicist in the services, was knitting for English children. Einstein's sister, who wished to talk about Italy, claimed my attention that evening, and I remember little about Einstein except the strong impact of his presence. And this is perhaps as it should be. To America also, Einstein's presence alone was all-important, not his actions or words. In this country he did not add significantly to the scientific edifice that he had built abroad and he participated only sporadically in American life. Since he did not teach classes he did not directly influence American youth, as other immigrants did, and in fact led a rather solitary and aloof existence in his home in Princeton. And yet Einstein's name is the only name in the migration wave that all Americans know and are likely to remember. He became a symbol of persecuted European genius and is a measure of the stature of the cultural migration.

AUSTRIANS

The intellectuals who were born in Austria proper — not in the whole Austro-Hungarian monarchy — form the second largest national group, comprising about 20 per cent of all the European-born in my survey. It is not always easy to tell them apart from the Germans, since they speak the same language, but once the distinction is achieved, it becomes apparent that as a group they are characterized by some different traits, much as American intellectuals differ from the British. The Austrian émigrés are on the average five years younger than the Germans because the Nazi persecution, the greatest single cause of emigration from Germany and Austria, did not hit them until the *Anschluss* in March, 1938, that is, five years after the first round of wholesale dismissals in Germany. And in fact about three-quarters of all Austrians in the wave came in 1938 or later.

Possibly because they are younger and endowed with a greater sense of humor, the Austrians are in general more cheerful and take themselves less seriously than the Germans: none of the Austrians I met tended to identify the Austrian émigrés with the entire migration and to give them credit, absent-mindedly, for all positive features of the wave, a misdemeanor that the Germans have indeed committed.

Perhaps as another consequence of their being young, the Austrians adjusted beautifully to America, promptly learned English, and came to speak it with a softer accent than the Germans; and few of them returned to Europe. (But the political situation in Austria after World War II was also an important reason in their decision to stay on here.)

The majority of Austrian émigrés were educated in Vienna, the one great cultural center of Austria. When Vienna was the seat of the Habsburg court she attracted the cultured aristocracy from all parts of the Dual Monarchy; and both before and after the dissolution of the Habsburg empire her excellent schools served a vast territory around her. Not only did the university acquire world fame, but also lower schools such as the Theresianum where children of the social, political, and military élite were prepared for the university; and even the Viennese kindergartens have made a mark in history: an American told me with assurance — or perhaps it was feigned assurance — that the most eminent Hungarian and Austrian intellectuals in this country as well as a few of those who were born in what is now Czechoslovakia attended the same Viennese kindergarten. (But when I investigated this story I was able to ascertain only that two immigrants from Austria and one from Hungary had attended the famous kindergarten. The dazzling generalization is an example of the formation of myth that too often finds a way into history.)

Of the several intellectual currents in Vienna in the early decades of this century the most important from the point of view of the cultural migration and its impact on the American cultural scene was undoubtedly the Freudian, and a later chapter is devoted to the arrival here of European psychoanalysis. In Vienna, Freud's influence acted directly on the group of psychoanalysts around him, and indirectly on a broader spectrum of intellectuals. The psychoanalysts in Vienna were relatively few but virtually all were forced to emigrate by the events of the thirties, and the majority came to the United States. And so America acquired, among others, the great analysts Paul Federn, Hanns Sachs, Robert Waelder, Heinz Hartmann, and Ernst Kris. But to America also came many Austrians of different professions who had acquired a psychoanalytic outlook through training or other association with analysts. The most common form of association was an analysis, for to the young Viennese intellectuals being analyzed had become a way of exploring life, of tasting all that life could offer, on which they insisted even while Hitler was threatening at their doors. The psychoanalytic knowledge they derived often proved useful in America: it led into social work a group of young lawyers who gave up the idea of a law career in this country because they would have had to begin their legal education from scratch. It gave psychologists, educators, and young social and political scientists a tool with which to broaden their fields. Whether intentionally or not, this young generation of Austrian intellectuals did much to spread the Freudian viewpoint in America. Most of the lawyers with a psychoanalytic background who went into social work remained in this field, but at least one made a remarkable switch: Robert Kann worked for a while among the prisoners at Rikers Island, then turned to history and became an eminent historian of the Austro-Hungarian monarchy and its successor states. Historical research gave him cause for frequent visits to his homeland.

Other influences besides the psychoanalytic were to move from Vienna to the United States. One was the influence of the famous Vienna Circle, which came into existence in the early twenties. Its members were philosophers, scientists, and mathematicians who attempted to apply to philosophy the methods of mathematical logic and became known as logical positivists. Among the members of the Vienna circle who eventually settled in America were philosophers Herbert Feigl and Rudolf Carnap, who though German-born lived and taught in Vienna for several years; the physicist Philipp Frank; mathematicians Karl Menger and Kurt Gödel, a Czechoslovakian-born, Vienna-educated man of fantastic mind who was to revolutionize mathematical logic. Once in the United States, these men had a considerable part in determining current trends in American philosophy and contributed to the establishment of the philosophy of science, which before the thirties had not been recognized as a field of research.

Vienna had also a strong tradition of economic studies, rooted in the 1880's, when Carl Menger initiated the "Austrian school," now identified with the theory of marginal utility, the deductive method, and the psychological approach. Many émigré economists were reared in the atmosphere of the Austrian school and were to make its theories better known in this country. By coincidence, three young men who were to become well-known economists and were to emigrate to the United States attended the same famous seminar conducted in 1905–6 by the eminent economist Eugen von Böhm-Bawerk: they were Joseph Schumpeter, who spent the last eighteen years of his life at Harvard University; Ludwig von Mises, who was professor at New York University; and Emil Lederer, for whose sake Alvin Johnson founded the University in Exile. A fourth student in the seminar was the Socialist leader Rudolf Hilferding, who was caught by the Nazis as he prepared to sail from Europe. In the following years students from many parts of Europe went to Vienna to study economics and several later settled in America. An Austrian among them was Gottfried Haberler, who after receiving his doctoral degree stayed on in Vienna as a teacher until 1936, then came to Harvard University.

Many other Austrian-born émigrés came to this country from Vienna and other cities. A most remarkable group were the musicians, including composers Erich Korngold, Ernst Krenek, Arnold Schoenberg, and Ernst Toch; conductors Kurt Herbert Adler, Paul Breisach, and Erich Leinsdorf; pianist Artur Schnabel; and musicologists Karl Geiringer, Hans Tischler, and

107

Emmanuel Winternitz. Most musicians prospered in America, where they found recognition and applause, but some suffered in the transplantation. One example is provided by the distinguished composer Karl Weigl, who after emigrating here led a precarious existence in New York, giving piano lessons, though in Vienna he had received numerous prizes for his work and had been the teacher of famous pupils, among them Kurt Adler (no relation to Kurt Herbert Adler), now a conductor at the Metropolitan Opera in New York. Weigl received some recognition long after his death, when in 1968 his symphony "Apocalyptic" was produced in New York, Leopold Stokowski conducting.

The world of Austrian theater and letters has been well represented in the migration. The great producer Max Reinhardt came to America in 1933 and in the ten years before his death spread the influence of the Viennese theater and its traditions. One of his young assistants, John Reich, came to the United States in 1938, produced many plays, and in 1957 became head of the Goodman Theater of the Art Institute in Chicago. A few Austrian literary men were only passing figures on the American scene. Writer Stefan Zweig, after a stay of a little over a year, moved on to South America and self-inflicted death. The poet and dramatist Richard Beer-Hoffmann and the dean of European music critics Julius Korngold (Erich Korngold's father) died one day apart in 1945. Both were Viennese and had been in America since 1939 and 1938 respectively. (The same issue of the *New York Times*, September 27, 1945, recorded the deaths of three great Europeans: Beer-Hoffmann, Korngold, and Béla Bartók.) Many other Austrian literary men lived long in this country, and some of their names will be encountered later in this book.

Two Austrian-born scientists, physicists Wolfgang Pauli and Victor Hess, were Nobel laureates. Pauli, gruff and round-shaped, more lavish of criticism than of praise, was one of the most brilliant theoretical physicists in the second quarter of this century. He came to America in 1940, and in 1945, while at the Institute for Advanced Study, was awarded the Nobel Prize for his exclusion principle. Pauli had been educated in Germany, but since 1928 he had been teaching at the Federal Institute of Technology in Zurich and had not lived in Austria for a long time. Hess, on the other hand, remained fully Austrian until he came here; he was educated in Vienna and taught at Austrian universities until 1938, when he emigrated to America to join the faculty of Fordham University. Two years before coming here

108

he had received the Nobel Prize for his discovery of cosmic radiation. Both Pauli and Hess became American citizens, but while Hess settled permanently in New York, Pauli returned to Europe shortly after the war.

Pauli and Hess made their main contributions to science while they were still in Europe, but this is not true of biologist Paul Weiss whose scientific career has taken place almost entirely in the United States. In Vienna, where he was educated, he had been an assistant director of the Biological Research Institute of the Vienna Academy of Sciences. He came to America in 1931, worked at Yale for a few years, at the University of Chicago for over twenty years, and in 1954 became a member of the Rockefeller Institute for Medical Research (now Rockefeller University). During World War II, when the repair of severed nerves in battle casualties had become a major surgical problem, Weiss was commissioned by the Office of Scientific Research and Development to study nerve growth and regeneration. Working with a nationwide team of scientists, Weiss devised methods to repair severed nerves by using a live artery as a sleeve within which the ends of the nerve could grow and join together, and by freezing and storing nerve sections to be used as grafts. His findings have given surgeons new approaches and allowed them to attempt surgery not possible before. Weiss, who is also an authority on normal and abnormal growth of cells, has held several influential positions (from 1958 to 1960, for instance, he was a member of the board of scientific advisers to the President of the United States). Most relevant to the cultural migration, he participated in many postwar international cultural undertakings.

Before closing the present list I shall mention an Austrian who in a most surprising shift of career turned from a lawyer into a mentor of the English language. The Viennese Rudolf Flesch was in the process of being admitted to the Austrian bar when the *Anschluss* forced him to change his plans, and six months later he landed in America, where his Austrian degree was of no value for a career in law. Twenty-seven-year-old Flesch knew little English and was "without resources — and certainly without the chance of going through an American law school all over again," as he wrote me. He worked as a stock clerk in a commercial book-bindery at sixteen dollars a week, then applied for and obtained a one-year scholarship at the School of Library Science at Columbia University.

Once qualified as a librarian he got a job doing bibliographical work at the Readability Laboratory of the American Association for Adult Education, and began to take part in the work that was being done at the laboratory. "The end result of that was a doctoral dissertation 'Marks of a Readable Style,' a Ph.D. in educational research, and a workable statistical formula to test the readability of English prose. The obvious next step was a trade book to put my findings before the public, and so I became the author of *The Art of Plain Talk*." The book was published in 1946 and by 1948 it had sold nearly 50,000 copies. Encouraged by this success, the following year Flesch published *The Art of Readable Writing*. Alan J. Gould, executive editor of the Associated Press, stated in a Foreword: ". . . the impact of Dr. Flesch's ideas on simpler, clearer ways of writing represents one of the most significant developments of our journalistic times."

In 1960, with nine books to his credit, Flesch evaluated the effect of his work himself. In an Introduction to *How to Write, Speak and Think More Effectively* he wrote: "Since [the publication of *The Art of Plain Talk*] my readability formulas have penetrated into schools of journalism, advertising agencies, textbooks on business writing, and many other places. Gradually, they contributed to a tremendous change in newswriting, business writing, and practical writing in general. . . . What was a novel approach in 1946 has become the accepted practice among professional writers." The amazing revelation in this statement is not Flesch's success but the willingness of American writers to accept the counsel of a foreigner in matters concerning their own language. Only one of his books, *Why Johnny Can't Read*, aroused considerable criticism. The book contained a strong plea for the phonic method to teach children to read, a method which had proved effective in European schools and which Flesch himself had successfully used on his twelve-year-old son Johnny after the boy had failed to learn to read in an American school. Flesch's sweeping criticisms of the methods used in American elementary schools irritated many educators. By 1965 *Books in Print* listed fourteen books by Flesch, most about writing and speaking — one, *The ABC of Style*, in the spirit of Fowler's *Modern English Usage*. Flesch agrees that he could not have done the same kind of work in Vienna, but he has reason to hope for a change. In Europe, along with the growing interest in Coca-Cola and supermarkets, "there is a faint beginning of interest in readability testing," and Flesch has received letters of inquiry from Germany, France, Belgium, and Finland.

110

HUNGARIANS

In my search for clues to the mystery of Hungarian talent I talked to so many Hungarians and heard mention of so many more that I gained the impression of a large representation in the cultural wave. But I must have confused quality with quantity. Though they constitute the fourth largest national group, the Hungarians in my file are fewer than a hundred, about 5 per cent of the total wave. They themselves explain that they seem more numerous because they have the gift of ubiquity — and some do seem to be in more than one place at the same time — which multiplies the effect of their presence. Indeed, they travel so frequently, so fast, and so unexpectedly that there is certain ground for this belief. But there may be a better explanation. Hungarian intellectuals began to emigrate earlier than those from other countries (except Russia), impelled by the political events that have tormented their country since the end of World War I; the Béla Kun revolution, the Whites' reprisals, and the veiled dictatorship and open anti-Semitism of Admiral Horthy's regime. Some of these early emigrants reached the United States in the twenties, so that there are actually more Hungarians in this country than my file indicates, but not all belong to the wave under study.

Not all the early Hungarian emigrants came directly to this country. Among those who did not, there were many students who sought to finish their education outside Hungary: while the Hungarian gymnasiums were excellent, the universities were poor and the *numerus clausus* excluded from them all but 5 per cent of the Jewish students. German universities were the most favored by Hungarians, though some students went to Austria, Czechoslovakia, and elsewhere. The fact that many went to Germany was ground for a casual remark made recently by one of my Hungarian friends: "Why make so much fuss about the Hungarians? They were all educated in Germany anyhow." But this is too broad a generalization.

True enough, the most brilliant Hungarian physicists, Eugene Wigner, Leo Szilard, and Edward Teller, and the great aerodynamicist Theodore von Karman obtained their doctoral degrees at German universities, and mathematician-physicist John Von Neumann received part of his university education in Germany (and part in Switzerland). Most outstanding Hungarians, however, studied in Hungary or went to universities within the territory of the old Austro-Hungarian state. In the strong group of mathematicians who were to emigrate to the United States, Von Neumann was an exception:

Paul Erdös and Cornelius Lanczos hold degrees from the University of Budapest; George Polya, Tibor Rado, Otto Szasz, and Gabor Szegö studied at the University of Vienna. The prominent psychoanalysts Franz Alexander, Therese Benedek, Sandor Rado, and Géza Róheim received their education at Hungarian universities. Alexander underwent his psychoanalytic training in Berlin many years after receiving his Hungarian medical degree. All Hungarian musicians whose background I could check, including composer Béla Bartók, conductor Antal Dorati, and violinist Joseph Szigeti, were products of Hungary.

If the German education of Hungarians is an unwarranted generalization, it is a fact that many spent time in Germany before coming to the United States, and only Béla Bartók and Géza Róheim, among the men mentioned above, remained in Hungary until the last moment, after the outbreak of war in Europe. Polya was in Switzerland from 1914, Erdös went to England in 1939, and Szigeti spent several years in Switzerland. But all the others lived in Germany before deciding to cross the ocean, and so did other famous Hungarians I have not yet mentioned. I need to name only those connected with the German Bauhaus, whose spirit they were to bring to the United States: artists and designers László Moholy-Nagy and Gyorgy Kepes, and architect Marcel Breuer (all trained in Hungary). When Hitler came to power in Germany, the Jews and leftists among the Hungarian émigrés were forced to leave the country. A few came directly to the United States, but larger numbers went to England and spent several years there.

A very colorful, "very Hungarian" man of the older generation was playwright Ferenc Molnár. His family name had been Neumann, but he had changed it to the Magyar word Molnár ("miller") so that his works would not be thought those of a German. In his years in New York, where he settled in 1940, he was surrounded by Hungarian émigrés and American intellectuals who were attracted by his charm as much as by his fame: his plays were popular in New York and as early as 1908 four companies were performing *The Devil* simultaneously. Later the Hungarian setting of his *Liliom* was a challenge to American stage designers, who responded to it with great success. *Liliom* was further Americanized as the musical comedy *Carousel*. Among Hungarians notable in fields not yet mentioned are economists William Fellner, George Katona, Karl Polanyi, and Tibor Scitovsky; musicologists Ernst Ferand and Otto Gombosi (they followed a fellow Hungarian musicologist who came to this country in the late twenties, Paul Henry Lang); physicians George Gomori, Imre Horner, and Stephen Rothman; physicist Marcel Schein; and art historian Charles de Tolnay.

Economist Karl Polanyi belonged to an exceptionally talented Hungarian family, several members of which "made good" in the United States. Legend has it that the Polanyis' intellectual heritage came from their mother, "Cecil-mama," an extraordinary Russian-born woman who introduced Freudian views in her renowned salons and was still devouring books at the rate of three or four a day while lying on her deathbed in Budapest. In the tradition of the Hungarian upper classes she kept two homes, in Budapest and in Vienna, and so it happened that her oldest son Karl was born in the Austrian capital. (But after her husband's business collapsed, the Polanyi family lived in poverty.) In his early years Karl, the founder and animator of the Galileo Club which did so much to stimulate young Hungarian talent, was secretary of the Radical Citizen's Party in Hungary. In the thirties he settled in England and became a co-founder of the Christian Left Movement in 1936. In 1940 he came to America where he taught first at Bennington College, and then (after a few years back in England) at Columbia University from 1947 until his retirement in 1961. In Bennington he wrote his first major work, *The Great Transformation*, widely influential in America as a critique of laissez-faire economics, as his brother Michael commented in a letter to me. "It powerfully appealed for including in any consideration of economic principles the effects of economic action on social life. . . . This work was followed by thirty years of study bent on elucidating the ubiquitous balance between strictly economic and purely social values. . . ." This study and its applications to examples of primitive societies affected the course of economic anthropology.

Among American scientists Karl was known as "Polanyi's brother." The "real Polanyi" was Michael. Michael Polanyi studied medicine and physical chemistry in Budapest and at the end of World War I settled in Germany where he won his reputation for work as a physical chemist at the Kaiser Wilhelm Institute. But he was interested in economic questions, and when he moved to Manchester he was appointed professor of sociology. Since his retirement he has given himself to the philosophy and epistemology of science and has lectured extensively in England and in the United States. Karl and Michael were the best known of the Polanyi family, but it is their sister,

Laura Polanyi Striker, who accomplished the most unusual feat. Cecil-mama did not think much of her daughter, or so the gossip goes, and nicknamed her "Mausi" (Mousy), but Mausi became a historian, was active in peace movements, and came to this country. Here she was called upon to rule, once and forever, on the veracity of Captain John Smith and his account of his adventures. A bitter controversy had flared up at various times on the credibility of his stories of voyages, fights, loves, and captivity in Hungary and Transylvania. It was claimed by some scholars that the battles he described were never fought. If so, Captain Smith was a fabricator of tales whose whole account, including information about early Virginia, could not be trusted. Captain Smith's biographer Bradford Smith felt that only a Hungarian scholar would be able to investigate the matter satisfactorily. He turned to Karl Polanyi for advice, and Polanyi suggested his sister Laura. Though she was almost seventy years old, she accepted the assignment with zest. She delved into old documents in Hungarian, Latin, and English that she found in the United States and into the material that was sent to her by J. Franz Pichler, archivist of the Central Archive of Styria in Graz, Austria, whose research she directed by correspondence. She established dates of battles and other events, and found conclusive evidence in favor of Captain Smith's stories. Thus she reaffirmed his reputation. When Bradford Smith's biography was published in 1953, it contained a scholarly appendix about Captain Smith's travels in Hungary by Laura Polanyi Striker. Four years later, she published as corroborative evidence her own translation of the Latin manuscript of Henry Warton's *The Life of John Smith, English Soldier* and accompanied it with a learned essay on Captain Smith in seventeenth-century literature.

The Polanyi tradition continues. Laura Polanyi Striker's daughter Eva Zeisel is a successful designer in New York, where she settled in 1938. Trained as a painter at the Academy of Fine Arts in Budapest, she was attracted by the craft movement in central Europe of which the Bauhaus was the inspirer and acquired experience in designing china for mass production. China and pottery remained her chief specialty, but she has also designed tubular metal chairs, lamps, and other household articles. She is one of only two industrial designers for whom the Museum of Modern Art has arranged a one-man show, and she has participated in many exhibitions in America and abroad. Through her fifteen years of teaching at the Pratt

Institute her influence has spread and her pupils are in leading offices of industrial design.

In the hearts of most Hungarians in America there lingers a pride in their national origin, which is somewhat different from the mild nationalism of other foreign-born. It is as if they felt that being a Hungarian was an asset in American life. Géza Róheim, the psychoanalyst, is said to have cultivated his national character consciously and proudly and pushed Hungarianism to its extremes. When László Moholy-Nagy was compelled to raise funds for the New Bauhaus only months after its opening and his arrival in America, all he could rely on for success, according to his wife Sibyl, was "his personality — alertness, enthusiasm, Hungarian accent, and personal magnetism. . . ." A saying attributed to Eugene Wigner and widely circulating among Hungarians puts the matter in a nutshell: "To be a Hungarian is not all, but it helps, it certainly helps."

Not only the jokes about themselves and their peculiar traits but also their great contributions to America single out the Hungarians as a group. The names of Wigner, Szilard, Teller, and Von Neumann are in all histories of the wartime atomic project. Outside the atomic field, Von Neumann's greatest influence was as principal inventor of the large computers that smooth the functioning of modern life. Before his death in 1964, Szilard launched the idea for and directed the organization of the Council for a Livable World, an imaginative plan by which our relations with the Communist world might be improved through an intelligent steering of American foreign policy. Wigner is still moving ahead on that path of physics and technology which has already given us atomic weapons and atomic reactors. And Teller may yet see one of his great projects come true: world government achieved through temporary military strengthening, the manipulation of weather by man, and the abatement of air and water pollution in the state of New York (he was a consultant to Governor Rockefeller). To von Karman also Americans have a debt of gratitude: he is regarded as the man who had the greatest influence on the development of high-speed aircraft in the United States and was repeatedly an adviser to the air force and the leader of programs to develop the first jet propulsion and rocket motors. If Béla Bartók and the United States did not understand each other in his lifetime, after his death he has made a triumphant comeback and is now a favorite of American musical audiences, who acclaim him as one of the great modern composers.

ITALIANS

One day in 1939, shortly after my arrival in New York, a friendly woman asked me what my husband's business was and upon hearing that he was teaching at Columbia University she exclaimed: "How interesting! Does he teach music or Italian?" One peculiarity of the Italian intellectuals in the wave of the thirties, which distinguishes them from those in previous waves, is the scarcity among them of music and Italian teachers. In a very broad sense Giuseppe Antonio Borgese, an early exile from fascism who was in this country from 1931 until his retirement in 1948, was a teacher of Italian. In Italy Borgese had taught German literature and aesthetics but was better known as a literary critic and contributor to the *Corriere della Sera*, then one of the best dailies in Europe. He had also written several novels which to my knowledge did not attain immortal fame, possibly because *nemo propheta in patria est*; in this country I have heard it said that he deserved the Nobel Prize in literature more than certain writers who received it. In the United States Borgese did actually teach courses in Italian literature at several colleges. In his twelve years as professor of Romance languages at the University of Chicago, he also gave courses that delved deeply into Dante's works, and wrote a book *Goliath, the March of Fascism*, the best, least dated part of which is a vivid picture of Italian culture through the centuries. It is likely, however, that Borgese will be remembered not as a man of letters but as a political figure, a bitter and early foe and merciless critic of fascism, who at the end of the war fought strenuously and a bit unrealistically for a world federation, drafted a much too premature world constitution, and founded the magazine *Common Cause* to launch his political ideas.

Renato Poggioli, a Slavicist, also taught Italian literature. Born and educated in Florence, he had been a teacher of Russian in Florence and of Italian in Wilno and Warsaw before coming to America in 1938. Here he was on the faculties of Smith and Brown, and at Harvard from 1946 until his death in an automobile accident in 1963. He acquired a reputation among American scholars for promoting the translation of Russian and Italian works and for his own translation of Italian poetry. But other than Borgese and Poggioli, very few Italians in the migration were teachers of Italian or Italian culture.

An even more puzzling fact is that artists and musicians, and therefore art and music teachers, were equally scarce despite the great Italian tradition. In music I can think only of Toscanini, composer Mario Castelnuovo-Tedesco, and conductor Massimo Freccia. As for the visual arts, no Italian-born sculptors or architects belonging to the wave are listed in the 1954–55 edition of *Who's Who in America*, and the one painter listed, Lino Sigismondo Lipinsky de Orlov, is of Polish extraction. One possible explanation is that music and the visual arts were not among the fields to which Italian Jews were traditionally attracted and therefore were not hit as hard as other cultural areas by the racial laws. Moreover, as a group, the artists must not have been strongly politically minded, since few emigrated for purely political reasons. Toscanini is an exception.

The majority of Italians came to the United States after the promulgation in 1938 of racial and other restrictive laws, but a few like Borgese who opposed fascism from its beginning arrived in the early thirties. The major figure among them was the historian Gaetano Salvemini. A liberal socialist, Salvemini first taught history in Messina, where he lost wife and children in the great earthquake of 1908, and then in Florence, and was the editor of the liberal newspaper *L'Unità*. At the end of World War I he was an Italian representative at the Versailles Conference. The most nationalistic Italians of that time reckoned him among the *rinunciatari* and dubbed him "Slave-mini," for he professed himself willing to renounce some Italian ambitions in the Adriatic in favor of new-born Yugoslavia. For these views and his liberalism, he became a target of political persecution upon the advent of fascism. In 1925 he was implicated in the publication of the clandestine anti-Fascist paper *Non Mollare* (*Don't Let Go*) and arrested. Shortly after being released he managed to slip out of Italy by eluding two Fascist agents assigned to follow him and went to live in London. Between 1926 and 1933 he paid several visits to the United States and in 1934 became Lauro de Bosis lecturer in Italian civilization at Harvard. (Lauro de Bosis was a young anti-Fascist, and a friend of Salvemini's, who died in 1931 after flying his plane over Rome to drop anti-Fascist leaflets. His American fiancée, Ruth Draper, established the Harvard chair to honor his memory and proposed Salvemini as the first occupant.)

117

In England and America, Salvemini used the historian's craft to unmask the Italian dictator and offset his propaganda outside Italy. Patiently and systematically, he uncovered facts, gathered documents to prove them, and was among the first to write books about fascism that may truly be called historical — not an easy feat while Mussolini was in power. Around Salvemini rallied the forces of anti-fascism in America. From New York the younger Max Ascoli added his written and spoken word to those of Salvemini and Borgese. Ascoli, who came to this country with a fellowship from the Rockefeller Foundation in 1931, did not return to Italy and became instead an original member of the University in Exile. Much later, in 1949, he founded the magazine *The Reporter*.

Salvemini, Borgese, and Ascoli were the most prominent anti-Fascists in the intellectual wave until the arrival of an even more militant group, which strictly speaking does not belong in the wave. They were not immigrants but men itching to return to Italy, old-time *fuorusciti* who in Paris or London had done all they could to fight fascism and were driven to America by the collapse of France. They did not stay long in America; some went back to Italy as early as 1943 in the wake of the landings at Anzio, others after the liberation of Italy. Nevertheless, they are important and must be mentioned because in the period of reconstruction they participated in one capacity or another in the assemblies organizing the new Italian republic and in its initial government. To their task they brought a clear understanding of the United States and its policies and intentions that they would not have acquired had they not lived on its soil.

The group was led by Count Carlo Sforza, a liberal aristocrat of Republican convictions who had been Minister of Foreign Affairs before the advent of Mussolini and had lived in France since 1928. Sixty-seven years old in 1940, tall, straight, with a short, snow-white beard and firm lips from which the pronoun "I" flowed in striking profusion, Sforza gave an immediate impression of great vigor and intelligence, of a strong drive steered by mature reflection and supported by self-confidence. Another colossus of Italian politics was Don Luigi Sturzo, the priest who in 1919 founded the Italian Popular Party — the precursor of the Christian Democratic Party — and had been an exile in London since 1923. Among the less famous were Alberto Tarchiani and Alberto Cianca, both former members of Carlo Rosselli's movement *Giustizia e Libertà* in Paris; Randolfo Pacciardi, a Republican like Sforza, who had fought against Franco in Spain; and Aurelio Natoli, who arrived in New York a few months after the others, by way of the Spanish battlefields and a concentration camp in Morocco.

The arrival of these militant *fuorusciti* stimulated the anti-Fascist intellectuals settled here, and the two groups joined efforts in an intense political campaign. The Mazzini Society was created in 1940 to combat Fascist propaganda and educate Italo-Americans. Its membership was small but sincerely dedicated to the cause of a free, democratic Italy as envisioned by Mazzini. Max Ascoli was appointed its first president and Salvemini its honorary president, in recognition of his leadership in the fight against fascism. (Max Ascoli recalled that when two members of the Mazzini Society went to the appropriate office of the United States Court to register the society, an official rejected their application because it did not bear "Mr. Mazzini's" signature!) In early 1941, before America entered the war, the Mazzini Society was broadcasting from Boston to Italy to "tell the truth about the struggle between the democracies and the totalitarian powers." In March of the following year the society began publishing its own weekly, *Nazioni Unite (United Nations)*. An editorial in the first issue set the tone by stating that all contributors to the new paper were "men who uncompromisingly stood against Fascism all their adult lives." Probably more important than this weekly were the extensive lecture tours undertaken by many of the members. Sforza and Borgese spoke mainly at colleges and universities, but others reached all sorts of audiences — a New York union of clothes manufacturers, for instance. Through these speeches and at the many anti-Fascist rallies sponsored by the Mazzini Society, its members presented Italy's case and pledged their loyalty to the United States. Political contacts with the American government were not extensive and, at least at the beginning, limited to the Intelligence Service. In 1942 the parallel Free Italian movement was organized. Unlike the Mazzini Society, it included Italian Communists and assumed the character of a government in exile. At a congress in Montevideo in August, 1942, Sforza was named the leader of the Free Italians.

When the liberation of Italy began, the first *fuorusciti* returned and a channel of direct communications was opened between them and anti-Fascists in America. The information received about the true state of affairs in Italy was passed on to the United States government in an attempt to

119

dispel American distrust of the leaders of the liberated parts of Italy. It is hard to say how effective this attempt was. More evident are some results of the *fuorusciti*'s sojourn in America: they could assure their countrymen of American good will and push pro-American policies. Sforza, as the president of the Italian Constituent Assembly, spoke to that body in 1947, strongly propounding the ratification of the peace treaty. In mentioning the favorable attitude of the United States toward Italy, he recalled, "with emotion," Columbus Day, 1942, "a day still living in my spirit," when Italians in America were overjoyed by Roosevelt's declaration that they would no longer be considered enemy aliens, that the United States was fighting fascism and not Italy. A few days later, Sforza reassured the Constituent Assembly, which had expressed doubts about the United States' financial solidity, and he showed a thorough understanding of the American stock market, credit policies, and taxation system. Speaking in favor of world government weeks later at the Paris Conference, Sforza invoked once more his knowledge of the United States in support of his arguments. "You are not unaware, Gentlemen," he said, "that I lived long in the United States and that consequently I am perhaps not devoid of a certain understanding of the Americans' way of thinking. . . . I dare tell you that I am acquainted with the present attitude of the United States . . . the Americans will pay greater attention to facts than to words. . . ."

In the men to whom she gave asylum in the years of turmoil America had staunch supporters. I have little doubt that they facilitated and hastened the good relations that prevailed in the postwar period. The political activities of the Italians in America were of course not unique. Statesmen and politicians from many countries took refuge in America in the years in which Europe was ravaged by war, or settled here for good. The Italian group was characterized by a greater unity than others, but the unity did not survive the liberation of Italy and the unleashing of political rivalry. The personal prestige and stature of some men also singled out the Italians. However, their case is offered here only as an example.

Other Italians, as well as Salvemini, Borgese, and Ascoli, came to America before the crucial 1938. Among them were conductor Arturo Toscanini, professor of government Mario Einaudi, and science historian Giorgio de Santillana, known to many American readers for his brilliant study *The Crime of Galileo*. The largest part of the Italians in the migration, however, came to

120

the United States after Mussolini's frenzied promulgation of "Prussianizing" laws in the second half of 1938. Many were either Jews directly affected by the racial legislation or Aryans with Jewish members in their families; but others left Italy for their political convictions or because they were hit by one of the many Fascist laws of the time — those prohibiting marriage between Italians and foreigners, or hindering the advancement of unmarried persons in government positions, including university teachers.

Prominent among these latecomers were three nuclear physicists whose wartime and postwar roles in atomic developments are described in Chapter VII: Enrico Fermi, who on his way into exile stopped in Stockholm to pick up a Nobel Prize; an expert in cosmic radiation, Bruno Rossi; and Emilio Segrè, who received a share of the Nobel Prize in 1959 for the discovery of the anti-proton. There were other Italian physicists. Sergio De Benedetti spent two years at the Curie Laboratory in Paris before coming to the United States in 1940; he was associated with the wartime Manhattan Project, taught and did research at several American institutions, and in 1949 joined the faculty of the Carnegie Institute of Technology. Franco Rasetti, Fermi's and Segrè's close friend and collaborator in Rome, spent the war years at Laval University in Quebec and was then at Johns Hopkins where he gained a reputation not only as an experimental physicist but also as a paleontologist: his collection of fossils is second only to the collection of the Smithsonian Institution. Two men, both born and educated in Turin, learned physics with Fermi, Rasetti, and Segrè at the University of Rome: Ugo Fano, of the Bureau of Standards in Washington, D.C., then of the University of Chicago, noted for his studies in theoretical physics, radiobiology, and physical chemistry; and Eugenio (now Eugene G.) Fubini, at the time of this writing a vice-president of International Business Machines.

Fubini attained one of the two highest positions in government reached by émigré intellectuals: in 1963 he was appointed Assistant Secretary of Defense and Deputy Director of Defense Research. (The other high position was John Von Neumann's as a commissioner of the Atomic Energy Commission.) When I first met him, in 1931, Fubini was a plump, short, and extroverted eighteen-year-old. His somewhat older friends used to pay him an Italian penny for every minute he kept silent — and never lost much money in that way. After receiving his doctoral degree in physics, he switched to electronics. In this country he joined the special wartime group at the Harvard Radio Research Laboratory, served with the American armed forces in Europe as a civilian consultant and technical adviser, became vice-president of Airborne Instruments Laboratory, served four years in the Pentagon, two as Assistant Secretary of Defense, and was a member of several government advisory boards.

When I asked him what had pushed him up the steep rungs of his career, he answered, "I was lucky, shorter and noisier than most people, and talked too much." He also believed that he understood complex issues more rapidly than most other people and could explain them to those who did not understand at once; and he stressed the generosity of the United States in giving him an opportunity to make good use of his abilities. What always struck me was his dynamism (even at fifty-three, he used to work thirteen hours a day) and his almost naïve purposiveness, totally devoid of doubts or uncertainties. When we met for the first time in this country he said as if with clenched teeth "I am studying English." Then he went on to explain that he was studying English day and night, with dictionaries and grammar books, reading all that came to hand, listening to commentators on the radio, and watching movies. His friends say that with the same furor he tackles the reorganization of industrial and governmental research projects, devouring reports faster than seems possible and pouring out a vast number of ideas for improvement.

Among the other Italians in the migration wave are biochemist Camillo Artom, who has been at the Bowman Gray School of Medicine since coming to this country in 1939; the composer of music on Jewish, Indian, and folk themes, Mario Castelnuovo-Tedesco; astronomer Luigi Jacchia of the Smithsonian Institution; virologist Salvador Luria, a professor at the Massachusetts Institute of Technology and 1969 Nobel laureate who as a teacher and researcher has contributed greatly to advances in virology; historian of medicine Arturo Castiglioni; economist Franco Modigliani; Mario Salvadori, a professor of civil engineering and architecture at Columbia; Raffaele Lattes of the College of Physicians and Surgeons of Columbia University; physiologist Piero Foà, who had a fruitful career at institutions in Ann Arbor, Chicago, and Detroit; and cardiologist Aldo Luisada of the Chicago Medical School.

After this long section on the Italians, I hope to be forgiven if I confess that they are far from being numerically important in the wave: in my files they represent approximately 3.6 per cent of the total. My only reason for giving them a disproportionate amount of space is that I know them better than I do other nationalities.

THE FRENCH

A remark widely circulating among the European-born in this country is that all Frenchmen went back to France at the end of the war. Although the statement contains more than a grain of truth, it is a generalization to which there are extremely important exceptions. In modern times the French have evinced an unmistakable disinclination to emigration and assimilation by other national groups. It seems safe to state that many of those who came here in the cultural migration had no chance to deliberate their course of action: ill-fated winds forced them to leave home and sent them in the only possible direction, toward the last open haven, America. Unlike other exiles, they did not harbor resentment against their government and had no reason not to return home once there was an end to German domination.

When Charles de Gaulle established a Free French provisional government in North Africa at the end of 1943, the patriotic feelings of French émigrés were stirred, and not a few hastened to join him. Later, when communications with Europe were reopened, many Frenchmen went home and the large crowds that had swamped New York and its vicinity thinned out. Many painters of the Paris school, Fernand Léger, André Masson, and the Russian-born Marc Chagall among them, went back to Paris. Departures decimated the faculty of the École Libre des Hautes Études, founded by Alvin Johnson in response to the plight of French intellectuals. Many others who left would have added prestige to American culture had they stayed: poet André Breton, the father of the surrealist movement; writers André Maurois and Jules Romains; atomic physicists Pierre Auger and Francis Perrin, who after their return to France were to assume leading positions, one with UNESCO, the other as French High Commissioner for Atomic Energy. Our culture would have been the richer had we still among us the French (Belgian-born) anthropologist Claude Lévi-Strauss, "whose stature in anthropology is in the heroic mold," in the words of the British historian J. H. Plumb, and whose book *The Savage Mind* is considered a classic in its field; but his stay here, though not very long, may have been of consequence: as a cultural attaché to the French embassy to the United States between 1946 and his departure from America in 1947, Lévi-Strauss was in the best position to make use of the knowledge of American culture that he had acquired since his arrival in 1941. We might have liked to keep here the great French mathematician Jacques Hadamard, though we paid little attention to his presence: he was seventy-five years old when he arrived after the fall of France, with the assistance of Varian Fry and Fry's committee, and his name had been in books of mathematics so long that his existence seemed to belong to the past. He had done outstanding work by the turn of the century, had solved the problem of distribution of prime numbers, and in 1903 had published a book of lectures on wave propagation that foreshadowed modern ideas on shock waves; by World War I he was famous, but by World War II his fame had declined, and America could offer him only a small position at Columbia. When he died in 1963, almost a centenarian, there were no obituaries in American mathematical journals, and the usually accurate *New York Times* failed to mention that Hadamard had spent the war years in the United States.

Many other Frenchmen returned to France, sometimes leaving little or no record of their stay: some French émigrés came so late and went back so early that they had no opportunity to make a mark and leave a trace of their sojourn; or, if they did leave a trace, it was so faint that it could not be followed. For these reasons the French account for only 3.5 per cent of the group under study, although they may have been a larger portion of the actual wave.

There is no doubt that the French re-emigration from America was of large proportion. And yet many Frenchmen who came to the United States of their own free will before the war or driven by war conditions remained and continued to contribute to American cultural life. Léon Brillouin, a theoretical physicist who in Paris had taught at the university and the Collège de France, in this country was a professor at the University of Wisconsin, Brown, and Harvard, and during the war was a member of the mathematics panel of the National Defense Research Committee. Physician André Cournand won a share of the 1956 Nobel Prize in medicine for research at the Medical College of Physicians and Surgeons of Columbia University. Marcel Duchamp, the Dadaist, settled in New York and lived a French life, while quietly steering the artistic taste of the city. Painter Yves Tanguy made his home in Connecticut, and did much to popularize surrealism in America. As if unable to decide between two strong loves, composer Darius Milhaud divided his postwar time between the United States and France, and has resided in France and at Mills College in California. Conductor Pierre Monteux joined the San Francisco Symphony Orchestra in 1936, was naturalized, and lived in the United States though in 1960, at the age of eighty-five, he became the conductor of the London Symphony. Henri Peyre, a highly regarded expert in French literature, is a long-standing friend of America: he visited here in the twenties and early thirties, then he returned, as he wrote, "to his own country where he had intended to make his career." Instead, in 1938, he joined the faculty of Yale. Philosophers Jacques Maritain and Yves Simon had long, fruitful careers in the United States. So did educator Philippe LeCorbeiller, who in this country taught mainly at Harvard; he is a gentle-mannered man of many interests whose judgment is respected and whose advice is sought in education projects. Among other Frenchmen who chose the United States for their home is statesman Camille Chautemps: in the fantastically kaleidoscopic French political scene between the two wars Chautemps was twenty times a minister, four times a prime minister, and held the post of vice-president of the council at the time of the fall of France. He went on holding this post for a short while after it no longer had official existence, because by then the government of Marshal Pétain had been established (and for this action he was called to account after the war). He came to the United States at the end of 1940, on an official mission from Pétain, then broke with the Vichy government and settled as a refugee in Washington, continuing to use his high contacts — President Franklin D. Roosevelt was the highest — and his friendship with Undersecretary Sumner Welles to serve the cause of the French resistance and heighten understanding between the French and American people.

RUSSIANS

The Russian intellectuals in my file are only approximately 5 per cent of all intellectuals, though I count as Russians those who were born in the once independent Baltic states, Estonia, Latvia, and Lithuania. (A further breakdown of figures did not seem advisable, considering the smallness of the numbers involved.) Nevertheless, they are the third largest national group.

A characteristic that distinguishes the Russians from other national groups is how early it was that emigration was barred to them. As Stalin's regime turned into a personal dictatorship and he tightened the screws, escape from Russia became more and more difficult and by the early thirties it was virtually impossible. So those among the Russian intellectuals who came directly or almost directly to America arrived before the thirties. Chemist George Kistiakowsky, conductor Serge Koussevitzsky, the aviation expert Igor Sikorsky, mathematician Oscar Zariski, and the inventor of the electron microscope, Vladimir Zworykin, were among the early arrivals. By the same token, most Russians who came here with the migration of the thirties and early forties had spent many years in European countries. A conspicuous exception is George Gamow, who managed to escape from Russia in 1933 by sleeping car, with a regular passport and his wife, and arrived in the United States the following year after a brief stay in England. But then he was a man of inventive perseverance and had not allowed himself to be deterred by several earlier frustrated attempts to escape.

If the migration of Russian intellectuals ceased much sooner than that of other Europeans, it had also begun much earlier, chiefly as a consequence of social unrest in Russia in the first two decades of this century. Some of the future emigrants to America left czarist Russia as children or young adults at the time of the revolution in 1905. Because they lived long in European countries, some of them are now identified with other nationalities. Marc Chagall, who settled in Paris in 1910, is generally considered a French painter. Economist Abba Lerner received his education in England, and the question was raised whether he is "too British" to be listed in the migration from continental Europe. Wolfgang Köhler, the renowned leader of Gestalt psychology born in Estonia, was "so German" and had the fate of Germany so much at heart that in 1933 he openly warned the Nazis of the danger of their course — that the purges would throw overboard much that was truly German. And Waclaw Jedrzejewicz, who in this country taught Russian at Wellesley, although born in the Ukraine was a Pole by stock and education: he was a vice-minister of finance and minister of education in the Polish government and as a Polish army officer he fought Russians and Germans.

126

In this early emigration there was a pattern, however faint: the intelligentsia favored life in Germany; artists and the establishment — aristocracy, army, and administrative personnel — preferred to settle in Paris; bright students and truly cosmopolitan Russians scattered over a wider range of European countries. Many of those who made their homes in Germany were forced to leave in the early thirties. Astronomer Sergei Gaposchkin, political scientist Waldemar Gurian, and Wolfgang Köhler were among the Russians who came directly from Germany to the United States. Others stopped a few years in other countries on their way: in England, economist Jacob Marschak, biophysicist Eugene Rabinowitch, and Slavicist Sergius Yakobson, later of our Library of Congress; in Switzerland, economist Wladimir Woytinsky; in France, biologist David Nachmansohn and writer Alexander Schiffrin, who in America became known by his pen name Max Werner.

Many Russians settled in France at an early date. They included, among others, artists Eugene Berman, Marc Chagall, and Ossip Zadkine; historian of science Alexandre Koyré and professor of law Boris Mirkine-Guetzévitch, both of whom became distinguished members of the École Libre des Hautes Études in New York; publisher Jacques Schiffrin; and the best known of all Russians to emigrate to America, composer Igor Stravinsky. Russian students were able to enrol at universities in many countries beside Germany and France. Thus philosopher Max Black, architect Serge Chermayeff, economist Abba Lerner, historian Andrew Lossky, author Vladimir Nabokov, and others went to schools in England; economist Alexander Gerschenkron and psychoanalyst Paul Kramer are among those who studied in Vienna. The best known of the young Russians who received degrees in Prague are mathematician Lipman Bers, linguist and literary historian Roman Jakobson, and biophysicist Alexander Kolin.

The devious route by which Roman Jakobson, Sergius Yakobson's brother, came from Russia to America may serve as an example of the Russians' lively, often involuntary travels and as a proof of their adaptability to changing environments and their facility in learning languages. Jackobson was twenty-three years old in 1920 when he left Moscow. There he had studied and initiated a teaching career that included his being a research associate at the university and a professor of orthoëpy (phonology) at the Moscow Dramatic School. He lived the next thirteen years in Prague, where he became co-editor of the *Slavische Rundschau*, wrote several scholarly books and papers, and received a doctoral degree (in 1930). From 1933 to 1939 he was at Masaryk University in Brno, teaching subjects that included Russian philology and old Czech literature. Then Hitler occupied Czechoslovakia. With great difficulty Jakobson fled the country, was a visiting lecturer first at the University of Copenhagen, then at the University of Oslo, and became a Norwegian citizen. The Nazis invaded Norway. Jakobson had his second dramatic flight, this time through Norway, reached Uppsala, lectured at the university, and through the Swedish Ministry of Foreign Affairs arranged to sail to America with his Czechoslovakian wife. On the trip there were moments of excitement: pleasant excitement when the Jakobsons met the famous German philosopher Ernst Cassirer and Cassirer's wife and the two men gave themselves to scholarly conversation; awesome excitement when the Germans stopped the ship for an inspection of passports and the Jakobsons feared for their lives. They were Norwegian citizens, and had the Germans recognized them as such they would have been removed from the boat. Instead, the Germans took at face value the Swedish passports for foreigners with which the Jaksobsons had been provided and let them continue their voyage. In the relief that followed, the very real dangers of mine fields and submarines were discounted. But after reaching New York the captain of the ship thought the voyage to have been so hazardous that on his advice the Swedes suspended wartime transportation of civilians across the Atlantic.

These were Jakobson's last wanderings and last trepidations. In America he could pursue at will his scholarly work; at the time of his adventurous sea-crossing, Jakobson had been engaged in the study of a language spoken by only 4,500 persons, and showed an interest in it which seemed grotesque under the circumstances, as Mrs. Cassirer remarked much later. He has published many other books and papers and has had an outstanding career in teaching. He taught first in New York, at the École Libre des Hautes Études, at the Institut d'Histoire et de Philologie Orientales et Slaves, and at Columbia University; in 1949 he became a professor of Slavic languages and literatures and of general linguistics at Harvard and more recently he also joined the faculty of MIT. He is a member of an amazingly large number of academies and learned societies in America and in many European countries.

In this description of Russian intellectuals on the go I have not been able to mention all those who were to make distinguished contributions to Ameri-

128

can culture. Many others will be encountered in the surveys of special fields, but here I shall point out a few of my more conspicuous omissions. They include several musicians, among them pianist Vladimir Horowitz; conductor and teacher of conducting Nicolai Malko; violinist Nathan Milstein; cellist Gregor Piatigorsky, who has trained many American pupils; and cellist Alexander Schuster. Although I have mentioned several economists, the list should be much longer, for the economists are the largest Russian group, representing 15 per cent of the Russian wave, a fact that may arouse speculation. Paul Baran, Alexander Erlich, Leonid Hurwicz, Wassily Leontief, Ragar Nurkse, and others belong in this group.

OTHER NATIONALITIES

The remaining national groups will not be treated separately for one of two reasons: either they fail to present strongly differentiating traits, or they are too small for meaningful generalizations. Two groups are relatively large: the Poles represent about 5 per cent of the whole cultural migration and are nearly as numerous as the Hungarians. The Czech migration is somewhat larger than the French and Italian and accounts for a little more than 4 per cent of the total. None of the other group reaches 2 per cent, and the percentages of some are considerably smaller.

The Czechoslovakian wave followed the pattern of most other waves and presented a crest in 1938 and 1939; the Polish wave, like the Russian and the French, reached its peak somewhat later, in 1940 and 1941 (the last two years considered in this study), suggesting that the Poles refused to flee until Hitler invaded Poland. The national characteristics of the Polish and Czech émigrés are less easy to define than most. Poland underwent several drastic partitions and lost its autonomy in modern times, and it is often difficult to determine whether an émigré is primarily a Pole, German, Russian, or Austrian (though, I am sure, "true Poles" will not subscribe to this remark). The difficulty is the stronger because some Polish intellectuals were educated and spent many years outside Poland. Under these circumstances, I often find myself embroiled in such definitions as "the Polish-born French mathematician Szolem Mandelbrojt" and "the Polish-born German physicist and Nobel laureate Maria Mayer."

The difficulties are even greater in the case of the Czechs. After centuries of obliteration from the maps, Czechoslovakia emerged as a nation from the ruins of the Austro-Hungarian edifice at the end of World War I. By that time many future Czech émigrés had already been born as the subjects of the Habsburg monarchy and had been shaped by the forces of the old order. The new state included strong German, Austrian, Magyar, Ukranian, and Polish minorities, and many intellectuals were never reconciled to their new national status. Their sentiment is typically expressed by something that my friend Hilde Schein said of her late husband, physicist Marcel Schein: "He was a Hungarian but traveled with a Czech passport because he was born in a part of Hungary that was given to Czechoslovakia after World War I." In order to adhere to the rules I have set myself for this study, when counting how many Czechoslovakian intellectuals came to this country I must include Marcel Schein in the lot. This is clearly an absurdity, but an absurdity that was created jointly by the Versailles treaty, United States immigration practices, and common usage in American biographical directories. In any more personal considerations I must call Schein a Hungarian. Likewise, there is no point in insisting that Joseph Schumpeter was a Czech economist or that Kurt Adler is a Czech conductor, since they are known as Austrians to the world.

The most salient feature of the Poles in the migration is that about 15 per cent are mathematicians. A measure of the stature of the Polish mathematicians in this country may be obtained by examining the composition of the class of mathematics of the National Academy of Sciences: in 1966, seven of the fifty-two members of this class were Polish-born; Salomon Bochner, Richard Courant, Samuel Eilenberg, Mark Kac, Alfred Tarski, Stan Ulam, and Antoni Zygmund. But outstanding Poles are met in many fields. In music, I need to mention only harpsichordist Wanda Landowska, pianist Artur Rubinstein, and musicologist Hugo Leichtentritt; in art, sculptor Jacques Lipchitz, painters Sigmund Menkes and Harry Mintz, and cartoonist Arthur Szyk, upon whose head Hitler put a price; in history, Ernst Kantorowicz, a medievalist and historian of ideas, who was by education a German, and Bernard Weinryb of Dropsie College, an expert in the social history of the Jews in Europe: in chemistry, Kasimir Fajans. In other fields, I may point out author Józef Wittlin; neurologist Kurt Goldstein; archeologist Bronislaw Malinowski, who spent the last four years of his life in America; and Louis Sohn, a professor of law and lecturer on world organization at Harvard. Sohn has been a consultant and legal adviser to agencies of the United Nations and a member of a committee of scientists and political scientists advising President Kennedy's co-ordinator of United States disarmament activities, John McCloy. Sohn is the author of several books, *Cases on World Law* among them, and co-author of *World Peace Through World Law*.

Like the Polish-born, so did the Czechoslovakian-born scatter over many sectors of the American cultural scene. In music they claim composer Bohuslaw Martinu, pianist Rudolf Serkin, conductors George Schick and George Szell, and musicologist Paul Nettl; in art, if the Czechs have given America outstanding painters or sculptors, I must have missed them: in my file I found only the name of Hugo Steiner-Prag, illustrator, lithographer, etcher, and book-designer. The writers are well represented among the Czechs: Franz Werfel was born in Czechoslovakia, though he lived for the most part in Austria and is claimed by the Austrians; but Hans Natonek is truly a Czech and wrote in his native language until he learned English in this country. Franz Weiskopf was the author of books in several languages, including the novel *Dawn Breaks* based on the German invasion of Slovakia; in this country Weiskopf kept busy writing and was on the staff of and a frequent contributor to *Books Abroad*; he returned to Czechoslovakia in 1949 to enter the diplomatic service of that country, first as ambassador to Sweden, then as a minister plenipotentiary at the Czech embassy in Washington, and finally as ambassador to China; after settling in Berlin he wrote *Unter fremden Himmeln*, a compendium of exile literature in the German language and a useful contribution to the scanty literature about the cultural migration. Among other Czech writers is novelist Egon Hostovsky, who settled in New York and became an American citizen but does not write in English: he is regarded as the most important contemporary Czech writer.

Perhaps as a consequence of the country's copious literary achievements, Czechoslovakia could give America one of the highest ranking contemporary scholars of the history and theory of literary criticism: René Wellek. Born in Vienna of Czech parentage and schooled in Prague, Wellek held a chair at the University of London at the time of the Munich crisis and the dismemberment of Czechoslovakia. He then decided to come to the United States, where he taught at Iowa and, after 1946, at Yale. His impressive knowledge of European, English, and American literature is demonstrated in his works, all highly distinguished and one monumental: *A History of Modern Literary Criticism* in five volumes. He is also conversant with literatures of earlier periods than the modern — one small example out of many possible is his urbane and learned essay "Bohemia in English Literature."

The economists are also very well represented in the Czech wave, of which they form more than 13 per cent; among them are such men as Joseph Schumpeter, Karl Přibram, and Joseph Schneider. Czechoslovakian-born who stand out in other fields include an expert in international relations, Hans Kelsen; historians Hans Kohn and Otakar Odložilíc; psychoanalysts Bernard Kamm and Emanuel Windholz; a specialist in German literature, Erich Kahler; professor of law and sociology at the University of Chicago Hans Zeisel; mathematicians Kurt Gödel, František Wolf, and Charles Loewner; and astronomer Zdeněk Kopal.

The list of Czechoslovakian-born notables could be much longer, but I shall close with physicist George Placzek. I met him first in Rome, where he came several times in the very early thirties, and again in America, at various places under varying circumstances. He was a remarkable man, easygoing and careless in appearance, sometimes even mocking and untidy, but warmhearted and with the intellectual refinement of the truly cosmopolitan European. He was respected by his colleagues for his profound grasp of theoretical physics and was able to talk on any subject; in his travels over the world he had made many friends and learned almost as many languages. I was always amazed at the way in which he could abruptly shift from one language to the other, without mixing them and with great fluency. He studied in Prague and Vienna, spent time in Holland, Germany, Italy, Denmark (where Niels Bohr attracted the best theoretical physicists of all countries), France, and Russia, then drifted to this country. He joined the faculty of Cornell University, then successively the atomic projects in England, Canada, and at Los Alamos. On this New Mexican mesa where a large number of his friends from many lands had gathered in the wartime atomic effort, Placzek could put to use both his scientific and his linguistic skills. Later he became a member of the Institute for Advanced Study, but illness increasingly plagued him until his premature death. Unlike most of his colleagues, he did not have a long teaching career in America, and his humanizing European influence was felt more by men and women of his own age than of the younger generation.

Belgium, Denmark, Greece, Holland, Norway, Rumania, Spain, Sweden, Switzerland, and Yugoslavia each contributed less than 2 per cent of the total migration and taken together they account for slightly more than 7 per cent. However, they include seven Nobel Prize winners, or almost one-third of the twenty-four that added distinction to the migration. The Danish physicist Niels Bohr (who was in this country only temporarily, during the war); writers Maurice Maeterlinck from Belgium and Sigrid Undset from Norway; and the Dutch-born chemist Peter Debye had already received the prize when they came to this country. Hendrik Dam from Denmark was awarded the prize in 1943, while he lived here, for the discovery of vitamin K, a discovery made in Denmark several years earlier. The remaining two earned recognition for work done in America; the Swiss-born Felix Bloch for his extremely accurate measurements of the magnetic characteristics of atomic nuclei and for the method by which they were carried out; and the Spanish-born Severo Ochoa for studies of the constitution of DNA and RNA, the genetic material responsible for transmitting instructions in the reproduction of cells (Bloch, Dam, and Ochoa shared the prize with others).

The largest of the small groups in the migration is the Dutch: the flow of intellectuals from Holland to America began in the twenties, when several Dutch scientists, especially astronomers and physicists, accepted positions at American universities. If my file tells the complete story of Dutch migration, the flow continued at a rather even pace in the thirties, slightly crested in 1940 and 1941, and brought here a more varied representation of Dutch culture than it did in the twenties. Orientalist Henri Frankfort, psychoanalyst Elizabeth Geleerd, professor of bio-organic chemistry Arie Haagen-Smit, economist Tjalling Koopmans, astronomer Gerard Kuiper, and painter-designer Piet Mondrian are a few of the distinguished Hollanders in the migration. I shall have an occasion to mention them again when reviewing the fields in which they made contributions, but not the work of Haagen-Smit who, to my knowledge, is the only émigré who has been long and persistently active in a relatively new field, the chemistry of air pollution. Here then is my opportunity to call attention to his work.

133

Haagen-Smit has been on the faculty of the California Institute of Technology since 1937 and he was therefore a resident of the Los Angeles area when the first serious episodes of smog occurred in 1943. The smog was attributed to the wartime increase in population and industry in the Los Angeles region, but the conditions that caused it were not well understood until, in 1951, Haagen-Smit proved that smog is formed by the reaction of unburned hydrocarbons and nitron oxygen in strong sunlight. In these and successive studies he identified and followed step by step many chains of photochemical reactions that take place in the atmosphere and some of which transform non-toxic substances into others that cause the pernicious effects of smog. His findings led to the incrimination of automobile exhaust as a major factor in the formation of the Los Angeles type of smog. In this and other ways — including the study of plant damage caused by smog — Haagen-Smit has substantially helped advance understanding of the extremely complex problem of air pollution, its causes and effects.

The Swiss-born include, to mention only a few, psychoanalyst Raymond de Saussure, biologist Gerhard Fankhauser, artist Fritz Glarner, surrealist painter Kurt Seligmann, physicist Hans Staub, and professor of international law Arnold Wolfers. Among the Belgian-born are physicist Maurice Biot, composer Desiré Defauw, economist Raymond Goldsmith, painter Alfred Jonniaux, and the famous anthropologist Claude Lévi-Strauss, already mentioned among the French. Norway and Denmark seem to have favored the sciences and have sent here, among others, the Norwegian geologist Thomas Barth and physicist William Zachariasen and the Danish botanist Jens Clausen and astronomer K. Aa. Strand — and, in a non-scientific field, Assyriologist Thorkild Jacobsen. Among the distinguished Spanish-born I may mention painters Salvador Dali and José de Creeft, conductor-pianist José Iturbi, physiologist Rafael Lorente de Nó, and architect José Sert. Mathematician William Feller, musicologist Dragan Plamenac, and sociologist Dinko Tomasic are a few among the Yugoslavian-born. A most distinguished representative of Sweden was the Shakespearean scholar Helge Kokeritz, an authority on English morphology who in his many years at Yale wrote *Shakespeare's Pronunciation, A Guide to Chaucer's Pronunciation*, and similar learned books. If Sweden seems scholarly inclined, Rumania appears artistically bent, and the Rumanian wave brought here such artists as painter André Racz, sculptor Bernard Reder, and the satirical artist Saul Steinberg, who has delighted the readers of the *New Yorker* since 1941. The Rumanian wave also brought statisticians Jerzy Neyman and Abraham Wald and briefly political scientist David Mitrany. The Greek migration is the smallest of all and entirely musical: the two Greek-born in my file are conductors Maurice Abravanel and Dimitri Mitropoulos.

Many of the émigré intellectuals and artists mentioned in this section will be met again in these pages.

PART II
ACHIEVEMENT

VI

-»»

European Psychoanalysts on the American Scene

The second part of this book is devoted to the achievement of the intellectual wave in America, and as the achievement is substantial this part is long. I prefer to use the world "achievement" rather than "impact" because the judgment implied in "impact" presupposes, in the present case, a detailed appraisal of conditions and trends in the American cultural scene before and after the arrival of the Europeans as well as a considered guess about the evolution that might have taken place in the absence of the migration. It would have been much too complicated to attempt to carry out consistently such an analysis of all cultural areas in which European émigrés have worked. There are, however, two fields where changes instrumented by the European-born are more clearly discernible and where I feel justified in saying that the Europeans did have an impact: psychoanalysis * and atomic science.

I have therefore chosen these fields as my two major examples of achievement. Further examples are offered in briefer surveys, but these are not intended to cover all areas in which Europeans have made contributions: I have selected those in which the concentration of émigrés appeared the greater and the consequences of their presence in America more widely distributed. Hence I have regretfully by-passed distinguished contributions that stand in relative isolation. In no case by mentioning or failing to mention the work of a European have I meant to pass judgment.

PSYCHOANALYSIS TODAY

Psychoanalysis, "that Freud stuff," as the American physician Frederick Peterson called it in 1907, was born in Vienna in the late nineties but by the

* In this chapter the word "psychoanalysis" and its derivatives are used loosely to include orthodox Freudian theories and analysts as well as ideas and men in revisionist movements.

middle of this century had taken strongest root and grown most vigorously not in Austria or in other European countries but in the United States. It is in America and not in Europe that Freud's ideas, as they developed along orthodox as well as revisionist lines and through popular interpretation, have so subtly and thoroughly permeated our culture that it is now difficult to identify areas where they have had no influence or to recognize elements in our thinking that have not been shaped by them. It is in America more than in any other country that one can speak with some justification of a Freudian revolution.

Perhaps I am especially aware of the impact of psychoanalysis on American culture because I came to this country from Italy, where before the last war psychoanalysis had made little headway and had practically no effect on the people and their mores. (An Italian Psychoanalytic Association was in existence, but its members could be counted on the fingers of one hand.) When I reflected in recent years over the differences between the Italian culture and the American that I noticed as an immigrant, I came to recognize that an appreciable part of these differences were not intrinsic in the two traditions but were due to the assimilation of psychoanalytic thought in America. The symptoms of this assimilation, visible as they were at the end of the thirties, have become much more conspicuous in the years that have intervened.

I see them in the home, where, one of the biggest changes has been fostered by the psychoanalytic views on childhood and child care, from the prenatal stage to adulthood. We have been led to recognize that childhood is a crucial and most vulnerable phase of human development, and as a consequence we allow ourselves to be moved by a new tenderness and anxiety for our children. We have replaced guidance by instinctive love alone with guidance by loving awareness and insight into the psychological needs of the young. Having acquired a better understanding of childhood needs and of the rebellious behavior of adolescents, we allow a greater tolerance to enter the family and enrich the source of feelings and emotions shared by parents.

The gamut of signs that I see outside the home spreads from the immense growth and transformation of the field of public relations — sales promotion is based on study of buyers' motivations, and commercial persuasiveness has become an art — to the change in our views about crime and criminals: the recognition that man may act under impulses or drives of the unconscious, over which he has no control, has led to a shift of emphasis from punishment to rehabilitation. The gamut of changes encompasses the new tendency to introspection and rationalization that pervades the cultured middle classes and the increasingly widespread feeling that we all have a right to self-fulfilment and happiness.

Many are the ways in which millions of Americans have been exposed to psychoanalytic influence: counseling services, rapidly proliferating since the war, have provided a net of capillary channels penetrating deeply into American life; television programs have popularized psychoanalytic interpretations of modern issues; motion pictures, the theater, and literature have done the same; and mass education has helped immensely in the absorption of new ideas. But before psychoanalysis could reach this stage of thorough dissemination, it had to affect the very roots of our culture.

In 1952, a prominent American analyst Henry W. Brosin remarked: "Psychoanalysis, through its influence upon psychiatry, psychology, pediatrics, education, the social sciences, and literature has been one of the most powerful humanizing forces of the twentieth century. It has compelled a more sensitive handling of the individual and has consequently forced a more respectful attitude toward the dignity of the individual man."

Another distinguished American psychoanalyst, Lawrence S. Kubie, stated in 1961: "With psychoanalysis, for the first time in human history a scientific technique of the study of man himself evolved. . . . Today we are seeing psychoanalytically informed studies of human behavior entering into the research programs and the curricula of our greatest scientific institutions . . . and many medical schools. The same influence is at work in law schools, theological seminaries, graduate departments of many disciplines in our major universities, and down the academic line to colleges, schools and kindergartens. It reaches out to social agencies, courts, and penal institutions. Its influence is felt in art, literature, and music, and in the behavioral and social sciences, such as anthropology, economics, law, government, and history."

HISTORICAL PERSPECTIVES

In the impact that psychoanalysis has made on American culture what has been the part of European analysts? Ideas may travel in different ways, and it is not always necessary to transport the men in order to transfer their doctrines. Was a displacement of men necessary or useful in this case? Although it will not be easy to give exhaustive answers to these questions, the Europeans' role may be placed in some perspective by two sets of considerations, one of which tends to limit its importance, the other to stress it. First, America was an extremely fertile soil in which psychoanalysis had already begun to develop long before the onset of the immigration wave in 1930. Second, at the outbreak of World War II, European psychoanalysis found itself in the unenviable position of being the only discipline, to my knowledge, that Hitler virtually exterminated in continental Europe. The political events of the thirties drove most analysts from their homes, and eventually a large proportion of them settled in the United States — about two-thirds, according to some estimates.

An elaboration of the second point will appear later in this chapter. The first point requires some comments. Many factors rendered America a fertile ground for psychoanalysis. At the turn of the century the humanitarian trends of the preceding decades were transformed into scientific movements. Out of organized charity social work emerged; the concern over the neglect of the mentally ill gave impetus to the mental hygiene movement; and from the enormous concern with children sprang the child guidance movement. Because they were still in the process of forming and crystallizing, of shifting from the missionary to the scientific spirit, these movements were especially open to new ideas. Psychoanalysis, appearing on the scene at the right moment, strongly interacted with them, receiving their support and assistance and contributing to their scientific development. In this respect, the comparison of some dates may be of interest.

In the early history of American psychoanalysis, the year 1909 was a milestone. Freud came to the United States, accompanied by Carl Gustav Jung and Sándor Ferenczi, at the invitation of the American pioneer child psychologist G. Stanley Hall, and delivered five lectures at Worcester, Massachusetts. The invitation to Freud was an expression of existing interest in psychoanalysis and called further attention to it. Significant events in other fields took place at about the same time. The first school of social work, the New York School of Philanthropy, opened in 1904, and in the years that followed schools of this type multiplied rapidly. The National Committee for Mental Hygiene (now the National Association for Mental Health) was founded in 1909. The first child guidance clinic was established in 1909 in Chicago as the Juvenile Psychopathic Institute, later changed to Institute for Juvenile Research.

Another factor favoring the acceptance of psychoanalysis in America was the attitude of American psychiatry, less rigidly oriented toward an organic interpretation of mental disorders, more willing to collaborate with psychology, more open to new ideas than the European. It is true that at first most American psychiatrists resisted Freudian views, but while in Europe resistance was intransigent, in the United States it was often attenuated by interest, discussion, and evaluation, which are preliminaries to acceptance. As one important result, psychoanalysis developed within the medical profession in America, not removed from it, as in Europe. The flexibility of the American educational structure, free of much of the rigid and stultifying hierarchical organization which characterized prewar European systems, also facilitated the establishment of psychoanalysis at the academic level.

In spite of these propitious conditions, the development of psychoanalysis in our country was at first slow and contested. The American Psychoanalytic Association and the New York Psychoanalytic Society were both founded as early as 1911, yet the interest in psychoanalysis was then sporadic and not always positive, and it waned during World War I. But the decade of the twenties saw a number of developments that were to favor its growth. After the reopening of communications with Europe, disrupted by the war, a number of Americans went to study psychoanalysis in Vienna and Berlin. An essential part of psychoanalytic training was the didactic or training analysis. Most of the Americans who went to Vienna were analyzed by Freud himself and a few by his close disciples; those who went to Berlin had their analyses with training analysts at the Berlin Psychoanalytic Institute (founded in 1920). The number of Americans involved, while sizable in proportion to the psychoanalytic movement of the time, was small in absolute figures: about ten went to Freud, and a few to other analysts in Vienna; a somewhat larger group went to Berlin. Analysis fostered a close relationship between American trainees and European teachers, and the friendship so established was soon to prove a valuable asset for the teachers who came to the United States.

In the twenties, a few European analysts came to the United States, some on their own, some invited by the New York Psychoanalytic Society or the

New School for Social Research. Otto Rank came to America on frequent trips starting in 1924 and later, in 1935, settled in New York, where he died in 1939. Before 1924 he was a member of Freud's inner circle but then broke away from the psychoanalytic movement. The Hungarian Sandor Lorand arrived in 1925, shortly afterward joined the staff of Mount Sinai Mental Hygiene Clinic, and remained in New York, contributing to the growth of American psychoanalysis. In 1948 he became the first director of the Division of Psychoanalytic Education of the State University of New York College of Medicine at New York City.

In the fall of 1926 another Hungarian, Sándor Ferenczi, arrived at the invitation of the New School for Social Research. He was an early friend of Freud's, the initiator of the psychoanalytic movement in Hungary, and one of the most distinguished analysts of all time. His eight-month stay in New York was fruitful; through lectures and personal contacts he aroused much interest in psychoanalysis in the medical world and among the general public. His series of weekly ninety-minute lectures at the New School was the first comprehensive discussion of psychoanalysis in the United States before a lay and professional audience.

In 1928, the eminent analyst and neuropathologist Paul Schilder settled in this country and became a pioneer in the field of psychoanalytically oriented group therapy. In the same year, Fritz Wittels, one of Freud's earliest disciples and well known for his application of psychoanalysis to literature, came to give a course of lectures at the New School and stayed on in America.

The popular appeal of psychoanalysis in the United States began to develop in the twenties, while the early movement of analysts was in progress. In the first years after World War I, the liberal thinkers were in search of new moral codes to replace the old that the war had shattered. Freudian teaching, with its emphasis on the needs of the individual and the role of sexual drives, appealed to those who considered themselves progressive and to introspective young adults, especially college students, concerned with their past and future, their social and sexual adjustment. Soon interest spread from these groups to others in the cultured classes. A measure of this popularity was the fleet of limousines that Ferenczi's lectures drew to the doors of the New

School, described by the school's director, Alvin Johnson, in *Pioneer's Progress*.

It is clear that psychoanalysis was taking root in America before the beginning of the immigration wave in 1930 and had already made a mark on several areas including social work and child guidance. Probably it would have continued to grow even in the absence of the wave. Yet its progress would have been slower and might have taken a different direction. By the end of the twenties American psychoanalysis was still in its formative phase and had not yet acquired recognition as a discipline. It was a young movement, restricted mostly to the eastern part of the United States and accepted only to a limited extent by American physicians and psychiatrists. As treatment, it was often considered a pastime of the wealthy. Then the great wave of immigration brought to our shores a good portion of Europe's psychoanalytic teachers, leaders, therapists, and students.

PSYCHOANALYTIC ROADS TO AMERICA

The analysts' reasons for coming to this country were not very different from those of other intellectuals. Early comers arrived on their own, moved by their wanderlust or attracted by the opportunities that America offered, although often the European situation had been instrumental. The first two eminent analysts of the wave, Franz Alexander and Sandor Rado, were Hungarians, a fact that may be relevant. In Hungary, as in a few other countries, political unrest at the end of World War I had borne its sour fruit very early. Franz Alexander left Hungary in 1919, during Béla Kun's short-lived Communist regime, Rado in 1923, during Horthy's Fascist dictatorship.

Once Hitler rose to power in Germany, outside help in preparing to escape and resettle became indispensable. Most analysts were Jewish and the victims of Nazi racial laws. The proportion of Jews in psychoanalysis was considerably greater than in other intellectual professions, though in all intellectual fields the proportion was much greater than might have been expected considering the total number of Jews in Europe. Freud himself accepted as a fact the assumption that Jews are especially suited for psychiatry, and the American Karl Menninger attempted an explanation of this belief based on the special social and traditional environment in which most Jewish children grow and the consequent tensions under which they struggle.

145

Whatever the reasons, the preponderance of Jews among European analysts is unquestionable. Another remarkable fact is that most Jewish analysts managed to escape Hitler and many fewer ended in concentration camps than did members of other professions. One possible explanation is that Freudian psychology may have given the analysts a better sense of reality and enabled them to see the writing on the wall in clearer letters than others did.

European psychoanalysis received its first blows before the advent of Hitler: in Russia the practice of psychoanalysis was prohibited as contrary to state political ideology, and the Russian Psychoanalytic Society faded away about 1927. In Germany a few analysts with Communist affiliations or leanings left the country when Hitler began persecution after the burning of the Reichstag. The first Nazi orders affecting psychoanalysis through the Jewish and foreign members of the German Psychoanalytical Society were enacted in April, 1933. In May of that year, Freud's books and other psychoanalytic literature were burned in the great bonfire in Berlin. The society functioned for a time, but German psychoanalysis was already doomed. Austria seemed to offer safety and some analysts moved there, but with the *Anschluss* of March 11, 1938, even the cradle of psychoanalysis, Vienna, fell into Nazi hands. A few months later Freud, then eighty-three years old, and the group of faithful who had remained with him escaped to London with the assistance of his ex-pupil and close friend, the French analyst Princess Marie Bonaparte.

Early help to psychoanalysts came from the free countries in Europe, as it did to intellectuals in general. The English analyst, Ernest Jones, best known to the American public for his monumental biography of Freud, had always kept an eye on international psychoanalysis. Once persecution began, he helped a large number of psychoanalysts find positions outside Germany. And so did others in England, France, and Switzerland. They tried to distribute the refugees widely, so that they would bring their contributions to many lands. Initially most analysts preferred to move to European countries rather than to America, despite mounting danger on the continent. Freud himself was against emigration and every departure saddened him, especially if the United States was the destination. He had a low opinion of America, and feared that if she were to accept his teachings, it would be at the cost of compromise and dilution. As late as 1935 he disapproved of the decision of his close associates Helene and Felix Deutsch who had accepted an invitation from the Boston Institute so that their young son Martin, now a well-known atomic physicist, would receive a democratic education. Helene, a founder of the Vienna Psychoanalytic Institute in 1924, and its director, now felt obliged to abandon it. (That choice, between duty to one's family and duty to one's students or institution, between leaving and staying, was a hard one to make, and the leaving was often accompanied by the disapproval of those who remained behind.) Freud, of course, did not object to emigration from Nazi Germany, and later from other countries occupied by the Nazis.

An idea of the diaspora of analysts can be had from news published in those years in the *International Journal of Psychoanalysis*. As early as August, 1934, Ernest Jones, addressing the Thirteenth International Psychoanalytical Congress, stated: "In the last few years the German Society has lost by emigration nearly a half of its former membership." At that time Wilhelm Reich, well known for his *Character Analysis*, was in Malmö, Sweden; Sandor Rado was already in New York; Otto Fenichel, who was eventually to settle in California, was in Oslo; Theodor Reik, the prolific writer now well known in America, was in the Hague; and Ernst Simmel, one of the founders of the Psychoanalytic Institute of Berlin, had left Germany (he was to arrive in California the same year). Siegfried Bernfeld was in Vienna (but shortly would go to southern France and then to the United States). All these came sooner or later to the United States. Of those who were not to immigrate to this country, some had scattered to Palestine and South Africa. Membership rosters for 1936 published in the journal indicated that Beata Rank had gone from Vienna to Paris, Annie Reich to Prague, Edith Weigert to Turkey; all three later came to the United States. By 1939, the journal no longer listed the German Psychoanalytical Society — its vestiges were under Nazi supervision and unrecognized by the international association. It did list the members of the Vienna Society, though the society itself had dissolved; their addresses indicated that they had left Austria: twenty were in the United States; two each in France, England, and Yugoslavia; and one each in Poland, Belgium, Rumania, and China. Of the sixty-nine members of the Vienna Society in 1937 (the last year in which the membership list was published before the dissolution of the society) only three were in Vienna in 1945.

The most devout in the Vienna group stayed on with Freud until after the *Anschluss*. They then went with him to London, and only after his death in 1939 did the last of those who were to come to America take the final step across the ocean. A considerable number of European analysts who moved to England throughout the years of Nazi persecution remained there and created the strong British movement in analysis which is still flourishing. A few eventually went to South America and other parts of the world including Ceylon, but by far the largest contingent gathered in the United States.

Assistance to refugee analysts was organized very early in the United States. Around 1932 or 1933, members of the New York Psychoanalytic Society established an informal committee to collect money upon the request of their president, Abraham Brill, who foresaw future problems. Bertram Lewin, who chaired this committee, recently recalled that for a while there was little use for the money collected. "Indeed," he wrote in a letter to me, "the first use of it was to stake a Dutchman who wished to go to South Africa." In 1935, a letter from Ernest Jones in London brought the plights of certain analysts to the attention of the society, and work began in earnest. In March, 1938, immediately after the German annexation of Austria, the American Psychoanalytic Association took over and organized the Emergency Committee on Relief and Immigration. Three persons were its driving force: the two co-chairmen, Lawrence S. Kubie and Bettina Warburg, and Bertram Lewin who "continued to deposit money and was, so to say, its treasurer." The three of them did an impressive job. They made all decisions, handled correspondence, interviews, and funds, all very informally and confidentially. There was no staff, and they did all business over the telephone, keeping each other informed about hardship cases and raising the amounts they felt were needed in each case. "Extraordinary for a committee of this sort," Bertram Lewin wrote, "we committee-members even paid the postage and the secretaries for their work." They created and maintained a revolving fund: the recipients of financial assistance regarded the money they received as a loan which most of them repaid after they had resettled in this country. In this way the sums collected went a long way and reached to the four corners of the world. Many prospective immigrants abroad were sent money for passage and sometimes for travel by roundabout, expensive routes — two families came from Central Europe via the Trans-Siberian Railroad and Japan. Upon arrival in America, and occasionally in other countries, numerous refugees were given loans to ease the difficulties of starting life anew. In several instances the assistance took another form: an assured position in

Top,
Marc Chagall, refugee from the fall of France.
Bottom,
Franz Alexander, 1930. Psychoanalysis in the universities?

Top,
Konrad Heiden at the time of his arrival in 1940. He revealed the true Hitler to the world.
Bottom,
Pierre Monteux, 1941. Not all the French returned to France.

Top,
Bruno Bettelheim, healer of autistic children.
Bottom,
Rudolf Flesch. Americans learned plain English from him.

Béla Bartók, the stranger who could not adjust to America.

Top,
Stan Ulam, early thirties. Poland sent great mathematicians to this country.
Bottom,
The intellectual bride: Maria Goeppert Mayer, 1930.

Top,
Hannah Arendt, a few years after arrival. She knew totalitarianism well.
Bottom,
Felix and Helene Deutsch. Austrian psychoanalysis moved to America.

Top,
Intellectuals in their European habitat: George Gamow and Wolfgang
Pauli before emigrating.
Bottom,
Felix Bloch, *ca.* 1940. Was the cyclotron out of order?

Top,
Max Delbrück, 1951. From atoms to the phage.
Bottom,
Leo Szilard with the American A. D. Hershey. The dissemination of ideas.

Alvin Johnson, a great friend of the migration.

Top,
Rudolph Carnap. The ideas of the Vienna Circle flourished in America.
Bottom,
George Szell. New life for the Cleveland Orchestra.

Top,
Max Rheinstein. Teachers can be extremely influential.
Bottom,
Marcel Duchamp. He smuggled his art out of occupied France.

Albert Einstein. His mere presence could fill a room.

Top,
Hans Morgenthau, a powerful critical voice.
Bottom,
Igor Stravinsky. Music for young elephants.

Top,
Paul Tillich, 1938. A long and fruitful American career.
Bottom,
Thomas, Erika, and Katja Mann, members of an extraordinary family, 1939.

Top,
Rudolf and Irene Serkin. A Czechoslovakian boy makes good in the United States.
Bottom,
Enrico Fermi and Emilio Segrè, early forties. European intellectuals in their New Mexico habitat.

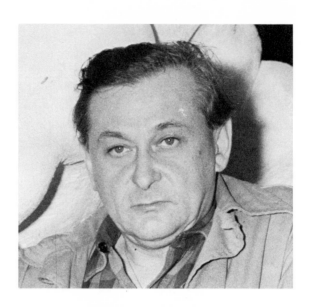

Top,
Jacques Lipchitz, leader of expressionism in sculpture, 1946. One of the many refugees rescued by Varian Fry.
Bottom,
John Von Neumann, 1953. The mystery of Hungarian talent.

the United States was a magic key to the gates of the country; to obtain positions for qualified persons the committee had often to advance as much as two years' salary and had to find special donors, individuals or foundations. Other forms of financial help ranged from support to psychoanalytic students to enable them to complete their training in the United States, payments for the cure of persons who had arrived from Europe in poor health, and the acquisition of dictionaries for a translator. The money still available in the spring of 1943, when immigration from Europe was at a standstill, was transferred to a fund to insure the care and education of the two children of a lay analyst who had died not long after his arrival in this country. By that time the Emergency Committee on Relief and Immigration had given financial aid to some sixty-five persons and many families. (I have not been able to ascertain how many received loans or gifts from the informal committee of the New York Psychoanalytic Society, which was active until 1938.)

Many more — about 150 persons and their families — received other kinds of assistance, often more valuable than money itself, largely connected with problems of immigration and resettlement. The committee obtained countless affidavits for individuals who had no personal friends in the States; kept in touch with other agencies assisting refugees, especially those helping physicians; found jobs and secured invitations from hospitals, psychoanalytic institutes, and other teaching institutions; intervened with the State Department in difficult cases; and wrote letters to or cabled consulates abroad. Newcomers were assisted in every conceivable way: more than one, for example, asked that manuscripts they were preparing for publication be read, edited, or criticized.

The committee did not limit its aid to analysts alone but extended it to relatives and friends of analysts and even to non-analytically affiliated persons. To have been analyzed abroad, for training or treatment, fully or partially, was a sufficient qualification for psychologists, teachers, lawyers, and social workers to apply for and receive assistance. Several physicians, some of them psychiatrists with no analytic training, were also aided, and so was at least one writer. Those who were assisted came from most of the countries where psychoanalysis was sufficiently established to survive the war or be revived after it but also from countries like Poland and Czechoslovakia where there is now no organized psychoanalysis.

"Thirty years ago," Bertram Lewin commented, "there were not so many psychoanalysts as there are now, things were not so strictly organized, on the whole we knew each other personally. . . . I don't believe we thought in terms of committees, reports and all that. . . ."

In this exceptionally bright story of good will and success a sad note is struck by the failures met by the committee; many persons were deported to Nazi concentration camps from Germany, Belgium, Holland, and France while the committee was engaged in attempts to bring them to safety in the United States.

Assistance to European analysts came also from individuals and institutions outside the American Psychoanalytic Association. The Menninger Clinic (now the Menninger Foundation) of Topeka, Kansas, is a signal example. This large center for both the treatment and study of psychiatry was established in 1919 by Dr. Charles Frederick Menninger and his two sons, Karl Augustus and William Claire. Psychoanalysis gained early admittance through the interest of its founders, and later the two sons were fully trained as psychoanalysts. Throughout the years in which psychoanalysis was liquidated in Europe, the clinic provided appointments for many émigré analysts (the Menningers themselves wrote a large number of the required affidavits of support) and invited so many others for briefer stays that the airport at Topeka came to be known as the "International Psychoanalytic Airport of the World."

But not all those who were urged by the Menningers to leave Europe for Topeka did so. A woman analyst, for one, declined the invitation because she was afraid that her laundry would not be done properly in Topeka. I think I can understand her: to emigrate is very difficult; between Vienna or Berlin and the unknown Midwest there is an abyss of habits and traditions the crossing of which requires more courage than the woman in question could muster. The laundry was the concretization of her fears, and around it she rationalized her decision.

The traffic at the Topeka airport was a symptom of the turnover of Europeans at the Menninger Clinic. With its psychoanalytic tradition and the Menningers' warm hospitality, the Topeka institution should have been a veritable heaven for Europeans. And it was, as far as working conditions were concerned. The Menningers smoothed all difficulties, found homes, calmed down the zealous FBI, and provided patients and income. All this strengthened the Europeans' self-esteem. They gained further satisfaction from the realization that as teachers and therapists they could be a true asset to the clinic. The Menningers also were aware that their clinic profited by the new arrivals. Reminiscing about those times, Dr. Karl told me: "We did not know whether we were extending a helpful hand or taking advantage of a situation. . . ." A most miraculous fact, he pointed out, was that Kansans, who in the last generations had hardly seen any foreigners, allowed themselves to be treated by doctors who spoke little English only because Dr. Karl and Dr. Will vouched for them. But Topeka, an oasis for intellectuals in the vast Midwest, was too "100 per cent American," as one European put it, too alien to Europeans still at the beginning of the process of Americanization.

I mention these matters only to show that the mutual adjustment of Europeans and Americans did not always go smoothly. America to many Europeans was at first a difficult experience, more of a purgatory than a heaven after the Nazi hell. To those Americans who had been unconditional admirers of European culture and its eminent exponents it must have been a shock to find themselves occasionally with a prima donna on their hands. It was inevitable that over the years the different outlook of European and American analysts should cause some disagreement, conflict, or dissension. It is to the credit of both groups that they did not let this interfere with their relationships and collaboration.

THE BEGINNING OF THE WAVE

By the end of the twenties European psychoanalysis was still something of a family affair. The rosters of the International Psychoanalytic Association for 1929, the year before the beginning of the wave, show that there were a total of 205 active and associate members of societies in Europe and Russia. (In comparison, the New York society, which had been in existence since 1911, then the only such society in the United States, listed 38 active and 12 associate members; the American Psychoanalytic Association, which listed only active members, had 46.) Psychoanalysis was, of course, expanding everywhere, and many young people were in training, but the growth was moderate. The largest European group, the Vienna Society, had 56 members in 1929 and 69 in 1937. Accordingly, the absolute number of persons who came to the United States in the psychoanalytic wave is not large. In my files I collected some 190 names of lay and medical analysts and psychiatrists with a psychoanalytic practice or interest.

Their arrival was far from being evenly distributed in time: about two-thirds came in the four years starting from the beginning of 1938 and one-third in the eight years before 1938. In the first four years (1930–33) there were eleven arrivals, and ten in 1934, at a time when the German Psychoanalytical Society had already lost half its membership to emigration. This uneven distribution reflects circumstances and events both in Europe and America. In Europe, Freud's negative feelings about emigration and the analysts' preference for exile in European countries after the rise of Hitler greatly slowed the wave until after the *Anschluss*. Then, as the number of European nations safe for the Jews began rapidly to shrink, the immigration to the United States doubled and redoubled. The events in America, from 1930 on, must be examined in some detail.

At the opening of the thirties, interest in psychoanalysis was on the ascent, and two more societies, one in Boston and the other in the Washington-Baltimore area, were established in 1930. In May, 1930, the first International Congress of Mental Hygiene took place in Washington, D. C., with important consequences for the migration wave. A large number of psychiatrists and analysts came from Europe to attend, among them persons whose names are now well known in American psychoanalysis: Franz Alexander, Helene Deutsch, Sandor Rado, and René Spitz. They were very favorably impressed. They saw a greater dynamism and freedom from dogmatic preconceptions, a more sincere eagerness for new ideas than they were used to at home; eventually they were to settle in the United States. Many years later Alexander wrote in his autobiography *The Western Mind in Transition* that at the 1930 meeting American psychiatrists had expressed the belief that American psychiatry was about ready to assimilate Freud's teachings. To him this was a novel experience, because in Europe the rift between psychoanalysis and psychiatry was wide and no attempt to bridge it was in sight. It was not only a novel experience, it was also a lure: during the congress he received and accepted a one-year appointment at the University of Chicago. When he returned to this country the following September he became the first professor of psychoanalysis at an American university. He was also the first immigrant psychoanalyst in the wave of the thirties.

Alexander and two other Europeans, Hanns Sachs and Sandor Rado, took an active part in a new venture, the founding of the first three American psychoanalytic institutes, in New York (Rado), Boston (Sachs), and Chicago (Alexander), between the fall of 1931 and the fall of 1932.

Psychoanalytic institutes originated in Europe. The very first institute was organized in Berlin by Max Eitingon, Karl Abraham, and Ernst Simmel. Its first training analyst was Hanns Sachs, and Franz Alexander was the first student. In the next few years members of its faculty — Alexander and Rado among them — devised a curriculum including a training analysis, supervised clinical work, case seminars, and theoretical courses. The Berlin institute was to serve as a model for other institutes in Europe and America for several years after its foundation and to have a great influence on American psychoanalysis. A good part of its faculty was to immigrate to the United States, not only Alexander, Rado, and Sachs, but Ernst Simmel, Karen Horney, Therese Benedek, Siegfried Bernfeld, Otto Fenichel, and Theodor Reik.

The first American institutes were founded in response to the growing interest in psychoanalysis and the recognition of the need for more systematic training than had been available in the United States in the twenties. Collaborating in early planning were American psychiatrists who had received psychoanalytic training in Europe and the few European analysts already settled in this country. The New York Institute was the first to open its doors, in the fall of 1931. The Hungarian Sandor Rado was called from Berlin to be its educational director.

Rado, an outstanding teacher, organizer, and leader, was exceptionally well-suited for this role. In 1913, when a young man of twenty-three, he had lent Ferenczi a hand in founding the Hungarian Psychoanalytic Society and became its secretary. Ten years later he moved on to Berlin to join its institute; throughout his life he made numerous contributions to psychoanalytical theory; in the United States he advocated, with Alexander, the incorporation of psychoanalysis in the universities. Alexander described him as "an aggressive, uncompromising debater" (Rado had obtained a degree in law before receiving a degree in medicine), a lucid scholar, a loyal friend, and a sympathetic therapist, "the active, determined ally of the patient." In New York, Rado set himself to mold the new institute on the Berlin pattern and devoted many years to it. Much later, in 1944, he left to organize the first psychoanalytic center within a university, the Psychoanalytic Clinic for Training and Research of Columbia University.

The Boston Institute was the outcome of a "Freud seminar" conceived in the winter 1930–31 by a small group of young Americans just back from psychoanalytic training in Europe. The seminar gained impetus in the fall of 1931, when Alexander went to Boston, at the termination of his initial appointment in Chicago, to conduct a psychoanalytic study of juvenile delinquency. The assumption among his Boston friends was that he would remain to direct the institute. Instead, he received a call from a Chicago group to return and organize a psychoanalytic institute. To his disappointed friends in Boston he suggested that they invite his old Berlin teacher and analyst, Hanns Sachs, and they did.

Sachs arrived in Boston from Berlin in the fall of 1932. Some twenty years older than Alexander, Sachs was heavy-set and balding, with a quiet, almost apologetic expression. He was not a physician but a lawyer who had been led to psychoanalysis by his love of literature: in his "boundless admiration for Dostoevski," he hoped to understand the secrets of the soul, which Dostoevski had sought to reveal. He had belonged to the intimate circles of Freud's disciples which formed the nucleus of the first psychoanalytic society in Vienna, and was also one of the "Seven Rings" (Freud, Abraham, Ferenczi, Jones, Rank, Eitingon, and Sachs), pledged to develop and defend psychoanalysis, each of whom wore a ring with an ancient engraved stone from Freud's collection. Sachs remained a most devout admirer of the master, whose biography *Freud, Master and Friend* he wrote in 1944. In it he also told his own story and the details related above.

Sachs called himself "a psychoanalytic hermit" and was wont to say "My home is where my desk is." In *Birth of an Institute*, Ives Hendrick, one of the founders of the Freud seminar and the psychoanalytic institute in Boston, described him as "aloof and intellectually austere, though not lacking in pungent humor." But Fritz Moellenhoff, who was Sachs' student in Berlin and came to the United States upon Sachs' advice, painted a much warmer picture in *Psychoanalytic Pioneers*: Sachs appears as a kindly man who could lecture with easy elegance and was able to create "an atmosphere filled with the unverbalized entreaty that his pupils experience what he felt" and as a therapist humble before his patients, fully aware of his responsibilities to them. A prototype of the European humanist and contemplative thinker, Sachs could apply psychoanalysis to literature, art, and the knowledge of man. This distinguished European scholar brought to Boston his conservative attitude and determination to adhere to Freud's precepts.

The third American institute was founded in Chicago in 1932. While the New York and Boston institutes were created within an existing psychoanalytic society, as its teaching arm, in Chicago there was no existing society. Nor had psychiatry made its appearance in Chicago in its modern form; there was nothing comparable to teaching and research hospitals, and most psychiatric students went elsewhere for their graduate work. Upon his return from Boston, Alexander was confronted with a new and challenging task. But novelty and challenge were the best food for his mind.

Stocky, with a heavy head sunk on rounded shoulders, Alexander was an extremely dynamic leader, a born experimenter and innovator. His formal training was in medicine and his background humanistic; he was the son of a professor of history and philosophy at the University of Budapest and at an early stage in his life he had been exposed to the effervescent intellectual milieu of Budapest. His life dream was to introduce psychoanalysis in a university.

The invitation to the University of Chicago had seemed a step toward the realization of this dream. To President Hutchins, Alexander had insisted that his appointment be as visiting professor of psychoanalysis rather than as visiting professor of psychiatry, and his request was granted. But the chair of psychoanalysis stood on shaky legs: Alexander was more warmly welcomed by social scientists, philosophers, and lawyers than by the medical faculty (with a few exceptions). His year at the University of Chicago gave little indication of the great impact Alexander was to make on American psychoanalysis.

In organizing the Chicago Institute for Psychoanalysis, Alexander was helped by men and women whom he had analyzed in Berlin and in his year at the University of Chicago. Because he was an independent spirit, he kept the institute independent from the psychoanalytic society, a unique innovation. From its inception, the Chicago institute has been both a teaching institution and a research center, and this was another innovation. As Alexander was to say at the twentieth-anniversary celebration, "The Chicago institute was founded to create a model which might show the way for the future incorporation of analysis into the traditional places of teaching and lecturing, the universities."

MORE ARRIVALS

In the intricate mechanism of the great cultural migration the first institutes were the one gear specific to psychoanalysis. Their high educational standards and aims increased the respect of the American professional world for psychoanalysis and the interest of young psychiatrists in psychoanalytic training. The need for therapists and teachers grew accordingly, and the expansion in the demand for psychoanalytic services facilitated the immigration of many more European analysts. Having organized the Chicago institute, Alexander, for instance, felt the need for an associate director, and Karen Horney came from Berlin at his invitation. (It was 1932, a depression year, and yet he called her long-distance across the Atlantic, a feat that is still cause for wonder among European-born analysts.)

Horney, born in Berlin, the daughter of a Norwegian sea captain, was endowed with an independent, critical spirit. Upon entering the psychoanalytic profession, she began questioning accepted views and stressing cultural factors in addition to the sexual, thus establishing a pattern for her career which after her death was to earn her recognition as a pioneer in psychoanalysis. During her life it also caused difficulties. Although Alexander called her to Chicago because he admired her qualities, her collaboration with him was not successful, and after two years she left for New York, more difficulties, and eventually the founding of the American Institute of Psychoanalysis, which is not approved by the American Psychoanalytic Association. The void she left at the Chicago institute was filled in 1936 by Therese Benedek, Hungarian-born like Alexander, who had brought psychoanalysis to Leipzig and, like Alexander and Horney, had been connected with the Berlin Institute. A small woman with a great drive and outstanding abilities, she embarked on her work as teacher, researcher, and therapist for which she is considered one of the very distinguished analysts of her generation. Many other European-born analysts gathered around the Chicago institute including Gerhart Piers, who was to succeed Alexander as its director.

A circumstance favorable to the European analysts was that many members of the early American institutes had been trained abroad. When the need arose, they did much to help their European friends to come over here, providing affidavits of support, teaching opportunities, or patients. They could not, however, solve all difficulties: as the early thirties gave way to the late thirties and early forties, tightened state requirements for licensing foreign doctors affected the analysts no less than other physicians. Eventually, in many states the only road to a license was through an internship in a hospital. Possibly the most dramatic illustration of what this could mean to a European is Otto Fenichel's case. When he arrived in Los Angeles from Oslo (where he had sought refuge from the Nazis) at the end of 1937, not quite forty years old, he was well known as an exceptionally able teacher with an encyclopedic knowledge of psychoanalysis. In 1946, when forty-eight years old, he felt that he would not be able to exert his full influence unless he obtained an American license and so decided to intern for a year though he was not in good physical condition. The strenuous hospital work, with its night duty and emergency calls, was too much for him, and he died of a heart attack before the year was up.

Among the many analysts who came in the big wave were several who, like Otto Rank and Hanns Sachs, had belonged to the original group of disciples who gathered around Freud in the first decade of the century: Ludwig Jekels, who came to America after the *Anschluss*; Edward Hitschmann, who went first to London with Freud, then came to this country; and the most venerable of all, Paul Federn, who began to practice psychoanalysis in Vienna as early as 1903. Other analysts of the heroic times of psychoanalysis had not belonged to the original group. Hermann Nunberg was one of that class. He was the first to suggest, in 1919, that no one should practice psycho-analysis unless he has been psychoanalyzed himself. He arrived in the United States in the early thirties and as a teacher in Philadelphia and New York he attracted to psychoanalysis many young American doctors. Another is Theodor Reik, who came from Germany after a long stop in the Hague. Reik was trained and taught in Vienna and in Berlin, but most psycho-analysts of the first generation belonged solely to the Vienna group, since Vienna was the birthplace of psychoanalysis. In the second generation of analysts, those trained after World War I, many of the great were Viennese — Robert Waelder, Felix and Helene Deutsch, Heinz Hartmann, and Ernst

Kris among them — but quite a few were Germans or spent their European psychoanalytic years in Germany: Franz Alexander, Karen Horney, Therese Benedek, Erich Fromm (criticized by orthodox psychoanalysts), Frieda Fromm-Reichmann, Edith Weigert, Edith Jacobson, Ernst Simmel, and others. Edoardo Weiss came from Italy: he had been trained in Vienna under Paul Federn and during the thirties had been the president of the Italian psychoanalytic society.

Many psychoanalysts of the third generation completed their training in this country. Despite their status as "psychoanalytic students," they had obtained university degrees in Europe and thus belong in the class of European intellectuals. One example is Gerhart Piers. He had received his medical degree from the University of Vienna, had qualified as a psychiatrist, and was well on with his psychoanalytic training when the *Anschluss* interrupted his career. Gerhart and his fiancée Maria had waited to be married for several years. Before the Anschluss the reason had been mainly financial, as the semi-Fascist Austrian government withdrew Jewish doctors' salaries. Hitler introduced "legal" obstacles to the wedding. But friends of Gerhart's in England and America were working for a visa in the name of Dr. and Mrs. Gerhart Piers, and they strongly advised an immediate marriage. With the connivance of Austrian magistrates the obstacles were overcome, the newlyweds spent a year in Switzerland, then came to the United States, and Gerhart completed his psychoanalytic studies at the Chicago institute.

Heinz Kohut, a Viennese like Piers, had received his medical degree in Vienna but had not initiated his specialization in psychoanalysis before coming to this country. For several years after his arrival in 1940 — by way of England and an adventurous crossing on a boat in an English convoy that zigzagged the Atlantic at the speed of the slowest tanker — he remained in the field of neurology and neuropathology. Eventually, led by his strong literary and artistic inclinations, he sought training at the Chicago Institute of Psychoanalysis. He became a professor of psychiatry at the University of Chicago and in 1964–65 was president of the American Psychoanalytic Association.

This series of examples may give the wrong impression that all European analysts came from either Austria or Germany. In reality, they came from many countries, including Hungary, France, Switzerland, Holland, Czechoslovakia, and Poland.

MORE TRAINING CENTERS —
MORE PSYCHOANALYSTS

Of considerable significance to the dissemination of psychoanalysis in America was the westward drive of European-born analysts. It extended psychoanalysis outside its eastern limits and dotted our country with institutes. The first westward step was taken by Alexander when he established the Chicago institute. When the two Menninger brothers, Karl and William, graduated from it, the influence of this institute reached further west. In 1938 the Topeka Psychoanalytic Society and the Topeka Institute for Psychoanalysis were founded under the protective shadow of the Menninger Clinic. Of the thirteen charter members of the Topeka Society, including the two Menningers, six were Europeans: Bernhard Berliner, Siegfried Bernfeld, Otto Fenichel, Bernard Kamm, Fritz Moellenhoff, and Ernst Simmel. The following year two more Europeans, Irene Haenel and Ernest Lewy, were added to the membership, and no Americans. By 1942, Berliner, Fenichel, Kamm (who subsequently went to Chicago), and Simmel had moved to California. With the Czechoslovakian Emanuel Windholz, who had already been in California a couple of years, and with five Americans — thus in perfect balance with native forces — they organized the San Francisco Psychoanalytic Society. The San Francisco Psychoanalytic Institute was founded that same year.

In 1946 the Los Angeles Psychoanalytic Society and the Los Angeles Institute for Psychoanalysis were founded. European charter members of the society were Frederick Hacker, Ernst Lewy, and Ernst Simmel — for the fourth time Simmel, a founder of the Berlin Institute, was involved in organizing an institute. A study group had been active in Los Angeles before the opening of the institute; its three training analysts, Otto Fenichel, Ernst Simmel, and Frances Deri, were all from Europe. Meanwhile, other institutes and societies sprang up in the East too, in Philadelphia and Detroit (under the leadership of Richard and Editha Sterba), and more were to come into existence throughout the United States, from Seattle to New Orleans, from southern California to Long Island. By 1966 the American Psychoanalytic Association had approved twenty-six societies, and there were a few groups outside the fold of the association. The great majority reckoned Europeans among their charter members, past presidents, or active members.

Before American psychoanalysis attained its present degree of unification and standardization, the groups organized by Europeans frequently reflected the experience and European setting of their founders in the selection of curricula and teaching procedures and in theoretical orientation. The European influence of the founders was even more pronounced in the institutes established by émigré dissidents and not recognized by the American Psychoanalytic Association, including Karen Horney's American Institute for Psychoanalysis and Theodor Reik's National Psychological Association for Psychoanalysis.

With the advent of the institutes, the number of students in training soared and was followed by a great increase in the number of trained analysts. Since the middle fifties, an average of nearly one hundred students a year are graduated from institutions approved by the American association.

The multiplication of societies and training institutions during and after World War II paralleled the growth of a demand for psychiatric services stimulated by the war. The psychiatric problems that came to light early in the war were of totally unexpected magnitude: in the years 1942–45, according to official figures, 1,850,000 men were rejected for military service because of neuropsychiatric symptoms, representing 38 per cent of the rejections for all causes; as of December 31, 1946, some 54 per cent of all patients in veterans' hospitals were being treated for neuropsychiatric disorders. The return home of men discharged because of psychiatric problems made millions of people understand for the first time the nature of psychiatric disorders. At the same time, in an effort to expand its rehabilitation services, the army enlisted the help of all the psychiatrists and psychologists it could find, and so singled them out for their usefulness. Psychiatric and in particular psychoanalytic literature was especially prepared and distributed to physicians and psychologists in the army. The desperate need for more psychiatrists, psychoanalysts, and well-qualified teachers was met more easily because so many European analysts were available in this country.

The high level of teaching in the institutes and the stature of many of their members, Europeans included, greatly raised the status of psychoanalysis. Only eight years after the end of the war, in 1953, Karl Menninger could write: "Psychoanalysis as a technique is still taught only in psychoanalytic institutes. . . . But the theory of psychoanalysis, the psychoanalytically derived concepts of personality structure and psychodynamics, are taught in practically every medical school and residency training center. And whereas it was formerly impossible for any psychiatrist contaminated with psychoanalytic ideas to be offered a university appointment, today the medical schools are choosing as professors and heads of psychiatric departments men who have had psychoanalytic training."

CONTROVERSY

In the events described so far, European-born analysts made decidedly constructive contributions. On a less positive side was their participation in debates that created dissension and disunity in the psychoanalytic camp. The two main issues causing controversy were lay analysis and the question of autonomy of local institutions versus central control. The first reached its climax and was settled in the thirties, but the fight over the second still persists. The group of analysts from Vienna, who had been under Freud's direct influence, took a conservative position toward both issues, adhering more closely to the master's directives, than did the Berlin group which had shown from the start a greater interest in experiment and innovation.

In psychoanalytic parlance, a lay analyst is a person who practices or teaches psychoanalysis but does not have a medical degree. Freud, himself a physician, foresaw that his discoveries would affect all fields of intellectual endeavor. He welcomed and encouraged "the incursion" as Ernest Jones wrote, "into the therapeutic field of suitable people from walks of life other than the medical, and he proclaimed as a principle that in his opinion it was a matter of indifference whether intending candidates for psychoanalytic training held a medical qualification or not; nor did he even think that any kind of academic qualification was at all necessary for membership. . . ."

As a result of Freud's stand, many European analysts were not physicians. Freud's own daughter Anna was a teacher — in 1938 she fled to London with her father, settled there, and exerted a great influence on further developments in psychoanalysis. Of the analysts who came to America, Theodor Reik, the Hungarian David Rapaport, and the Viennese Rudolf Ekstein were psychologists, Hanns Sachs was a lawyer, Géza Róheim an anthropologist, Robert Waelder a physicist, and Erik Erikson a social scientist. Ernst Kris, in his early career as an art historian and museum curator, became such a well known expert on cameos, intaglios, and goldsmith work that he made his first trip to America in 1929 at the invitation of the Metropolitan Museum of Art which sought his services. Many other European-born were lay analysts, and most would have liked to see this openness to the profession perpetuated in America. A notable example was Hanns Sachs, who after becoming the director of the Boston institute fought strenuously for the admission of candidates without medical degrees, and when he lost this battle to his American colleagues fought for the recognition of the training that these lay candidates would receive if they went to Europe. But he lost this battle also. The fact is that conditions were not the same in Europe and in the United States. Freud placed emphasis upon the acquisition of knowledge as the first goal of psychoanalysis, whereas America stressed treatment from the moment psychoanalysis began to be acclimatized here. The humanitarian trends that had brought about the mental hygiene movement were then still at work, and immediate relief of the suffering of mental patients was of much greater concern than theoretical developments. If psychoanalysis was to effect a cure, it had to be handled by physicians.

Thus, the American medical profession, including the majority of American analysts, waged a war against lay analysis. This issue was settled once and for all in 1938, against lay analysis, but the consequent need to establish standards for American psychoanalytic education differing from those prevailing in Europe before World War II brought the American Psychoanalytic Association very close to a declaration of independence from the International Association. The American Psychoanalytic Association decided not to grant official recognition to analysts and candidates who were not medically trained — it made a few exceptions, granting membership to several but not all, European-born lay analysts, allowing research training for behavioral scientists, and permitting some non-medical analysts to become training analysts. In spite of the official ruling against them, European-born lay analysts made many useful and important contributions to American psychoanalysis. The field into which they went in the largest numbers and to which they made the greatest contribution is child analysis, possibly because the value of collaboration between psychiatrists and psychologists in work with children was recognized at an early date by the organizers of American child guidance clinics. At present there seems to be a tendency among older psychoanalysts to leave child analysis to the clinical psychologists and the younger analysts.

The second controversy, about the question of central control of local institutions, was a consequence of the first. Having ruled against lay analysis in 1938, the American Psychoanalytic Association published "Minimal Standards for the Training of Physicians in Psychoanalysis," which, with minor revisions, remain in effect. In order to be eligible as a student or candidate, an applicant must have received a medical degree, have served one year's internship at an approved hospital, and have completed one year's work in psychiatry. Psychoanalytic training is at the postgraduate level and is offered on a part-time basis while the student continues his psychiatric work. Psychoanalytic training on a part-time basis spans a considerable number of years, and seldom is a student graduated before he reaches his late thirties.

The majority of analysts in this country, the Vienna group among them, felt that these uniform standards, controlled by the American Psychoanalytic Association, would protect American psychoanalysis against the dangers of branching in wrong directions and attacks upon its integrity. But there was a minority advocating greater independence of local institutions and a more flexible attitude in training practices. Several in this minority belonged to the Berlin group, and Rado and Alexander were prominent among them. In 1961 Alexander wrote: "Just because so much still has to be explored, we must not only tolerate but encourage individual differences, personal initiative of teachers and also of the students, instead of insisting on strict uniformity and conformity. We must return to local autonomy of institutes from a uniformly systematized centrally regulated educational system."

Alexander's stand was related to his conviction that psychoanalysis belonged in the universities and to his and Rado's efforts to bring it there. In 1944 Rado left the New York institute to organize the Columbia University Psychoanalytic Clinic for Training and Research, the first of its kind. In a sketch of Rado in *Psychoanalytic Pioneers*, Alexander commented: "He met a great deal of resistance in this new venture; many of the psychoanalysts felt strongly . . . that universities were not yet ready to assimilate psychoanalysis. They feared compromise and dilution." Perhaps the resistance that Rado encountered was not as strong as Alexander suggested: by the late sixties psychoanalytic institutes had been established within the State University of New York, Western Reserve University, and the University of Pittsburgh; and all four, the Columbia institute and the later three, were approved by the American Psychoanalytic Association.

To his very last days Alexander held on to his hope. In a letter in answer to my queries, which he wrote shortly before his death in March, 1964, he asserted that the isolation of psychoanalytic institutes from other centers of academic training was a historical relic which of necessity would be gradually liquidated, and that psychoanalysis would become a fully integrated part of psychiatric training and practice. The opposing majority states that psychoanalysis is rooted in several different disciplines and that it cannot be squeezed into a conventional academic setting without danger of distortion and of curtailment of its services; that the institutes have preserved the special relationships with students and patients necessary to the development of psychoanalytic knowledge, which would not be possible in other settings. The Viennese Robert Waelder may have reached the heart of the matter when he remarked in 1955 that the standard psychoanalytic course of study would fit in a university organization if it were not for the training analysis.

CONTRIBUTIONS

As a group the European analysts have been immensely prolific writers. "It was easy to be prolific when the field was still young and not yet saturated with publications," Therese Benedek explained to me. But perhaps there were other reasons as well. Perhaps in their new home in America the Europeans experienced a sense of mission and felt that it was their duty to share with others the intellectual patrimony that had been entrusted to them. European humanism and scholarly traditions may have done the rest. Whatever the reasons, they have contributed a great deal to American psychoanalytic literature.

Some have written at the level of the enlightened lay reader, without descending to easy popularization. Outstanding, though not unique examples, are Theodor Reik and Erich Fromm. Neither Reik, who at one time was very close to Freud, nor Fromm, with his sociological outlook, is considered an orthodox analyst within the main stream of psychoanalysis; but Reik is closer to it, while Fromm is a prominent neo-Freudian revisionist. Reik introduced the American public to the techniques of psychoanalysis through several books, particularly *Listening with the Third Ear*. His literary skill, avoidance of technical language, and candid introspection

164

when relating his own experiences have stimulated psychoanalytic thinking in America and helped to prepare the way for the widespread acceptance of psychoanalysis. Fromm, probably even better known than Reik, has written many books since his arrival in America — *The Sane Society, Man For Himself, May Man Prevail?* and others; his *The Art of Loving* was translated from the German. He shows himself an acute analyzer and critic of our society but retains a hopeful optimism about man's possibilities and his future.

A large part of the psychoanalytic literature produced by Europeans is highly technical, dealing either with theory or with the technique of treatment, and it is not possible to attempt to evaluate it here. One more promising approach may be to go back to some of the areas of culture influenced by psychoanalysis — as suggested in the quotations from Brosin and Kubie — and see what part of the influence on each is to be attributed to Europeans. One area is medicine itself. Here psychoanalysis, together with other scientific movements, has promoted a return to the concept of man as a whole — of the inseparability of body and mind — which the emphasis on organs, cells, and laboratory findings in the second half of the last century had tended to efface. Psychoanalytic studies of personality illustrate the role of emotions in health and disease and show that pathological phenomena must be interpreted both from the physiological and psychological point of view. Thus psychosomatic medicine, which introduced a scientific psychological approach to disease, owes much to psychoanalysis.

A true pioneer in modern psychosomatic medicine was Felix Deutsch, who started his professional career in Vienna as an internist. Deutsch's early lectures on "Mind and Body" aroused great hostility among his colleagues. He did not let himself be deterred, and by the time he came to the United States in 1935 he had written extensively on the application of psychoanalysis in medicine. It seems probable that he was the first to use the term "psychosomatic" in its modern context. In Boston he continued his research and published books and numerous papers on his psychosomatic studies. As a teacher at Harvard University and at schools of social work he exerted his influence over large numbers of students.

Franz Alexander organized psychosomatic research at the Chicago institute for Psychoanalysis, following his own postulate "that both the psychological and the physiological processes must be studied and described precisely with controlled methods of observation." The studies carried out in Chicago on many psychosomatic conditions have set a pattern for research elsewhere and have been so important that, according to Brock Brower, "Franz Alexander . . . brought about a small revolution in the healing arts." Among the many who worked in this field under Alexander's leadership was Therese Benedek, who studied the sexual cycle of women from the psychoanalytic-endocrinological point of view.

To literature, psychoanalysis has given a wealth of new materials and new angles from which to interpret and present them. "The Freudian psychology," Lionel Trilling wrote, "is the only systematic account of the human mind which, in point of subtlety and complexity, of interest and tragic power, deserves to stand besides the chaotic mass of psychological insights which literature had accumulated through the centuries." The widest and best known use of psychoanalytic insight in literature has been made by the writers of fiction, novels, short stories, and drama. A towering figure among them is Thomas Mann, who was Freud's friend. But the analysts themselves, starting with Freud, have given shining examples of how to apply psychoanalysis to the interpretation and creation of literature.

Of the Europeans who settled in our country, some explored the field of biography. The Viennese pioneer psychoanalyst Edward Hitschmann, of Freud's original group, began writing analytic biographies of great men as early as 1912. Among his subjects were scientists, philosophers, musicians, and writers. He continued his biographical studies in the United States, which he reached only in 1940, being one of the devout who stayed with Freud in Vienna and fled to London with him following the *Anschluss*. As was his intention, by showing the psychoanalytic approach to biography he stimulated others to follow his path. Among those who also explored biography, Theodor Reik published in 1929 a psychoanalytic study of Goethe's love for Frederike and in 1940 incorporated it in *Fragments of a Great Confession* in which he analyzed his own love affairs, drawing frequent parallels with the life of Goethe. The German-born Erik Erikson, whose main body of writings springs from his studies of children, wrote *Young Man Luther*, a powerful study of Luther's early development and reaction to the historical and religious forces at work in his time. The Sterbas, Editha and Richard, wrote *Beethoven and His Nephew: A Psychoanalytic Study of*

Their Relationship, and Kurt Eissler published a two-volume psychoanalytic study of ten years in Goethe's life.

Literary criticism has also been popular among European analysts in America. Examples that come to my mind are Heinz Kohut's brief essay on Thomas Mann's "Death in Venice" and Edmund Bergler's *The Writer and Psychoanalysis.* Ernst Kris, a man of many interests and a signal example of a modern humanist on the Renaissance pattern, has shed light on creativity in *Psychoanalytic Explorations in Art* and in the article "Psychoanalysis and the Study of Creative Imagination."

It was the Hungarian-born Géza Róheim who from the first did much to introduce psychoanalytic thinking in anthropology. Having become acquainted with both anthropology and psychoanalysis before beginning his career, he worked all his life to show that the two disciplines could be combined. He studied the dreams and unconscious material of primitive people in Africa, Australia, Melanesia, and Arizona and wrote many works about them and the evolution of cultures. His influence on American anthropology has been great, but the circle of his close followers is small. Prominent in this circle are two younger men from Europe, one of whom, Warner Muensterberger, came to this country after the war and does not belong to the migration under study. The other is the Hungarian-born analyst George Devereux whose double preparation in anthropology and psychoanalysis merged in his current research in ethnopsychiatry. Róheim's work foreshadowed, and Devereux's exemplified, one trend influenced by psychoanalysis: the breaking down of previously strong boundaries between the disciplines concerned with man's development and activities, now collectively called the behavioral sciences.

Sociology and psychoanalysis interacted at an early stage. The impact of American social science on psychoanalysis is no less great than the impact of analysis on social science. Much has been written about the relation of the two disciplines, and a large body of literature has resulted from the recognition that one is relevant to the other. Of the many anthologies exemplifying this relevance, one is impressive for its duration in time: the series *Psychoanalysis and Social Science,* later retitled *The Psychoanalytic Study of So-*

ciety, with five volumes published under the old title and four by 1967 under the new.

The interplay between sociology and psychoanalysis is most evident in the work of the so-called neo-Freudian revisionists, especially Erich Fromm and Karen Horney. Both came to the United States at the invitation of the Chicago Institute, shortly after its opening, both witnessed a good part of the American depression, and were strongly influenced by our society. They have created currents of psychoanalytic thought that attribute a greater role to social and cultural factors in the development of personality than does Freudian psychology. Horney has been called the most successful émigré revisionist because she founded both her own institute and a lasting psychoanalytic movement. Fromm seems to me the more influential of the two, in a general way, for he has written extensively about the most pressing problems besetting our society. In addition, he has had remarkable influence as a teacher; one of his students was David Riesman, co-author of *The Lonely Crowd*, a now famous study of contemporary society.

The direct application of the methodology of psychoanalysis to specific sociological issues is not an easy task, according to another well-known European analyst, Bruno Bettelheim. In 1964 he and the American-born sociologist Morris Janowitz stated in *Social Change and Prejudice*: "When [fifteen years ago] we were planning the *Dynamics of Prejudice*, our design was to. remove psychoanalysis from its social isolation, to apply it to the field of social analysis, and to show that it has application to the field of social action. Unfortunately the state of psychoanalytic theory at that time made this a difficult task and, despite progress in theory, continues to do so . . . theory has been slowly changing . . . While these changes are highly theoretical, they actually have far-reaching consequences. They will eventually bring sociological and psychoanalytic theory much closer together and may even contribute to their integration." (The original book, *Dynamics of Prejudice*, is one of five volumes in a series entitled "Studies in Prejudice," initiated by Max Horkheimer.)

The theoretical changes to which Bettelheim and Janowitz referred are in the field of psychoanalytic ego psychology. After Freud's solid construction of this psychology and the publication of his daughter Anna's *The Ego and the Mechanism of Defense* in 1936, the main advances took place after the war and are linked to four European analysts who settled in the United

States: Erik Erikson, Heinz Hartmann, and Hartmann's collaborators, Ernst Kris and Rudolph Loewenstein.

Ever since the early thirties, when August Aichhorn began to use psychoanalysis in his work with wayward youths in Vienna, numerous analysts have searched into the motivations for the behavior of delinquents and explored appropriate ways of treatment. The first systematic study of juvenile delinquency in the United States was done by Franz Alexander at the Judge Baker Guidance Center in Boston, with the collaboration of the director, William Healy. Alexander, who had already applied psychoanalysis to criminology in Berlin, analyzed eleven offenders over a period of nine months in 1931–32. His results were published in the book which he wrote with Healy, *The Roots of Crime*, but Alexander did not continue to pursue this study. Among other European analysts in this country who have searched for the roots of delinquency, the Viennese Fritz Redl is notable for his sustained efforts: he arrived in the United States in 1936 and since then has spent much time observing and treating "children who hate." This is the title of the book he wrote with the American David Wineman to report his work at Pioneer House in Detroit — a residential institution for a small group of pre-adolescent boys, which he organized and directed during its nineteen months of existence — within the framework of wider studies in the therapy of aggressive children.

In 1944 Bruno Bettelheim, a Viennese like Redl, entered a field related to that of Alexander and Redl: he became the director of the Sonia Shankman Orthogenic School of the University of Chicago, devoted to the rehabilitation of autistic children and the training of persons for work with such children. Bettelheim, whose early career in Vienna was in aesthetics, arrived in the United States in 1939 after a year in German concentration camps. Soon thereafter he established a wide reputation with a report on these camps titled *Individual and Mass Behavior in Extreme Situations*, which General Eisenhower made required reading for members of the military government in Europe. Bettelheim has been exceptionally successful, and reports that about 80 per cent of the children admitted to the school have recovered. Both Bettelheim and Redl have greatly advanced the understanding and treatment of autistic children. Both wrote several books in clear, effective language in which they illustrate their observations of disturbed children and draw conclusions of value in the handling of normal children in daily life. A third Viennese works among psychotic children on the West Coast: Rudolf Ekstein was associated with the Menninger Foundation from 1947 to 1957, and in 1957 became the co-ordinator of training and research at the Reiss-Davis Clinic in Los Angeles. The study and psychotherapy of the borderline child are his specialties, and among his numerous writings is a review of the literature on childhood schizophrenia and allied conditions.

The work and writings of these three lay analysts, Redl, Bettelheim, and Ekstein, have influenced American education in the home and school and improved the expectations for disturbed children everywhere. With other European analysts and social workers, they have done much to overcome American opposition to the institutional care of children, which was rooted in a past when this care was mainly custodial. Susanne Schulze was so insistent in asserting that foster homes could not provide what seriously disturbed children need that her colleagues called her teasingly "Mrs. Institution."

A striking feature of the psychoanalytic wave is the large number of women who formed a part of it: about 30 per cent of all analysts in my file are women. This is an extremely high proportion, not since maintained: in 1958, the last year for which I have seen a breakdown of figures, women accounted for only 9 per cent of all students in training institutions approved by the American Psychoanalytic Association. It seems reasonable to conclude that women felt strongly attracted to psychoanalysis as long as it remained a small, informal profession, but once its strict organization became crystallized they were discouraged by its demands and the length of training.

Women in the wave contributed to most fields of psychoanalysis — Frieda Fromm-Reichmann, for instance, advanced a theory and treatment technique for the psychoses. But they flocked principally into two areas, the psychology of women and child analysis. It was often stated that Freud's psychology was weakest on women, and so it is not surprising that several women have tried to remedy this weakness. Helene Deutsch's two-volume *Psychology of Women* (1944–45) is the result of over twenty years of study and observation in Austria and later in Boston, where she drew material from the social casework she supervised. Her book, which her colleagues consider the most comprehensive on the subject, examines the emotional development of women from childhood to the climacteric. Therese Benedek worked with gynecologist Boris B'. Rubinstein to do the first psychoanalytic-endocrinological research into the emotional response of women to the fluctuations of hormones during the sexual cycle. The result of this study was published under the title *The Sexual Cycle in Women* and later included in Therese Benedek's *Psychosexual Functions in Women*. The work of Karen Horney is also outstanding, although most of it is outside the main stream of psychoanalysis.

The other field favored by women, child analysis, was developed in Vienna in the second decade of the century, at about the time when in this country child guidance clinics were being set up. It was inevitable that the two movements should interact: young American psychiatrists working at guidance clinics went to Vienna to be trained by Anna Freud and the group around her, many of whom were women (and lay analysts). When the analysts of this Vienna group were compelled to leave Austria, several came to this country and some joined their former students at child guidance clinics. Not that all émigré child analysts were women. Redl, Bettelheim, Ekstein, and Erikson prove the exception. Another great analyst, René Spitz, made an epochal study of infants in institutions which proved unequivocally that love is essential to the normal physical development of babies. (Spitz was born in Vienna, but studied and lived in so many other European cities, including Budapest, Prague, Trieste, and Paris, that he could claim he had no national allegiances when he arrived in the United States.) In child analysis, however, women were even more numerous: Jenny Waelder-Hall, Berta Bornstein, Edith Buxbaum, Margaret Mahler, and Elizabeth Geleerd were among them. Their work greatly contributed to the understanding of the emotional needs of young children and their normal and abnormal responses to parental attitudes and environmental forces. It has been a factor in the revolution that psychoanalysis has brought about in child rearing.

As it is often the case, some women, busy for years with family responsibilities, remained on the fringes of psychoanalysis and yet did useful work. One example is Maria Piers, who in the course of her activities as teacher and lecturer filmed several series of talks shown on National Educational Television. More recently, she organized the Chicago Institute for Early Childhood Education (now the Erikson Institute) to train highly skilled teachers with a psychoanalytic orientation and administrators for nursery schools, kindergartens, and day-care centers. The ultimate aim of the institute is to alleviate the difficulties of underprivileged children.

PSYCHOANALYSIS AND THE MELTING POT

"It is amazing how much we European analysts have accomplished here," Rudolf Ekstein once said. "We could not have done as well had we remained in Europe." And this sums up the situation. The European analysts, America, and the melting pot were the three ingredients essential to the final product: a psychoanalysis so thoroughly Americanized that its effects on our culture are no longer recognizable because they have fused so perfectly. The psychoanalytically slanted advertisement can no longer be separated from typically American capitalistic initiative or the purchasing ability of our society; the psychoanalytic approach to the aggressiveness of children is based on a deep understanding of American society, the pressures under which it labors, racial tensions, living conditions in the slum, and the like.

It is often difficult to discern how the melting pot acts on newcomers and their intellectual baggage, but in this case one fact stands out: American psychoanalysis is the product of two essentially different trends. In Europe, Freud and his doctrines had attracted men with humanistic leanings. Franz Alexander, Heinz Kohut, and others explained that they were led to psychoanalysis by their interest in man as a thinking being and in all products of the human mind; as one result, they stressed the importance of acquiring more and more insight into man and deepening both knowledge and theory. In America it was the humanitarian tradition that drew psychiatrists and psychiatric social workers into psychoanalysis. After the arrival of the immigration wave, the Europeans' theoretical emphasis was channeled into an effort to preserve the doctrine and structure of psychoanalysis in their original form, while the Americans' more optimistic and practical approach stressed the value of therapy, creating the demand for psychoanalytic treatment that gave psychoanalysis its *raison d'être*. The two trends complemented each other and catered to each others' needs.

In the light of these considerations, the presence of European psychoanalysts in America appears essential. It is true that ideas can often be transplanted without transplanting the men who have originated them. It is also true that Freudian doctrine had aroused interest in America and psychoanalysis was taking root here even before the arrival of the wave. Yet the wave made a real difference. Without the Europeans' preoccupation with the preservation of Freudian theories, psychoanalysis might have become more fully absorbed than it is by psychiatry and be taught in all medical schools as one of the medical specialties, though probably at the price of considerable adaptive modifications. Or it might have remained on the fringes of recognized science, as it was in the twenties, accepted by few and frowned upon by many. The arrival of the Europeans conferred upon it a dignity that it lacked before, raised its status in the public eye, made it an attractive profession, and greatly contributed to its expansion. The Europeans' willingness and ability to meet the mounting needs for teachers and therapists during the war and in the early postwar period further aided the diffusion and strengthening of psychoanalysis in America.

The Americanization of psychoanalysis was facilitated by several circumstances. Training and occupation sharpen the psychoanalysts' perceptiveness, and European analysts were probably the most perceptive intellectuals in the migration. Practicing analysis on American patients opened a window on the most intimate aspects of American life, its conflicts and motivations. Many patients were eager to be treated by Europeans, because the famous among them cast a bright aura on others. Finally, the American medical and lay professions demonstrated a considerable willingness to accept outsiders. The acceptance was not always immediate or smooth, and European analysts did meet resistance and encounter difficulties. Isolationism was still strong in the thirties, and opposition to anything foreign is indeed in the American tradition; but America often proves willing to give a fair trial to her foreign importations, whether men or ideas, and so it did to psychoanalysis.

VII

$\ggg\ggg\ggg\ggg\ggg\ggg\ggg\ggg\ggg\ggg\ggg\ggg\ggg\ggg\ggg\ggg\ggg\ggg\ggg\ggg\ggg\ggg\ggg\ggg$

European-Born Atomic Scientists

Much more spectacular than the effects of psychoanalysis were the consequences of the wartime release of nuclear energy. They may have not reached as deeply into our culture or modified our mores to the same degree, but they struck us more directly. There was nothing subtle in the way they acted. Unlike the invisible elements of the "Freudian revolution," the atomic bomb, the cold war, and the awesome destructiveness of future warfare are brutal facts of which we inevitably feel the impact. The peaceful consequences of some wartime developments are just as striking and important, although their beneficial nature may make us feel them less keenly: atomic power for industries, utilities, and the propulsion of ships; and radioactive materials for scientific research, medical diagnosis, and the treatment of disease.

No one can doubt the importance of atomic energy. The question here as in the case of psychoanalysis is: What was the role of the European-born scientists in making possible its release? I have been too close to atomic science and at the same time too much on the outside of it to trust my own judgment. Before undertaking to answer this question, I talked to many scientists. They agreed on three fundamental points.

1. Atomic energy was not the most crucial scientific contribution to victory in World War II. It was radar that from 1942 on changed the fortunes of war in favor of the Allies, in the deserts of Africa, the submarine battle in the Atlantic, the invasion of France, and the fight in the Pacific. Our radar was superior to the German, of shorter waves and of greater power of definition. In the wartime development of radar in the United States, the European-born had a limited part. Hans Bethe, the Nobel laureate physicist whose balanced voice has often been heard in questions of science and poli-

174

tics, worked a few months at the Radiation Laboratory of the Massachusetts Institute of Technology, where radar was developed. Bethe estimated that at all times more than 90 per cent of the leading scientists were American and that among the younger group the European representation was even smaller. The outstanding exception in the almost entirely native staff was Samuel Goudsmit, a theoretical physicist from Holland, who joined the faculty of the University of Michigan in 1927. (Felix Bloch, Nobel Prize winner in 1952, went into radar work at a later date, long after Bethe had moved on, and was engaged in research on defenses against radar rather than in the development of it.)

2. Europeans had a decisive role in the development of atomic energy. For better or worse, without their presence in this country the release of atomic energy would have been delayed by many years, and the Americans would not have produced atomic weapons before the end of World War II.

3. On the other hand, had the Europeans stayed each in their own country, they would not have achieved the release of atomic energy. The uncertainties and the difficulties to be overcome were so great that even researchers in the richest and most industrialized nations might have given up efforts to attain it, as the Germans gave up. Atomic energy might have been delayed for generations. For a speedy success several factors were essential: an enormous concentration of brainpower in one country; the close collaboration of European and American scientists with their different skills and intellectual traits; their unity in their striving to defeat the dictators; formidable American industrial potential; no-less-formidable American financial power; and the co-ordinating supervision of the American army.

EARLY ARRIVALS

I thought until recently that the story of atomic energy in the United States began on January 16, 1939, when Niels Bohr arrived from Denmark and brought the news that Otto Hahn and Fritz Strassmann had discovered the fission of uranium in Hitler's Germany and Lise Meitner had explained it: Fermi, whose work in Rome four years earlier had set the three German researchers on the path of discovery, had immigrated to the United States only two weeks earlier. Leo Szilard, who in the past had had intuitions of chain reactions and atomic explosions, had been in America since 1937. I had no doubt that Bohr's arrival marked the beginning of atomic work in America.

But then a physicist pointed out to me that I was overlooking the important preparatory activities of European nuclear physicists, mostly theoreticians, who preceded Bohr and Fermi to this country. Among them were Eugene Wigner, George Gamow, Felix Bloch, Hans Bethe, Edward Teller, and Victor Weisskopf, who arrived in this country in the order in which I mention them, between 1930 and 1937. With others who came in the same period, they initiated a most fruitful interaction with American colleagues, an essential prerequisite to wartime success.

My account of this period is in great part pieced together from information that I gathered through conversations with European physicists or by reading their recollections. Physicists are quite fair in judging their colleagues' work, but in evaluating their own contributions they follow the dictum attributed to Fermi: "Honesty comes before modesty." So European-born honesty may occasionally color the following paragraphs.

The timing of the early arrivals was exceptionally good, and America was well prepared for them. The outstanding feature of American physics in the early thirties was the development of powerful accelerating machines and other large-scale apparatus for the study of nuclear phenomena. For its quality, power, and profusion the equipment of American laboratories was the object of admiration of foreign visitors. So were other features: European physicists in general had been lone wolves, working in isolation or in small groups; the absolute number of physicists at each European university was small. In the United States, large teams of able experimental physicists formed around the big machines, teams skilled in working in a new type of scientific collaboration.

The Europeans had been accustomed to compartmentalization within the universities and had had little contact with experimental work. It was to them a most agreeable experience to meet with American experimental teams and exchange views with them. Machines yield the best results if experiments are carefully planned to advance theory and if the experimental data obtained are interpreted in the light of theory. American experimentalists felt the need of theoretical advice and sought it, but before the coming of the Europeans it was scarce. At the beginning of the thirties, American theorists of stature were not lacking. They advanced theory, taught courses, and maintained in general closer contact with experimental work than did their colleagues in Europe. But there were not enough of them to fill the needs of American universities, many of which did not have theoretical physicists on their faculty. American theoretical literature was wanting. Most graduate students who chose to specialize in theoretical physics went to Europe for their training.

Then the Europeans began to arrive. They were young. Only George Gamow was thirty when he reached America; the others were in their late twenties. They were happy to have left the political insecurity of Europe, grateful for the freedom here, and determined to become Americans as soon as possible. Eugene Wigner, the only one in this group to come before Hitler's ascent to power, may have been an exception: America, his "country on paper," really existed but was not easy to take: for five years his halftime position at Princeton University forced him to commute between Princeton and Berlin and to repeat the experience of emigrating. To a Hungarian, Berlin is home; in his periods in America, Wigner, a bachelor then, missed the easy intellectual exchanges with persons of his own background. Not until he went to live in the more *gemütlich* Madison, Wisconsin, with a full position at the state university, did he begin to enjoy American life.

To George Gamow, the Russian, America must have made an entirely different impression. He had no reasons for wanting to return to Europe. I met Gamow at a Solvay Congress on physics in Brussels in the fall of 1933, when he had "just escaped from Russia," as a delegate of the Soviet government to the Solvay meeting. The fact was a great surprise to Gamow himself: from 1928 to 1930 he had spent much time in Germany, England, and Denmark, but in 1931 he was refused permission to attend a conference on nuclear physics in Rome and given to understand that Soviet scientists were no longer to "fraternize" with capitalistic western European colleagues. Other refusals followed, and his attempts to leave the country failed. In 1933 he seized an opportunity offered him, probably through the intervention of western scientists. He had already an established reputation as theoretical physicist for his theory of the decay of alpha particles and had worked with the great of Europe, Niels Bohr in Copenhagen and Ernest Rutherford in Cambridge. After the Solvay Congress, the couple did not go back to Soviet Russia, and a year later they settled in Washington where he had an appointment at George Washington University. When I first saw him in Brussels, Gamow was tall and as thin as a reed. After more than thirty years in this country, he admitted to at least 220 pounds. Some other characteristics did not change. Though he became the author of a number of popular scientific books, his incredibly colorful spelling always created serious trouble for his publishers. There is a story circulating among friends that at one time his frantic publishers sent him a dictionary. Gamow wrote them to complain that some of the most common words were not included, and mentioned one. He received a return wire: "Try a-p-p-l-e."

The Swiss Felix Bloch went to Rome in late 1933. He was then an aristocratic-looking young man of twenty-eight with refined tastes and a growing dislike for dictatorships. In Switzerland there were not many satisfactory openings for a bright theoretical physicist like Bloch, who had the rare ability of combining theory and experiment. He had begun his teaching career in Leipzig, but as early as 1932 the growth of nazism made him realize that his days in Germany were nearing their end. He applied for, and received, a Rockefeller fellowship for Rome and Cambridge. Meanwhile, having left Germany, he was in Copenhagen at Niels Bohr's institute when he received a cable from Stanford University offering him an appointment on its faculty. Bloch had no idea where Stanford was or what it was like, but Bohr, who had visited there, recommended it. Bloch arrived at Stanford in the spring of 1934 after his stay in Rome and became popular at once, especially among the coeds. He also began his sustained theoretical and experimental activities there and at nearby Berkeley, which were eventually to lead him to the discovery of the principle of nuclear magnetic resonance. For this work he shared the 1952 Nobel Prize in physics with Edward M. Purcell who had made the same discovery independently. American industry has built equipment based on this principle, which it distributes to laboratories all over the world, and Bloch thinks that he can "honestly" claim considerable credit.

Hans Bethe, the descendant of a long line of German university professors, seems to me the living picture of the thinker. Not that he despises the practical side of life: I have seen him and the aristocratic Felix Bloch stage an eating contest at Thanksgiving and do very well indeed. But Bethe goes at everything with thorough deliberation. When solving scientific problems he explores all avenues: no possibilities escape him; when answering questions he speaks slowly, and each word leaves his lips as a separate unit; he never goes back on what he says, and what he says is never muddled — later, if given more time to ponder, he may add details or start on a branching line of thought, but he never contradicts himself. He was in Rome in 1931 and 1932, a big young fellow with a chestnut mane, and already a good eater and undoubtedly a thinker. He too, like Bloch, saw the writing on the wall earlier than most, left Germany in 1933, spent two years in England, and was there when he received an invitation from Cornell University. While in Germany he worked with Lloyd Smith, a young American physicist from Cornell who afterward returned to that university. When the head of the physics department proposed to expand it, Smith suggested Bethe. Hans Bethe arrived in Ithaca in 1935, and immediately felt at home. To him being a bachelor was not the painful hindrance that it was to Wigner. (Bethe was to remain a bachelor until 1939.) He felt no ties with the past and was happy to be in a country that accepts people completely, makes them part of itself. He made friends at once, though at first the fact that he was a foreigner aroused the antagonism of some members of the department.

Edward Teller, whose bushy eyebrows and intense expression are now known to most television watchers, left Hungary as a student and went to Germany. He was teaching in Göttingen when Hitler came to power and was rescued by the English chemist F. G. Donnan. He enjoyed his stay in England, his association with Donnan, the weekly tea parties of the chemistry department, and Donnan's insistence that his friends from Germany mix with his British colleagues. But Teller, a young man endowed with a most original and imaginative mind, was always restless. In 1935 he left London and joined the faculty of George Washington University which offered him a position at the suggestion of his friend Gamow. As Teller himself put it, he was a survivor of the shipwreck of Hungary, and had escaped fascism and communism after having had a horrifying look at a world that was not free. He was well prepared for the role he was to assume many years later, when he pushed the work on the hydrogen bomb and advised strong armament for the United States.

Victor Weisskopf is the most talkative in the group, but talkative in the best sense of the word, the one who most easily establishes relationships with other people. His disposition is sunny and his appearance dark: his hair, eyes, and stubble are very black. Born in Vienna, he studied and did research at important European centers of theoretical physics, Göttingen, Zurich, and Copenhagen, where he met and talked with most theorists of the time. He knew their scientific problems, the theoretical questions on their mind, and the experiments needed to answer them. He had also a special ability, according to his friends: he could "smell" the results of some experiments even before they were performed. Weisskopf arrived in Rochester in 1937 and soon achieved a reputation as the theoretician who talked with the largest number of experimentalists. Years later, in the corridor of the theoretical building in Los Alamos, there was a sign pointing to Weisskopf's office. It read "Los Alamos Oracle."

The newcomers, fascinated by American scientific equipment, explored its possibilities and discussed them with experimental physicists, thus acting as a link between theory and experiment. Several of them gravitated toward the big machines. The accelerators of the thirties were a far cry from those of the sixties, and Bloch once asserted that in 1939, to his knowledge, the cyclotron in Berkeley was the only one that worked at least part of the time and then by the sheerest chance. All the same, the Europeans were fascinated by the American machines that appealed to their highly developed imaginations. In Europe they had seen nothing comparable and they knew that a judicious use of these big beasts might yield the answers to the theorists' questions. Those who were invited to have a hand in the planning and construction of new machines jumped at the chance. They designed accelerators according to the type of experiments for which each was intended, and because it was still depression time and money was scarce they sweated over calculations to save materials without impairing efficiency. Later these machines were used for highly secret work connected with the war effort. There were no cyclotrons in Washington, D.C., but the city housed a large number of otherwise well-equipped experimental laboratories at the Bureau of Standards, the Carnegie Institution, the Office of Naval Research, and so on.

Another activity of the theoretical physicists was to present the latest European developments in quantum mechanics to their colleagues and pupils. Quantum mechanics was then still a sacerdotal body of knowledge entrusted to the hands of a chosen few. Their mission was to spread the gospel and recruit proselytes through informal speeches and lectures. The American-born theoretical physicist Robert Sachs, who did his postgraduate work at George Washington University, recalled that teacher Edward Teller was never in his office but spent most of his time at other institutions, offering ideas and providing inspiration. (Sachs stressed how lucky he had been to have learned theory from Europeans without the necessity of going abroad — Teller, Maria Mayer, James Franck, and the early comers Karl Herzfeld and Gerhard Dieke were his teachers in America.) In connection with their mission to spread the gospel or in other responsibilities as teachers, the European theorists wrote many articles packed with information and gave courses in quantum mechanics and in other fields of nuclear physics. Students took notes of some of these courses and later published them. Slowly the lacunae in theoretical literature began to fill.

THEORETICAL MEETINGS IN WASHINGTON

Some more specific and limited activities of the theorists in this period led directly into wartime work. In 1935, a depression year, the American physicist M. A. Tuve of the Carnegie Institution's Department of Terrestrial Magnetism was fortunate enough to have that prime American asset, "a little money." He initiated a series of annual Washington conferences on theoretical physics. To organize them he first enlisted Gamow's help, then, after Teller settled in Washington, Gamow's and Teller's. The meetings were successful, but Tuve's two assistants were eager for novelty and easily tired of well-trodden paths. When the time came to plan the fourth conference, to take place in March, 1938, they suggested that both theoretical physicists and astronomers be invited and the subject be "The Problem of Stellar Energy." Almost ten years earlier, while still in Russia, Gamow had become interested in the mechanisms of energy production in the stars and had reported to the Soviet Academy of Science a theory advanced by an Austrian physicist and an English astronomer that the energy that causes the heat of the sun is produced when light, small nuclei fuse together to form larger nuclei at the very high temperatures obtaining in the solar interior. Bukharin, one of the Soviet officials whom Stalin was to put to death, was in the audience. He must have had intuitions of thermonuclear power, perhaps of the explosions that it might cause: he offered Gamow the use of the electrical works at Leningrad to try and reproduce solar reactions. Gamow did not think this was feasible at the relatively low temperatures that can be reached on earth and declined the offer. But his interest in stellar energy persisted, and in the United States he communicated it to Edward Teller.

By 1938 physicists were agreed that the energy production in stars must be due to some thermonuclear fusion reaction but did not know which one.

When Teller and Gamow called the 1938 meeting, their idea was that the astronomers would tell the physicists all the known facts about stars, and the physicists would tell the astronomers all the known facts about nuclei. A good many foreign-born attended the conference: astronomers Bengt Stromgren and S. Chandrasekhar; physicists Teller, Gamow, Bethe, Dieke, and Herzfeld; and mathematician John Von Neumann whose wide scientific interests included theoretical physics. The exchange of ideas was fruitful, and within a few months several physicists came up with plausible explanations of the production of energy in stars. The most widely accepted theory was Bethe's "carbon cycle," in which one atom of carbon causes the fusion of four hydrogen nuclei into one helium nucleus. His systematic examination of every possible reaction was "so complete," according to Teller, "that nothing useful could be added to his work during the next decade." It is these studies by Bethe and others, fostered by the 1938 meeting, that later inspired physicists to attempt thermonuclear reactions on earth and led to the construction of thermonuclear weapons after 1952.

The next Washington conference (the fifth) led in another direction. According to plans, it was to revert from astrophysics to a more orthodox topic, low temperature physics; but when it opened on January 26, 1939, Bohr and Fermi dropped a bombshell: they discussed the newly discovered uranium fission and the possibility that neutrons were emitted when it took place. As a result this meeting turned into a forum for the disclosure of atomic fission and its potentials to the scientific community. The way was opened to work on chain reaction and the atomic and hydrogen bombs.

SCIENCE AND GOVERNMENT

When the meeting opened, Bohr had been in this country ten short days and had talked only with colleagues at Princeton and Columbia. The implications of fission and its meaning for Germany, where it was discovered, were not yet fully explored. The atomic bomb entered the dreams of only the most prophetic physicists. Leo Szilard was one of them: the day before the opening of the Washington meeting, he was confined in bed in New York with a high fever. From there he wrote to his friend and scientific protector Lewis L. Strauss, the future chairman of the Atomic Energy Commission, to inform him of the discovery of uranium fission. Szilard stated that one aspect of fission "so far does not seem to have caught the attention of those with whom I spoke. . . . I see potential . . . possibilities . . . [which] may lead . . . perhaps to atomic bombs. This new discovery revives all the hopes and fears in this respect which I had in 1934 and 1935. . . ."

Less than three weeks later, on February 13, Szilard wrote another letter to Strauss: ". . . in Washington I spent a day with Dr. Teller there and another day with Dr. Wigner in Princeton. . . . On my return to New York I went to see Fermi. . . ." Szilard's itinerary is of interest. He got in touch with Strauss, Teller, Wigner (who in 1935 had returned to Princeton as Jones Professor of Theoretical Physics), and Fermi. At that moment Strauss, the only American-born among them, represented American financial support. The scientific brainpower was furnished by three Hungarians and an Italian.

In a sense this was natural. Hungarians and Italians knew dictators well. Though only Szilard may have considered the atomic bomb more than a vague specter of the future, Wigner, Teller, and Fermi were as well acquainted as Szilard with both Hitler's ruthlessness and the capabilities of German scientists. The idea that fission had been discovered in Germany was deeply disturbing to them. It is this profound concern, this vision of Hitler with an atomic bomb in his hand, that led physics into politics in the spring of 1939. The going was hard. In America scientists and statesmen seldom spoke to one another. While in Europe most universities operated within the framework of government, American universities were independent bodies; channels of communications between them and the federal government were all but non-existent, and effective channels had to be opened.

The story has been told many times but is worth recalling briefly, for as years go by perspectives change. In March Fermi approached the navy in Washington and gave a talk to a group of navy and army men. He did not have Szilard's assurance in making predictions, and his evaluation of future results was filled with question marks. His report to the navy was thorough but cautious, and the meeting was called inconclusive. In later years Fermi was to say repeatedly that nothing much had come of it; but two men at the meeting felt differently. Captain Garrett L. Schuyler and Ross Gunn, a young physicist from the Naval Research Laboratory, immediately realized the importance of fission. Schuyler wrote an extremely clear summary of Fermi's remarks, which remained secret for a long time (it was published in part by Lewis Strauss in his *Men and Decisions*). Within three days of the meeting, Gunn had prepared a memorandum outlining a project for a nuclear reactor for submarine propulsion. It seems now established that from that meeting sprang the first serious idea of using atomic energy for propulsion.

Szilard rightly felt that the government had not been sufficiently alerted. On the advice of economist Alexander Sachs, Szilard and Wigner prepared a letter to President Roosevelt, and Einstein signed it. (Sachs, who was interested in atomic developments, believed that Einstein was the only scientist of sufficient stature in the United States to be able to gain the ear of the President.) Einstein's letter was dated August 2, 1939, but did not reach the President at once. It was not intrusted to the mails but to Sachs' hands, and before Sachs could obtain an audience, war broke out in Europe. The President was very busy, and it appeared even less probable than before that the matter would receive proper attention unless Sachs delivered the letter in person and spoke with the President. Eventually, in early October, 1939, Sachs handed to Roosevelt both Einstein's letter and an explanatory memorandum prepared by Szilard, and read aloud his own covering letter. "Alex," the President said to Sachs, "what you are after is to see that the Nazis don't blow us up." The European-born physicists had made their point. An Advisory Committee on Uranium was established at once, but the total appropriation in the first year, until November, 1940, was a pittance, only six thousand dollars.

The smallness of the sum seems incredible in retrospect, but it should not be taken as a measure of what the physicists had achieved with their move: the Executive's eyes were open to the dangers and potentialities of atomic energy, and army and navy were represented on the new committee. The channels of communication between science and government were well established. About a year later the Advisory Committee on Uranium was reorganized under Vannevar Bush and the new National Defense Research Committee, and several scientists were added to it. The reorganization gave the uranium program official status in the defense effort of American science. By then Europe had crumbled under Nazi attack; Poland, the Netherlands, Belgium, Luxembourg, and France were occupied; Mussolini had entered the European war in order not to miss a share in the loot; the eyes of the world were turned on England, where Hitler's next move was expected; and America was preparing to take measures that were to involve her in the war before she entered it, the first peacetime draft and the lend-lease agreement with Great Britain.

COLLABORATION AND CONFIDENCE

Approaching the government was the first political contribution of European-born atomic physicists. Their initiative in proposing a voluntary censorship of information pertaining to their work may also be regarded as a political move. On the scientific side it happened that interest subsided after the first outburst of excitement caused by the news of fission. The chain reaction seemed a vague possibility for a distant future, and many felt and hoped that atomic explosions might never be achieved. Perhaps some American scientists thought that the European physicists were overly nervous about conditions in Europe, that the devil, Hitler, was not as black as depicted and could still be stopped, though by the spring of 1939 he had already annexed Austria and Czechoslovakia.

Several American physicists who had taken up work on fission returned to earlier fields of research. For months the further exploration of the possibility of a chain reaction was in the hands of a few at Columbia and Princeton. The leaders at Columbia were Fermi and Szilard — Szilard's vision of the future was too clear to allow him to stand by when he could put his fantastic mind to work; and to Fermi the investigation of fission meant the resumption of work he had done in Rome in 1934, the very work which had led to the German discovery. At Princeton, where Bohr's presence had sparked a lasting interest in the problems of fission, the men principally involved were the versatile Wigner and the American theoretician John A. Wheeler. Other Europeans had not yet come into the field. They were either too absorbed by research or, like Teller, hesitant to undertake work that might eventually lead to destructive weapons.

Slowly, through 1940 and 1941, more people were drawn into atomic work. Notable was the group studying the separation of uranium isotopes under Harold Urey at Columbia, and the group at the University of California trying to make plutonium. (Plutonium does not exist in nature, but in 1940 theoretical considerations indicated that it might be created in uranium under neutron bombardment, and that it might be a most suitable material for making atomic weapons. If making plutonium were at all possible, Lawrence's big cyclotron at Berkeley would be the best means to make it.) Each group had a European member: the Russian-born chemist Aristid Grosse worked with Urey, the Italian physicist Emilio Segrè was on the California team. As Fermi's collaborator in Rome, Segrè had shared in the discovery of artificial radioactivity produced by neutron bombardment and in the work with slow neutrons. He continued his research in nuclear physics as a professor at the university of Palermo until Mussolini and his laws made Italy unpleasant as a place to live and work. When the Fascist laws were promulgated, Segrè was spending the summer in the United States and he decided not to return to Palermo but to stay on at the University of California. He has been there ever since, except for a few years during the war, and it is at the University of California that he and the American Owen Chamberlain carried out the experiments that demonstrated the existence of the anti-proton and led to the joint award to the two men of the Nobel Prize in physics for 1959. In 1940, when the California group turned to the problem of producing plutonium by nuclear bombardment, Segrè was a great asset to the team.

Regardless of the proportion of native and foreign-born scientists, the closeness of the collaboration between them was a salient feature of the atomic project from the very beginning. The collaboration was so close that it could be called a symbiosis, so close that it is not possible to separate the contributions of the newcomers from those of the American-born. Such a degree of collaboration is unusual and almost inconceivable outside America. It is true that the European physicists who had come in the earlier thirties (or, like Karl Herzfeld, Sam Goudsmit, and George Uhlenbeck, in the late twenties) had done much to establish good relations and to dispel any diffidence that might have existed. But there was also something else, more basically American. An example may clarify what I have in mind.

When Fermi came to New York, he left in Italy his laboratory, equipment, and collaborators. He knew it would be difficult to start again as an experimentalist at Columbia, and was considering the resumption of theoretical work. Since this is usually done "in the quiet of one's own small room," it could help him avoid any feeling of being a "groping and isolated outsider" among experimenters at work on a going project. But two weeks after we arrived, Bohr also landed in New York, on his way to Princeton, and soon the physics department at Columbia was astir with talks of fission. Fermi thought at once that in the fission process neutrons might be emitted, and that if they were, it might be possible to attain a chain reaction. The first thing to do was to look for these hypothetical neutrons, and this required an experiment. A graduate student came to him and said that he had had a hand in building some equipment for John Dunning's cyclotron at Columbia and felt that he was entitled to some say in its use. He suggested that Fermi use Dunning's cyclotron to look for fission neutrons, and Fermi did.

Fermi had just received the Nobel Prize and his name was in the news. In Europe (or at least in France and Italy, the countries I know best) should a foreign professor with a Nobel Prize join a university, colleagues and students would take off their hats and bow to him but otherwise would leave him alone to cope with his own difficulties. In Europe, one expects deference, in America encouragement and help. I must admit that in Fermi's case the circumstances were favorable: the Nobel Prize winner was at least outwardly modest, and the student was Herbert Anderson, who was not troubled by false modesty. Herbert Anderson's collaboration with Fermi started the moment Anderson offered the use of Dunning's cyclotron and lasted until Fermi's death. Dunning too behaved in typical American fashion and did not object to the intruders but gave them his full support. In fact, he and Fermi agreed on some division of work: Fermi would study the feasibility of a chain reaction in natural uranium, Dunning would investigate the fission properties of uranium 235. Dean George Pegram added his approval and soon afterward his collaboration and moral guidance. It was Pegram who arranged for Fermi's meeting with the navy; and it was under Pegram's general leadership and with his sharing of the actual work that exploration of the chain reaction was pursued at Columbia. Fermi's early going in America was very smooth.

The Dunning-Anderson-Pegram-Fermi arrangement represents one of many examples of close collaboration. At every point where European and American scientists came together, there was the same high degree of acceptance. As the atomic project grew and many more Americans and Europeans joined it, co-operation became even more prominent. The foreign-born were not judged by their accents or odd habits or by the land they came from but by their scientific worth. They were respected and often given leading roles. The determination to defend America at all costs spurred the newcomers no less than the Americans, and the European-born may have come to this determination somewhat earlier than the native-born, driven by stronger personal emotions. The picture of their country under Nazi power in the event of a German victory was something the Americans could imagine only with difficulty. As a nation they had never suffered defeat or been invaded by an enemy; they had never lived under a totalitarian regime. The Europeans did not have to rack their brains to visualize the consequences of defeat; they were sure that if the dictators won the war the United States would become a Fascist-dominated country even if allowed to remain technically independent. And if America failed them, where would they go? It was not only gratitude to the country that had offered them asylum or pride in their new citizenship but also the fear of dictators that drove them to work to the limit of their physical and mental endurance.

Their new citizenship was slower in coming than they might have liked. The foreign-born individual must reside at least five years in the United States before he can be naturalized, and it happened often that in the waiting period new security regulations caused difficulties for European scientists and their American collaborators. Germans and Italians who were not yet naturalized were considered enemy aliens, and the new restrictions sometimes hampered their work. Fermi, for one, worked in New York City and lived across the Hudson river in New Jersey; after eight o'clock in the evening neither he nor his family could cross a state line, and every time he went on a trip he was obliged to secure a permit from the state attorney. He had to travel a great deal in those first months after Pearl Harbor, for as a consequence of the stepped-up pace of the uranium project all work on the chain reaction was being moved to Chicago. For six months, until all experiments could be wound up in New York and all men and equipment shipped to Chicago, Fermi shuttled between the two cities. He traveled for war work but because of security regulations he could not reveal this fact to the Justice Department. On the Pacific Coast, Germans and Italians, as well as Japanese had to observe an early curfew. (In October, 1942, President Roosevelt, running for reelection, exempted the Italians from the status of enemy aliens.)

Bethe had relatives in Germany and could not be cleared for secret work until he became a citizen in 1941. Before that time he was forced to work on his own. From the *Encyclopaedia Britannica* he gathered information on the properties of the armor plate that reinforces the hulls and decks of war vessels, and to what he learned he applied theories concerning elasticity and shock waves. The paper he then wrote was considered so useful to the navy that it was classified Secret, but for lack of clearance Bethe could not see it in its final form.

These were only episodes. They reveal the probably unavoidable complications arising when security restrictions are imposed on any field of endeavor, no matter how urgent. In general, however, the display of confidence was much more striking than the occasional suspicion or harassment.

While a symbiosis developed between American and foreign-born scientists, another exceptional collaboration came slowly into being: the collaboration between science and the world of industry and technology. At an early stage, the search for materials needed by the project reached as far as mines in the Belgian Congo, the United States, and Canada and involved the co-operation of American industry. The search was undertaken at what may have seemed the whim of Fermi and Szilard: they wanted huge amounts of uranium and graphite, and they wanted them of an inconceivable purity. It was not a whim. Fermi and Szilard had studied various ways of achieving a chain reaction and came to the conclusion that the most promising was to build a pile of graphite and uranium. Uranium at that time had only one practical application, as a coloring agent for ceramics. Scientists knew little about it; its properties had not been exhaustively studied; and not even its melting point had been determined. Graphite was used more extensively, as lead for pencils and as insulating material, but nobody had ever attempted to purify it to the degree demanded by the specifications of Fermi and Szilard. To obtain enough materials of a sufficient degree of purity became one of the major concerns of atomic workers and a limiting factor on the pace of their progress. Procurement developed into one of the biggest operations of the uranium project. That the operation was successful and eventually filled all needs is due to the goodwill and dedication of the industries involved. The bulk of industrial contribution, however, was to come a little later.

AFTER PEARL HARBOR

These outstanding aspects of the project, confidence in the foreign-born, symbiosis between American and European scientists, and collaboration between science and industry were greatly heightened after Pearl Harbor, which followed by one day the government decision to make an all-out effort to produce atomic energy. Once America was at war, scientists, putting aside earlier scruples, interrupted their current pursuits, abandoned the classrooms, and hastened to one of the laboratories doing war work. Because the uranium project was being enormously expanded at that very moment, the largest number flocked to it. In fact, many flocked to Chicago, where all work on the chain reaction was being moved. To many, this work was the most alluring aspect of the atomic project, the part that was still within the field of fundamental scientific research, while other parts were already on the borderline of technology. It held all the excitement and appeal of a voyage of discovery to a land of great hazard and enormous promise. The vision of the land was clear, but the path to it was known only in general, and travelers would have to feel their way step by step, basing the choice of each step on what they found just before.

For the work on the chain reaction a new project was established at the University of Chicago, the Metallurgical Laboratory. Here the numerical proportion of European-born to natives fell to a low. Yet the Europeans were unabashed. For security reasons, none of them could be appointed director of the lab, so the choice fell on an American Nobel Prize winner, physicist Arthur H. Compton, who was a member of the Chicago faculty. But Fermi remained the leader of the work to construct the pile, and he, Szilard, and Wigner formed an exceptional team: Szilard threw out ideas; with his practical intuition Fermi turned them into rough theories that served immediately to guide experiments; and Wigner, more patient and rigorous, refined them into mathematically cogent theories that would stand the test of time. At the peak of activity, hundreds of Americans worked with them or on parallel phases of the chain reaction program.

It was under Fermi's guidance that on December 2, 1942, the atomic pile under the stands of Stagg Field at the University of Chicago released controlled atomic energy for the first time in history. Wigner's role that day, the role of which he was most proud, was as a provider of Chianti for the toast. It was by great foresight, he said much later, that he had bought the famous bottle before Italian wines disappeared from American stores.

Wigner's primary energy was directed at designing large atomic piles of industrial scale, a huge extrapolation from Fermi's rudimentary pile. This jump was necessary. The Chicago pile was only an experiment proving that a chain reaction was feasible and atomic power would be available for peace-ful pursuits in the future. But at the end of 1942, America, deeply involved in war, wanted weapons. And there was still the fear that Germany might be ahead of the United States in atomic research. A small, experimental pile was not enough. The possible role of a large atomic pile was implied in the results of investigations conducted at Berkeley by the group that included Emilio Segrè. In early 1941 the group was trying to discover plutonium, whose formation in uranium 238 had been postulated theoretically. Soon not only was this new element discovered but small amounts were separated and its properties studied. The Berkeley scientists concluded that plutonium would be excellent material for bombs if produced in sufficient amounts and that the best way to produce it was in large atomic piles, if it were proved that the piles would work.

The successful operation of the atomic pile at Chicago was to remove some of the "ifs" in the uranium project, and before this success, while the uncertainties were still overwhelming, all eyes were turned in expectation on Chicago as on a crucial test. It seemed impossible to make predictions and decisions before the performance of the pile was known, despite several attempts elsewhere. One attempt was made at Berkeley, where in the sum-mer of 1942 Robert Oppenheimer gathered a group of theorists to study the physics of a bomb. They were men of high caliber, including the Euro-peans Hans Bethe, Edward Teller, and Felix Bloch. Their goal was to make a realistic estimate of the amount of fissionable material needed for a bomb, although experimental data on which to base their studies were scarce. Re-search on plutonium and uranium 235 was still done on infinitesimal amounts, and the investigation of the modality of fission was a slow and painstaking process.

The summer and fall of 1942 were indeed times of great uncertainty. It is therefore the more astounding that in those months the decision to begin production should be taken, in an act of immense faith in science and scientists.

ARMY, INDUSTRY, AND EUROPEAN SCIENTISTS

In the summer of 1942, the Corps of Engineers began to take over the con-trol of the uranium project and formed a special unit for this purpose, which it named the Manhattan Engineer District. In the following September General Leslie Groves was placed in charge. Even before his appointment, the army displayed an uncommon faith in "enemy-alien" scientists, as when it placed the Nobel laureate chemist James Franck in a leading position.

Franck, whose courageous stand against Hitler's racial discrimination was known to the scientific world, for many years had been on the faculty of the University of Chicago. He was a man of such patent sincerity, of such balanced judgment, that no one who knew him could have any doubt of his devotion to America. But he was not known to the army, and Arthur Compton expected a rebuttal when he suggested Franck for the post of head of the chemistry division at the Metallurgical Laboratory. But the army accepted Franck on the word of men who were acquainted with him, without going through the lengthy procedure of a regular clearance.

General Groves' faith was even more remarkable. He paid his first visit to the Metallurgical Laboratory on October 5, 1942, and met with about fifteen of Compton's senior men. "Among them" he wrote in his book *Now It Can Be Told*, "were two other Nobel Prize winners [in addition to Arthur Compton], Enrico Fermi and James Franck, together with the brilliant Hungarian physicists Eugene Wigner and Leo Szilard, and [American-born] Dr. Norman Hilberry, Compton's assistant." It is significant that Groves does not mention other men at the meeting by name. Perhaps the keen sense of rank ruling the army made him attribute undue importance to the Nobel prizes. Perhaps he felt as if he had found three generals in an outfit so small that at the time it could be housed in one university building. At the end of the meeting he was left with a very high opinion of the scientific attainments of the Chicago group. "It was obvious that it would not need major strengthening in any scientific area, and that the existing organization was more than adequate as a basis for any build up. . . ." There is no evidence that General Groves ever questioned the advisability of retaining the "enemy aliens" already on the project or of hiring others. His confidence was to prove entirely justified; there was to be one German-born atomic spy in the project, Klaus Fuchs, but he was a member of the British mission to the American project, not an immigrant or resident in the United States.

General Groves' faith in the scientists, both native and foreign-born, must have been greater than he himself realized. In a British documentary on the atomic bomb, more than twenty years after he was appointed to head the Manhattan District, he stated that until the bomb was tested he never estimated the chances of success at more than 60 per cent. But he acted always as if he had complete confidence in the outcome. The facts speak for themselves: when he took over the project, Fermi, Szilard, Wigner, and their co-workers in Chicago were still waiting for the material with which to build the atomic pile and had not proved that a chain reaction was feasible. If the pile worked, large atomic piles would eventually produce plutonium in quantity, but so far plutonium was being made with the cyclotron in Berkeley in only extremely small amounts. Several methods for the industrial separation of uranium 235 from uranium 238 were under study, but none seemed entirely reliable, and the minute samples of uranium 235 so far produced were only of scientific value. To top these uncertainties, scientists on the project said that their evaluations of the amount of fissionable material needed for a bomb were accurate only within a factor of ten. General Groves writes: "This meant, for example, that if they estimated that we would need one hundred pounds of plutonium for a bomb, the correct amount could be anywhere from ten to one thousand pounds."

This was the situation when General Groves took over, and yet he went ahead at once with plans for industrial production of both uranium 235 and plutonium. The meeting with the Chicago scientists had impressed him.

Many industries had already been brought into the picture before the summer of 1942. They had been engaged mainly in mining, treating and refining uranium, and in refining graphite. Once Groves began putting his plans into effect, their number multiplied.

In the fall of 1942 another industry was needed for the construction of production piles, and the choice fell on I. I. Du Pont de Nemours. Their eventual acceptance of the task, after much hesitation, is a good example of the trust of industry in science.

Du Pont's first reaction after being approached and briefed in late October and early November was that "the entire project seemed beyond human capability," according to Groves. In late November a group of men from Du Pont was appointed to a review committee and taken to meet scientists at Berkeley and Chicago. Among those with whom they spoke was Arthur Compton, who in answering their fire of questions quoted figures calculated by Fermi, and perhaps opinions of Wigner and Szilard. As Compton himself wrote in his book *Atomic Quest*, the Du Pont men "were concerned also about the trustworthiness of recommendations made by recently arrived émigrés." Compton did not say directly that Fermi was all right — perhaps because for a long time he himself had been uncertain whether to trust Fermi — but he replied that he had gone through Fermi's calculations independently and found the same results.

Still the Du Pont company demurred. What may have decided them in the end was to see the physicists at work. On December 2, at Compton's invitation, C. H. Greenewalt of Du Pont witnessed Fermi's pile experiment and the first controlled release of atomic energy. Greenewalt, who years later was to become president of Du Pont, was duly impressed by Fermi's competence and the Chicago scientists' performance as a team. Still many questions remained. Although the feasibility of a chain reaction was proved, it did not advance engineering knowledge on how to build production piles; nor could anyone say for sure whether it would be possible to make a bomb even if plutonium were available in quantity. But the scientists were optimistic, and the Du Pont men had come to trust the judgment of scientists, even of the foreign-born and the accuracy of their predictions. The Du Pont Company agreed to construct the piles at Hanford at no profit, and the contract with the government established the fixed fee at one dollar. The irony is that at the end of the war Du Pont was paid its dollar, but since the time mentioned in the contract had not run out, the company was subsequently asked to return a third of its dollar.

PRODUCTION

The year 1943 saw the beginning of the last stage in the atomic program, production. This is the stage that Europe could not have matched — jumping directly from laboratory experiments to immense industrial plants, even before the small experiments were complete; the decision to try different approaches and costly large-scale processes in order to see which would work best; and the sudden multiplication of scientists, engineers, technicians, and business and military men needed to turn atomic research into a huge crash program. European nations did not have the money, the broad vision, or the faith that were required, nor did they have the concentration of brain power. Its best brains had emigrated. It is true that Europe had started with an advantage: European science lived and developed within the framework of government, while in the United States of 1939 science and government hardly knew how to speak to each other. It is a typically American achievement that in a short time science and government had established excellent means of communicating and full understanding through men of wisdom who respected one another.

To achieve production, not only did General Groves multiply the number of industries involved, but he also ordered the construction of three atomic cities. The production piles would be built at Hanford, Washington; the separation of uranium 235 from uranium 238 would be the main role of Oak Ridge, Tennessee; and to Los Alamos, New Mexico, would fall the responsibility to construct the bomb. The spring and summer of 1943 saw the exodus of scientists from city laboratories and of industrial personnel from plants all over the country to these three secret sites.

The Los Alamos assignment was the most critical, the one that would certainly require a great deal of brain power and close collaboration with all other parts of the project and with the army. For the post of director of research at Los Alamos General Groves chose Robert Oppenheimer. Oppie, who was to prove one of the greatest assets of the Manhattan project, was of European background and taste and had spent several years in Europe where he met and learned to appreciate many of the future immigrant scientists. Perhaps because of this, or for other reasons, of the three secret sites Los Alamos was the one with the greatest concentration of European talent.

Szilard stayed in Chicago. Wigner traveled between Chicago and Oak Ridge. Until the summer of 1944, Fermi kept his residence in Chicago and made trips to Hanford, Los Alamos, and Oak Ridge to advise and assist in all phases of research; he then joined the Los Alamos staff as associate director of research and division leader. Von Neumann, being a versatile mathematician and physicist, was busy at several other projects and gave Los Alamos only part of his time. To Felix Bloch, life on the Los Alamos mesa, under strict army rule, was hard to take and soon he left to join the radio research laboratory at Harvard. But Hans Staub, Emilio Segrè, Hans Bethe, Bruno Rossi, Edward Teller, Victor Weisskopf, and Stan Ulam stayed in Los Alamos from the beginning until well after the end of the war. Niels Bohr, who was never an immigrant or a resident in the United States, paid frequent visits to Los Alamos, bestowing advice and inspiration and greatly contributing to the prestige of the group. In 1944 the European contingent was enlarged considerably by the arrival of the British mission of which Bohr was a member. It included, besides a few true British specimens, men from Switzerland, Poland, Germany, and Denmark and the Russian wife of one scientist (but the work of their mission is not considered in this account).

It looked and sounded as if the Europeans were overflowing the mesa, and bad English was the prevalent language. In reality Americans were in the great majority but not as colorful or conspicuous. General Groves must have had the Europeans in mind when he is said to have remarked, "At great expense we have collected here the greatest collection of crackpots ever seen." The more equanimous Henry Smyth certainly included the whole scientific community of Los Alamos, American as well as European, when in his famous report he mentioned the "extraordinary galaxy of scientific stars gathered on this New Mexican mesa." In *The New World, 1939–1946,* the official history of the atomic project, there is a page of four photographs with the caption "Four Los Alamos Scientists": they are Hans Bethe, Enrico Fermi, John Von Neumann, and George Kistiakowsky, the Russian-born chemist who came to this country in the middle twenties, made explosives his special field, and in recent years was a scientific adviser to the government. It is clear that the photographs were not chosen at random but were meant to stress the contribution of the European-born.

When the Los Alamos laboratory was reorganized for the last time during the war, only three of its seven divisions were placed in charge of American-born scientists. Another was under the joint leadership of an American chemist and the British metallurgist Cyril Smith. The remaining three were under Bethe, Fermi, and Kistiakowsky. Other Europeans were group leaders or held sensitive positions.

Of the two divisions in the hands of European physicists of the cultural migration Bethe's was the first established and the one of broadest scope. There was no previous technical experience of atomic bombs, and the word "bomb" was the closest link between atomic and conventional weapons. All other characteristics of atomic bombs, size, materials used, and means of detonation, were entirely different from the conventional and in many respects unknown. There was no possibility of gaining information from a small-scale explosion, because unless a mass of fissionable material is of critical size, namely about as large as a bomb, it does not explode at all. Bethe's division had to extrapolate from the results of experiments on infinitesimal amounts of materials and make predictions for an actual bomb. Victor Weisskopf was a group leader in this division.

Fermi's division, which was set up in the early fall of 1944 when he went to live at Los Alamos, was called the Advanced Development Division. In fact it was a problem-solving outfit. Other groups passed on to it both difficult problems that did not fit into their work and "problem children" they could not handle — men who under the pressures of work and the stress of life under army rule had developed personality difficulties. One of these was Edward Teller. His non-conformist mind responded more to the challenge of what seemed impossible than to the demands of what was on the way to solution, more to the call of the hydrogen bomb than to the problems of the atomic bomb. Under Fermi, who was also attracted by the scientific unknown, Teller could explore at will the new field of thermonuclear physics. But this is part of a story that comes later.

One serious impasse at Los Alamos in 1944 was how to spark the explosion of a plutonium bomb. Studies of samples of plutonium and theoretical considerations indicated that the gun method — the firing at a mass of fissionable material — would work well in the uranium bomb but not in the plutonium bomb. Unless another method was found, plutonium could not be used as material for weapons. The only hope was to achieve implosion, the bursting inward of some explosive substance enveloping the bomb, but that hope was very tenuous in late 1943. The "father of implosion" was the American Seth Neddermeyer who in 1943 proposed the implosion method to detonate plutonium bombs. In February, 1944, Kistiakowsky was persuaded to join the Los Alamos staff for the specific purpose of pushing implosion. The leader of the experimental division, Robert Bacher, lent him four group leaders, among them the Italian-born Bruno Rossi, who had been a professor of physics at the University of Padua until the Fascist laws had forced him to leave. In Los Alamos Rossi was to obtain the first encouraging results on implosion. But the spiritual godfather of the implosion program, the man without whom the whole program might have been abandoned, was, of course, a Hungarian. In his visits to Los Alamos, John Von Neumann pushed the idea of implosion, suggested the use of explosive lenses (to direct explosion waves toward the center of the bomb material), helped with the design and calculations of these lenses, and at all times infused confidence in the solution of the problem. His friend and countryman Edward Teller gave him a hand by predicting some advantages of the implosion method. The actual working out of the practical problems, the day-by-day tests and approximations to reach the final solution, remained the task of Kistiakowsky and his division.

During production, European scientists occupied a very small space in what has been called General Groves' sprawling empire and were but a tiny fraction of its population. Yet they were a most influential minority. It is difficult to conceive of the atomic project without them, without the correlation between theory and experiment that the early comers had promoted, or the stubbornness that Szilard, Wigner, and Fermi displayed in the first few years after the discovery of fission, when they stuck to research that others deemed unpromising, without their dedication and hard work, their intellectual leadership and confidence in the ultimate outcome of the project and its power to end the war. On the other hand, it is even more difficult to imagine a group of foreign-born scientists attaining the same degree of success in isolation, outside the great compound of American industry, without the leadership of men like Compton and Oppenheimer and without the collaboration of hundreds of American scientists, the young as well as the mature, the obscure as well as the prominent.

A very significant comment came from a German scientist, one of several captured by the Alsos mission at the end of the war. For purposes of interrogation, the group was flown to Farm Hall in England, which had been thoroughly prepared for their arrival with a number of hidden microphones. (The Germans had considered this possibility and discarded it. Werner Heisenberg said: "Microphones installed? . . . I don't think they know the real Gestapo methods; they are a bit old fashioned in that respect.") Among opinions secretly recorded about the atomic bomb, there is one by Dr. H. Korsching: "That shows at any rate that the Americans are capable of real co-operation on a tremendous scale. That would have been impossible in Germany. Each one said that the other was unimportant . . ."

A SECOND ROUND OF POLITICAL ACTIVITIES

Not long before the end of the war, foreign-born scientists became thoroughly involved in a second round of political activities. In this more than in the first they shared the initiative, planning and acting with other American scientists and non-scientists, extending their field of operations over a much wider geographical range. (The doings of this time, and the consequent explosive emergence of the "movement of atomic scientists" immediately after Hiroshima are described in *A Peril and A Hope* by Alice Kimball Smith.)

Concern about the use of the bomb and its consequences preceded by many months the certainty that a bomb would be achieved. One of the first to give a great deal of thought to the implications of atomic energy and to express his ideas persistently was Niels Bohr. It is probable that his ideas traveled far and influenced other scientists, though some of them were unaware that they were being influenced. Bohr did more than hold discussions with fellow scientists; in the spring of 1944 he sought and obtained an interview with Churchill, and the following July he spent over an hour with President Roosevelt. While he was not able to talk at length with Churchill, his conversation with Roosevelt was more satisfactory; he presented to the President his views on the need for international control of atomic energy and the need to inform the Russians of our atomic program.

By the end of 1944 a few scientists began to formulate their thinking in reports of various kinds. Anxiety and agitation increased in early 1945 when it became evident that thoughtful planning was urgent: on the one hand, there was little doubt by then that we would build the bomb: on the other, in the face of crumbling German resistance, it became increasingly unlikely that the Germans would use atomic weapons against our country. In fact, in mid-April 1945, the American mission Alsos was able to ascertain that German scientists had long since given up work on the production of atomic energy.

Alsos was a scientific intelligence unit under General Groves, and its name is the Greek word for grove. Like many other intelligence groups, Alsos made use of men born and raised in Europe. Its scientific chief for the operations in France and Germany was the Dutch-born physicist Sam Goudsmit, who came to America in 1927 to join the faculty of the University of Michigan and was working on radar at the Radiation Laboratory when he was recruited for Alsos. Another member was the astronomer Gerard Kuiper, also a native of Holland, who immigrated to the United States in 1933 and before and after the war spent many years at the University of Chicago.

From France, where it had set up headquarters, Alsos moved into Germany in the wake of the Allied advance. Goudsmit, who knew personally many German physicists, helped to locate and question them. Only then, about three weeks before the surrender of Germany, did we learn that our fears of German atomic weapons had been unfounded. In reality, since Alsos was a secret mission and the army was extremely compartmentalized, very few persons in the United States could have known of Alsos and its outcome. I doubt very much that knowledge of its findings could be a motive for the atomic scientists' political action. But the trend of war events spurred them on. In the early months of 1945, Hanford and Oak Ridge were under ever-increasing pressure to produce materials, and Los Alamos was preparing for the final test at an accelerated pace. At the Metallurgical Laboratory, after the successful experiment of the atomic pile, the demands of work had somewhat eased, and there more time and deeper thought were devoted to atomic policies than anywhere else, although opinions and suggestions came from many universities and laboratories.

There were three main considerations. We had undertaken the development of atomic weapons because we were afraid that Germany would make them before we did, but now Germany was on the point of surrender and the war against Japan was likely to last a long time. Should we, then, use atomic bombs against Japan? Whether we used them or not, how should we deal with atomic energy in peacetime both at national and international levels? Men in government did not seem sufficiently informed about the implications of atomic energy; why were they not taking full advantage of scientists who knew the facts, why were the scientists cut off from the shaping of atomic policy?

In the discussion of these questions and formulation of replies to them, Leo Szilard, James Franck, and Eugene Rabinowitch emerged as leaders. Leo Szilard, a good prophet but an individualist and according to his friends a lover of intrigue, started alone, battling along devious paths, enlisting the help of various persons. In 1939 he had been worried because he felt that the United States government was not informed of the military potentialities of atomic energy. Now that these potentialities were almost a reality, he was eager to give the government the full benefit of his advice. His progress was hampered by President Roosevelt's death, on April 12, and the fact that Roosevelt's successor, President Truman, had been kept completely in the dark about the atomic project. Eventually Szilard talked with James Byrnes, a few days before Byrnes became Secretary of State, but the meeting was not a success.

Meanwhile, Arthur Compton was conducting opinion polls and organizing study committees. The most active was the Committee on Political and Social Implications of Atomic Energy, headed by James Franck. When Arthur Compton asked Franck to join the Metallurgical Laboratory in 1942, Franck put as a condition that if and when use of the bomb was considered he would be allowed to present his views to the policy makers. Much more sedate than Szilard, and more willing to weigh different opinions, Franck discussed matters with many scientists at the lab, then drew up a memorandum with the help of Eugene Rabinowitch. Rabinowitch had already tried his hand at expressing atomic scientists' opinions in November, 1944, when he helped to draft a document known as the Jeffries report, entitled "Prospectus on Nucleonics." (The committee in charge of preparing the report consisted of six members besides the chairman, Zay Jeffries. James Franck and Enrico Fermi were members; Rabinowitch was not.) Now Franck and Rabinowitch prepared a report advising the government not to use the atomic bomb against Japan without warning, on the grounds that such an action would present us in a poor light to the world, precipitate an armaments race, and prejudice international control of atomic energy. The so-called Franck report was signed by seven scientists, three of whom were Europeans: Franck, Rabinowitch, and Szilard.

It is difficult to say whether these political endeavors had any immediate impact on the government. Bohr's interviews with Churchill and Roosevelt failed to bring the decisive results he had hoped for. Some of the many reports sent to Washington were shelved before they reached the decision-makers, and it is not known who read the others or how much attention they received. Yet the scientists' activities in the last part of the war were important on two grounds: first, their detailed planning helped smooth the transition from the wartime organization of atomic work to a vast program of peacetime research and industrial participation. (Fermi and Szilard were among the first to evaluate and stress the industrial value of atomic energy.) Second, their reports, including the memorandum that Bohr prepared for his talk with Roosevelt, constitute the first formulation of ideas to be advocated, after the war, by those who adhered to the movement of atomic scientists. Besides,

201

the call for free exchange of information with other nations, which was reiterated in most memoranda, has been heeded with excellent results, and the prediction that without international control we would be launched into an armaments race has come true to a degree that was unforeseeable in 1945.

Although many persons were involved in the early thinking and formulation of ideas, the leading roles assumed by the European-born, their clear vision and labor, have been of undoubted importance.

THE DECISION TO USE THE BOMB

On the need for control of atomic energy after the end of the war all scientists agreed, but on use of the bomb in wartime there was disagreement. Many saw in the new weapon our only chance to end the war and stop the enormous loss of lives on both sides. The American people were tired. The terrible strain of the long, depressing years of Nazi advance in Europe and Allied losses in the Pacific were still telling, although the fortunes of war had changed; the cruel fight with Japan gave no signs of relenting, and there was the expectation of a landing on the Japanese islands, which would mean an enormous multiplication of losses and casualties.

In the spring of 1945 the atomic bomb was almost ready. It had not been tested, but the strategists were preparing to decide how best to use it to terminate the war. Early in May, four scientists were appointed to form a scientific panel to assist the newly created Interim Committee of the War Department of which Secretary of War Henry L. Stimson was the chairman. Three of the four were American-born: Arthur Compton, Robert Oppenheimer, and Ernest Lawrence. One member was Italian-born: Enrico Fermi. His appointment to the panel seems to me a great act of faith on the part of the government toward one of the many to whom it had given asylum. True, Fermi was one of the best-informed men on atomic energy and his knowledge was basic, deriving from over ten years of research, more than half before the creation of the American project. True, no one could have taken his knowledge or insight away from him. Still, it was a different matter to give him a chance to have his say, though likely not a strong say, in one of the most crucial decisions our country ever had to make.

The scientific panel was asked to examine a specific proposal in the Franck report: that the bomb be used in a technical demonstration on wasteland or a desert island, before representatives of the United Nations. The panel debated possible ways of preparing such a demonstration but felt obliged to discard them all. Not only did they consider the possibility that the bomb might "fizzle," produce a weak explosion or prove altogether a dud, but they also had doubts that a demonstration on uninhabited land would produce signs of destruction sufficiently dramatic to shock the Japanese nation into surrender. (The Trinity test in the desert at Alamogordo one month later confirmed this opinion: not even the scientists who witnessed the test were able to anticipate the tragedy of Hiroshima.)

The panel's reluctant conclusion: ". . . we can propose no technical demonstration likely to end the war; we can see no acceptable alternative to direct military use."

AFTER THE WAR

As scientists returned to the universities and other institutions of learning, the concentration of European talent at project sites scattered over our vast land. European-born and native Americans mixed even more thoroughly than they had before, and the end-product of their labors became even less separable. Another factor contributed to a greater intermixing: when atomic energy ceased to be the secret property of the Manhattan District under the guardianship of a few strategists, atomic scientists were propelled outside the world of science. They rubbed elbows with all sorts of men, politicians, legislators, statesmen, social scientists, and members of other enlightened groups. In this maze of relationships, actions, and reactions, the individual paths are not clearly seen, and I shall not try to follow them. Instead, I shall indicate some fields in which the European-born were conspicuous.

The main field was of course science itself, and scientific achievement continued to be very great: five nuclear scientists who came here with the migration added prestige to American science by receiving the Nobel Prize: Felix Bloch in 1952, Emilo Segrè in 1959, Maria Mayer and Eugene Wigner in 1963, and Hans Bethe in 1967. The feats of four of them were related in this account, and the other, who was mentioned only in passing, needs an introduction, especially since she is a type of emigré not considered so far, an intellectual woman whose reason for emigrating was marriage. Maria Goeppert was working for her doctoral degree in physics in her native Göttingen when Joseph Mayer arrived from California to spend a post-doctoral year and became a boarder in her home. When I met them in Ann

Arbor in the summer of 1930, the Mayers had been married about six months. She was blonde and slender and looked decidedly delicate. But in the following years she managed to raise a family, run a household, and keep up with physics. After Pearl Harbor both husband and wife did their share of war work, but in different fields, and only Maria, associated with the Manhattan Project, spent some time in Los Alamos. While reunited for a vacation on Nantucket Island, Joe and Maria heard the news of Hiroshima. He was completely surprised but she was not, and her knowledge must have added to his surprise. After the war, in Chicago, she worked on a cosmological theory with Edward Teller and through a painstaking examination of data and calculations, and with the help of a chance remark of Fermi's, arrived at the discoveries concerning the shell structure of atomic nuclei which earned her a share of the Nobel Prize.

Through the years since it was first awarded in 1901, the Nobel Prize has acquired such an aura in the public eye that no other prize competes with it. Nonetheless, it is pertinent to mention here a distinguished award established by the Atomic Energy Act of 1954 for recognition of achievements in the development of atomic energy. Its first recipient was Enrico Fermi, and after his death the Atomic Energy Commission decided that it should bear his name. Up to 1963, that is, as long as the policy was to recognize scientific achievement only (excluding contributions to engineering and technical management), eight men received the Enrico Fermi Award and five were European-born: Fermi, John Von Neumann, Eugene Wigner, Hans Bethe, and Edward Teller. (The three American-born were Ernest Lawrence, Glenn Seaborg, and Robert Oppenheimer.)

In the socio-political field, European-born atomic scientists took as great a lead as their American-born counterparts. Two factors made the ferment of atomic scientists erupt into the open immediately after Hiroshima and Nagasaki: the moral impact of the destruction caused by the atomic bomb and the partial lifting of wartime secrecy. At sites of the Manhattan Project and other places, scientists immediately formed local organizations to discuss solutions to the global problems created by the release of atomic energy and explore ways to persuade the men in power to adopt these solutions. Soon the local groups merged into the Federation of Atomic Scientists, which later broadened its scope and became the Federation of American Scientists.

The activities of the local groups and those of the federation are collectively known as the "movement of atomic scientists." Its long-range consequence was to shape public thinking to a remarkable degree by presenting the new concepts of the atomic age, which are now an integral part of our culture. Among its short-range achievements was its victorious battle against the May-Johnson bill, which might have placed control of atomic energy in military hands and made insufficient provisions for the freedom of science and the exchange of scientific information with other countries.

Many foreign-born scientists were prominent participants in the movement from its very beginnings. At the Metallurgical Laboratory, Rabinowitch and Szilard had prominent parts in the founding of the Atomic Scientists of Chicago and contributed to its development. In Los Alamos, before the exodus of scientists returning to the universities, Bethe, Weisskopf, Teller, and George Placzek were very active in the Association of Los Alamos Scientists. Other European-born scientists co-operated in efforts to inform the public.

Geographically dispersed and protean as it was, the movement of atomic scientists soon had a central organ and a lasting record of its activities, the *Bulletin of the Atomic Scientists*. It was founded in 1945 by Eugene Rabinowitch and Hyman Goldsmith (killed in a tragic accident in 1949) and sponsored by a group of scientists among whom were the foreign-born Albert Einstein, James Franck, Hans Bethe, Leo Szilard, Victor Weisskopf, Sam Goudsmit, Edward Teller, and several American-born. Since its first issue, the *Bulletin* has provided a vehicle for authoritative presentation of atomic issues and a forum for enlightened discussion. Scientists from all parts of the world have contributed articles, and newspapermen everywhere have drawn upon it as a most reliable source of scientific-political information. Close friends of the *Bulletin* know that Eugene Rabinowitch has been its spirit and driving force since its start. Somehow, achieving the impossible, he was able to combine his duties as professor of botany at the University of Illinois in Urbana (until his retirement) and the demanding tasks of editor of the *Bulletin*. He read every article to be published and wrote editorials for most issues. Rabinowitch, who was born in Russia, educated in Germany, and lived in England for several years before coming to the United States, has a visionary's conception of the international role of science: the language of science is truly international in his opinion, and once people come to understand and speak it, difficulties can be solved and differences settled. The *Bulletin* assumes the task of training the American public and politicians in the use of this language. Although his dream has not come true and science has helped to solve only a few international conflicts, Rabinowitch exerts his intellectual influence over a wide horizon and to him goes a good part of the credit for the educational accomplishments of the *Bulletin*.

THE HYDROGEN BOMB

Another area in which European-born atomic scientists have been influential is the development of thermonuclear weapons. Interest in thermonuclear reactions antedated the idea of using fission to produce atomic energy; in the late thirties speculation remained an intellectual game played by theoretical physicists (mainly Bethe, Gamow, Teller, and the American Charles Critchfield). These men did not expect to be able to produce on earth the great concentrations of energy and heat found in the interior of stars without which light nuclei cannot fuse. Yet the challenge of the problem stimulated their imaginative minds. The discovery of fission diverted their attention and channeled their energies into the war effort. By early 1942 fission had progressed to the point where the achievement of an atomic explosion was a definite possibility. At that time Teller was working with Fermi on fission problems at Columbia, and they were in the habit of discussing scientific matters over lunch. One day Fermi posed a question: once an atomic bomb was developed, could the explosion be used to initiate something similar to the reactions in the sun? The suggestion intrigued Teller and soon it became his central preoccupation. Wherever he happened to be, at the Metallurgical Lab, in Berkeley, or in Los Alamos, he engaged in discussions with other scientists. Out of what he called "conversational guesses" and "inspired guesses," the concept of the thermonuclear bomb began to take shape. Teller worked on it in Los Alamos during the war, and after the war he considered how the thermonuclear program could be supported and pushed. But, "Hiroshima," as he himself wrote, "filled many scientists with a moral repugnance for weapon work." Fermi and Bethe, who had contributed to the thermonuclear effort, and Oppenheimer, who had urged it, were among those who left Los Alamos, preferring not to work on arms in peacetime. Only a small group pursued thermonuclear research.

In September, 1949, the news that Russia had achieved and exploded an atomic bomb caused a re-appraisal of thermonuclear possibilities. Scientists were divided. Some were in favor of a crash program — Teller and John Von Neumann were its exponents; others were firmly against it, among them Oppenheimer; and others were uncertain. The Atomic Energy Commission sought the opinion of its General Advisory Committee, which was then chaired by Oppenheimer. It convened in October, 1949, and unanimously recommended that the United States not take the initiative in precipitating the development of hydrogen bombs, but it offered two reports. The majority report explained the committee's recommendations on practical and political considerations, the minority report on ethical reasons; the minority report began with the sentences: "The fact that no limits exist to the destructiveness of this weapon makes its very existence and the knowledge of its construction a danger to humanity as a whole. It is necessarily an evil thing considered in any light." It was signed by I. I. Rabi and Enrico Fermi.

The controversy about the thermonuclear program was then secret. It became known in part through the publication of the hearings before the Personnel Security Board in the Oppenheimer case. Since Oppenheimer's opposition to the hydrogen bomb program was one of the reasons for investigation, this issue was discussed at length. In sampling scientific opinion expressed at the hearings, I shall draw only from the testimony of foreign-born scientists. Von Neumann, whose testimony is considered one of the most impartial and significant, placed the issue in the proper light. "I was in favor of a very accelerated program," he said. "Like everybody else I would have been very happy if everybody had agreed with me. However it was evidently a matter of great importance. It was evidently a matter which would have consequences for the rest of our lives and beyond. So there was a very animated controversy about it. It lasted for months. That it lasted for months was not particularly surprising to my mind. I think it was perfectly normal that emotions should run rather high."

Fermi referred to the minority report of the General Advisory Committee, which he had signed, and said: "My opinion at that time was that one should try to outlaw the thing before it was born. I sort of had the view at that time that perhaps it would be easier to outlaw by some kind of international agreement something that did not exist. My opinion was that one should try to do that, and failing that, one should with considerable regret go ahead."

Bethe described his feeling in greater detail. In October, 1949, he recalled, Teller asked him to join full time the project to develop thermonuclear weapons. "I had very great internal conflicts what I should do," he said at the hearings. He was impressed by Teller's ideas, which seemed to make hydrogen bombs technically feasible. "On the other hand, it seemed to me that it was a very terrible undertaking. . . . It seemed to me that the development of thermonuclear weapons would not solve any of the difficulties that we found ourselves in, and yet I was not quite sure whether I should refuse. . . ." In the end he did refuse. "I was influenced in making up my mind after my complete indecision," he stated, "by two friends of mine, Dr. Weisskopf and Dr. Placzek. I had a very long conversation with Dr. Weisskopf [on] what a war with the hydrogen bombs would be. We both had to agree that after such a war even if we were to win it, the world would not be . . . like the world we want to preserve. We would lose the things we were fighting for. This was a very long conversation and a difficult one for both of us." Later Bethe had a conversation with both Weisskopf and Placzek on a drive from Princeton to New York. "Essentially the same things were confirmed once more. Then when I arrived in New York, I called up Dr. Teller and told him that I could not come to join his project." (Later when the Korean war broke out, Bethe changed his mind and did co-operate in the thermonuclear program.)

At the Oppenheimer hearings, Teller mentioned his "almost desperate interest in the undertaking" (the thermonuclear program), and his being "dreadfully disappointed about the contents of the majority and minority reports" of the committee, "which in my eyes did not differ a great deal. . . . Not only to me, but to very many others who said this to me spontaneously, the report meant this: As long as you people go ahead and make minor improvements (to atomic weapons) and work very hard and diligently at it, you are doing a fine job, but if you succeed in making a really great piece of progress, then you are doing something that is immoral." (In this testimony Teller pronounced words that many colleagues judged very unfair to Oppenheimer and that resulted in a deep and lasting rift in the scientific community. This result is a negative entry in the balance sheet of the cultural migration.)

But the ultimate decision on the thermonuclear program was taken away from the scientists, as had been the decision on the use of the atomic bomb in 1945. In January, 1950, only a few months after the negative report of the General Advisory Committee, President Truman by-passed its recommendations and gave the green light to a crash thermonuclear program. Four days earlier, in England, Klaus Fuchs had confessed that at Los Alamos he had passed information to Communist agents on the work at the laboratory, and Fuchs was well acquainted with all that was done there in wartime, including work on the hydrogen bomb.

The presidential directives did not end Teller's woes. Technical difficulties arose. Teller was pushing a design of his own invention for the hydrogen bomb, but several of his collaborators in Los Alamos doubted that it would work. A review of his design required complex mathematical computations, and information about it was fed to the fastest computer of the time, the Eniac in Aberdeen, Maryland. Simultaneously, Stan Ulam and his American colleague Cornelius Everett started the same calculations without computers, in a race between man and machine. When Ulam proved that Teller's design would not work — it would use so much tritium that its cost would be prohibitive — Teller would not believe him; men often make mistakes in abstruse mathematical operations. But then came confirmation from the Eniac at Aberdeen. Teller went through a brief period of depression, and meanwhile Ulam kept thinking about the problem of achieving a thermonuclear explosion. He came up with a new idea, which received Teller's approval. The paper that the two wrote jointly is the basis for the construction of present-day hydrogen bombs.

If in an emergency the human brain can beat a machine, in the long run the machine can do much more "thinking" at a much faster speed than a brain. The first modern computers, which can store and process fabulous amounts of data, were being completed at about the time the thermonuclear program was recuperating from its setback, and they were used frequently. The great jump from the old calculating machines to computers is due mostly to ideas conceived by John Von Neumann. His knowledge of thought processes and of the brain itself led him to plan a computer using as a model the human brain and substituting electronic tubes for brain cells.

Von Neumann proposed the construction of the electronic brain as a means of handling information to predict the weather. Availability of accurate weather predictions is an important factor in war operations requiring good weather, such as air-borne assaults and landings, and Von Neumann obtained funds for his future computers on this basis. The first two computers to be completed were the Johnniac, named after Von Neumann and built in Princeton, and the Maniac (mathematical and numerical integrator and calculator) of the Los Alamos Scientific Laboratory. The first big problem they solved was not in the field of weather forecasting but in that of thermonuclear weapons.

At the Oppenheimer hearings, Von Neumann himself colorfully described the role of the computers in the thermonuclear program. He said that during about two-thirds of the period in which the hydrogen bomb was developed the conditions were such that fast computers "were not generally available and that it was necessary to scrounge around to find a computer here and find a computer there which was running half the time and try to use it. . . . The last third of the development computers were freely available and industrially produced . . ." As for the Johnniac, Von Neumann said, "this computer came into operation in 1952, after which the first large program that was done on it, and which was quite large and took . . . half a year, was for the thermonuclear program. Previous to that I had spent a lot of time on calculations on other computers for the thermonuclear program."

Without Von Neumann and his computers the thermonuclear program would have progressed at a much slower pace than it did. (Later, when the Maniac was free of weightier tasks, Stan Ulam taught it to play chess.)

Once progress in the thermonuclear program was achieved, a new laboratory was created at Livermore, California, for the development of thermonuclear weapons. In 1952, Teller, who had worked hard for the establishment of such a laboratory, became its first director and held that position for over ten years. During this time he saw the realization of many of his ideas, the achievement and testing of hydrogen weapons, and the first explorations into the possibility of using thermonuclear explosions for constructive projects. In *The Legacy of Hiroshima*, he writes imaginatively of possible peaceful applications of thermonuclear power: the opening of harbors and canals; the uncovering of mineral and oil deposits; the modification of world geography, the irrigation of deserts, and action upon the weather.

IN THE GOVERNMENT'S SERVICE

As a director of the Livermore laboratory, Teller was in the service of the Atomic Energy Commission. Many other foreign-born atomic scientists served in official positions within the commission or on advisory boards and committees of other government branches.

The civilian Atomic Energy Commission was established in 1946. As heir to the wartime Manhattan Project, it sought the assistance and advice of those who had been leaders in that project and had given thought to the peacetime administration of atomic energy. Foreign-born talent had made substantial contributions in these areas and was therefore represented among those serving the commission. At various times Fermi, Teller, Von Neumann, and Wigner served for longer or briefer terms on the General Advisory Committee, the commission's most important advisory body. Teller and Wigner were also appointed to technical committees. Others contributed in different ways: many, for instance, spent periods of time in Los Alamos as consultants in various phases of its work.

Outside the Atomic Energy Commission, foreign-born scientists have held a wide range of official positions. Von Neumann, Bethe, and Teller served on the Scientific Advisory Board of the air force, members of which were also Kistiakowsky and the prominent aviation expert Theodore von Karman, who had greatly contributed to the improvement of American airplanes. Bethe served in other official capacities. Perhaps his major role was as member of the President's Science Advisory Commitee, when he became the principal scientific proponent for the cessation of atomic tests on an international scale. As a consequence, he participated in the conference of international experts in Geneva exploring the feasibility of a test ban and was later the principal scientific adviser in the political negotiations on the ban. He was also an adviser to the disarmament agency established in 1961. Another of Bethe's interesting assignments was as a member of a committee to evaluate Russian atomic tests and analyze debris, a committee which reported to both the Department of Defense and the Atomic Energy Commission. These and other foreign-born scientists served the government in other ways. Several were advisers or researchers in the National Air Space Administration — among them Bruno Rossi, who for some time was also a member of the President's science advisory board.

It was John Von Neumann who reached one of the two highest positions in government attained by intellectuals in the wave. (The other was attained by Eugene Fubini, as previously described.) In 1954, Von Neumann was appointed one of the five commissioners of the Atomic Energy Commission.

"The fact that he was a naturalized citizen," Admiral Strauss wrote in *Men and Decisions*, "caused some eyebrows to be raised in the Joint Congressional Committee, but he was confirmed and quickly gained the respect of the Congress." Not only was he the "most normal" of Hungarian scientists, in the opinion of his non-Hungarian friends, but he was also one of the very few men about whom I have not heard a single critical remark. It is astonishing that so much equanimity and so much intelligence could be concentrated in a man of no extraordinary appearance, short, with a round face and a round body. His qualities of genius include a prodigious mental speed and an enormous depth and adaptability of thought. His early fame was due to purely mathematical achievements, but over the years his mathematical insight has affected many fields, from games and strategy to automation and operations research.

Besides contributing to the development of atomic and thermonuclear energy and computers, he exerted a great influence in the program for the development of Intercontinental Ballistic Missiles. "The United States immediately after World War II," Teller wrote, "made a start on rocket projects. The program remained modest indeed until we proved the capabilities of the hydrogen bomb. Then such farsighted men as John Von Neumann and Trevor Gardner realized that missiles tipped with thermonuclear bombs would be decisive weapons." Hans Bethe was most eloquent about Von Neumann's impact on the ICBM program. He said once that Von Neumann was the forceful member of a committee that formed "spontaneously" and whose other mover was Trevor Gardner, an assistant secretary of the air force. Von Neumann made strong recommendations, said that the ICBM program was in a mess, that it had to be reorganized as a crash program, and that several companies had to be called upon to do the job. Because of the forceful action of Von Neumann and his committee, Bethe said, the United States had the missiles only a matter of months after the Soviet Union; otherwise there would have been a lag of several years. During these years the balance of power might have been upset, the Russians might have dictated their policies, and we might have been shaking in our boots. The ICBM program was accelerated also by the fact that we had the fast computers, to the development of which Von Neumann had made the greatest contribution. In his effectiveness as an Atomic Energy Commissioner, his equanimity and common sense counted more than his genius. Those were the years when McCarthyism and the Oppenheimer case had aroused great animosity and split the scientific community. Von Neumann was neutral, and more important, equally acceptable to the opposing forces: at the Oppenheimer hearings he had made one of the most balanced statements, putting each issue in the right perspective, although he had disagreed with Oppenheimer on the question of the hydrogen bomb. As commissioner he took it upon himself to be a conciliator and because of his reasonable attitude toward conflicts he succeeded to a remarkable degree. He did not hold his post of commissioner for long; he died in 1957 after a long illness. Nevertheless his influence in the last years of his life was great and beneficial.

ATOMIC SCIENCE IN A LAND OF OPPORTUNITY

In this chapter I have related episodes in the story of European-born atomic scientists and their assimilation and contributions to American life. A full evaluation of their impact would require much more. For one thing, I have not mentioned all of the European-born atomic scientists, several of whom collaborated in less spectacular phases of the war effort or remained in the universities, which were sorely depleted and in great need of teachers. But the completeness of the Europeans' story does not seem essential to me. Much more important would be a full picture of the activities of their American counterparts in the same period and a detailed description of the settings in which members of the two groups came together. But I shall leave this task to the historians and instead stress some points.

Most European atomic scientists were a remarkably brilliant lot because at the time they first began to specialize atomic science was a new field bristling with difficulties, which would attract only the most intelligent and ambitious, those willing to work the hardest; and because selective forces were at work on the intellectual migration. Individuals of initiative and self-reliance, with a spirit of adventure and great adaptability were more likely than others to leave Europe, and these qualities are important assets both in one's personal life and the life of science. On the other hand, the American academic world, which helped Europeans to emigrate, has always placed a high premium on intellectual worth, so that invitations and appointments are first offered to the best.

Europeans were accepted in American intellectual circles more fully than they had expected and felt much gratified. The trust of the American government was a further reason for gratification, and gratitude made of them especially loyal citizens, anxious to channel their productivity into the service of America. Wartime conditions threw together scientists of great worth who might otherwise have stayed in distant parts of the United States, occupied with varied pursuits. The advantage of the Europeans over their American colleagues consisted in their knowledge of two cultures, which put them in a position where they could integrate the European scientific approach with the American scientific praxis. Contacts with Americans and Europeans of different backgrounds were highly stimulating. (When Fermi's Latin brain and Teller's Magyar brain came together they sparked, like two electrically charged bodies.) European-born scientists were extremely productive under these conditions, certainly more productive than they would have been at home. The fact that in the United States money was at no time a limiting factor gave free rein to the scientists' imagination. Because American policymakers in science were farsighted and the American industrial complex was formidable, the Europeans saw some of their most fantastic ideas (even Fermi's and Teller's sparks) become reality. It is difficult to think of another country and of other circumstances in which this could have happened.

VIII

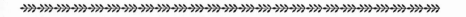

In the World of Art

MUSICIANS

According to a table published by Maurice Davie in his *Refugees in America*, the number of immigrant musicians from Europe who were admitted to the United States between 1933 and 1944 was estimated to be as high as 1,501. Davie's Study Committee was able to obtain the names of 1,015 musicians who had immigrated in this period. Were similar figures available for the more active period 1930–41, they would be even higher. Davie did not publish his list of musicians, but we may assume that many were primarily performers and not, strictly speaking, "intellectuals." I gathered the names of about 125 "intellectual musicians," a much more modest number than Davie's, but indicative of a large wave, which could not but make an impact on the American musical world.

The wave of musicians must be viewed in a different light from other groups; though its size was a novelty, it was in part the continuation of an old tradition. Long before the thirties, America welcomed European conductors and performers, and only the arrival of composers and musicologists was an essentially new phenomenon. An inherent characteristic of conductors and performers is their mobility. They have always been international itinerants, spending a good deal of their time and energy on tours that introduced them to audiences over the face of the world. Indeed, it seemed to be of little consequence to them from what place they took off on their wanderings or where they eventually settled. (This unconcern is evident in their peculiar selection of biographical data for publication. Musicians, or at least the European-born, tend to indicate the age at which they became child prodigies, the extent of their tours, and the applause they received rather than the countries in which they have lived or the year they settled in the United States, a habit irksome to the historical researcher.)

America was a favored goal of musical wanderings. As the young country began her fabulous climb up the economic ladder, the emoluments she could offer visiting celebrities outdistanced European stipends. Enticed by the seemingly inexhaustible flow of dollars, European conductors and performers came on visits, made it a point to stop here on their transatlantic voyages, and returned year after year for musical seasons. These were the traveling musicians, but there were also the settlers. When one of the mushrooming American symphony orchestras needed a conductor it often turned its eyes to Europe. And after each great European political convulsion some musicians came to this country even if they did not have formal invitations. Important to the development of American music were the German Forty-eighters, who founded musical societies and schools and in many ways promoted musical education. A group of twenty-five joined to form the Germania Orchestra that toured America for several years, and then disbanded, scattering its members to many American cities where each continued to raise the standards of American musical culture.

European-born conductors and performers were no novelty on the American scene. When in the thirties they became more numerous, more frequently evincing the determination to stay here permanently, and were joined by composers and musicologists, America accepted the lot with good grace. In fact, American friendliness toward foreign musicians grew considerably. In World War II there was practically no open hostility, whereas during World War I German conductors Karl Muck and Ernst Kunswald were interned for the duration and most German music was banned from stages and concert halls. Yet few were the musicians and musicologists who upon their arrival from Europe did not have to go through an initial period of hardship. In the United States of the thirties, ravaged by the depression, there were much fewer openings than now for musicians and musicologists, even for those of first rank. This situation was to improve rapidly because the arrival of the wave coincided with a new era in American music, an era in which music attained a popularity and diffusion that would have been inconceivable before. (All the same, full-time musical careers are still difficult in many cases.)

The sudden demand for music in America was so dramatic that Jacques Barzun called it a cultural revolution in his *Music in American Life*. Barzun did not specify when he believed the revolution began, but 1926 seems to me a good date, since that was the year of the first network broadcast of a symphony orchestra and marks the advent of the radio as a means of musical education. Subsequently, electrical recording, long-playing records, television, and complex high-fidelity systems have taken a part in the revolution and made music available in the home, in cars on the move, and from jukeboxes in public places. But they did not supplant the demand for the live performance. On the contrary, both the availability of mechanically reproduced music, which increased the appreciation of music, and the limitations of its quality whetted the appetite of the public for live music. And the expansion of the demand created new possibilities in all areas of the musical field.

CONDUCTORS

Viewed against the background of this mechanical revolution, the migration of Europeans to this country may seem irrelevant. Would we not have heard their music even though they had remained in Europe? Certainly we might have heard their music, or some of it, but I think that European musicians in this country played roles in which their presence was essential.

The conductors had a part in the expansion of American music and contributed to raise it to its present standards in several ways: by the high quality of their performances and the introduction of music until then unknown to American audiences; by strengthening the orchestras of many American cities and commissioning music for them; and, to a much more limited extent, by their teaching activities. For all this, their physical presence was necessary. They had to be here, on American soil, they had to learn our American needs and adapt to them. They had to come back in the thirties, those who had already been here, because by the thirties our musical needs had changed drastically.

Toscanini had been a habitual conductor at the Metropolitan Opera House in New York from 1908 to 1915 and at the New York Philharmonic Society from 1926 to 1936. He was already admired and loved, and the Toscanini legend — the repertoire of invectives he shouted at his musicians, the broken batons, his physical vigor, and his magnetism — was already shaped. Yet it was essential to American music that he return in 1937 and

217

give fully to America the last two decades of his life: the National Broadcasting Company organized especially for him a radio orchestra of highly paid, first-class musicians, and performances of excellence were transmitted throughout the United States week after week for seventeen years, in a sustained and outstanding output of music that reached wherever there was a radio set. And this was an unprecedented feat. By the time of Toscanini's return to America to stay the legend about him had been enriched by his acts of defiance against his onetime running mate Benito Mussolini (on the first Fascist ballot presented to Italian voters) and against Mussolini's friend Hitler. When in March, 1948, a few days before his eighty-first birthday, Toscanini appeared on television for the first time, he reached the apogee of a fantastic popularity that would not die with him. The desire for his musical interpretation still persists and can still be satisfied by high-fidelity recordings.

Bruno Walter, ten years younger than Toscanini, was a true intellectual who not only conducted, making a specialty of Mozart and the Viennese school, but was also a distinguished composer and the author of several books — among them a sensitive biography of Gustav Mahler, the composer who had been his teacher, and his own autobiography, *Theme and Variations*, a penetrating commentary on the political and intellectual events of his time. Among his close friends with whom he was reunited in this country were such writers as Thomas Mann (who turned to him when he needed musical information for *Doctor Faustus*), Franz and Alma Werfel, and Bruno Frank. Walter had visited the United States several times in the twenties and early thirties and returned to stay after the outbreak of World War II. He left Germany to settle in Vienna after his engagement with the Leipzig Gewandhaus Orchestra was canceled as a result of the Nazi racial laws, and when the *Anschluss* drove him out of Austria he went to France. The influence he exerted on American music was of a different sort than Toscanini's. Walter did not have his own orchestra but moved around as a guest conductor in many cities from Los Angeles to New York; through performances and rehearsals he influenced the musical understanding and interpretation of a large number of musicians.

Most European conductors appeared in New York at one time or other, for longer or shorter periods, at the Philharmonic or the Metropolitan Opera.

But perhaps more important was their work outside New York, for New York had lived a rich musical life before their coming. Their contributions to other American cities is brilliantly exemplified by Pierre Monteux's long conductorship in San Francisco. In the early thirties the symphony orchestra in San Francisco was in bad shape, "with a vanishing personnel" and "beyond the point of rallying to a periodic shot in the arm by a guest conductor," according to John Mueller in *The American Symphony Orchestra*. In 1934–35 San Francisco suspended concerts entirely. But the voters passed legislation to raise a half-cent tax for the benefit of the orchestra and an invitation was dispatched to Pierre Monteux, then conducting in Amsterdam and Paris. Monteux was well known to American audiences, having conducted at the Metropolitan Opera Company (1917–19) and with the Boston Symphony Orchestra (1919–24). He accepted the invitation and arrived in San Francisco in January, 1936. Upon taking up his new duties he announced that he intended "to restore the San Francisco orchestra to its former place among American ensembles, to give the public the best of the classics and a suitable allotment of modern compositions." He kept his promise, and transformed the San Francisco Symphony into a major orchestra, which he conducted steadily from 1936 to 1952. Then, though seventy-seven years old, he resumed his tours of Europe and America. "With Monteux," Mueller wrote, "the [San Francisco] public was introduced to a more sophisticated inventory, commensurate with the growth in stature and security of the orchestra and the international eminence of the conductor." In that period more French music was heard in San Francisco than in any other place in the United States.

The passage of time often causes a change of perspective. In recent years Monteux' impact upon the San Francisco Symphony may not appear as dramatic as George Szell's on the once-provincial Cleveland Orchestra, which Szell has transformed into an orchestra comparing favorably with any in the world. Szell was born twenty-two years later than Monteux and although he had been on the European musical stages as a pianist, conductor, and composer since he was ten years old, he was not well known in America when he arrived in the summer of 1939, not a glamorous guest but a stranded man without a job: after years as director of the German Opera in Prague he had moved on to the Scottish Orchestra in Glasgow and was returning there from a trip to Australia. He had meant to stop briefly in New York, but he learned that the British had mobilized and the Scottish Orchestra had suspended its season. He stayed on and, sustained by his great passion for music, began reworking his way to musical fame. He accepted teaching positions and engagements as a guest conductor until, in 1946, he was appointed permanent director of the Cleveland Orchestra. Painstakingly, by choosing and re-choosing his musicians and working incredibly hard with them, and by imposing on them the same high standards he had set for himself, he gradually drove his orchestra to the high position it has attained.

Other European-born conductors had a revitalizing effect on American orchestras. Vladimir Golschmann, who in Paris had established the Concerts Golschmann in 1919 and led them as "the youngest conductor," revived the failing taste for the symphony orchestra in St. Louis. He turned a repertoire in which popular music was predominant into one featuring avant-garde composers. In 1957, after twenty-six years in St. Louis, he moved to Denver.

It is said that Minneapolis was "put on the [musical] map" by the great Athenian conductor Dimitri Mitropoulos who led its orchestra for twelve years. When Mitropoulos left in 1949 — for the New York Philharmonic and later also the Metropolitan Opera — he was succeeded by Antal Dorati, who had been five years in Dallas and stayed in Minneapolis until 1960. Other conductors had beneficial effects on their orchestras: Otto Klemperer in Los Angeles; William Steinberg in Buffalo and Pittsburgh; Massimo Freccia in New Orleans and Baltimore; and Erich Leinsdorf and José Iturbi (best known as a pianist) in Rochester, New York. From 1961 to 1969 Leinsdorf led the Boston Symphony Orchestra, which he drove to perfection and brilliant performance.

In our era of mass culture there are larger audiences than ever before and not as discriminating, but the European-born conductors have not compromised on their account. By insisting on performances and repertoires of high quality and by commissioning great quantities of music from American composers they have influenced musical taste and provided outlets for musical talent.

Several conductors took up teaching as a side activity, or at times as their main occupation. The Russian Nicolai Malko taught at De Paul University of Music in Chicago, established a conducting class and published the manual *The Conductor and his Baton*. George Szell, who had spent years as a teacher in Germany and Czechoslovakia, taught at the Opera Workshop of the New School for Social Research as well as at the Mannes School of Music; Monteux opened his own summer school at Hancock, Maine; the Greek Maurice Abravanel became a professor at the University of Utah (while conducting the Utah Symphony Orchestra); Fritz Mahler, nephew of the famous composer and conductor Gustav Mahler, taught at the Juilliard Summer School of Music. These are a few out of many possible examples.

COMPOSERS

If the European composers had not come to America, much of their music might have been heard here all the same, but arriving from such a distance it might have seemed somewhat cold and remote. The presence of the composers made all the difference. We know who they are and occasionally see them or hear them perform. They may make public appearances as conductors of their own compositions or as soloists. Igor Stravinsky has appeared a great many times, for instance in the summer of 1966 at the age of eighty-four, venerable, leaning on a cane, to conduct his *Symphonie des Psaumes* at the New York Philharmonic. Paul Hindemith also took up the baton several times to direct his own compositions; and so did Darius Milhaud — as in 1940, when arriving from France on his way to California he stopped in Chicago to direct the world premiere of his *First Symphony*. Béla Bartók, Milhaud, and Mario Castelnuovo-Tedesco have played the piano at concerts of their music, and Hindemith played the viola. By their appearances they spurred a great enthusiasm and a consequent demand for their compositions. Many of the most important works they produced here were commissioned by American orchestras or foundations.

There is another reason why the presence of the European composers in this country was important: since they seldom could make a living by writing music alone, many went into teaching and influenced a generation of young American musicians. Royalties on the Europeans' past compositions were often frozen in countries that did not let money out, and families could not be fed on the hope of future income from not-yet-created music. Bartók, who refused to teach, died in poverty. Most others had fruitful careers at American schools — even Stravinsky, who we are told did not need the extra income, was for a while a lecturer at Harvard University and taught at the Berkshire Music Center.

221

Some had previous teaching experience. Paul Hindemith, composer and musicologist, had been a professor at the Berlin Hochschule für Musik. He was a great scholar, and his music was very popular in Germany; but the Nazis considered it degenerate and called him "a cultural bolshevist." When his music was banned from Germany he went to Turkey where he helped organize music teaching and research and taught at the conservatory in Ankara. In America, where he arrived in 1939, he joined the faculty of Yale and taught advanced theory until his return to Europe in 1953. "The School of Music at Yale during the years of his presence was practically identified with his name," Annemarie Holborn, wife of Yale historian Hajo Holborn, wrote me. "His impact . . . was tremendous. For the general public the concerts Hindemith organized and where he conducted and played at the same time were joyful occasions." Arnold Schoenberg too was a teacher of long standing and while living in Vienna was surrounded by admiring pupils and devoted disciples; he came to America in 1933, taught a year at the Malkin Conservatory in Boston, and then joined the faculty of the University of California at Los Angeles. Ernst Krenek, a composer and musicologist like Hindemith, and Nicolai Lopatnikoff, Bohuslav Martinu, and Ernst Toch were also teachers, and Darius Milhaud had a long association with Mills College of which he wrote with great warmth in his autobiography *Notes Without Music.*

Important as their teaching role was, the composers' fame is unquestionably tied to the music they produced. In this respect too America was good to them. Feeling welcome, relieved of the most stringent financial worries, pleased by their experiences on the American campus, they often added new elements to their music and were prolific. True, a few felt pushed the other way and lost their voice in the wilderness of a new environment, as Karl Weigl did. But in general they were far from silenced. Even Bartók, the foreigner who could not adjust to America, composed here some of his best music. Bartók's biographer Halsey Stevens states that the *Concerto for Orchestra*, which Bartók composed in 1943 for the Koussevitsky Foundation, "is a strong, vital work, contemporary in the best possible sense, since in it are amalgamated into a homogeneous fabric all the diverse elements which touched Bartók from his earliest creative years to the end of his life. . . . [It] is a good work, one of the greatest produced in this century."

Stravinsky came to the United States several times before making it his permanent home in 1939 and some of his compositions were especially written for his American tours, as the *Jeux de Cartes*, which he composed in 1937 for the Stravinsky festival at the Metropolitan Opera House; or they were on American subjects, as his concerto for sixteen instruments *Dumbarton Oaks*. After 1939 the American influence continued to be evident; his *Circus Polka* "for a young elephant" was commissioned by the Ringling Brothers Circus; he was approached by the choreographer George Balanchine, a fellow Russian émigré with whom he had worked on the ballet *Apollo* in Paris and on *Jeux de Cartes* in New York. According to Balanchine's biographer Bernard Taper, upon hearing that the ballet was to be for elephants, Stravinsky asked: "How old?" "Very young," Balanchine replied. After some thought, Stravinsky answered gravely: "If they are very young elephants I will do it." The collaboration with Balanchine did not stop after the *Circus Polka*: one of Stravinsky's major works in America, the ballet *Orpheus*, was commissioned by the Ballet Society of which Balanchine was a founder, and once more the two men worked together.

A few of Stravinsky's compositions were on American subjects, among them an arrangement of the *Star-Spangled Banner*, which he prepared at the time he applied for American citizenship; the *Ebony Concerto*, composed in 1946 for the band leader Woody Herman; and the song in memory of Dylan Thomas written shortly after the poet's death in 1954. Among the major works of Stravinsky's American period are, aside from the ballet *Orpheus*, the *Symphony in Three Movements*, his first major liturgical work, the *Mass*, and *The Rake's Progress*, his first opera in twenty-five years, for which W. H. Auden and Chester Kallman wrote the libretto.

Schoenberg too benefited from his transplantation to American soil. He became more human, entering into a closer contact with the contemporary world. Undoubtedly the impact of his European experiences had much to do with this change: when the Nazis passed their anti-Semitic laws, Schoenberg, a Catholic for years, returned to the fold of Judaism. In 1947 he composed the cantata *A Survivor from Warsaw*, for which he also wrote the text, a starkly realistic and emotional description of Nazi concentration camps. Among the other works he wrote in America are *Quartet for Strings*, *Concerto for Piano and Orchestra*, and *Theme and Variations for Orchestra*.

Many years before coming to this country, Paul Hindemith had casually coined the term *Gebrauchsmusik* (functional music) which was soon forgotten in Germany. But upon his arrival here the word hit him wherever he went, "it had grown to be as abundant, useless and disturbing as thousands of dandelions in a lawn." (Hindemith felt "like the sorcerer's apprentice who had become the victim of his conjurations.") That this man with his fine sense of humor and profound learning did not remain unaffected by the American scene is proven by some of his minor works, as the American requiem after Walt Whitman's "When Lilacs Last in the Dooryard Bloom'd," and the *Apparebit Repentina Dies* which he composed for a symposium at Harvard. Among his major works written here are *The Four Temperaments, Symphony in E Flat Major, Quartet No 5*, and *Symphonia Serena*, commissioned by Antal Dorati for the Dallas Symphony Orchestra.

Milhaud is one of the most prolific composers of our time and writes music with exceptional facility in the most difficult circumstances, even in what he called his "age of illness" — since the early thirties he has been plagued by attacks of arthritis and compelled to conduct while remaining seated. In the French edition of his *Notes sans Musique* he lists no fewer than 182 works for the period from his arrival in the United States in the fall of 1940 to 1962, a period which he spent mostly in this country although after the war he did a considerable amount of shuttling between Paris and Mills College. Some of the titles of his compositions in this period are suggestive of his warm feelings for America and adaptation to her culture: *Opus Americanum, Mills Fanfare, Bolivar, La Libération des Antilles* (two Creole melodies), *Pledge to Mills* (students' song), the Man Ray sequence for "Dreams that Money Can Buy" (a film), *Carnival à la Nouvelle-Orléans, Kentuckiana, West Point Suite, Aspen Serenade*, and *Un Français à New York*.

Ernst Toch, self-taught composer who began as a student of medicine and philosophy, was known to American audiences since 1932, when he came on a visit and introduced his *Concerto for Piano and Orchestra* at the Boston Symphony. He returned to make his home here in 1934, at the invitation of the New School for Social Research, and continued his activities as teacher and composer. Among his American works are *Pinocchio, A Merry Overture* and four symphonies — the third of these was introduced by the Pittsburgh Symphony, William Steinberg conducting, and won the Pulitzer Prize. The Czechoslovakian Martinu arrived in 1941 in the United States, where a pleasant surprise awaited him: the Boston Symphony was preparing to give the world premiere of his *Concerto Grosso*. Martinu had composed it in 1938 but the *Anschluss* prevented its publication in Vienna. A premiere arranged in Prague could not be realized because the Munich crises intervened, and plans for a premiere in Paris in May, 1940, had to be abandoned when the Nazis invaded France. Fortunately, although Martinu was not aware of the fact at that time, conductor George Szell, a Czechoslovakian like Martinu, managed to smuggle a copy of the score out of Prague and took it along on a tour of Australia before coming to America. Martinu, prolific in the past, in this country further increased his productivity and wrote some of his best and most ambitious works.

In Italy Mario Castelnuovo-Tedesco composed music influenced by the traditions of his native Florence and by his Jewish background; here he widened his vision to embrace the American scene and wrote such works as *American Rhapsody* and *Indian Songs and Dances*. Kurt Weill, already known for *The Three-Penny Opera* before his arrival here in 1935, soon became one of the most creative and popular Broadway composers: of his numerous stage hits it will suffice to mention *Knickerbocker Holiday* and *Lady in the Dark*.

The warmth and gratitude of European composers toward America seems commensurate to their success here, at least if Milhaud's feelings were shared by others. In his *Notes sans Musique* Milhaud wrote of the celebrations and festivities in 1962 on the occasion of his seventieth birthday — held in France, Belgium, Switzerland, Germany, Finland, Canada, and the United States. And it is quite evident which touched him most deeply: while he only mentions in passing other events and devotes three lines to the naming after him of a street in his home town, Aix-en-Provence, he describes in delightful detail the Aspen Festival as seen through eyes that remained very French despite his long years in America. The mayor of Aspen, Milhaud wrote, decreed that Bastille day should be a holiday in Milhaud's honor. In friendly manifestation, Aspen residents organized a flea market with booths where a bit of everything was sold: pancakes, records, French books, and puppies; a local physician built a cardboard guillotine as a prop for picture-taking; in what Milhaud considered a typically American gesture a child adorned the composer's head with a wreath of aspen leaves; and the mayor ceremoniously presented the keys of the city to him.

225

INSTRUMENTALISTS

The cultural wave brought to America unprecedented numbers of instrumentalists. Some had been here on tour and were already well known —
violinists Joseph Szigeti and Nathan Milstein, pianists Artur Schnabel, Vladimir Horowitz, and Artur Rubinstein, and others. But some of the very
famous in Europe, Adolf Busch and Wanda Landowska for instance, and
many of the not yet famous were on their first American visit. Soon they
scattered (although many established headquarters in New York), went on
tour, joined American orchestras or appeared with them as guests, united to
form chamber music groups, founded schools, and took up positions or
performed at music festivals. It is indeed a matter of record that Black Mountain College, one of many musically oriented colleges, was able to give performances of excellence with the participation of numerous Europeans.

Violinist Adolf Busch, who in Germany had founded the internationally
known Busch quartet, made many American appearances in joint recitals
with his son-in-law pianist Rudolf Serkin; in New York in 1938 they played
the complete series of Beethoven piano and violin sonatas. Their association
started when Serkin, a young Czechoslovakian still in his teens, went to
see the already famous Busch and asked to be allowed to play the piano
in his presence. Busch, greatly impressed, kept the boy in his household
(Irene Busch, Serkin's future wife, was then a child of five). In 1933 Serkin
was forbidden to play in Germany because he was not German-born,
and Busch, who could have stayed, followed his son-in-law into exile. Adolf
Busch died in 1952, without having recaptured in the United States the
popularity he had enjoyed in Europe. Serkin, on the other hand, has had
one of the longest and most fruitful careers among émigré pianists. Not only
has he continued to tour in the United States, year after year, but he has also
become a teacher, the head of the piano department of the Curtis Institute
of Music in Philadelphia and the founder of a music school in Marlboro,
Vermont. With his passionate enthusiasm and profound loyalty to the composers whose music he interprets, with his great generosity and honesty,
Serkin could not fail to give immensely to audiences and students alike. His
school, which he calls a "republic of equals," attracts European musicians as
well as American. Artur Rubinstein is another brilliant pianist who has been
in this country since the fall of France and is well known to American au-

diences for his extraordinary command of his instrument from which he extracts resonant sounds and subtle nuances. Among his musical activities in this country, he has undertaken to record the entire work of Chopin.

Wanda Landowska had an enormous influence here as she had in Europe. She was the first pianist of rank to realize the possibilities of the harpsichord in the concert hall, and she revived the use of this instrument which had been neglected since the eighteenth century. In Berlin, where she was a professor at the Hochschule, and in Paris, where she founded her own École de Musique Ancienne, she trained a number of European harpsichordists. Some of them preceded her to America. When she arrived, Erwin Bodky, for one, was teaching at the Longy School of Music and was later to join the faculty of Black Mountain College. With her own presence and through that of her ex-students she created a great appreciation of and demand for the harpsichord. Landowska's recordings of the *Goldberg Variations* sold 20,000 sets in the first three months they were on the market. Another European harpsichordist, Yella Pessl, has performed frequently here, written many articles on harpsichord music, and been associated with the department of music at Columbia University.

Of the several cellists who came here from Europe at least two were Russian-born: Nikolai Graudan and Gregor Piatigorsky. Graudan had formed a duo with his pianist wife Johanna which was heard in Europe, the United States, and in Asia. Graudan was a member of the Aspen festival quartet and the Aspen Institute of Music and a cellist with American orchestras. Piatigorsky, who has been in this country since 1929, has given concerts, toured the world as a virtuoso, and been a guest soloist with the major orchestras in this country. His influence as a teacher has been very great; he was for many years the head of the cello department of the Curtis Institute of Music, where he had numerous students, some of whom have won international prizes. In the summer of 1966 Piatigorsky, who fled Russia when little more than a boy, was on the jury of the third Tschaikowsky competition in Moscow where three of his American students were singled out for prizes. These and other cellists from Europe have made the cello popular in America.

Trios and quartets from Europe or established here by European musicians "created an enormous appetite for chamber music," musicologist Gerhard Herz pointed out. Of this fact he has a firsthand knowledge, for he arranged for concerts of the Budapest quartet (founded by four Russians) on the campus of the University of Louisville where he has been teaching since 1938 and helped to set up chamber music concerts at the University of Indiana.

All these artists, conductors, composers, and performers contributed to the expansion of American music and helped to elevate its standards. But another fact must be considered, Herz stressed: the impoverishment of European countries. Germany, Austria, and Hungary "lost some tremendous artists. Germany was left without a decent violinist or cellist. Not one single great string quartet remained in Germany and Austria," Herz said. "The Germans would have given anything to keep Busch who was not a Jew." The high level of American music after the migration appears even higher when compared with the depletion in Europe.

MUSICOLOGISTS

The conditions that émigré musicologists found in this country were substantially different from those encountered by the performers. By the beginning of the thirties American music was already in a phase of rapid expansion which would have gone on even without the arrival of the Europeans, though it was accelerated by them. American musicology was instead at its start. Musicology, the youngest discipline among the humanities, is to the musical arts what art history is to the visual arts: a scholarly study of musical achievements in different times and places; an analysis of their styles, characteristics, and relationships; and a search for and re-interpretation of old texts. It may give all music lovers a deeper appreciation of musical works and a more intimate contact with them. Born in Europe, and introduced in the United States in the early part of this century, musicology has retained a good many of its original traits. But American musical scholarship long antedated musicology proper and developed parallel with music. In the last century American scholars wrote some histories of music, biographies of musicians, and catalogues and bibliographies of musical works. These were, however, mainly sporadic efforts of a few individuals, and as recently as the twenties musicology had not yet attained academic recognition. Although the first American musicologists appeared on the scene in that decade, they had obtained their degrees in Europe, and at least one, Otto Kinkeldey, had taught for several years in Germany. A few younger men coming from other fields, psychology, history, or one of the languages, completed doctoral dissertations in musicology, but their number was very small — only three in the year 1927–28, for instance. (In comparison, in the United States there were 42 theses in musicology in 1950–51, and by the end of 1965 the total number of theses in musicology was 1,204.)

European musicologists arriving in the thirties gave an enormous impetus to their discipline, greatly hastening the process of its growth and its acceptance in the academic world. The first chair in musicology was created at Cornell in 1930 for the American-born but German-trained Otto Kinkeldey: to the second chair, established in 1933 at Columbia University, was appointed the Hungarian-born Paul Henry Lang, who had settled in this country in 1928. By the early forties musicology had entered many universities and colleges as well as music schools, and at that time most teachers were exiles from Europe. Among those from Germany who produced the present generation of American musicologists and gave a strong theoretical and historical background to hosts of young musicians were Willi Apel of the University of Indiana; Manfred Bukofzer, who taught at the University of California from 1941 until his death in 1955; Hans David of the University of Michigan; Alfred Einstein of Smith College; Erich Hertzmann of Columbia University; Gerhard Herz of the University of Louisville; Paul Hindemith of Yale; Edward Lowinsky of the University of Chicago; Hans Nathan of Michigan State; Curt Sachs of New York University; and Leo Schrade of Yale. Karl Geiringer of the University of California at Santa Barbara; Ernst Krenek, formerly of Hamline University; Hans Tischler of the University of Indiana; and Eric Werner of the Hebrew Union School of Sacred Music were born in Austria. Ernest Ferand of the New School for Social Research and Otto Gombosi of Harvard were natives of Hungary. Hugo Leichtentritt of Harvard was born in Poland; Paul Nettl of Indiana University was from Czechoslovakia; and Dragan Plamenac of the University of Illinois came from Yugoslavia.

Some of the older musicologists from Europe were already renowned for their achievements before coming to this country, notably Alfred Einstein and Curt Sachs. In Germany Einstein had acquired an early reputation for great scholarship and was the brilliant, influential musical critic of several papers as well as the much acclaimed author of *A Short History of Music* and other books; but in 1933 he was obliged to go into exile. He arrived here in 1939, after a short stay in England and somewhat longer in Italy, and although already fifty-nine years old, he was to have his most productive period in America. He was engaged in the monumental work *The Italian Madrigal*, on which he spent several decades of research in libraries throughout the world, unearthed music, and edited and transcribed it. An appointment at Smith College enabled him to complete the writing of this three-volume study which was published in 1949. (All the source material Einstein collected is now deposited in the Smith College library.) Curt Sachs, who like Einstein was exiled from Germany in 1933, arrived here in 1939 (after spending the intervening years in France) and taught at New York University. He was probably the greatest expert then living on musical instruments: as the head of the Berlin State collection of ancient musical instruments he had them restored so that they could be heard again. He reorganized the collection according to his own method which, described by him and followed by others, proved to be very useful. He also wrote many books about the musical instruments of the Indians and Indonesians and of ancient Egypt, some of which were published in this country.

The majority of European musicologists were young men, not yet known at the time of their arrival. Some had been at the beginning of their careers when the political events in their countries had disrupted their work, and their formal advancement and possibility of gaining recognition were suspended for periods that were occasionally as long as a decade. In this country they had to stand on the record of their performance, a record which in general was excellent. Their interests were wide, and their intellectual output was conspicuous. Through their publications and lectures they deepened American knowledge of European composers and stimulated the study of most phases of European music as well as music of other parts of the world. America was not neglected: a survey of Indian music was made by the Hungarian-born George Herzog, who does not really belong to the wave under consideration because he came to America in the mid-twenties. But two researchers into early American music do belong: Hans David edited twelve volumes of music of the Moravians in America and was co-author of a catalogue of Moravian music, and Hans Nathan wrote a book on the rise of early Negro minstrelsy.

As educators, the European musicologists strove for high humanistic standards. ("I made myself unpopular wherever I went," said a musicologist

230

who taught at several colleges and universities, "because I pressed for Latin for musicology students. But how could they go into Church musicology without Latin?") Under their competent direction, universities and public libraries acquired or enriched their musical collections. At least one musicologist took pains to make musical instruments and their history better known to Americans: as the curator and head of the department of musical collections of the Metropolitan Museum of Arts, Emanuel Winternitz organized exhibits of musical instruments from all countries and wrote articles about them. Winternitz' is a singular story: in Vienna he was a corporation lawyer by profession and a musician only by avocation; arriving in this country in 1938, he led at first a precarious existence as did many other European lawyers (friends say that he played the magician for a living) until his extraordinary, humanistic approach to music and its relation with visual arts earned him a position at the Fogg Museum and later at the Metropolitan. His understanding of musical instruments is so profound that he alone was able to identify certain strange devices in Leonardo's notebooks as musical instruments, thus revealing a new facet of Leonardo's complex personality. In many towns and cities Europeans were responsible for strengthening local orchestras and arranging for performances of outside groups that further increased the desire for chamber music. Since most musicologists are also performers, conductors, or composers, they were able to organize concerts or direct productions of operas by student groups and engage in other activities that promoted music appreciation. With the collaboration of the Europeans, American musicology matured and from a succession of isolated scholarly achievements it changed into a recognized discipline.

A scanning of the musicology journals, book lists of publishers, and historical editions of music reveals the extent of the Europeans' contribution. Of the five volumes in Norton's history of music series published through 1965 three were by European-born authors: Curt Sachs' *The Rise of Music in the Ancient World — East and West*, Manfred Bukofzer's *Music in the Baroque Era*, and Alfred Einstein's *Music in the Romantic Era*. The first monographs of international significance published in this country were by émigré scholars and include those by Einstein on Mozart and on Schubert, those by Karl Geiringer on Haydn and on the Bach family, Eric Werner on Mendelssohn, and Leo Schrade on Monteverdi. Willi Apel's *The Notation*

231

of Polyphonic Music and *Gregorian Chant,* and Curt Sachs' *The History of Musical Instruments* and *The Wellsprings of Music, or an Introduction to Ethnomusicology* are some of the first music textbooks published in this country. Among the works focusing attention on genres, Einstein's three volumes on the Italian madrigal may well be regarded as the proudest achievement of European musical scholarship in America. Ernest Ferand raised the problem of the significance of improvisation in the history of music and Lowinsky that of the interpretation and definition of Renaissance music. Kathi Meyer-Baer and Emanuel Winternitz wrote on the iconography of music and musical instruments. Among the outstanding editions of the works of musical masters of the past are Dunstable's and Ockeghem's complete works published respectively by Manfred Bukofzer and Dragan Plamenac. And among the important anthologies are those edited by Einstein (*Canzoni, Sonetti, Strambotti et Frottole, Libro Tertio*), by Gombosi (*Compositione de Meser Vincenzo Capirola, Lute Book*), by Apel (*Keyboard Music of the Fourteenth and Fifteenth Centuries*), and by Schrade (*Polyphonic Music of the Fourteenth Century*). The last addition is the series *Monuments of Renaissance Music,* edited by Edward Lowinsky, presenting critical editions of major sources of fifteenth- and sixteenth-century music.

This small gleaning from a richer harvest testifies both to the energy and talent of European musicology and the degree of reception and absorption by American universities and publishing houses. If the European musicologists made many contributions to America, they in their turn gained much by living here. They shed the aloofness frequent among European scholars of their generation, which tended to maintain a distance between masters and disciples, and found that they enjoyed meeting American students in friendly partnership, as is proved by the willingness of some musicologists to teach at institutions like Black Mountain College, where teachers and students led a sort of communal life; they shifted their main concern from the learned detail discussed over and over again among the erudite to broader vistas and discovered that they were reaching much wider audiences. But these experiences were not peculiar to musicologists: scholars in other fields made similar adjustments to the positivistic attitudes of this country and the demands of its rapidly expanding education in a fruitful process of cross-fertilization.

ARTISTS

The wave of European artists was slightly smaller in number than that of musicians. Davie wrote that "some 717 sculptors and artists migrated from Europe to the United States during the period 1933–44." This does not take into consideration the architects from Europe, who were approximately 380, according to Davie's figures. In my file for the years 1930–41, I gathered about one hundred names of artists, including architects and art historians. The artistic wave appeared aggrandized by its quality, for it brought to our shores the greatest of Europe, and they heightened the cultural prestige of our country. Large numbers of painters and sculptors were latecomers, Frenchmen by birth or election, and refugees from many countries who were driven out of France by her collapse. A sizable part of this group returned to their European homes at the end of the war, Marc Chagall, André Masson, and Fernard Léger among them, and so America lost some of the luster she had acquired. But their influence was felt long after their departure. Others in the group and the majority of those who arrived in the thirties settled in the United States, and among them there are persons no less outstanding than those who left.

ARCHITECTS AND DESIGNERS

One group of artists — as distinct from the historians of art — made the strongest imprint on the American scene: the architects. Architecture is the most visible and tangible form of art. Its work is everywhere, not enclosed in galleries and museums, and may be seen by all. Its interrelation with the broad scene on which it develops, that is, the action of socio-cultural forces on it and its own on them, results ultimately in modifications of the urban horizon. It is modern architecture that has shaped our American cities and is both the creator and mirror of their greatness. It expresses the characteristics of each, their wealth and degree of industrialization, the amount of effort each is willing to devote to social equality, the pride each places in cultural achievements, and the stringency of aspirations to health and beauty. Our modern cities are well on the way to expressing "the will of an epoch translated into space," which Ludwig Mies van der Rohe considers the proper role of architecture.

An outside observer, the British Ian McCallum, commented in 1959 in his book *Architecture USA*: "The new architecture stems from three main sources — Germany, France, and the American Middle West. Among the men who have made it there are four pioneers. . . , Walter Gropius, Mies van der Rohe, Frank Lloyd Wright, and Le Corbusier, all but the last resident in the United States of America. In America then, we can see working out within a highly industrialized society such as the new architecture always pre-supposed, ideas which sprang, not only from the American, but also from the European, forcing-ground of the nineteenth century."

The two European-born giants of modern American architecture, Walter Gropius and Ludwig Mies van der Rohe, were both German-born and both started their careers in the office of the architect Peter Behrens. They had already achieved a solid reputation before coming to this country, Gropius in 1937, Mies in 1938, to become respectively chairman of the department of architecture at Harvard University and director of the Department of Architecture of Chicago's Armour Institute, now the Illinois Institute of Technology. In the years at these institutions before their retirement, Gropius in 1952, Mies in 1958, they both trained large numbers of architects, many of whom now are in leading architectural firms throughout the country. But the nature of the enormous influence that each exerted in America is different. Gropius, whom James Marston Fitch called one of the few inventors of modern architecture, had evolved intellectually and artistically in Germany. In the United States he pursued ideas and techniques with which he had experimented in Germany, expanding and adapting their application to the new setting but without introducing significant innovations. On the other hand, Mies van der Rohe matured in America. Here he continued to refine the expression of his style, striving toward purity of form, toward rectilinear geometric perfection achieved through an inexorable process of simplification and drastic elimination of all that to him seems inessential to structure. He evolved patterns of buildings apparently so simple that they could easily be repeated or imitated, as in fact they are. And in this rests a great part of influence.

But Gropius' influence has been the more humanizing of the two. Gropius attained fame as early as 1911 with the Fagus Works, a factory of steel and glass, possibly the first achievement of transparency and the appearance of weightlessness in architectural form. He established himself as a master of architecture in 1925 with the complex of school building and staff homes and studios for the Bauhaus at Dessau, a classic in its perfect correlation of function and architectural form. The most significant activity of his German period, however, was not as builder but as director of the Bauhaus from 1919 to 1928. He was animated by an idea the novelty of which it may be hard to recognize in our times. It was a novel and radical idea when Gropius launched it in the Germany of 1919, especially radical because he formulated it as the program for a state art school, the Bauhaus. He thought that designers should accept the machine as a modern tool to produce design and should work out a new set of aesthetic criteria. Craftsmanship and creative art should not be separated and the education of designers should include manual training in workshops together with theoretical instruction in the laws of design. In view of the scale and complexity of modern problems, collaboration was a necessity. To further his idea he called to the Bauhaus some of Europe's finest architects, designers, and painters, and the Bauhaus became the leading school of design in the world. Under Gropius' slogan "art and technology — the new unit" it was to transform product design in the western world. But its liberalism soon aroused official opposition in the rapidly deteriorating political climate of Germany. In 1928 Gropius resigned. Mies van der Rohe became its director in 1930, and on him fell the painful responsibility of closing the school in the fall of 1933, when ideological clashes with the Nazis became too frequent and disrupting.

Gropius was fifty-four years old when he came to America, but long years of achievement were ahead of him. He built a great deal — private homes, educational buildings (among them the Harvard Graduate Center), and housing projects in New England and Pennsylvania. He was a consultant or planner for the reconstruction of large city areas in Boston and in Chicago and received important commissions from other countries. As an architect he worked mostly in collaboration: from 1938 to 1942 with his former pupil and colleague at the Bauhaus, Marcel Breuer; after 1945 with a group of younger architects with whom he formed the Architects Collaborative (TAC). But he exerted the greatest influence on America as a philosopher and teacher. For Gropius was a humanist of great thoughtfulness, with a great sensitivity to the social implications of architecture. He conceived the architect as the co-ordinator of all human problems connected with building, and this conception, he himself wrote, "inevitably led me on, step by step, from the study of the function of the house to that of the street; from the street to the town; and finally to the still vaster implications of regional and national planning." It is his vast approach to the building and designing arts in an age of technology as well as his dedication to his convictions and ability to infuse them in others that made Gropius the greatest and most influential educator in architecture in our time.

The reputation that Mies van der Rohe earned in his German years was based on a smaller number of buildings than Gropius' and on several models that were not executed, but his basic style and techniques were already firmly established. They were amazingly well suited to American technology and the continuing development of skyscrapers. In the United States, Mies built mainly in Chicago (the most notable exceptions are the Seagram Building in New York and the Bacardi Building in Mexico City) where his own apartment buildings and those of others influenced by him have contributed much to the present appearance of the Chicago lakefront. Away from the lakefront is his first Chicago project and first expression of his own Americanization: the campus of the Illinois Institute of Technology. It is convincing proof that he, the newcomer, could become one of the major interpreters of American building technology.

In his *Architecture USA* Ian McCallum concluded a biographical sketch of Mies with the sentences: "America could not have nurtured Mies, Europe could not have fulfilled his promises, he has perhaps gained more, and given more, to the US than any other *émigré* outside the realm of atomic physics. He has produced a lyricism of two constituent US psychological facts — unlimited space and unmitigated technology — in a form that . . . can be held up to the rest of the world as an example of a convincing machine-age architecture. The rest of the world has taken note and, wherever architectural thought is on the move, the influence of Mies — American Mies — can be felt." There are signs now that Mies' influence is on the wane. But his past influence and his achievements cannot be canceled. The story of his achievements is of special interest because it may furnish some clues to the puzzling fact that so many émigrés have accomplished more in America than they themselves feel they might have done in Europe.

If Gropius and Mies were giants, other foreign-born architects were men of high stature, casting long shadows on the American scene. One of them is Marcel Breuer, once Gropius' pupil, then his friend, and entirely a product of the Bauhaus. He was born in a small town in Hungary and met technology back to front, so to speak: he flew in a plane before he rode in an automobile and had done both before he first used a telephone. At the Bauhaus he was given to riding a bicycle. In 1924 when he was twenty-two years old he was placed in charge of the carpentry shop and the next year he got an inspiration from his bicycle: to bend the tubing of the handlebars in different shapes and use them for furniture. So he invented the tubular-steel chair, which in subsequent versions is now so common that most American housewives can hardly recall the time when it was not in their kitchens. In the United States Breuer joined the department of architecture at Harvard at the same time Gropius did and until 1942 was a partner in a firm they established together. Then, while they remained colleagues at Harvard, their roads as architects parted. Breuer went on building, mostly on his own. He was strongly impressed by the wooden houses blending so well in the New England setting and he greatly admired Frank Lloyd Wright. Deeply affected by the cultural elements that he encountered in America, he developed a new style and used more wood and stone and less glass and steel than other architects from Europe. He has become best known and exerted his greatest influence as an architect of residential houses, but he also built larger units for colleges, universities, and religious institutions here and abroad. The most famous among them is the UNESCO building in Paris in which he collaborated with Pier Luigi Nervi and Bernard Zehrfuss. A more recent achievement is the new Whitney Museum of Art in New York.

In a somewhat different category is the Viennese architect Victor Gruen, for neither in Austria nor in the United States was he associated with teaching and the academic life. He began to assert himself in private practice with important residential and commercial projects in Austria, Germany, and Czechoslovakia; then Hitler and the *Anschluss* forced him to move to the United States. Here, with offices first in New York and then in Los Angeles and Chicago, he spanned a wider geographical area than his European colleagues and gained a reputation for his activity in a typically American architectural field, the modern shopping center. He planned and built many centers in many states, including California, Minnesota, Texas, Michigan, New York, and Florida, and he also collaborated in the book *Shopping Towns U.S.A.*

One of the great European architects, Erich Mendelsohn, spent the last twelve years of his life in America, but his production here did not equal his European reputation. In Germany where he lived until 1933 he was numbered among the most influential and productive in his profession; his commercial and industrial buildings were admired, his department stores were famous, and the Einstein Tower, an observatory and astrophysics institute, was called poetic (though to me its bulky walls cut by recessed windows like gun emplacements, topped by a helmet-shaped cupola, suggest a fortress rather than a scientific building). Between 1933 and 1941 Mendelsohn continued to erect enduring monuments in England and in Palestine, where his numerous and varied projects have greatly contributed to the modern architecture of present-day Israel. In America, where he came in 1941, his influence was limited and identified almost exclusively with Jewish architecture. First he built the Maimonides Hospital in San Francisco, then Jewish temples in St. Louis, Cleveland, Grand Rapids, and St. Paul. Refusing to imitate Greek temples or Gothic churches, he infused new life into this type of construction and brought a modern approach to it. But he hardly affected modern American architecture as a whole.

Gropius, Mies, and Breuer were not the only staff members of the Bauhaus who came to this country. Josef Albers, the painter, joined the faculty of Black Mountain College in 1933, and three more colleagues arrived between 1937 and 1938: painter-designer László Moholy-Nagy, architect-typographer-designer Herbert Bayer, and the abstract expressionist painter Lionel Feininger, who was born in America but as an artist was a German product: he left the United States at sixteen to study music in Germany and a year later decided to turn to painting. He returned to America for good in 1937, a refugee artist among countless others.

After they arrived in America, Herbert Bayer worked and taught mainly within the industries: Feininger, who was sixty-six years old at the time of his return, went on painting but did not teach; and Albers and Moholy-Nagy devoted themselves to organizing art schools in the spirit of the Bauhaus. Of the two, Albers had the longer American teaching career, at Black Mountain College until 1949 and at Yale from 1950 to 1960, and taught the larger number of students; as a painter and one of the leaders of geometric abstraction he developed an interpretation and philosophy of art in which vision is more essential than expression and is non-representative, based on the relation between simple shapes and their interaction with pure hues; his many paintings on the theme of "celebration of the square" are among his best-known works. In his brief career, ended in 1946, Moholy came closer to creating a Bauhaus in this country. He was one of the principal forces of the German school to which he devoted himself and from which he resigned in 1928, in accord with Gropius and in protest against government pressures. When, in 1937 the Association of Arts and Industries of Chicago decided to establish a school on the Bauhaus model, it turned to Gropius for advice, and Gropius suggested Moholy for its director. Then came the cable that I quoted which originated the mix-up in Sibyl Moholy-Nagy's mind between Marshall Field and a field marshal. Moholy disregarded his wife's misgivings and arrived in Chicago with his family in the fall of 1937, in time to open the "New Bauhaus" for the academic year.

To the faculty of this school Moholy called several Americans and his countryman and collaborator, designer Gyorgy Kepes. Moholy's Hungarian optimism, tinged with a touch of fanaticism, did miracles. When the stature of the staff and the fitful financial support of Chicago industry proved insufficient to maintain the school, and the New Bauhaus was forced to close after only one academic year, it was Moholy's faith and stubbornness that succeeded in re-opening it the next year as the School of Design and with a faculty pledged to give their time without pay for at least one semester. The School of Design, like the New Bauhaus, had no easy life and struggled for survival. To its financial difficulties others were added, due to America's entry into the war and the consequent departure of many students and faculty members for war duties. Once again, it was the devotion and abnegation of its faculty, of Moholy and his wife Sibyl in particular, that saved it. They adjusted its work and output to wartime needs, making it possible for the staff to do its part in war work. In 1944 the school was reorganized as the Institute of Design, with college rank, and it was under this name that it became famous. During the years of difficulties, in spite of the great teaching load, both Moholy-Nagy and Kepes managed to continue their work, experimenting in new forms of art that combined different mediums, painting, collage, photography, and typography. In those years Moholy realized some of his most lucid concepts in painting and construction.

Moholy-Nagy's successor as head of the Institute of Design was the Russian-born Serge Chermayeff. Trained as an architect, but probably better known in this country for his painting and industrial design, Chermayeff was educated and lived in England until he came to settle in America in 1940. He had had no formal connection with the Bauhaus but fully subscribed to its principles, and so his appointment at the Chicago Institute of Design insured the continuity of Moholy-Nagy's ideas. However, Chermayeff remained in Chicago only until 1951. Two years before that, Moholy's school had undergone its last metamorphosis and became a department of the Illinois Institute of Technology. It is now housed with the department of architecture in Crown Hall, Mies van der Rohe's most famous building on the campus.

When Chermayeff left Chicago he went to the Massachusetts Institute of Technology, where Kepes had been teaching since 1946. Two years later Chermayeff was named chairman of the department of architecture at Harvard, to succeed Gropius who had retired the previous year. Harvard had a most "Europeanized" Graduate School of Design. Between 1938 and 1950, besides Gropius and Breuer, another European architect, the German Martin Wagner, was on the Harvard faculty and taught housing and regional planning. Wagner shared with Gropius and other Europeans a strong interest in prefabricated, mass-produced housing and designed a very original, circular one-room house unit that could be sold, he thought, for under seven hundred dollars; as many units as were wished could be joined to form a variety of house patterns. In 1953 the Spanish-born architect and city planner José Luis Sert was appointed to the Harvard faculty and became the dean of the Graduate School of Design and chairman of the department of architecture. (In 1963 Chermayeff moved on to Yale.)

The influence of European architects and designers in America has been threefold: first, through their works — buildings forever on display as a part of the American landscape, paintings and designs in permanent and temporary exhibits, and industrial products with artistic qualities have affected the taste of the general public. Second, as most of them were teachers, they have had a great influence on younger men, and through their pupils their theories have irradiated from a few schools to wider reaches. Third, almost all have left enduring records of their thoughts in books and articles that are consulted by teachers, students, and professionals everywhere. The one outstanding exception is the taciturn Mies, whose most articulate language is that of steel and glass.

In the success of these men in the United States, American technology had a leading part. Without the tools and products of the machine age and the co-operation of industry, the Europeans would not have fulfilled their intellectual capabilities. But Gropius himself seemed no longer the assured propounder of "art and technology — the new unit" when in 1953 at a symposium on the occasion of his seventieth birthday he launched a warning: ". . . we need to muster all our strength and originality in trying to keep creative impulses active and effective against the deadening effect of mechanization and over-organization that is threatening our society . . . . I mean that the misuse of the machine is creating a soul-flattening mass mind, which levels off individual diversity and independence of thought and action."

PAINTERS AND SCULPTORS

The first painter with an established reputation to arrive in the cultural wave was Hans Hofmann who in 1930 was invited to teach at the University of California. An abstract painter and an exponent of Central European expressionism, he was well known as a teacher who had founded a school in Munich as early as 1915. At Berkeley he taught only two years, then opened his own school in New York, with summer sessions in Provincetown. Hofmann was one of the European-born artists who exerted the greatest influence as a painter and even more as a teacher and whose career in the United States was one of the longest (he died in 1966). I can think of only one European artist who in America had a longer career than Hofmann's: Boris Margo, painter, sculptor, printer, and teacher, came here in 1930 and was still living at the end of the sixties. Twenty-two years younger than Hofmann at the time of his arrival, Margo was more susceptible to the artistic influences acting in America; although he was educated in Russia, some art historians classify him with American artists. Hofmann, instead, was himself one of the forces that molded younger men in this country and a leading personality behind the emergence of abstract expressionism in America (but he allowed his students to paint in their own way, and their styles range widely from realism to abstraction).

There had been little abstract art in the United States in the twenties, but by the opening of the thirties it was gaining favor: a few Americans were taking it up, while it reached the public more and more through exhibits and reproductions of European works. The arrival of the Europeans sped up a process — some call it a revolution — that almost certainly would have taken place without them. Several abstract artists established residence in the United States after Hofmann. There were those from the Bauhaus,

Albers, Moholy-Nagy, Bayer, and Feininger. There were exponents of the Dutch group De Stijl, related to the Bauhaus, whose work in painting, sculpture, or architecture was based on rectangular shapes and primary colors: Fritz Glarner came to America in 1936 and Piet Mondrian, the founder of neoplasticism, who attained an unsurpassed precision of line and color, spent the last four years of his life in this country, from 1940 to 1944. Amedée Ozenfant arrived in 1938, taught at various American universities and art schools, and established his own school of fine arts in New York. In the first years in the United States he painted strange, abstract landscapes of Arizona, catching "the spirit of the corroded ancient monuments of nature," as Sidney Janis wrote.

The war in Europe and the fall of France brought to the United States some of the most famous among the painters who are considered French regardless of their place of birth. Though they were not all typical abstractionists, they were modernists of one school or another. Ferdinand Léger, a founder of cubism and preoccupied with the machine as a tool in art, painted highly stylized objects with the hard appearance of mechanized forms. He had paid several visits to America before returning in 1940 to spend the war years, and here he gave himself to painting with great alacrity. Of his oil *Les plongeurs circulaires* he wrote, "The concept of forms like birds and clouds which rotate out of a fulcrum is a part of the *new realism* of the time. The picture may be hung on any one of its sides." To the suggestion that it might also revolve like a mobile painting he answered, "Why not?"

The most famous refugee artist is Marc Chagall. He was profoundly depressed when he landed in New York in 1941 by the tragedy which had befallen the European Jews and the trauma of his own uprooting from France. In this country he suffered the loss of his wife. Nevertheless, his American period, which lasted until 1947, was very productive. He composed here some of his best paintings, part of the great fantastic world he has built over the years, in which the fundamental elements are the cows, girls, cocks, and houses of his provincial Russia, as he himself once said.

Marcel Duchamp, who is sometimes called "the perennial Dadaist," was well known in New York from the time of the Armory Show in 1913, when his "Nude Descending a Staircase" caused an explosion of criticism that bordered on a scandal. Duchamp gave up painting in 1923 but continued his artistic activity, related to the playful, iconoclastic Dada movement, which he had begun earlier. He was the last of the artists to arrive in the United States to settle, trailing behind the wave: after the invasion of France it took him almost two years and a great many trips to smuggle his art from the occupied to the unoccupied zone, a feat he could achieve only by posing as a cheese merchant. Finally he went to Marseilles, then Lisbon, and in 1942 arrived in New York.

Especially pertinent to later American development was the group of surrealists who aimed at expressing the process of thought through psychic automatism. Salvador Dali, who joined the movement in 1929 when he moved from Spain to Paris, painted what he calls "literal pictures of his dreams," leaving little doubt, if doubt there ever was, of the debt the movement owed to Freud and the psychoanalysts. Among the surrealists who like Dali came to America from France were such leaders of the movement as André Masson, Max Ernst, and Yves Tanguy, and the Chilean Matta Eucharren; a less "French" surrealist, Kurt Seligmann; and the poet André Breton, who in 1922 composed the surrealist manifesto. By their presence and their teachings these men gave impetus to the American surrealist movement which, not large in itself, pervaded other forms of American art. Their direct influence varied, for Breton and Masson returned to France right after the war, Max Ernst in 1949, and Tanguy died here in 1955. In this country Dali has been active in several artistic fields beside painting: he has made drawings — including his interpretation of atomic particles; he has designed costumes for the theater, and has given himself to writing. (Shortly after his arrival he created window displays for a leading department store in New York; but when he found that his displays had been altered because they were considered risqué, he became so angered that he pushed a bathtub from the display through the show window, falling after it himself, and landing first on the sidewalk, then on the front pages of most newspapers.)

Seligmann remained active on the American scene for a long time. Born in Basel, educated in Switzerland, Italy, and France, Seligmann lived for several years in Paris, where he joined first the group called "abstraction-creation," then the surrealists. He arrived in this country in 1939, taught at Brooklyn College and the New School for Social Research, and exhibited his work in the most important American museums.

Among the many other painters in the wave, the Italian-born Enrico

Donati, who has been connected with various art schools and university art departments in the East and has exhibited internationally, belongs to the New York School (abstract expressionism). The Russian-born and Russian-educated Eugene Berman, a leader of the neo-romantic movement, lived in France before coming to the United States; composer Darius Milhaud, who in America seemed particularly alert to anything pertaining to French culture, wrote in 1953 that Berman's painting was daily growing in greatness, "wringing tragic expression from all the pomp of baroque and the distress of suffering humanity, in sublime amalgam of tattered clothes and crumbling palaces." And Karl Zerbe, whose art was described as being a "little colder and more reserved than most expressionism" by John Baur, had considerable influence on painting in Boston, where he was head of the department of painting of the school of the Museum of Fine Arts from 1937 to 1954. The German impressionist, George Grosz, was a terribly effective satirical caricaturist, a commentator on social and political questions, who expressed his desperate criticism in paintings and drawings. When he came to settle in America in 1932, *Times* magazine announced "Mild Monster Arrives." He was regarded as one of the most powerful expressionists and an inveterate pessimist who showed little hope for humanity and no compassion for those whom he considered exploiters of society. With his arrival in this country "something of that spirit had died." In Germany, he explained, he "had poured forth venom" in the form of caricatures. But in the United States "hate and proselytizing rancor seemed out of place."

Several of the painters did some sculpture at some time or other in their careers, but the sculptors in the migration wave were not numerous. The greatest figures in the field are José de Creeft, who arrived in 1929; Jacques Lipchitz, a resident of the United States since 1941; Bernard Reder, a latecomer in 1943 after waiting in Cuba for over a year for an American visa; and Ossip Zadkine, not as widely known in this country as the other three because he returned to Europe after the war. Zadkine had acquired an early reputation in Paris as one of the first to apply to sculpture the principles of cubism, from which he later freed himself. In this country he continued to produce, and the Museum of Modern Art owns some of his major works. Lipchitz's career in Europe was not dissimilar to that of his contemporary Zadkine, although he was somewhat slower in accepting cubism. Lipchitz's sculpture, as that of Zadkine, soon evolved toward a greater expression of movement. In the United States he "has built an art of extreme emotional intensity, using massive rhythms, anguished gestures, and primitive dislocations of anatomy," according to Baur; his art has gained him recognition as one of the two leaders of expressionism in sculpture. The other one is Bernard Reder. Somewhat younger than Lipchitz, he worked for years in his native Czernowitz and arrived in Paris only in 1936; massive, rounded sculptures, with no frontal view, equally important on all sides, were beginning to earn him recognition when the German occupation of France set him on a three-year odyssey that included imprisonment more than once in Spain and the long wait in Cuba for an American visa. Meanwhile the Nazis destroyed a good part of his French sculpture. After his arrival in this country he was enormously productive and gave free rein to his imagination, depicting nature in fantastic forms. José de Creeft came to the United States after years of study and work in Spain, where he was born, and in Paris. He has produced solid, rounded, and rhythmic figures, carved in stone or hammered in metal, inspired by the classical tradition that emphasizes human figures and stresses the importance of tactile values.

Although it would be very difficult to evaluate the total impact of these European painters and sculptors and the many more whom I have not mentioned, a few general considerations are possible. The majority of these men lived in the East, many around New York, and though they are widely known through exhibits and reproductions of their work, their influence is felt mainly in the East, especially on the expressionist New York School. A distinction must be made between the artists who came to America to stay and those who were "guests" during the war years and returned afterward to Europe. Of the former, those who were young when they arrived here and not already strongly shaped by the European tradition became identified with American art; Margo and Donati are examples. Another is the realist painter Henry Koerner, who was twenty-four years old when he left Austria in 1939. Older men, or men who settled here at a later date, were formed by one of three main streams of influences — the abstraction of the Bauhaus and De Stijl; German impressionism; and the successive, often overlapping modernistic movements of the school of Paris, mainly cubism, Dadaism, and surrealism. In the United States they gave impetus to the currents closest to those they had known in Europe. There were among them great teachers, who may have been more influential here as such than for their works.

Hofmann, Zerbe, Ozenfant, and Albers come readily to mind (although Albers is often classified with the designers). Those who did not teach — and they were in the majority — have been important in proportion to the length of their American careers, the quality and quantity of their output here, and the number of followers they sparked: Grosz, Tanguy, Seligmann, Berman, Lipchitz, and Reder are prominent in this group. But at least one painter, Marchel Duchamp, exerted an influence although he neither taught nor painted after settling in New York. His enigmatic personality, which remained French despite twenty-six years in the United States; the memory of the scandal at the Armory Show; the fame of his "ready-mades" and past artistic pranks, as when he painted a beard and mustache on a reproduction of the *Mona Lisa*; and the retrospective shows of his work — in Pasadena in 1963 and in New York in 1965 — have kept interest in him alive. He has exerted the greatest influence as an adviser to important art galleries in New York which used to place complete trust in his judgment of new artists and of works of art.

Finally there was the group that could be called visiting celebrities, the artists who returned to Europe after the war. Their presence in this country had a catalytic action especially on the future abstract expressionists of the New York School. It was, in Robert Goldwater's opinion, one of two separate experiences that combined in the background of these American artists — the other was the Federal Art Project of the WPA, which brought them together and gave them a sense of belonging to a group. The Europeans' arrival had similar effects, for "to see, occasionally to talk with, Mondrian, Masson, Ernst, Tanguy, Léger, Lipchitz, Duchamp, among others, was, so to speak, to join the School of Paris, to join, that is, the central creative tradition of twentieth-century art." Robert Motherwell, in an interview for *Artforum*, estimated that there were some twenty celebrated European artists in New York during the war and recalled that "anybody who wanted to could join them walking the streets." Their meeting place was the French Canteen. Motherwell, a newcomer to New York himself, liked to join them in the beginning because they were more interested in ideas than were American artists. There were constant discussions. According to Goldwater, the Europeans "carried with them a warmth of feeling, an intensity and concern for matters esthetic, a conviction of the rightness of their own judgment and an unconcern for any others . . . [their] conviction of the importance of art even in the midst of a cataclysm . . . was sincere and contagious." It affected the Americans and gave them an assurance as artists that they had lacked. "On the foreign side," Motherwell stated, "surrealism, of course, took a position on everything. Mondrian's and Leger's followers were few but intense; loners like Chagall . . . had no influence on us."

Whatever consequences the influx of foreign artists may have had on American painting and sculpture, the parallel depletion in Europe was conspicuous. In the forties the German centers and the school of Paris were eclipsed. The eyes of the international world of art turned to America. And in the years of reconstruction, while Europe was trying to find a new balance, American art, growing ever stronger, attained international prominence.

ART HISTORIANS

Art history was one of the not overcrowded academic fields in America in the twenties and early thirties, and many Europeans found a place in it. Writing about the development of art history in this country, James S. Ackerman remarked: "In the course of the 1930's . . . European influence increased as the field developed in size and strength, due in part to the large-scale enlistment of Europeans by American college and university faculties. . . . Around 1930 several German scholars were regular visitors to graduate schools on the East Coast, and the appointment of Europeans on a permanent basis was accelerated at the close of the Depression by the rapid expansion of university programs in art history and by the willingness of outstanding scholars uprooted by Hitler to take up permanent residence and citizenship in the United States."

The American career of Erwin Panofsky, the best known émigré art historian, is an illustration of Ackerman's description of events. Panofsky first visited the United States in the fall of 1931 and for the next three years commuted between Hamburg and New York University. In New York, in the spring of 1933, he received a cablegram from Germany (with Easter greetings from Western Union) informing him that he had been dismissed from his chair at Hamburg. He went back for a few months, returned to this country with his art-historian wife Dora and two teen-age sons, and in 1935 became a professor at the Institute for Advanced Study in Princeton. In the years after his coming, a considerable number of European art historians gathered at New York University and Princeton. The director of the Department of Fine Arts at New York University was that Walter Cook who "picked the apples" when Hitler shook the tree. During their association Panofsky helped Cook expand and strengthen the Institute of Fine Arts, by advising him in the selection of the "apples" to be picked.

Since that time, numerous art historians and archeologists have been on the faculty of New York University. Julius Held, an expert in Dutch and Flemish painting, who later moved to Columbia, and Karl Lehmann arrived in 1935. Until his death in 1960 Lehmann was one of the mainstays of the institute; he had already had a distinguished career in Europe as a classical archeologist: after directing the German Archeological Institute in Rome and the Archeological Institute at Heidelberg University, he was a professor and director of the Archeological Museum in Muenster at the time of his dismissal. Lehmann's American reputation is mainly tied to his excavations and work in Samothrace (of which he became a honorary citizen), but in an excursion into pure Americana he wrote a biography of Jefferson and described him as a humanist whose contemplation of ancient civilizations lasted a lifetime. Thus he startled even serious students of American history who had not yet delved deeply into this aspect of Jefferson's extraordinary personality. The next addition to the Institute of Fine Arts was Walter Friedlaender in 1936. He was then sixty-two years old and had taught at the University of Freiburg from 1914 to 1933. Hitler's laws caused his dismissal and prevented the publication of the *Festschrift* that art scholars and students had prepared for his sixtieth birthday. He was to be more than repaid in 1963, on the occasion of his ninetieth birthday, when two *Festschriften* in his honor were published, one in Germany and one in the United States. Friedlaender, an exceptionally active and lively man, taught a large number of American students who filled high-ranking positions — several are chairmen of art history departments — and through them his influence spread over the United States.

The stream of Europeans to the Institute of Fine Arts continued. In 1937 Martin Weinberger arrived from London where he had taught since his dismissal from the University of Munich in 1933. The next year New York University engaged Alfred Salmony, internationally known authority on Far Eastern art and jade and the editor-in-chief of the international journal *Artibus Asiae*. Salmony was to remain its editor until his death at sea on the "Île de France," in 1958. Guido Schoenberger came in

248

1939 and José López-Rey in 1944. Horst Janson, the chairman of the under-graduate department of fine arts, also holds a professorship at the Institute of Fine Arts: he came to America as a graduate student and before joining New York University taught over ten years in the Midwest, mainly in Iowa and at Washington University in St. Louis. In 1952 the institute acquired Richard Krautheimer, an expert on early Christian archeology and the history of early Christian and medieval architecture, who also taught at Louisville and Vassar. Other European art historians were at the institute for shorter times: Richard Ettinghausen, to name only one, was there from 1937 to 1938, then moved on to other positions.

Long before the thirties, Princeton University had a strong department of art and archeology. As a center of studies in these fields the town of Princeton acquired further prestige when in 1935 Abraham Flexner decided to add a school of humanistic studies to his Institute for Advanced Study, and both Erwin Panofsky and the younger but already outstanding Kurt Weitzmann joined its staff. In Germany Weitzmann had published books on Byzantine and Armenian art, and in this country he continued to be a very prolific writer on subjects that ranged from classical and Early Christian archeology to the history of book illumination. Besides being a permanent member of the institute (since 1935), in 1950 Weitzmann became a professor of art and archeology at Princeton University. Soon other European art his-torians came to the institute: Hanns Swarzenski joined it in 1936 and re-mained there until 1948 when he moved on to the Museum of Fine Arts in Boston. From 1939 to 1948 the scholar Charles de Tolnay was there. He wrote a remarkably large number of books, mostly on Italian Renaissance art, published in many countries. Paul Frankl, an eminent specialist in the history of Gothic architecture and its literary sources, joined the institute in 1940 and Adolf Katzenellenbogen in 1953. Richard Ettinghausen; the art critic, editor, and historian Justus Bier; and Richard Bernheimer are among those who have been members of the institute for one-year terms.

European scholars in the field of art history gathered at other American academic centers, showing a marked tendency to form groups, although nowhere as large as in Princeton and at New York University. The University of Chicago is one example: in 1935 Ulrich Middledorf left Florence where he had been the curator of the German Institute for Art History to become a teacher of art at Chicago. A very active man, he built up the department of art of the University of Chicago, of which he was the chairman from 1940 until his return to Florence in 1953; under his leadership art history acquired a greater prominence at Chicago than it had in the past. A scholar of Far Eastern art, Ludwig Bachhofer, joined the Chicago faculty in the same year and was there until his retirement. A third art historian from Germany, Otto von Simson, was at Chicago from 1945 to 1954, when he returned to Germany, and a fourth, John Rewald, joined the faculty in 1963. Though this group was small, it was part of a larger group of German émigrés at the University of Chicago, mainly in the department of Germanics but also in other departments of the college and graduate school, who promoted high-level German studies in this country: Middledorf and von Simson, for instance, were among the contributors to Arnold Bergsträsser's *Deutsche Beiträge*.

Harvard had at least four European scholars: the medievalist Wilhelm Koehler was at that university some twenty years and Jakob Rosenberg, historian of painting in northern Europe from the late Gothic to the Baroque period, stayed even longer; archeologist George Hanfmann went to Harvard as a young Ph.D. in 1935 and stayed on there — only for a few years in wartime was he away, working with the Office of War Information and other agencies; Otto Benesch, a museum man, came to this country from Vienna in 1940 and in 1947 he returned to Vienna to resume his position as director of the Albertina. In his brief stay he worked intensely and published abundantly. He made studies of collections of European artists in America, and among his major works of this period is the book *The Art of the Renaissance in Northern Europe*.

Mills College had its trio: Alfred Salmony, before he joined the faculty of New York University; the historian of nineteenth-century art and Indian art, Alfred Neumeyer; and an expert in Far Eastern art and archeology, Otto Maenchen-Helfen, now at the University of California. Others scattered to many schools throughout this country. Ackerman wrote: "While the second generation of scholars in this country [those active between World War I and 1930] had been trained by Americans . . . few of their students completed advanced education without having worked with a distinguished foreigner."

Another group of European art historians, the "museum people," have been influential outside the strictly academic world. They are directors or curators of art museums and galleries, who have contributed to their scholarly operation by publishing catalogues and comments on art collections, recommending purchases, and organizing exhibits. Thus in New York City René d'Harnoncourt was director of the Museum of Modern Art and vice-president of the Museum of Primitive Art, which he helped to organize; Hans Huth had been at German museums and in the administration of former royal palaces and parks in Prussia before coming to this country; here he first joined the United States National Park Service and then was a curator at the Art Institute of Chicago from 1944 to 1958. In Germany George Swarzenski had been instrumental in the acquisition of many choice collections for the Städel Museum in Frankfurt and had gained a reputation as one of the connoisseurs and organizers of German art. In this country both he and his son Hanns held positions at the Museum of Fine Arts in Boston.

Wolfgang Stechow played the double role of teacher and museum man: in 1940 he joined the faculty of Oberlin College (after teaching in Germany, Holland, Italy, and at the University of Wisconsin), and he helped gather a collection of Dutch works of art for the Oberlin Museum. This jewel of an art museum cannot fail to startle the European visitor to whom the small town of Oberlin seems to spring up in the middle of nowhere. When in its museum he finds himself face to face with numerous masterpieces of Italian and Dutch art he will ponder on the reach of European influences and the dispersion of artistic patrimony.

Among émigré art historians there are first-rank scholars, their American colleagues agree, very important scholars, and others that deserve a nod. But, the Americans say, Erwin Panofsky is in a class by himself. A man of delightful wit rooted in the wisdom of two continents, Panofsky imported to this country modern iconology of which he was one of the creators in Germany and for which he revived the old word. It is a method of integral interpretation of works of art, not only of their forms, but also of the themes developed in them and of their symbolic value in the cultural context of their time and place.

Panofsky discussed his methodology and some of its applications in the book *Studies in Iconology* which he published in 1939. Since then iconology has become established as an important branch of the history of art, and Panofsky has gained the reputation of being one of the greatest art historians of our time. In this country he has many followers who have assimilated his

251

methods. An important group of iconological studies have shed a new understanding on early Flemish and Dutch art. Among the émigrés who have contributed to these studies are Panofsky himself, de Tolnay, and Stechow. Janson's *Apes and Ape-Lore in the Middle Ages and Renaissance* is an example of iconological scholarship in a more special field. Iconological methods have been applied also to the study of architecture and the content of churches, monasteries, and palaces. Panofsky, Otto von Simson, and especially Krautheimer have contributed to this field.

Iconology is only one of several areas in which art history may be divided and to which the Europeans have made contributions. Another is connoisseurship, a form of scholarship that grew out of the close intimacy with works of art which is acquired only by long association with museums and galleries. The American Bernard Berenson was one of its exponents. Ackerman lists among the works of connoisseurs Janson's *The Sculpture of Donatello*. Luigi Salerno, in the *Encyclopedia of the World of Art*, gives great prominence to the work of Lionello Venturi, the Italian-born art historian who refused to take the Fascist oath required of university professors and was in voluntary exile from 1932 to 1946. In this period, part of which he spent in this country, Venturi published works that extended connoisseurship to recent art, namely impressionism. Venturi's *Il gusto dei primitivi* furthered also the history of taste.

Walter Friedlaender is identified with more than one area: with the history of style, as the author of notable essays on mannerism and its relation to the baroque; and with the interpretation of art as the expression of a culture, for his interpretations of the work of Caravaggio in relation to the taste and religious movements of his time. Friedlaender was preparing to give a course on Caravaggio at the Institute of Fine Arts of New York University at the time of his death. He was an expert on the French painter Nicolas Poussin; and the author, among other works, of the monumental *Caravaggio Studies*; he finished a book on Titian a few days before he died.

The historians in these areas directed their attention to European art, but others were concerned with the art of other parts of the world. Ludwig Bachhofer studied and wrote books in the field of the art and archeology of India, China, and Japan. Alfred Salmony, who traveled extensively in China and Japan and in 1950 was an American exchange professor in Korea, wrote books on Far Eastern art, including two volumes on Chinese jade and on the interrelation of the ancient arts of Europe and Asia. A major exponent in the field of Byzantine art is Kurt Weitzmann, who also took part in an archeological expedition to Mount Sinai; among his more recent books are *Greek Mythology in Byzantine Art* and *Ancient Book Illumination*. The art of the western continent was not entirely neglected: in Europe, Pál Kelemen, art historian and archeologist, had been interested in early Christian art, but after coming to the United States in 1932 he turned to pre-Columbian and colonial art in Latin America, made many survey trips to Latin America, and published books among which is a two-volume history of medieval American art. Alfred Neumeyer explored the contributions of American Indians to Spanish colonial art. And Wolfgang Born, after arriving here from Austria, turned his back on everything European and published only on American painting.

European art historians made great contributions to America, but they have also gained much, and not only because they found the means to realize their capabilities and their plans — they obtained support for archeological or survey expeditions, and libraries, museums, and galleries assisted them and put a great wealth of material at their disposal. But in their contacts with colleagues and students their perspectives broadened. In the process of adjustment they have shed confining European habits and have assimilated the more democratic ways of American institutions. Erwin Panofsky described this process with great wit in a lecture "The History of Art," published in *The Cultural Migration*. His observations are of broader interest than the field of art history alone and apply to the Americanization of the countless scholars in many fields who came from Europe to the United States in the thirties.

IX

⟨⟨⟨

In the World of Books and Magazines

WRITERS

If every person who wrote a book or a few articles were to be considered a writer, most European-born intellectuals would come under this heading. Not only hosts of scholars and scientists but also musicians and artists have joined the free-lancers in their march on the printing press. Their output is astounding. Titles by the European-born have been persistently on the lists of most publishers; library shelves sag under the weight of their works; and newspapers and quality magazines have published a stream of shorter pieces. The question then is: are all those responsible for this tremendous flood to be called writers?

In an age when fiction has lost its primacy over non-fiction it would be unrealistic to deny the title to all those who are not creative writers, in the sense currently attributed to this class. The line becomes hard to draw. Paul Tillich's bibliography includes at least twenty-three books in German and English and countless articles, but posterity will almost certainly remember him as a theologian rather than a writer. On the other hand, it is not clear whether Erich Fromm is at present better known as a psychoanalyst and social scientist or as an author, nor how future generations will classify him. In many other doubtful cases the future may forget entirely academic and professional connections and remember some men and women exclusively as writers. In the last analysis, any definition of the word "writer" must be left to the usage and taste of the times.

In the early forties when America was crowded with refugees from the fall of France there was much ado about exiled writers and many articles appeared about their plight. These articles left the impression that "writers" meant those men and women who hoped to support themselves in this country mainly by writing, or, if willing to accept college, university, library, or other paying positions, hoped to establish a reputation in the writing field, as they had done or had hoped to do in the past. But it is evident that most authors of the articles made exceptions even to as tenuous a definition as this and extended it to their pet refugees. Those most frequently mentioned were poets, writers of fiction, and journalists, but statesmen, linguists, philosophers, historians, social and political scientists, and others were not excluded; the bio-bibliographical *Deutsche Exil-Literatur 1933–1945* has an entry even for Einstein and his politico-philosophical writings. (But then this manual, published in Germany in 1962, is not selective, and lists as German literature the works of authors who were born in Russia, Austria, Hungary, Poland, Czechoslovakia, Yugoslavia, and even France and Belgium. Indeed, the ideal of greater Germany is here fulfilled.)

The vagueness in the definition of the word "writer" permits inclusion here of émigré authors who played an important role before the end of World War II: they published a mass of reliable information about totalitarian countries. The dictators' propaganda devices suppressed or distorted news, and foreign observers in those countries were not always equipped with the necessary insight to understand the mentality of the people. The émigrés, on the other hand, were anxious to share with the Americans their knowledge of the political, social, and intellectual scene in their homelands. And so they wrote abundantly.

Among the Italians who presented Italy and her culture at an early date were Ascoli, Borgese, Salvemini, and Sforza; and somewhat later Niccolò Tucci began writing articles and short stories with an Italian background for the *New Yorker* and other magazines. The Russian-born Angelica Balabanoff who had lived for many years in Italy expressed her very personal point of view in chapters of her autobiography *My Life as a Rebel*. She was an extraordinary woman. After having relinquished her rights to her parents' estate out of sympathy with the Russian peasants, she became an active worker in international and Italian Socialist movements. For years, in Switzerland and in Italy, she was Mussolini's friend and political mentor, but when he turned his back on socialism she broke her ties with him. In Europe she collaborated with Socialist leaders of many countries, including

Lenin, in 1919 and 1920, in Russia (she reported that she had free access to the Kremlin). After travel in Europe and frequent returns to Italy, her country of adoption, she came to America in 1936, where she remained until the end of the war. Here she wrote her book, which flashes restlessly over the scenes of her European adventures. At the end of the war she returned to Italy, where she died in 1965. When I met her in Rome in 1958, she appeared to be just the little old woman over eighty that she was, complaining like other little old women that things had changed, and moving sluggishly, with some difficulty. But she was still full of contempt for the man Mussolini who had betrayed her ideals, and she was still traveling in uncomfortable Italian trains to speak at Socialist rallies.

Angelica Balabanoff's colorful glimpses of Russia do not form a coherent picture, but other Russian-born intellectuals have written on Russian affairs, either before the end of World War II or during the cold war. David Dallin wrote copiously about his country of origin — no fewer than seven books in the forties alone, and more later, books widely recognized as authoritative, scholarly, and well documented. Dallin was exiled twice from Russia, the first time in 1911 when he was still a student. After the revolution he went back and until 1921 was a member of the Soviet as opposition deputy. Forced to leave Russia a second time, he lived in Germany, Poland, and France before coming to the United States in 1940 — a good example of a refugee kept on the go by events. Among other scholars of Russian politics and economy, social scientist Waldemar Gurian wrote on Marxism, bolshevism, and Soviet foreign policy; and economists Alexander Gerschenkron, Michael Mirski, and others illustrated many aspects of the Soviet economy.

The French, although latecomers on the American scene, published exceptionally prompt comments on the fate of France and Europe: André Maurois' *The Tragedy of France* and Jules Romains' *The Seven Mysteries of Europe* appeared at the end of 1940.

More authors wrote about Germany than about any other country, which is not surprising in view of the size of the German migration. Among those who discussed historical, social, or political issues at an early date were Arnold Brecht, Ernst Fraenkel, Karl Frank (under the pen name of Paul Hagen), Robert Kempner, Hans Leonhardt, Paul Massing, Franz Neumann, Heinz Pol, Fritz Sternberg, and Hans Weigert. Hermann Rauschning, a conservative liberal since 1935 but originally an important member of the

Nazi party, wrote at least five books about Hitler and the Nazi revolution between 1939 and 1944.

Some of these writers were concerned with broad topics, Germany's form of government in the past and at the time of their writing, her politics, and her future. Others took up more specific historical events they had witnessed, as did Hans Leonhardt in his *The Nazi Conquest of Danzig*. But often a specific instance, such as this, could permit the observation, as if in slow motion and in great detail, of the process by which the Nazis infiltrated and subjugated Europe.

Several authors wrote about Hitler, and Konrad Heiden was one of the first. Well before coming to this country from France with the help of the Emergency Rescue Committee, Heiden had written a two-volume biography of Hitler, published in the United States in 1936 and 1939. By exposing Hitler to the world, Heiden placed himself in great personal danger, but he had vowed to fight Hitler by all the means at his disposal. Once safely in this country Heiden continued to write about Hitler, and his *Der Führer, Hitler's Rise to Power* (1944) is still one of the best sources of material on Hitler's personality. In other fields Otto Nathan and Gustav Stolper dealt with German economy and finance; George Eliasberg, Curt Riess, and Kurt Singer described the underground and espionage. Singer, a newspaper man concerned with espionage since 1933, reported that he actively participated in exposing Axis agents. Bruno Bettelheim published the already mentioned study of individual and mass behavior under the extreme stress of camp life; and Jan Valtin treated a similar topic in a more popular way in his unforgettable *Out of the Night*.

The many personal narratives published here in the thirties and early forties by émigrés from many European countries shed much light on little-known aspects of intellectual and cultural life in their homelands, aspects that are not usually discussed in factual exposés: how publishing houses were run; the resistance of newspaper staffs to Nazi pressure; the mechanism of university administration and how it allowed the rise or continuation of anti-Semitism in various countries; how the theater and music world was affected by political events. One of these accounts is Stefan Zweig's masterpiece, *The World of Yesterday*, describing an affluent Austrian and European upper middle class, and another is Leopold Infeld's *Quest: The Evolution of a Scientist*, giving the reader a vivid picture of Polish ghettos and schools.

In the same category fall the books by Klaus and Erika Mann (Thomas Mann's children) about their experiences after the rise of Hitler; and the autobiographies of the German book publisher Hermann Ullstein and of the literary magazine editor Franz Schoenberner (his two books were published a little later than the others mentioned, in 1946 and 1949).

A few émigrés wrote about their tribulations and early experiences in America shortly after their arrival, before memories could lose poignancy. Hans Natonek (*In Search of Myself*), psychologist Erna Barschak (*My American Adventure*), physician Martin Gumpert (*First Papers*), and Klaus and Erika Mann (*Escape to Life*) belong to this group. And to it belong also writers who have described the plight of refugees caught in the fall of France: Lion Feuchtwanger and Hans Sahl in their books already mentioned, and Leo Lania in *The Darkest Hour*. Gumpert and the Manns painted a segment of the migration that seemed the most prestigious in the early forties: the older group with an established European reputation, many of whom have later passed into oblivion.

The authors mentioned so far were singled out because they filled special roles. The group of conventionally defined writers is much larger.

According to an article by Walter Sorell in the *Saturday Review* in August, 1945, there were more than four hundred exiled writers in the United States at that time. In comparison, Maurice Davie stated that his study group had collected the names of 326 writers who had come after 1933 and that this figure was certainly much lower than the actual. Since not many writers came to America between 1930 and 1933 and probably even fewer in the war years 1942–45, it may be assumed that both Sorell's and Davie's estimates are representative of the writers in the migration wave.

It was the contention of many observers in the mid-forties that the writers' plight was much worse than that of other exiles, that the mind of a writer is shaped by the tongue he learned to speak as a child, by his land and its traditions; good translators are hard to come by; stylistic perfection cannot be transferred from one language to another; if a foreign writer manages to master English his foreignness will be reflected in the shape of his thinking; and although a few others may be cited, history records only a single successful transplanted writer, Joseph Conrad, the Ukranian-born Pole who had heard hardly a word of English before he was twenty-one. Although émigré lawyers and doctors may object to an indorsement of the writers' plight as the most difficult, there is some truth to these comments.

Well-established European novelists and other writers who had gained fame in Europe managed without difficulty to have their works translated, yet the problem of adequate translators was real and to each writer it became acute as soon as he learned enough English to read his translated works with a critical eye. The poets were understandably the worst stricken and would never be satisfied by the way in which their poems were rendered in English. Poets as well as prose writers often had to be content with having their works published only in their native tongue and read by limited audiences. Many American publishers were willing to publish in German or French; there were numerous foreign-language periodicals; and in the early forties several émigrés launched publishing ventures. Even so, the majority of writers lived under great financial hardship.

From a psychological angle, it is especially interesting to note that the more strictly a writer identified himself with writing per se, the greater were the difficulties he encountered in the transplantation. The scholar and the scientist could learn and perfect their English while gathering material for their next book. Lecturing and contacts with students and colleagues facilitated and sped up the switch from their native language to English. I am not aware of grumbling about writing difficulties from émigré academics, and indeed from these quarters came a spectacular output. On the other hand, the man with the writer's label, especially if not very young, went through a much tougher apprenticeship in this country. Pride demanded that he make good at once, the exigencies of life that he start earning money promptly, and he himself insisted on achieving both aims by writing. But writing is a terribly lonely job and compelled the newcomer to isolate himself. Unlike the teacher, the émigré writer did not have the benefit of close relationships with Americans. He was on his own. The conviction that style is tied to language rather than to mode of thought, that he should preserve his own style and writing qualities, hampered him. He could not take the time for a leisurely process of Americanization. Perhaps he did not even welcome the process.

Some of these feelings were expressed by the French novelist Marc Chadourne in a "Symposium on Transplanted Writers" in *Books Abroad*. Chadourne, who as late as 1948 was still publishing novels in French, commented on the position of the refugee writer: "If by chance he succeeds in asserting himself, in expanding through sheer persistence a few timid roots, a strange thing happens: In taking on a new life, a change comes over him, but this mimetic transformation breaks his spirit . . . he has to adapt his topics, his style to the taste of a public he is unfamiliar with. . . . Little by little, while doing his best to 'go native,' he loses his own touch, his style, his personality. Little choice is left to him between giving up writing and being no more completely himself." This opinion was not shared by all, and in the same symposium, an Austrian, Alfred Werner, stated, somewhat oratorically: "Whether we started writing in English . . . or whether we are working primarily for the restoration of freedom in the respective countries of our origin — we came under the wholesome influence of this hemisphere, we became 'Americanized,' often without noticing it."

Although opinions and personal situations varied, all indications are that in the early forties large numbers of foreign-born writers did not yet feel at home in America, were uncertain of their future, and bewildered by the present. Many were in a distressing financial situation, depending for their sustenance on grants or charity and torn between the lure of a regularly paying non-intellectual job and the stubborn determination not to abandon the career they had chosen for themselves — as Hans Natonek poignantly described in his *In Search of Myself*. At the same time younger men were gaining experience in the English language and American customs by serving in the United States armed forces, as Klaus Mann, his younger brother historian Golo, and many others did; or by participating in one branch or another of psychological warfare.

By the mid-forties, the early comers among the writers had settled in their new home, established new habits, a new circle of friends, and new contacts with publishers. They were as well acclimated as they would ever be. Some had been here for many years. Vicki Baum, for one, had long been a darling of American audiences for her novels of intrigue and adventure and the movies made from them. Trained as a harpist in Vienna, she had her first stories published when she was thirteen, the first book when she was eighteen, and later she became a magazine editor in Vienna. *Grand Hotel* was published in 1931, and that same year at the age of thirty-five she emigrated to the United States where she continued to write, at first in German, then in English, and published no fewer than thirteen books.

Early comers, however, were not very numerous. The writers were among the intellectuals who clung the longest to Europe, dreading to venture out of a cultural environment which they deemed essential to their thinking and its expression. In the end many were caught in the tragic events of the spring of 1940, and after sharing the misadventures of refugees from invaded countries they barely managed to reach America before Pearl Harbor virtually closed the passage across the Atlantic. Whether early or late, the cultural wave brought to these shores some of Europe's most important writers. Several continued to write and produced outstanding works in this country.

Thomas Mann, recipient of the Nobel Prize for literature in 1929 and one of the most significant figures of modern literature, arrived in America in 1937, after five years of exile in Switzerland. Soon after Hitler came to power, Mann left Germany on vacation and, warned of the danger in which his criticism of the Nazis had placed him, did not return. At that time Thomas Mann had completed *The Tales of Jacob* and *Young Joseph,* the first two parts of his tetralogy *Joseph and His Brothers,* which were to be published in Germany in 1933 and 1934. He was at work on the third, *Joseph in Egypt,* and the manuscript remained in his home in Munich when he left on what he thought would be a short vacation. His daughter Erika returned to the abandoned home under the protection of darkness to steal the manuscript, as it were, from the Nazis. Mann completed his work in Switzerland, and *Joseph in Egypt* was published in Stockholm in 1936. In America, after settling in Princeton where he was a lecturer at the university, he began work on the fourth part, *Joseph the Provider,* and completed it in California, where he moved in 1941.

In California Mann wrote two other books, the last of his major novels, *Doctor Faustus,* and *The Holy Sinner.* Years later, after he had returned to Europe, he gave an account of how *Doctor Faustus* came into being, describing the steps in the often painful creative process. From this account, published posthumously in the United States under the title *The Story of a Novel,* a striking fact emerges about Mann the émigré writer: his presence in America was not relevant to his work, and though he felt "the pressure and tumult of outward events" his conception of *Doctor Faustus* was not affected by any typically American element of his environment. (In *The*

261

Black Swan, which Mann wrote after his return to Europe, there is one American, but the characterization is weak, and the young man could be of almost any nationality.)

The idea of an artist's pact with the devil as a possible subject for a book dated back to a much earlier period of Mann's life; after having been shelved for over forty years, it gripped him in this country, when he went through old notes. He was then finishing *Joseph* and was seeking inspiration for further work. While exploring anew the old idea, he did much background reading, almost entirely of German works, and sought the advice, assistance, or simply the attentive ear of German or German-speaking émigrés: theologian Paul Tillich, conductor Bruno Walter, social scientist Theodor Adorno, writers Alfred Neumann, Franz Werfel, and Leonhard Frank, composers Ernst Toch, Ernst Krenek, and Arnold Schoenberg, physician Martin Gumpert, publisher Fritz Landshoff, and many others. Mann participated in the intellectual life of the exiles much more than in that of the Americans, and his friends belonged to émigré circles. When he was not working at his book, he was busy preparing forewords for books by fellow exiles, or commemorations of Germans who had died in America (Max Reinhardt's death provided one such occasion). Or he prepared lectures about Germany, broadcasts for Germany, addresses to sponsor relief activities; he had been a speaker at the launching of relief ventures at least since the time the Emergency Rescue Committee was formed. Contacts with Americans were incidental, and very seldom did they have anything to do with the writing of *Doctor Faustus*.

And yet it was within these years that Mann became an American citizen, renouncing the Czech citizenship which the Czech government had given him when he lost his German citizenship. The new nationality must have affected him to a certain degree, for he did deliver a speech in Roosevelt's campaign for a fourth term. But the new American remained what he was, a man whose roots reached deeply in the soil of German culture, who had no use for another culture: it would not help his writing. As a result, *Doctor Faustus* is, in Alfred Kazin's words "a most German book, bounded on every side by German thought . . . a great cry of love and despair over the country he fled."

Thomas Mann was the most famous member of an extraordinary clan; several other members also attained literary distinction and came to the United States. Thomas' older brother Heinrich was one of those writers whose traditions and loyalties bound them fast to Europe, and he did not consider a move to the United States until forced to do so by the debacle of France. Heinrich Mann, who had chosen Nice as his exile-residence, was such a European at heart that his niece and nephew Erika and Klaus Mann, writing about him in 1939 in *Escape to Life*, mentioned his "almost super-stitious fear of leaving France." Only under the pressure of events did he allow Varian Fry and his Centre Américain de Sécours to help him reach Portugal and a boat bound for the United States. He arrived on American soil in 1940, and here he was hailed as "Thomas Mann's brother." In Germany, however, there had been times when he had stood higher than his brother in political and literary circles. Thomas had been criticized for his conservative stand, for coming out too slowly at first, too waveringly against the rise of nazism. Heinrich as novelist, political writer, and spiritual spon-sor of the expressionist movement in German literature, was one of Germany's greatest liberal animators. He had always turned his skilful pen against the German forces of reaction, "Wilhelmism" first, then Hitlerism. But in America he was little known, and his presence here did not bring him additional recognition. In 1940 he was almost seventy. In the next ten years he wrote and published in German, but the echoes of his books hardly reached the American public. He died in 1950 in California, aware of the oblivion in which his work had fallen and the great silence around him — one of the many exiles who had suffered in the process of transplantation to America.

Thomas Mann's two oldest children were also gifted writers: Erika, who married poet W. H. Auden but kept her maiden name, and Klaus. Both preceded their parents to America by several months and both gave them-selves to the strenuous task of enlightening Americans on the state of affairs in Germany. They were interviewed, went on lecture tours, contributed articles, and wrote books. One of the books they wrote together is *Escape to Life* in which they described in detail, with the vividness of first-hand knowledge, the dispersal of German intellectuals just before the outbreak of World War II. Like a series of pictures at the beginning of a film reel, it shows the intellectuals settled in places from which they were to be wrenched and expressing sentiments that were to change sharply when war and the invasion of Europe gave them a violent jolt.

In the early forties Erika became a war correspondent and between trips to the European theater of war she assumed the role of sympathetic listener and editor of her father's work. For all his success, Thomas Mann needed the reassurance and encouragement of friends and relatives while his writing was in progress. Erika was his most critical admirer and "a skilled parer down of all pedantic excess," as Mann put it: she suggested cuts in her father's often too-long drafts for lectures or chapters of books, and he usually accepted her suggestions with gratitude. Klaus, who served in the American army, had become well established in his career as author, literary critic, and journalist by 1949, the year he committed suicide in Cannes.

Mann's other four children also came to the United States. Golo, a noted historian, who accompanied his uncle Heinrich in his flight from France to the United States, went back to teach in Germany. Monika, primarily a musician, has done some writing, including a book of reminiscences of her father, and writes poems in German. Michael is a violinist. Elisabeth, the youngest child, studied in this country, then married Giuseppe Antonio Borgese and assisted him in his literary and political ventures, including the editorship of *Common Cause*. After Borgese's retirement from the University of Chicago, he, Elizabeth, and their two daughters went to live in Italy, where he died in 1952. More recently she has published books on different subjects and become the director of studies in international relations of the Center for the Study of Democratic Institutions at Santa Barbara.

The migration wave brought to America two writers who, like Thomas Mann, had received the Nobel prize in literature, the Belgian Maurice Maeterlinck and the Norwegian Sigrid Undset. Maeterlinck, now an almost forgotten author, was celebrated throughout Europe in the first two decades of this century for his mystic plays and other works in which he revealed symbolically the mystery that lies beneath the surface of ordinary life. Among his most successful works available in English translation are his allegorical play *The Blue Bird* and the book *The Life of the Bees* that combines philosophy and natural history with fantasy. Old Count Maeterlinck, already seventy-nine years of age when he came to this country, did not publish here and except for attending performances of some of his plays — at least one was a benefit in aid of French children — he kept out of the limelight.

Unlike Maeterlinck, Sigrid Undset produced several books, some of them for children, while she lived in the United States. They are not of the same quality as the great novels that made her famous: those depicting the life of working girls in Christiania, of which *Jenny* is one, and those about medieval Norway, the most famous of which is the trilogy *Kristin Lavransdatter*. The books she wrote in the United States have distinction and charm. *The Return to the Future* was certainly timely when published in 1942, for it is the story of her flight across the Swedish border to Stockholm and then to America, and it describes how the German invasion trampled the beauties of her land. Both Maeterlinck and Undset returned to Europe after the war and both died in 1949, Maeterlinck in Nice, Sigrid Undset at her Norwegian home.

There were other great literary figures in the wave. Franz Werfel, the Czech-born poet, dramatist, and novelist, was well known to the American public for his *The Forty Days of Musa Dagh*, the epic of the Armenians' desperate resistance against the Turks on that now famous Syrian mountain. On his flight from the Nazis, Werfel, a Jew, found himself one day in Lourdes and vowed that he would write the story of Bernadette. *The Song of Bernadette* is the first novel he wrote on American soil. Published in 1942, it revived the popularity that Werfel had enjoyed six years previously with his story of the Armenians, but his close friend Thomas Mann was skeptical about his "playing with miracles." Mann thought that "intellectually there is something impure about it." Nevertheless Werfel played with miracles again in his posthumously published utopian novel *Star of the Unborn* describing a trip he takes into a future some hundred of thousand years from now and the technico-spiritual life he meets.

Lion Feuchtwanger was known for his historical novels, several of which have a Jewish background (*Jew Suess* is one); in the United States he published many other books after *The Devil in France*, among them *Simone* and *Proud Destiny*. Oskar Maria Graf, a Catholic left-wing writer of peasant Bavarian stock, surprised the world when he openly and vigorously protested because the Nazis did not burn his books in the great bonfire of May, 1933; in this country he wrote abundantly, but published mostly in German.

Some literary critics maintained that the Austrian Hermann Broch was more worthy of the Nobel prize in literature than several of those who received it. In Vienna he had been a mathematician, engineer, and director of a Viennese textile concern and had come under the influence of psychoanalysis. In Vienna he wrote the powerful trilogy *The Sleepwalkers*, depicting three stages in the dissolution of European society; in the best known book he wrote in the United States, *The Death of Vergil*, the dying Roman poet, in a state of exalted perception, depicts the age from which Christianity was to spring. Among the many other writers who were already well known by the time they came to America are Erich Maria Remarque, Emil Ludwig, Stefan Zweig, Jules Romains, and André Maurois and the poets Walter Mehring, Fritz von Unruh, and surrealist André Breton.

There are indications that Thomas Mann's aloofness from the American scene was shared by other émigré writers, especially German authors in the older age group. But the opposite tendency, the deliberate exploration of the environment, was also evident. This attitude is not surprising in younger authors not yet firmly entrenched in the literary traditions of their countries. One example is the Hungarian Stefan Lorant, a pioneer in America of picture textbooks, including a life in photographs of Lincoln and a pictorial biography of Franklin Roosevelt. On the occasion of the publication of Lorant's *The New World*, containing reproductions of drawings and paintings by early American settlers, the *Saturday Review* stated, "What bothers some American historians is the uncomfortable fact that one of the leading members of their group is a fellow who was born in Hungary and didn't come to the United States until 1940."

Another "fellow who was born in Hungary" invaded the American historical field, but at a later date than Lorant. Nicholas Halasz, a journalist and attorney at law, did not know English very well when he arrived in America in 1941; his major work, a history of Czechoslovakia, was in Hungarian. Not until 1955 did he publish a book in English, a biography of Dreyfus. But in 1960, after having written two more books in English on non-American subjects, Halasz published *Roosevelt Through Foreign Eyes* and thus entered American history. The foreign eyes were not his but those of newspaper writers, government leaders, and similar people who were spreading information and misinformation while Franklin Delano Roosevelt was President of the United States. More recently, in 1966, Halasz made a forceful incursion into old Americana and wrote *The Rattling Chains*, a study of slavery and the slave revolts in the South, whether real or imagined by slave owners, which ended almost invariably in the slaughter of Negroes.

266

Digging into American history and culture is less expected of an older author who had no intention of settling in America. I am thinking of the great French writer André Maurois, born Herzog, a man who has done a great deal to promote understanding between France and the United States. He had been in this country several times between 1927 and 1939, on lecture tours and to teach a semester at Princeton, and had then enjoyed the status of a famous visitor from Europe. He returned in the summer of 1940, an exile, downcast, crushed under the blows of the French disaster. Since his early visits he had felt that it was the duty of a French author who could speak English not to miss any opportunity to maintain a spiritual bond between America and France. Now, in his sorrow, he sought to plead the cause of France before divided public opinion. In a series of articles published as *Tragedy in France*, he related what he had seen of World War II as a French captain attached to the British Army (he had held a similar position in World War I) and what he believed had been the causes of the defeat. When he lectured he asked Americans to keep on loving France and help in saving her. To forget his heavy grief he began working furiously and produced, among other writings, a *Histoire des États Unis*. His aim was to answer questions in his own mind and to enlighten his countrymen, who knew little of the United States. Except for a period in 1943 in which he was an officer in North Africa, Maurois spent the war years in the United States and ended his exile in the summer of 1946. In France he continued to explain America to the French, and in 1962 he published a new history of the United States covering the period from Wilson to Kennedy. It was part of an ambitious project in collaboration with the French Louis Aragon, parallel histories of the United States and the Soviet Union between 1917 and 1960.

André Maurois is only one of many writers who went back to Europe and endeavored to make America better known to their countrymen. Others wrote from here in their own languages and served the same purpose. But together with our virtues they occasionally illustrated our shortcomings, as did the books in German by the brilliant Hungarian Hans Habe (pseudonym of Janos Bekessy) on our civil rights and race problems and on the assassination of President Kennedy. (In the cultural exchange Habe is a two-way participant, having written several novels in English with strong Hungarian and Austrian backgrounds.)

As the years went by, the writers who did not go back to Europe became more and more Americanized. Some went on writing their books in their own languages and used English for less extensive works, literary reviews, art criticism, short stories, and topical newspaper and magazine articles. Together with those who achieved a complete switch of language they form such a large group and have become so familiar to American readers that they are seldom identified as foreign-born. Occasionally a "Rudolf," "Erich," or "Ernst" suggests a fondness and attachment to a spelling that is an indication of long years lived in a distant country. Thus the spelling betrays a member of the intellectual wave, for younger people who had either all or a part of their education in this country often rebelled at a first name that not even their teachers could spell correctly (Italians whose first name was Giulio, Giuseppe, or Giovanni had indeed to anglicize or change it altogether to avoid spellings and pronunciations that seemed comical to them). A very partial list of writers who have contributed to American non-technical dailies and periodical (and have also written books, either directly in English or in their own language first) includes Martha Albrand, Hannah Arendt, Rudolf Arnheim, Hans Habe, Leo Lania, Stefan Lorant, Paul Massing, Vladimir Nabokov, Hans Natonek, Robert Pick, Richard Plaut, Franz Schoenberner, Niccolò Tucci, Ernst Waldinger, Joseph Wechsberg, Bella Fromm Welles, and Alfred Werner. (Niccolò Tucci is the author of novels on a European background — in *Before My Time* Tucci described the extraordinary, often theatrical situations in which his ancestors were placed by the eccentricities of his Russian grandmother and the marriage of his Russian mother to his Italian father.)

If I were asked to name the most successful author from a literary standpoint, I might choose the Russian-born Nabokov, for his mastery of the English language is so good that he has been praised as one of the best English stylists. But Nabokov is no Conrad. Although he lived in Russia until he was twenty years old, he had become acquainted with the English language long before then. When he was a small child his mother read English stories to him at bedtime; until the age of seven or eight he had English governesses; and in his early teens he discovered his life-long interest in Lepidoptera by chancing upon English periodicals on that subject. But several times he mentions in his books "governess English" and his allusion to the fear he experienced when he began writing in English that he would never be able to bring his English prose anywhere close to the level of his Russian give an idea of the huge distance he had to travel before he could write *Lolita*. His two years as a student at Cambridge certainly helped him, though they were followed by almost two decades spent in other European countries, mostly in Germany — decades in which he wrote in Russian and occasionally in French, and toward the end of which he began writing in English. His first novel written in English was completed almost a year before he came to the United States. He also translated two of his Russian novels into English while still living in Europe.

Nabokov's proficiency in English is such that he has undertaken something that extremely few foreign-born-and-educated persons have attempted: the writing of poetry. (The Italian-born Anna Maria Arni published one volume of poems she wrote in English, but no other poems by intellectuals in the wave have come to my attention.) He has published a volume of poems, has translated the poetry of Pushkin, and his "novel" *Pale Fire* consists of a commentary upon a 999-line poem. One of Nabokov's attractions, to the foreign-born reader at least, is the frequent piercing through of the European background in his English writings: in *Pnin* the main character is a European-born college professor, whose adventures on an American campus undoubtedly evoke memories of their own experiences in countless foreign-born intellectuals. Elsewhere the familiar note may be struck by a character in a novel pausing to translate yards and feet into meters and centimeters. Or here and there from Nabokov's verses may spring up an image almost invariably twisted by Nabokovian humor that no native-born and no European who had not become thoroughly Americanized could possibly evoke. No American would describe the death of an exile in a motel as Nabokov did in *Pale Fire*, the bits of light that remind the dying man of "hands from the past offering gems"; and the man's very last thought that he "conjures in two tongues." Finally in *Ada* Nabokov's real and imagined worlds fuse in a pastiche that affects universality.

On the whole, however, émigré writers have not done well in this country. Three received the Nobel Prize before their emigration from their homelands, none received the award after arrival. Recently the Book-of-the-Month Club published a list of 618 selections distributed in the first forty years of its existence, from 1926 to the middle of 1966. At least thirteen are books that were written in Europe by authors who later came to this country and span a period of thirteen years, between 1927 and 1940. In the next fifteen years ten books written here by émigré writers appear on the list. Of the ten, three were by Thomas Mann, two by Erich Maria Remarque, and one each by Franz Werfel, Stefan Zweig, and Vicki Baum, who had all been Book-of-the-Month Club authors before immigrating to America. The two new authors on the list were Jan Valtin (*Out of the Night*) and Lion Feuchtwanger (*This is the Hour*). It is puzzling that none of Feuchtwanger's better known novels of his European period were selected. No books by writers in the wave were chosen in the last eleven years.

All this seems to indicate that the only writers who did well in America were those who were entirely formed in Europe, had become set in their European molds, and could draw on their European experience for their writings. But no outstanding talent blossomed here, none found inspiration for a true masterpiece. Even Nabokov, who is probably the most popular of those who were not preceded by their fame, has attained a reputation that at best may be called uneven.

PUBLISHERS

In the war years, as communications with Europe became disrupted, the authors in exile lost touch with their European publishers; their contracts became worthless and the prospects of publishing future works became dim. Several American houses were then publishing foreign-language books, but in limited numbers, and could not meet the emergency created by the sudden arrival of hundreds of foreign-born authors. New outlets were needed, and in response to this need several émigré publishing ventures of one sort or another were launched. The Éditions de la Maison française, established in 1940, was a major wartime publisher of French works. Most other ventures of those years catered to the exiles from many countries who wrote in German. At the end of the war, as authors resumed their contacts with European publishers or went back to their countries, the publishing enterprises that had served exclusively or mainly émigré authors lost their *raison d'être* and were slowly extinguished. Viewed in retrospect the few firms in this class and the many *Selbstverleger* (self-publishing authors) appear as curiosities: they provided foreign-born writers with means of livelihood, however meager, and

German-reading audiences in America with books that might not have been available otherwise, but they were of little lasting consequence in the American publishing world.

Among these curiosities, Aurora Verlag reflects the spirit of the times in more than one way. It was founded in 1945 by eleven émigré writers from Switzerland, Germany, Austria, and Czechoslovakia. Its head was the Swiss-born Wieland Herzfelde, who had been a writer and publisher in Berlin from 1916 until 1933, then had moved successively to Czechoslovakia, France, England, and finally, in 1939, to the United States where he was to remain ten years. Here he engaged in various types of work and opened the Seven Seas Book and Stamp Shop in New York City before Aurora was started. Its other founders were the German social writer Ernst Bloch; the famous novelist and playwright Bertolt Brecht whose significant plays have turned the stage into a platform for social and political messages; the writer Ferdinand Bruckner; novelist Alfred Doeblin; Lion Feuchtwanger; Oskar Maria Graf; Heinrich Mann; the Austrian poets Berthold Viertel and Ernst Waldinger, a nephew of Freud; and the Czechoslovakian Franz Karl Weiskopf, who in his years in the United States was a frequent contributor to and staff member of *Books Abroad*.

An intriguing feature of Aurora was its motivation. In the German-language catalogue of the first ten publications the founders stated that "since in the country of their immigration there was no publishing house for German literature and art they decided to establish one themselves and called it Aurora. 'The name stands' as Heinrich Mann put it, 'for hopes not yet fulfilled. It denotes goals for which there has been struggling and suffering . . .' The founders . . . foresaw that after the collapse of the Hitler regime Germany and Austria would be afflicted by spiritual famine and, true to the great humanistic traditions in German literature, they wished to participate in the cultural reconstruction. They kept in mind the people of their own countries as well as the German readers scattered over the whole world." However, in announcing the foundation of Aurora Verlag, *Publishers' Weekly* quoted Herzfelde as saying: "With the arrival in this country of hundreds of thousands of German prisoners of war the demand for German books has suddenly risen to an unprecedented height without being met by an adequate increase in the supply of good German books . . . free from any vestige of nazism and devoted to the ideals of freedom, tolerance,

271

and truth. In order to cope, to a modest extent, with the task a number of writers . . . have launched . . . Aurora Verlag."

Whatever purposes Aurora Verlag may have served, the fact is that in the two years of its existence it published only books by its founders in the German language. A more professional initiative, showing a different kind of interesting sidelight, was taken by Gottfried Bermann-Fischer. Originally he was associated with S. Fischer Verlag in Berlin and when forced to leave Berlin in 1936 he established his own Bermann-Fischer Verlag in Vienna. Two years later he was compelled to flee again, leaving behind a stock of 400,000 volumes. He reopened Bermann-Fischer Verlag in Stockholm, but having been accused of anti-Nazi activities he was imprisoned and after his release had to leave Sweden. He came to this country, relinquishing the Stockholm house, which remained in operation. In 1941 Bermann-Fischer founded a new publishing firm in New York under the name of L. B. Fischer, in which *B* stands for Bermann and *L* for Fritz H. Landshoff, the firm's vice-president. Landshoff had been a publisher in Berlin and then the head of the German publications branch of Querido Verlag in Amsterdam. The war conditions drove Querido from Amsterdam to Batavia in the Dutch Indies and Landshoff to New York. Both Bermann-Fischer Verlag and Querido Verlag had their German-language books printed in Stockholm, while the new L. B. Fischer in New York published books in English and made available in the United States the German books printed in Stockholm for Bermann-Fischer and Querido. After 1945 L. B. Fischer's name no longer appeared on the lists of American publishers.

Of longer-lasting value than the emergency ventures were the publishing houses whose founders had stability in mind. Several are still in existence, though some have merged with American firms or have passed into non-émigré hands. The brief survey that follows does not claim to be exhaustive. In the earliest of these ventures, H. G. Koppell, who had been a publisher in Germany, came to America in 1936 and in 1938 founded Alliance Book Corporation of which he became the president. He made a hit with Jan Valtin's *Out of the Night* and published the works of such renowned authors as Emil Ludwig and Hermann Rauschning. After a brilliant beginning, he sold Alliance in 1942 to establish, shortly afterward, Arco Publishing Company.

Transatlantic Arts, Inc., was founded by the Hungarian George Vajna, who in his country had owned since 1919 the publishing and bookselling firm Dr. George Vajna & Company. When he established it, he once explained, the Hungarians felt that the injustice of the Versailles treaty was due to the peacemakers' complete ignorance of Hungarian history. Hence Vajna, "working under the principle of better understanding between nations . . . started to publish books in English, French, German and Italian." In 1939 he came to New York where his firm had an office which distributed books on Hungarian culture. The outbreak of World War II put an end to this enlightened mission; and Vajna, making use of connections he had established while in Europe, began to import British books and to distribute them under the joint imprint of Transatlantic Arts and the original British publishers. After George Vajna retired the firm passed into the hands of his younger brother, economist Ladislas Vajna.

Frederick Ungar arrived in America in 1939 from Vienna where he had been the founder of Phaidon Press. In 1940 he established the Frederick Ungar Publishing Company and began to issue books the following year. For him, as for most refugee publishers, the main difficulty was money: starting with a small capital, he was obliged to proceed very slowly. His early publications were mainly foreign-language grammars, textbooks, readers, and dictionaries. These books are still prominent on his list, although at present major publications are English translations of works in many fields.

Two exclusively scientific publishing houses, Interscience Publishers, Inc., and Academic Press were founded in the early forties by European refugees. They were related, for chemist Eric Proskauer, one of the two founders of Interscience, had been for many years with Akademische Verlagsgesellschaft, G.m.b.H., Leipzig, the parent company of Academic Press. The other founder of Interscience, Maurits Dekker, also a chemist, arrived in 1939 from Holland where he had been an editor of a chemical journal and founder and owner of the bookselling and publishing firm Dekker & Nordemann in Amsterdam. Dekker meant to become the president of Elsevier Publishing Company of New York, and Proskauer was to join him. Elsevier is the famous Dutch house that in 1638 published Galileo's *Two New Sciences*, after the Catholic Church issued a general prohibition against the printing or reprinting of any of Galileo's books. This remarkable display of independence had evidently been entirely forgotten three hundred years later: Maurits Dekker's scientific advisers here feared that Holland might become German and Elsevier with her, and they demanded that Dekker and Proskauer form their own American company. Thus, the foundation of an American branch of Elsevier was delayed for many years and left to the initiative of other men. In 1940, in its stead, Interscience Publishers, Inc., came into being, with Dekker as its president and Proskauer as its vice-president. They published a large number of scientific books, encyclopedias, and journals of high quality, and have continued to publish along the same lines and at an accelerated pace since Interscience merged with John Wiley & Son in 1961 and became an independent division of that company. Dekker retired in 1964, but Proskauer remained a vice-president of John Wiley & Son.

Academic Press was founded in 1942 by Walter Johnson and Kurt Jacoby, who are respectively the son and son-in-law of the founder of the parent firm. The Leipzig house was established in 1903; in 1938, under Nazi laws, it was obliged to oust its owners in order to survive. Jacoby spent the years between 1938 and 1941 in German concentration camps and prisons, and on a voyage around the world that brought him here by way of Japan. Like Jacoby, Johnson arrived here in 1941 by way of Japan. In America they were compensated for their tribulations. Of all publishing houses established by Europeans in the cultural migration, Academic Press has achieved the greatest expansion and is now a colossus in the scientific field. Johnson and Jacoby continued here the policy of the German house and specialized in multi-author volumes and multi-volume works. Academic Press laid the foundations for its treatises through the policy of seeking out capable editors and encouraging them to select the most competent authors, and this in turn led numerous authors to submit monographs on special subjects to the press. One useful venture is its series of "Advances," up-to-date reviews of developments in each of many scientific fields. An early example, *Advances in Protein Chemistry*, was initiated in 1944. With these publications, its highly specialized scientific journals, and the volumes of proceedings of symposia throughout the world, Academic has built an accurate and exhaustive record of scientific progress. In more recent years, it entered the fields of college textbooks and paperbacks. The founders of Academic Press never encountered serious difficulties after the initial financial strictures that beset most European-born publishers.

In 1945 Schocken Books Inc., another company of European parentage, appeared on the American publishing scene. Of singular appeal is its prehistory, as its president Theodore Schocken calls the story of the German parent house, Schocken Verlag. The founder was Salman Schocken, Theodore's father, an enlightened and scholarly merchant; together with a brother Salman owned a chain of department stores in various German cities and in the twenties could hire as the architect for some of his store buildings the famous Erich Mendelsohn, later an exile to this country. Salman Schocken's main interest outside his business was the dissemination of the Jewish cultural inheritance, and long before founding Schocken Verlag in 1932, he had "discovered" and signed up the Hebrew writer S. J. Agnon, who in 1966 was to share in the Nobel Prize for literature. The advent of Hitler created, on the one hand, difficulties for the Schocken department stores and, on the other, greatly increased the demand for books of Jewish content on the part of German Jews. Schocken Verlag filled the need until it was closed by the Nazis in 1938. Salman Schocken had meanwhile emigrated to Palestine and founded a publishing house. The plans that he soon began to make for an American branch matured in 1946, when his son Theodore, who came to this country in 1938, was released from service in the American army. Theodore became president of the American house, Schocken Books, Inc., under the guidance of his father who divided his time between New York and Jerusalem.

The success of Schocken Books as the publishers of Agnon's and Kafka's work is due to Salman Schocken's vision: not only had he recognized a potential great writer in the young Agnon, but in 1934, after the Nazi racial laws had proscribed Kafka's books, Salman bought world rights to Kafka's works. Schocken Books counts several émigrés among its editors and authors. Hannah Arendt was an editor between 1946 and 1948 and devoted much time and effort to the publication of Kafka. For almost twenty years Schocken's Jewish editor was the Austrian-born Nahum Glatzer, a professor of Jewish history at Brandeis University. The firm has published works by political scientist Leo Strauss, neurologist Kurt Goldstein, and art historian Walter Friedlaender.

Frederick Praeger was only twenty-three years old when he arrived in this country in 1938. He had studied law and political science in Vienna and Paris and for three years was an associate editor at a Viennese publishing house. In this country he did odd jobs and for a while was in the jewelry business. Then he joined the army and from 1946 to 1948 was with the military government in Germany. He put his experience to good use: in 1949 he was in charge of book exports of the Nassau Distributing Company in New York, which was then selling books and periodicals of forty-six American publishers in West Germany under contract with the Economic Co-operation Administration. The following year Praeger established his own publishing, bookselling and exporting firm, under the name Frederick A. Praeger, Inc., and took over all the export business previously conducted by the Nassau Distributing Company. Under the slogan "Books that Matter" the business flourished rapidly and gained distinction — art books of quality are one of the specialties for which it is known. Praeger was later bought by *Encyclopaedia Britannica* but continues to issue books under its own name.

Kurt Wolff and Pantheon Books, founded in 1942, chronologically preceded Praeger and Schocken, but I disregarded chronology to dwell at some length on Wolff's story as a remarkable example of European humanism in the book trade. Kurt Wolff, the son of a university professor and music conductor, studied at the universities of Bonn, Munich, Marburg, and Leipzig, and served his apprenticeship in publishing in the two-room office of a Leipzig publisher. In 1913 he established his own business, the Kurt Wolff Verlag, and soon became well known as the distinguished publisher and friend of expressionist poets, playwrights, and novelists. (He was a writer and editor himself.) In a German radio broadcast, the text of which was published in 1965 after his death, Wolff said that he disliked the word "expressionism" but it had pursued him like a shadow he could not escape. In the same broadcast he listed ten authors whom he said he was proud to have published and who are now considered expressionists. Of the ten, the best known to Americans is undoubtedly Franz Kafka. Of the other nine, two were to come to this country with the cultural wave, Franz Werfel and Heinrich Mann (who in Wolff's judgment stood much higher than his brother Thomas).

Werfel, one of Wolff's first authors, was hired as a reader by the Kurt Wolff Verlag, but he was a reader only in name, because no one wanted to divert him from his own writing. Other Wolff Verlag authors were eventually to come to America with the wave. They include, in order of their appearance on Wolff's lists, Kurt Pinthus, critic and historian of literature and the theater, who was on the first Nazi list of proscribed authors and in this country joined successively the staffs of the New School for Social Research,

276

the Library of Congress, and Columbia University. The poet Fritz von Unruh; the novelist, psychiatrist, and historian Richard Huelsenbeck, and the illustrator of one of his books, painter George Grosz; the poet Walter Mehring; Ernst Toller, the rebel writer who committed suicide in New York; the brilliant playwright and novelist Carl Zuckmayer; and Erwin Panofsky.

The Kurt Wolff Verlag flourished from its beginnings through the twenties, but the German economic depression forced it to close in 1930. Immediately after the burning of the Reichstag, Wolff emigrated to London, then moved to Nice with the family he had acquired; after vicissitudes similar to those of many others, he landed in New York in March, 1941. In December of that year he entered into an agreement with his German friend, antiquarian, book collector, literary critic, and teacher Curt von Faber du Faur and du Faur's stepson, Kyril Schabert. The agreement provided that if Wolff could match their offer, the other two would jointly advance him $7,500 for the establishment of a publishing concern to be headed by Wolff.

Wolff must have managed to match the funds, for in 1942 Pantheon Books was incorporated. It was no easy going. Wolff, like most recent arrivals, was technically an enemy alien, so he did not give his name to the firm. Kyril Schabert, who was an American citizen, became its president, Wolff vice-president, and Wolff's wife Helen was placed in charge of editorial work and promotion. Contacts with possible authors were hampered by language difficulties. Pantheon could not afford offices, and business was started in one room of the Wolff's apartment in Washington Square. But, slowly, things moved on. In 1943 Wolff published his first book in America, and by the spring of 1944 had fifteen titles on his list. In 1944, Jacques Schiffrin entered the firm as a partner to edit a series of French Pantheon Books. Russian by birth and French by adoption, Schiffrin had founded in Paris the very successful *Éditions de la Pleiade*, deluxe hardbound editions of classics and modern literature. In this country, where, like Wolff, he had come after the fall of France, Schiffrin had planned to publish on his own. But he started later than Wolff, too late to be eligible for a quota of paper when rationing was introduced; he became a partner in Pantheon and shared its quota.

"Recollecting those initial years," Helen Wolff wrote me, "I find it hard

277

to answer your question about the thinking in founding a publishing house in America. Thinking itself was a luxury at the time. For both Wolff and Schiffrin, it was a question of survival. For both of them, publishing was their profession. No American publishing house offered them an opportunity to use their experience. They had no choice but to start their own — European methods were introduced not by special planning but because of previous experience. They consisted mainly in the fundamental approach, which was the same for Kurt Wolff and Jacques Schiffrin: that a publishing house had to have a physiognomy, that it should reflect the tastes of the publishers, and that it should not publish indiscriminately whatever promised to sell. Books were not considered merchandise, but objects of permanent value, an attitude that dictated particular care in production. (One of my most vivid memories of those early days is a discussion between Kurt Wolff and one of our salesmen about using genuine or fake gold leaf as imprint on the spine of a book — the salesman pleading for fake, which would mean several cents less in production costs, Kurt Wolff saying it would fade. Which the salesman answered with the argument that by that time the people would have bought the book and be stuck with it anyway. He did not prevail.)"

Pantheon Books reflected European practices in several respects. In his new firm Wolff adopted his past policy of publishing bi-lingual editions of foreign-language poetry. In wartime, rather than lower the quality of his books, he reduced the size of the printings, since for small printings he could obtain decent paper. And, as he had done in Germany, he gave prominence to art books, or well-illustrated books. One of Pantheon's earliest publications was a two-volume edition of Grimm's fairy tales, abundantly illustrated by Josef Scharl, a noted German-born émigré artist. In 1949 Pantheon issued *The Arabian Nights* with thirteen lithographs by Chagall, and also a numbered edition of one hundred copies of *The Creation* with twenty-four woodcuts by the Flemish woodcutter Frans Masereel. This book was printed on the hand press of the Officina Bodoni in Verona, Italy; other Pantheon art books were also done in Europe. This fact is worth noticing: the now widespread practice of having art books published in Europe, where accurate reproductions may be obtained at lower prices than here, was introduced in this country by émigré publishers.

Wolff's knowledge of the European literary scene is mirrored in the large number of European works that he published in translation, and by the smaller, but not negligible, number of books by émigré authors, Eugene Berman, Hermann Broch, Jacques Maritain, Dora and Erwin Panofsky, Kurt Seligmann, Richard and Editha Sterba, and Otto von Simson among them.

Pantheon Books achieved its first great success with the publication in 1955 of Anne Morrow Lindbergh's *Gift from the Sea.* A most enlightened selection was that of Boris Pasternak's *Doctor Zhivago* in 1958, for although Wolff could not have known it when he made his decision, Pasternak was to receive the Nobel prize in the same year. In 1960 it was *The Leopard* by Giuseppe di Lampedusa that attained enormous popularity. By this time Pantheon Books, the once-small firm that could be housed in a single room, had taken its place among the most highly regarded American publishing houses.

In 1960 Wolff sold his firm to Random House; he was seventy-three years old. Schiffrin, whose health had never been good in America, had died in 1950. When Wolff retired from the publishing business — for good, he then believed — he received a letter from a business associate who professed to be not usually given to personal expression. "I feel and continue to feel a deep sense of personal loss," the man wrote Wolff. "Somehow, in our contacts there was always imparted to me an awareness of great wisdom, knowledgeableness, integrity, and nobility which one seldom experiences in business associations." Wolff's "retirement" did not last long: in 1961 he and his wife joined Harcourt-Brace and World at the invitation of its president, to head Helen and Kurt Wolff Books. Kurt died in 1963, and the series is now headed by his wife Helen. Pantheon Books preserves its distinguished identity as a branch of Random House.

This brief story of European publishers in the United States is limited to some of those who in America have established a new and independent publishing firm. Other European publishers have joined existing American houses and held from the beginning, or reached later, such influential positions as a presidency or vice-presidency. One example is Kurt Enoch, now a corporate vice-president of the Times Mirror Company, in charge of the book division. In Europe Enoch had had considerable experience with paper-bound editions, and he came to New York to assist in the operation of the American branch of Penguin Books. Later he and the American Victor Weybright bought the agency and formed the New American Library

279

of World Literature which publishes Signet and Mentor books and which was purchased by the Times Mirror Company in 1960. An exhaustive presentation of Europeans in the book trade would have to include editors and book designers and lead back to European artistic trends, mainly the influences of the Bauhaus, to Herbert Bayer, László Moholy-Nagy, and others. But such a thorough study is beyond the scope of this book.

The thirties and forties witnessed the birth — and often the death in infancy — of many publications founded by intellectuals in the wave. *United Nations*, the organ of the Italian Mazzini Society, is an example of a short-lived weekly springing up from the war emergency and not outlasting it for very long. The majority of these ventures into the periodical press, and especially the early ones, were in foreign languages — those in the German language were the most numerous. But intellectuals from Europe have also ventured into the field of American periodicals and have started publications in English, for the English-reading public.

In the first category, the foreign-language periodical press, the most important is undoubtedly the German *Aufbau* of New York. It is a weekly paper of tabloid format with a substantial circulation in the United States and other countries. Besides current events, music, theater and movie news, it contains literary articles, poems, and serial novels. (In the summer of 1966 it published in the original German Hans Habe's *The Mission*, a novel reconstructing the Evian Conference of 1938 at which delegates of thirty-two countries refused to accept the Nazi offer to sell German Jews for $250 each.) The *Aufbau* has a better coverage of German news than many American dailies. "When we come back from Europe," Irma Morgenthau told me, "and feel the need to keep in touch, we read the *Aufbau*. After a while the American papers will do." It was started in 1934 as a result of the intensified immigration from Germany and was then a bulletin of the German Jewish Club (later renamed the New World Club). It soon expanded, and in 1937 it acquired its first professional editor, Rudolf Brandl, who in Germany had been an editor of the *Frankfurter Zeitung* and chief librarian at the Ullsteinhaus. Brandl held his position for two years, and in 1939 was succeeded by Manfred George, who was to be the *Aufbau* editor for the next sixteen years.

It is Manfred George who was chiefly responsible for the distinguished character of the *Aufbau*. In Germany, George, the holder of a law degree, had been the editor, theater critic, and correspondent of several papers; but he had also been involved in the founding in 1924 of the Republikanische Partei Deutschlands (Republican Party of Germany) with Carl von Ossietzky, Hans Simons, Fritz von Unruh, and others. Having been denationalized by the Nazis, he fled to Czechoslovakia, then to Paris, and eventually arrived in New York in 1938 and soon became the editor of *Aufbau*. Within two years he could boast that his paper was read on five continents and that it was the public voice of the immigration from Germany. The best literary names among the German émigrés appeared as its contributors and used it as a forum for the expression of views and sentiments. On its advisory board were men of high stature, both native and German-born. The émigrés included Richard Beer-Hoffmann, Albert Einstein, Lion Feuchtwanger, Otto Loewi, Emil Ludwig, Paul Tillich, and Franz Werfel, all of whom are now deceased; and Fritz von Unruh, who lives in Europe.

Outstanding in the category of English-language periodicals is the magazine *The Reporter*, founded by Max Ascoli in 1949. Unlike the *Aufbau*, it is not identified with the migration from Europe, and in the twenty years of its existence there have been only a few émigrés among its contributors. And yet *The Reporter* is decidedly a product of the migration.

Over the years *The Reporter* remained very much Ascoli's own magazine and folded up when Ascoli decided to retire. It had always been influenced by his strong, somewhat ponderous personality and his liberal political views. Not only did he write an editorial for each issue, unless prevented by reasons beyond his control, but he decided on policies, read all articles, edited many, chose authors, gave the green light for publication. *The Reporter*, he said, "is always objective, never impartial," and its partiality reflects Ascoli's ideas. But Ascoli did not force his conclusions on his readers or consider world events in terms of black and white. The partiality he imparted to his magazine consisted in his refusal to compromise with principle. And principle may sometimes be very personal.

Ascoli, a tall man with broad shoulders on which a large head rests heavily, has had to cope since his youth with one of the worst adversities that can plague an intellectual, very poor sight. As a university student in Italy he was sometimes obliged to have friends read aloud to him. Nevertheless he obtained two degrees from Italian universities, one in jurisprudence, another in philosophy. In America he studied at several universities before initiating his successful career as a professor at the New School for Social Research and as a writer. He was named president of the Mazzini Society in 1940, but the following year resigned because the Mazzini Society was in New York while his wartime duties required his presence in Washington. His venture as founder, editor, and publisher of *The Reporter* was "an experiment in adult journalism." The many awards that his magazine received, the quality of its staff and readers, and its circulation testify to the success of his experiment.

The Reporter is an outstanding example of achievement made possible in America. Had Ascoli not settled in America, *The Reporter* would not have come into being; but neither could it have existed without the collaboration of the many distinguished American-born writers and editors or without the never-sufficiently-eulogized assistance of American money.

X

≪≪-≪≪

More Natural Scientists

The scientific contributions of the European-born are not limited to the development of atomic energy, which was singled out in this book as the most dramatic example. The European-born worked in practically all areas of science, making an impact on several, and to survey the entire field would be a tremendous task. So in this chapter I am going to describe only their work in a few limited areas, although by doing this I shall be obliged to leave out many prominent and deserving scientists. In particular, I shall not deal with the extensive and often very important achievements of men who in this country have been employed exclusively in industry.

MATHEMATICIANS

American mathematics was well developed long before the cultural migration. Americans had distinguished themselves in most fields of mathematics and on some frontiers had done the pioneering work. They had taken their place in the international society of great mathematicians and were preparing younger men to do the same. The arrival of European mathematicians further raised the stature of American mathematics and gave it unprecedented impetus, contributing to its penetrations in fields other than the exact sciences of physics, astronomy, and chemistry. (A measure of the Europeans' importance is obtained from the records of the National Academy of Sciences: in 1965, well over one-quarter of the members of the class of mathematics — fourteen out of fifty-one — were European-born who had reached the United States as part of the cultural wave.)

Most European countries contributed mathematicians to America, but the relatively larger groups came from some of the least wealthy nations. In my sampling, for instance, the mathematicians from "poor" Poland represent about 15 per cent of the Polish-born intellectuals, an extraordinary percentage. By way of comparison, the mathematicians from "rich" Germany are less than 3 per cent of all German-born intellectuals. Since, however, the German-born intellectuals in the wave were over ten times as numerous as the Polish-born, in absolute figures the German-born mathematicians are more numerous and account for about 30 per cent of the mathematicians of all nationalities, while the Polish-born account for only about 16 per cent.

According to Stan Ulam and Antoni Zygmund, my informants on Polish mathematical affairs, there is no simple explanation of the extraordinary blooming of mathematics in Poland. It is due in part to one of those fluctuations that may happen anywhere and are not clearly understood and in part to the fact that mathematics is one of the most "inexpensive" intellectual occupations, which "poor" Poland could well afford. In the early twenties, a few eminent teachers, including S. Banach, Waclaw Sierpiński, and Hugo Steinhaus, developed a Polish mathematical school which specialized mainly in set theory, mathematical logic, and topology. It soon acquired international fame. The expansion in Polish mathematics was not met by a comparable expansion in mathematical careers, and mathematicians began emigrating long before the rumble of war was heard.

Witold Hurewicz, who received a Ph.D. in Vienna, went to Amsterdam as early as 1928 and came to this country in 1936; he was teaching at the Massachusetts Institute of Technology at the time of his untimely death in a freak accident: while in Mexico for a meeting he climbed to the top of the Magician's Pyramid in Yucatan, slipped, and was killed in the fall. Jerzy Neyman left Poland in 1934 and spent four years in London before crossing the Atlantic to join the University of California. Born in Rumania but a Pole by education, Neyman made important contributions to several areas of modern statistics, in particular to the theories of testing hypotheses and estimation. Stan Ulam, self-styled "somewhat practical mathematician," taught at Princeton for a semester in 1935 and later returned to settle in this country. Statistician William Birnbaum came in 1937 and taught mainly at the University of Washington in Seattle. Mark Kac, a widely known expert in mathematical analysis and probability theories, arrived at Cornell in 1938 and later moved to the Rockefeller Institute. The year 1939 saw the arrival of several latecomers: the Russian-born and Polish-educated econometrician Leonid Hurwicz whose longest association was to be with the University of Minnesota; algebraist Samuel Eilenberg, chairman of the department of mathematics at Columbia; two applied mathematicians, Alexander Wundheiler, for many years a professor at the Illinois Institute of Technology, and Stefan Bergman, who eventually joined the faculty at Stanford; Alfred Tarski; and Anthoni Zygmund. Tarski, an eminent logician who was to settle at the University of California in 1942, had made important contributions to various fields of logic and had set the foundations for semantics as a branch of logic while he was still living in Poland. Here he continued his studies in the region that mathematics shares with logic and applied recently developed methods of logic to several areas of mathematics. He has written many books in Polish and English, and his imposing production earned him a high position among the philosophers of science. Zygmund was the last arrival: he had fought three weeks with the Polish army during the Nazi *Blitzkrieg* and after the collapse of Poland mingled with civilians to reach Vilno, taught there for a time, and then came to America on the last wartime trip of the Swedish boat "Drottingholm." In 1947, after a few years at other institutions, Zygmund settled at the University of Chicago where he has been an influential member of the department of mathematics and has led a large number of students to the doctoral degree.

Hungary is another not very wealthy country that produced outstanding mathematicians, as was to be expected considering the stimulating Hungarian intellectual climate. Those Hungary sent include Paul Erdös, Cornelius Lanczos, George Polya, Tibor Rado, Otto Szasz, Gabor Szegö, and John Von Neumann. It cannot be said, however, that these mathematicians were the product of a Hungarian school in the same sense that the Polish were a product of a Polish school, because most of the Hungarian mathematicians received their doctoral degrees from universities outside Hungary. Only Erdös and Lanczos, two important exceptions, completed their studies in Hungary.

Of the many European centers from which mathematicians moved to our country, one is the famous Vienna Circle of philosophers, scientists, and mathematicians who re-examined the foundations of logic and natural science using the strict methodology of mathematics. Through those among them who came to America, their influence spread to such seemingly unrelated fields of thought as linguistics and mathematics. The two mathematicians of the Vienna Circle who came here were Karl Menger and Kurt Gödel: Menger, who left Austria in 1937, went first to the University of Notre Dame, then to the Illinois Institute of Technology, and through his writings and editorial and educational activities has worked toward a better understanding of mathematics in America. Gödel, while still living in Vienna, made a fantastic discovery which changed mathematics: in 1931 he proved that in any sufficiently large system of mathematical axioms there will be statements that cannot be proved *or* disproved. James Newman wrote that Gödel's proof "is generally regarded as the most brilliant, most difficult, and most stunning sequence of reasoning in modern logic." And Ulam calls it the greatest mathematical discovery of this century.

The most important German center of mathematics until the early thirties was probably the Institute of Mathematics of the University of Göttingen, a model to similar institutes throughout the world until nazism virtually extinguished it. Mathematicians from all countries went to study at that institute and several of those who later settled here were graduates. Its director from 1920 to 1933 was Richard Courant and others on its staff who also came to America include Otto Neugebauer, Emmy Noether, William Prager, Hans Lewy, and Hermann Weyl.

The pattern of distribution in America of the mathematicians from these and other European centers is not dissimilar to that of other groups. (Indeed, the resemblance to the distribution of art historians is striking.) Certain American cities were like magnets around which clustered many mathematical newcomers. Possibly the strongest magnet and certainly the first to begin to act was the town of Princeton, New Jersey. It has two great mathematical centers: the department of mathematics of Princeton University and, since 1933, the Institute for Advanced Study. It was Princeton University that brought John Von Neumann to this country, and he was on its faculty from 1930 to 1933 when he moved to the institute. At the university he was succeeded by Salomon Bochner, who was born in Poland, educated in Germany, and had been teaching at the University of Munich. At Princeton Bochner has written many scientific books and papers dealing with a variety of questions in mathematical analysis and the theory of probability. His book *The Role of Mathematics in the Rise of Science* is a collection of essays several of which are delightful and intelligible to the layman. Other Europeans who have been on the Princeton faculty for long periods include Claude Chevalley, who was born in South Africa but is a French algebraist; the Austrian-born, German-educated Emil Artin; and William Feller, Yugoslavian-born and a Göttingen alumnus like many mathematicians of rank. Artin, who in the United States is remembered as a beloved teacher by many students, was already famous for his mathematical work when in 1937 he came from Hamburg to Notre Dame. He moved from there to Indiana and Princeton and in the middle fifties returned to Germany. Feller, who went to Princeton in 1950, is well known as a statistician, but at Princeton he taught some courses outside statistics. One of his students remembers him as a "colorful man" in whom native Yugoslavian traits were still very evident in spite of his many years in Germany and America, a teacher intent on maintaining the attention of his students: he seldom completed his demonstrations and often started them with such words as: "If ax [x] is any member of dot [that] lousy space. . . ."

The Institute for Advanced Study began functioning in 1933, and the first members included Albert Einstein, John Von Neumann, and Hermann Weyl. The *New York Times* recorded the appointments of Einstein (to head the school of mathematics), Weyl, and two American mathematicians, James Alexander and Oswald Veblen. The appointment of Von Neumann, who was then only thirty years old, passed almost unnoticed but his name is now familiar to a larger section of the American public than all the others save Einstein.

Einstein is in fact so well known that he needs no introduction. He had completed the bulk of his life work, including the theory of relativity, before coming to this country, and though he did continue some research in Princeton, he exerted his greatest influence as a unique person who attracted others by his mere presence and as the only scientist whose fame had reached American non-scientific quarters before the war: he was to be a link between science and our government in 1939, when physicists less well-known became aware of the potentialities of atomic energy.

Both Von Neumann and Weyl were encyclopedic mathematicians who had contributed to the advancement of many mathematical fields before joining the institute. But Von Neumann was also a practical mathematician, according to Ulam's definition. While mathematics tends to abstract itself from reality, Von Neumann was always sensitive and responsive to current human problems. Modern electronic computers are his most important practical invention. Automatic calculation was not a novelty: mathematician philosopher Blaise Pascal, who died in 1662, built a calculator, and much more recently the American Vannevar Bush designed mechanical relay machines. J. P. Eckert and J. W. Mauchly built an electronic computer during the war. But it was Von Neumann who devised a general logical code for all problems so that computers would not have to be reset after each problem. Large computers that solve problem after problem and store the results are due mainly to him. Without Von Neumann, modern computers might not have been developed at all, according to Hans Bethe, or at best they would have been delayed ten years or longer.

One of Von Neumann's practical contributions started as a piece of abstract work: in 1928, while still in Germany, he developed a theory of games (the first idea for which was advanced by Émile Borel). Thus he initiated a new branch of mathematics which aims to analyze problems of conflict having in common strategic features, that is, features which are controlled by the participants in the game. Later he was to extend this theory to economics.

Von Neumann died before he could complete work on one of his most imaginative conceptions: the theory of self-reproducing automata. These are automata that can each construct another automaton because they contain in their memory a description of the automaton to be built and are surrounded by an unlimited supply of parts from which they pick and assemble those they need. Recently Von Neumann's theory was edited, completed, and published by Arthur Burks, who worked with Von Neumann on the logical design of computers. Meanwhile some models described in Von Neumann's incomplete writings have been studied and may serve to explain in part how the human brain processes the information it receives.

Hermann Weyl, eighteen years older than Von Neumann (and six years younger than Einstein), had completed in Germany a good part of the work for which he has earned a place among the great mathematicians. His research was in many fields of pure and applied mathematics and mathematical logic; he had worked on Einstein's theory of relativity and its generalizations and had begun studies that constitute a link between mathematics and physics and influenced thinking in modern physics. In this country Weyl completed these studies and wrote some of his most important books. Among those published while he was in Germany is the now classic *Space-Time-Matter*; those issued after 1933 include *Mind and Nature, The Classical Groups, Algebraic Theory of Numbers, Philosophy of Mathematics and Natural Science, Symmetry* (an integration of science and art), and volumes of his lectures. About Weyl's books, Salomon Bochner wrote: "His distinctiveness came through better in his books, even synthesizing ones, than in his memoirs in periodicals; which is rare in mathematics." When Weyl died (in 1955), physicist Freeman Dyson of the Institute for Advanced Study stated: "Among the mathematicians who began their working lives in the twentieth century, Hermann Weyl was the one who made major contributions in the greatest number of different fields."

Since 1938 Kurt Gödel has also been a member of the institute which he had visited earlier. He pursued his fundamental work in mathematical logic and lectured on it. The notes of one of his courses were published under the title *The Consistency of the Continuum Hypothesis*. Later he turned to relativity and proposed a possible cosmological model. No recent book on the foundations of mathematics fails to mention Gödel and describe his work, and many books have been dedicated entirely to his revolutionary ideas in logic. Other European-born mathematicians who were at the Institute for Advanced Study either permanently or for long periods include the German-born Alfred Brauer and Carl Siegel and the French André Weil.

When Abraham Flexner founded the Institute for Advanced Study he envisioned a small permanent staff acting as the nucleus of a larger group of usually young though mature men who would stay for shorter periods. Flexner could have chosen no better men than Einstein, Weyl, and Von Neumann to form this nucleus together with prominent Americans. Over the years they attracted mathematicians and physicists, foreign-born as well as natives. The mathematicians from Europe who were temporary members of the institute include Lipman Bers, Richard Brauer (Alfred's brother), Claude Chevalley, Reinhold Baer, Paul Erdös, Guido Fubini, Witold Hurewicz, Hans Rademacher, Alfred Tarski, Stan Ulam, and Aurel Wintner.

In addition to being a center of attraction for European mathematicians, the Institute for Advanced Study acted as a clearing house or center of dispersion for them. Flexner's policy was to help Europeans come to the United States by inviting them to spend a year or two at the institute and then see

289

that they scattered far and wide. Thus Baer and Richard Brauer were respectively "scattered" to the University of North Carolina (later to the University of Illinois) and to the University of Toronto (later to Michigan and Harvard). Both German-born, they had studied together in Berlin, and in the United States they both influenced the development of group theory; although Baer went back to Germany in the middle fifties, Brauer stayed on here and trained an enormous number of students. Hurewicz moved from the institute (where he had gone from Copenhagen) to the Massachusetts Institute of Technology, and Tarski went to California.

No one did more to spread European influence in mathematics than Paul Erdös. A very colorful man, Erdös was at the Institute for Advanced Studies on several occasions. From there he moved about over the country, changed universities almost every year, and acquired the reputation of being a peripatetic mathematician. Between 1940 and 1946 he sent papers to mathematical journals from Pennsylvania, Michigan, Purdue, Princeton, and Stanford. While most mathematicians work in isolation and publish individually, Erdös collaborated with an amazing number of colleagues, American, foreign-born, and many still living in Hungary. After the war his peripatetic bent sent him traveling back and forth between Europe and America. It was politically risky to do this, for he was a man of strong leftist leanings and his mother belonged to the Hungarian Communist Party. During the McCarthy era he went back to Europe once too often and was barred from re-entering the United States, but more recently he was allowed to come back.

Occasionally one of these temporary invitations to the institute resulted in a decision to remain permanently in the United States. This was Ulam's case. He had not thought of leaving Poland when he was asked to come to the institute for a semester. He was then twenty-six years old and had received his doctoral degree in Lwów (Poland) only two years before, but he had been lucky, as he put it, to have had a paper published when he was an eighteen-year-old and had gained entry into the professional world before finishing his studies. While at Princeton in 1935 he received and accepted an invitation to lecture at Harvard the next year. The lure of a career in America, coupled with a foreboding of impending disaster in Poland, eventually decided Ulam to make his home in this country. His American activities have been in line with his being both a pure and a "somewhat practical" mathematician.

Two other American centers attracting European mathematicians in the thirties were New York and Brown universities. Both had a part in an important development, the rise of applied mathematics. In America before the thirties, the ties of mathematics with physics, mechanics, and technology had been loose. The arrival of key European applied mathematicians, coupled with the demands of the war, caused a rapid growth in the teaching of applied mathematics and the formation of two strong university centers for its study at New York and Brown.

In 1934, New York University extended an invitation to Richard Courant and thus initiated a transformation of its small department of mathematics. Courant felt keenly the challenge of his new environment and its needs and resolved to help change the situation of American applied mathematics by building a strong school at New York University. At first he worked alone, then in 1937 he was joined by the American James Stoker and the German-born Kurt Friedrichs. Friedrichs, who had received his doctoral degree in Göttingen, taught in Braunschweig until, unable to endure nazism any longer, he agreed to come to America. In time, and with the assistance of American colleagues and government support, these three men developed the best and largest department of applied mathematics in the United States as well as a substantial department of pure mathematics. By 1952 several specialized groups and divisions of mathematics had formed at New York University, and that year they were incorporated in the Institute of Mathematical Sciences, of which Courant became the director. (In 1958 it was renamed the Courant Institute of Mathematical Sciences.) This institute "is larger than the one we had in Göttingen," Courant said in an interview for Radio-Bremen in 1959, "and it unites all that was there with what springs from American opportunities." The institute, which now trains a large number of students, would not have been established, in Courant's opinion, had not the usefulness of applied mathematics been recognized, as it was in wartime, when Courant and his colleagues solved many mathematical problems of vital importance to our armed forces.

In recognition of his services Courant received the navy's Distinguished Public Service Award in 1958, the year he celebrated his seventieth birthday. He was honored because he had contributed modern mathematical methods and tools which greatly enhanced the capabilities of the navy as well as national defense generally. Courant established a wide reputation by writing in collaboration with the American mathematician Herbert Robbins the book *What is Mathematics?* which has become a classic read by countless American students and interested laymen.

Among other European mathematicians who over the years have been on the faculty of New York University, Fritz John arrived in 1946, and Lipman Bers in 1951 (from 1959 to 1964 he was chairman of the department of mathematics, then moved to Columbia); William Birnbaum, Alfred Brauer, and Wolfgang Wasow were there for shorter periods.

The Europeanization of mathematics at Brown University began in the late twenties when the Russian mathematician Jacob David Tamarkin joined its faculty. Tamarkin belonged to the great Russian school of mathematics and was so highly esteemed in Russia that in the early twenties he held four simultaneous professorships in Petrograd (now Leningrad). Nevertheless by 1924 he had come to the decision that as a Menshevik he would have to leave his country. He managed to escape and arrived in America in the early spring of 1925 after adventures upon the winter ice of Finland and at the American consulate of Riga. There, to establish his identity, the American consul submitted him to some sort of examination in analytical geometry, until Tamarkin threatened to reverse the roles and conduct the questioning. Once in this country Tamarkin was for two years a visiting lecturer at Dartmouth College and in 1927 joined Brown University. That same year Brown created its graduate school and the arrival of Tamarkin changed entirely the level of teaching of mathematics.

The arrival of a second European mathematician at Brown occurred over a decade later, when the Austrian-born Otto Neugebauer was driven there by his editorial activities. Neugebauer had received his doctoral degree in Göttingen and was teaching there when in 1931 he became the acting editor of the newly created *Zentralblatt für Mathematik*, an international journal of mathematical abstracts. After the exodus from Germany began, Neugebauer moved to Copenhagen and there edited *Zentralblatt* from 1933 to 1938. That year the publisher in Berlin was forced to drop from the list of *Zentralblatt* editors the name of the Italian mathematician Tullio Levi-Civita, who was a Jew. An event of this sort was not unexpected, and a group of European and American mathematicians had already prepared to transfer the activity of international abstracting to the United States. Neugebauer was invited to Brown University and arrived in 1939. (The invitation may or may not have been connected with the fact that since 1932 Tamarkin, at Brown, had been an assistant editor of *Zentralblatt*.) In January, 1940, *Mathematical Reviews* made its appearance under the sponsorship of scientific and mathematical societies in the United States, London, Amsterdam, and Lima.

The American Mathematical Society, in announcing in 1939 the forthcoming publication of *Mathematical Reviews*, did not mention *Zentralblatt* but stated that Tamarkin and Neugebauer would be the editors of the new American journal. Since both had been editors of *Zentralblatt* the implication was evident. (According to library records, *Zentralblatt* continued to be published under the Nazis; its publication was suspended between 1944 in 1948, but since 1948 it has been issued regularly.) In 1939 Neugebauer called William Feller to Brown University and invited him to join the editorial staff of *Mathematical Reviews*. This journal has been published steadily since 1940, first at Brown University, and since 1964 at the University of Michigan.

So far the story of the European mathematicians at Brown does not explain their concentration in the field of applied mathematics. Neugebauer, an expert in the history of Egyptian and Babylonian mathematics, joined the faculty as professor of the history of mathematics. Tamarkin, however, was interested in both pure and applied mathematics and William Feller had taught applied mathematics both at Kiel until 1933 and at Stockholm. And so the trend toward emphasis on application was already recognizable in 1941 when William Prager arrived from Istanbul. As one of the German university professors hired by the Turkish government, Prager had been a professor of mechanics and editor of scientific journals. At Brown he was named professor of applied mechanics and founded the department of applied mathematics. Feller remained at Brown until 1945, then moved to Cornell and later to Princeton. Another applied mathematician, Stefan Bergman, was at Brown from 1940 to 1945.

Not all the European mathematicians who settled in this country were connected with one of the three centers that I have mentioned. The mathematician Richard von Mises, for one, joined the faculty of Harvard University upon coming to the United States in 1939 and was there until his death. He was an Austrian of wide interests who in World War I had built the 600-horsepower airplane used by the Austrian army; had taught in Czechoslovakia, Alsace, and Germany; and from 1933 to 1939 had been Prager's

293

colleague in Istanbul. In this country he became well known both as a mathematician and a foremost expositor of the philosophy of positivism. He wrote several books on positivism, the theory of flight, the theory of probability, and the life of the poet Rainer Maria Rilke.

George Polya, who went to Brown in 1940 and two years later to Stanford, contributed to various fields of pure and applied mathematics and is outstanding for his teaching. His remarkably clear thinking and teaching ability are reflected in the little book *How to Solve It* in which he shows profitable ways to approach mathematical problems and teaches "tricks" that may help in solving what may seem impossible to solve if tackled directly. The Rumanian Abraham Wald, whom many consider one of the founders of modern statistics, was a pupil of Karl Menger in Vienna. He was doing work in econometrics at the Austrian Institute for Business Cycle Research (founded by Ludwig von Mises) when, in 1938, he accepted an invitation from the Cowles Commission. (The invitation may well have saved his life, for all but one of his close relatives later died in Auschwitz.) The same year he joined the faculty of Columbia and the next he developed the statistical decision theory, one of his major works. Another is sequential analysis, used by the armed forces in wartime. Wald was killed in an airplane accident in 1950 while on a lecture-tour in India.

As a footnote to the mathematical experts and an example of the sparking that takes place when brains from different countries meet on American soil, I might mention briefly the origins of the Monte Carlo method. This is a statistical, trial-and-error technique for solving complex problems now widely used in connection with large electronic computers. The technique was invented and its use initiated before computers were available by a Pole, a Hungarian, and an Italian. Right after the war, neutron problems were foremost in the minds of Los Alamos scientists; solution was essential, but their complexity was sometimes forbidding. In 1946 Stan Ulam suggested a statistical method for handling neutron problems. The fast, electric computers were definitely, if somewhat remotely, on the horizon, and Ulam's suggestions seemed promising. It was John Von Neumann who early the following year worked out all the necessary steps for the calculations proposed by Ulam. But then there was a lull, for the construction of the first computer, the Eniac, was not yet completed. Los Alamos scientists were "frustrated at having a computer technique and no appropriate computer on which to use it," as the Los Alamos monthly *The Atom* related in October, 1966. Then Fermi arrived on a visit and suggested building a quick and inexpensive device that would permit some use of the Monte Carlo method. Following Fermi's specifications, the American physicist L. D. P. King came up with a design, and his shop constructed a little brass gadget that moved on wheels and was sometimes-called "a trolley." (It was a physical analogue with some digital properties.) Ulam, Fermi, King, and others made use of it in the late forties and thus proved the value of the Monte Carlo method. Then the fast, multi-million-dollar electronic computers arrived, the Monte Carlo method surged to new dignity, and Fermi's trolley was forgotten. It was rediscovered in 1966, when one of the men who had used it moved to a new office.

ASTRONOMERS

European astronomers have long been attracted to America, and migration was already in progress in the twenties. By then America had some of the best equipped observatories in the world, but the number of astronomers was not large, and around her big telescopes there was often room for more researchers. The Europeans came to fill this room. A large proportion of the astronomers who settled here in the twenties were Dutch, for Holland had been in the vanguard since the eighties when the eminent astronomer Jacobus Kapteyn established a school in Groningen. For decades Holland had produced first-rank astronomers, and because there were not enough positions for them at home they scattered over the world. Peter van de Kamp, Jan Schilt, and Dirk Brouwer were among those who came to America in the twenties.

Several astronomers arrived from Russia in the same decade, including Alexander Vyssotsky, Nicholas Bobrovnikoff, and Otto Struve, who was to have the greatest influence on American astronomy. Struve was the descendant of a long line of astronomers, the best known of whom, his great-grandfather Wilhelm, was born in Germany but raised in Russia. Wilhelm's work as a student and young observer was so outstanding that Emperor Nicholas built an observatory near St. Petersburg largely for him and on his design, which when completed in 1839 was considered to be the finest in existence. Wilhelm and his descendants in Russia dominated astronomy for almost a century. Then came the revolution, and young Otto, who was serving in the White Army, found himself stranded in Constantinople, doing odd.jobs to survive, even chopping wood for the British Admiralty. But the name Struve was so well known among astronomers that he was soon rescued. The chairman of the department of astronomy at the University of Chicago, E. B. Frost, invited him to Yerkes Observatory, and he arrived in 1921 to work for his doctoral degree.

The department of astronomy at Chicago had been outstanding in its early years but by the end of World War I was only a shadow of what it had been. It was Struve who in the twenties and thirties gave it new life, and not only through the imposing body of his scientific contributions and the construction of the 82-inch telescope for McDonald Observatory in Texas (a joint enterprise of Chicago and the University of Texas), but also through his interaction with the wave of the thirties: in 1932 President Robert Hutchins of the University of Chicago appointed him director of the department of astronomy with the request that he seek out the best men available in the field. As a consequence the department became highly Europeanized. The foreign-born astronomers on its staff for longer or shorter periods included Hans Rosenberg, Gerald Kuiper, Bengt Stromgren, Gunnar Randers, Pol Swings, Gerhard Herzberg, K. Aa. Strand, and S. Chandrasekhar. Strictly speaking, not all of them belong to the wave as defined for this study, since Herzberg had taken Canadian citizenship before coming here; Stromgren was in this country for two years before the war, went back to Denmark, returned for a long visit in the forties, and did not settle in America until 1951; and Chandra was born in India and received his graduate training in England. But it would be inconceivable to consider major influences in astronomy and not mention Chandra, a most distinguished astrophysicist and an influential member of the department of astronomy of the University of Chicago, which he joined in 1936; or Stromgren, who was for several years the director of Yerkes and McDonald observatories, then joined the Institute for Advanced Study, and more recently returned to Denmark.

Chicago had no exclusive claim on the European astronomers who came in the thirties. Mount Wilson and Palomar observatories had on their staffs Walter Baade and for several years Rudolph Minkowski. Bart Bok, Sergei Gaposchkin, and Luigi Jacchia were at Harvard (but Gaposchkin alone settled there); Jacchia moved to the Smithsonian Astrophysical Observatory, and Bok, after ten years in Australia, returned to the United States as the director of the Steward Observatory in Tucson. Zdenek Kopal, born in Czechoslovakia, was briefly at Harvard and for a longer period at the Massachusetts Institute of Technology; Gustav Land was at Yale where Rupert Wildt settled after having been at several different observatories and universities; and Martin Schwarzschild, son of the eminent German astronomer Karl, was first at Harvard and Columbia universities, and in 1947 went to Princeton Observatory.

These Europeans trained many students and participated, in greater or lesser degrees, in the spectacular advances of modern astronomy. Several were versed in both observational and theoretic astronomy, although they were likely to have a preference for one of the two. A good example is Walter Baade, a native of Germany and one of the most stimulating astronomers of our time. Like Galileo, Baade knew how to use the telescope and other equipment to the best advantage of science. He made many observational discoveries and often proposed theories to explain his findings. In the early forties he turned the 100-inch telescope at Mount Wilson toward the amorphous nuclear region of the Andromeda nebula and by selecting suitable photographic plates was able to resolve it into stars. He found evidence of the existence of two stellar populations, which he called Population I and Population II and which differ in age, location, and in several of their chemical and physical properties. These findings greatly stimulated research and theories in many fields of astronomy. Other observations and theoretical studies led him to the conclusion that the distance between galaxies is 2.5 times greater than it was previously believed, and therefore the size and age of the universe must be multiplied by the same factor. When he announced these conclusions at an international gathering of astronomers in 1952 in Rome, the world of astronomy was startled, but his values for the time scale of the universe were found to be in agreement with the ages of rocks and meteorites as determined by geophysical methods.

Martin Schwarzschild has been a driving force in the expansion of American theoretical astronomy, which before the thirties was less developed than the observational. His name, together with that of the American Allan Sandage is tied to the rapid advances of the last few decades in the understanding of the main processes of stellar evolution and the production of energy in the interior of stars. Recent work springs from earlier research by many astronomers and in particular by Chandrasekhar. Around 1939 Chandra advanced a complete theory of stellar evolution in *Introduction to the Study of Stellar Structure* (re-issued as *Stellar Structure*), which is now considered a classic. Later theories and findings are presented in Schwarzschild's *Evolution and Structure of Stars* (1958). Among other theories advanced by Schwarzschild is an imaginative explanation of the extremely high temperatures of the gases forming the solar corona; according to him, these gases are heated by intense sound waves which are emitted by the turbulent surface of the sun. On earth, George Gamow has pointed out, "the idea that a symphonic orchestra playing a Beethoven concerto in the open, or the noise of a crowd at a county fair, might cause intense heating of the upper stratosphere sounds completely ridiculous, but in the case of the solar atmosphere it is just about what happens." Schwarzschild calculated that the sound waves emitted by the surface of the sun can keep the gases of the corona at a temperature of one million degrees. Although Schwarzschild is mainly a theorist, he is interested also in observational astronomy and has initiated a project to send balloons with telescopes above the atmosphere to make astronomical observations from the stratosphere.

Gerard Kuiper, a versatile astronomer born in Holland who has worked in many areas of astronomy, is an expert in the study of the solar system. He advanced a theory of its origin, discovered some satellites of Uranus and Neptune, and made intensive observations of Mars. He studied the green regions of Mars for indications of life and came to the conclusion that they are probably covered by some kind of primitive vegetation, lichen or moss, similar to those covering rocks on the earth, but that higher life is very improbable because of the low oxygen content in the Martian atmosphere. (Kuiper was at the University of Chicago Yerkes Observatory from 1936 to 1960 and then at the University of Arizona.)

Rudolph Minkowski, who was born in Strasbourg and educated in Germany, supervised a survey with the Schmidt telescope at Palomar Observatory which between 1949 and 1956 took 879 plate pairs and will keep researchers busy for some years. He has also made theoretical and observational studies of nebulae; in particular, he and Baade studied the Crab Nebula, which is the result of a supernova explosion in 1054. The Belgian Pol Swings was a professor at the University of Chicago during most of

World War II. He and Struve worked together at McDonald Observatory, which was inaugurated in 1939 just a few months before the war broke out in Europe. They spent hundreds of nights together at the reflector and published many joint papers on gaseous shells around single stars, spectrum analysis, and other topics. Swings returned to his old position at the University of Liège at the end of the war but continues to be a frequent visitor to the United States. Other European-born astronomers also made substantial contributions.

Several European-born physicists wandered into the field of astronomy and tried their hand at astronomical work. George Gamow did this consistently and, either alone or in collaboration with others, worked out theories and models to explain various cosmological phenomena. I have already related George Gamow's and Edward Teller's part in the successful meeting of physicists, astronomers, and astrophysicists in 1938 in Washington and Hans Bethe's consequent discovery of the carbon cycle. Enrico Fermi advanced a theory on the origin of cosmic rays, suggesting that the enormous energies of their particles are due to repeated acceleration by magnetic fields in clouds of ionized gas between the stars. He also collaborated with Chandra on calculations of the magnetic fields in the galactic spiral arm in which our planetary system is located. But in my opinion George Gamow is the European-born physicist who has done the most for American astronomy. Beside doing original work, he has written excellent and widely read books for laymen which have called public attention to astronomy. In present-day America the art of popularization is not too often practiced by the experts themselves. Gamow, a first-class atomic physicist and astrophysicist with a fondness for biology, has done a service to science by explaining many aspects to laymen. In recognition of this service, UNESCO awarded him the Kalinga Prize in 1956 for his work in the popularization of science. Among his books devoted mainly to astronomy are *The Birth and Death of the Sun, Biography of the Earth, The Creation of the Universe*, and *Matter, Earth, and Sky*.

IN THE FIELD OF MEDICINE

Physicians, including practitioners, specialists, and medical scientists, were the largest professional group coming to the United States from Europe; although different statistics indicate different total figures, it is certain that they ran in the thousands. According to a report of the National Committee for the Resettlement of Foreign Physicians (in the *Journal of the American Medical Association*, November, 1941), about 5,000 physicians came from Europe between 1933 and 1940, or as many as were graduated in one year from all the medical schools in the United States. The mere size of the group constituted an obstacle to its smooth resettlement, for it was inevitable that this inundation of foreigners, in a time of economic crisis when some American doctors charged only fifty cents a visit, should alarm the American medical profession. The protective measures that the profession was induced to take increased the difficulties faced by European physicians: they were obliged to comply with licensing and practicing rules which were always alien to them and became crippling as the years passed and many states began requiring more extensive examinations and internships and refused to consider candidates who were not American citizens. (The examination and internship requirements applied also to Americans graduating from medical schools, but the ordeal was of course much greater for the foreign-born, often older men, who had not been brought up in the American system.)

In the early thirties, some states, notably New York, recognized medical degrees issued by many European institutions, and the holders of such degrees were only asked to take a language examination. But other states recognized only degrees issued by American schools, and in general, to obtain a license to practice the Europeans had to take the state board examination in the state in which they resided — in the late thirties, even in New York. New York State never adopted the citizenship requirement, and several physicians of my acquaintance took the examination in New York City. Their ordeal became one of the liveliest topics of conversation in refugee circles: most physicians had been long out of school and it was a great effort for them to return to the study of medical subjects, for the approach was not the same in America and in Europe, and they were learning in a language that many had not yet mastered. When they felt prepared and took the examination, they were faced with a disconcerting experience: they were accustomed to oral examinations supplemented by written dissertations, but instead, they were given multiple-choice questionnaires which baffled them completely. Some of my physician friends boasted that they had passed the New York State board examination after failing it only once; but others took it a number of times before they were successful; and a few in the older age group, discouraged by what they heard, did not attempt to get a license.

The board examinations were not as difficult for those who had interned a year or two in American hospitals in compliance with the requirements of many states, but the internship itself was no joke. American interns work much harder than many young physicians in Europe, certainly harder than any of my Italian physician-friends had ever worked. An internship was a strenuous experience not only for men forty or fifty years old who sought an American license, but also for much younger men. The first internship of the Italian-born pathologist Conrad Pirani still haunts his dreams. Pirani is the chairman of the department of pathology at Michael Reese Hospital in Chicago and a professor at the University of Illinois College of Medicine, where he has been teaching since 1942. When he first arrived in New York from Italy in the summer of 1939, a young physician of twenty-five and only one year out of medical school, he went through a period of hunting job after job, to which he now refers as "extremely unpleasant." As a first job, he chanced upon a three-month internship at a small hospital in New York City and worked day and night as an ambulance surgeon (for board, room, and no pay, as American interns work). In "poor" Italy, Pirani, who belonged to a wealthy middle-class family, had never seen poverty, but in "rich" New York he was thrown into brutal contact with the grimmest aspects of the slums and with a violence he had never known before. He learned a great deal, he says, in terms of medical and human experience.

Internships and board examinations were not required if the candidate were seeking a position solely as a teacher. But the beginnings of academic careers in American colleges and universities were also slow and difficult, according to dermatologist Franz Baumann, and men with families were often compelled to seek more rapid roads to financial independence. Most beginnings are arduous (for foreign-born and Americans alike), and Baumann recalled how difficult his had been, although later he was to become well established and serve for a time as president of the Chicago Metropolitan Dermatological Society. In 1938, he was arrested in Germany but was fortunate enough to be released and escape to America with his wife and two little daughters. In Chicago he was introduced to the German-born physician Robert G. Bloch, who having arrived in the United States in the twenties was already established and was doing all he could for refugee colleagues. Through Bloch he obtained an internship at Provident Hospital, where he worked mostly among Negro patients. The needs of his family prevented Baumann from seeking an academic career, and once he had obtained his license he opened a small office near his home. Although the rent was only ten dollars a month, he could not afford a telephone; his wife took messages on their home telephone, rushed to bring them to the office, then rushed home in order not to miss other messages. In the evening she waited for her husband to return with his earnings of the day so that she could buy the family groceries.

Others met with difficulties of a different sort. A psychiatrist who had planned to open an office in a town in one of the most enlightened southern states had to give up the idea because the local medical profession was jealous of foreigners, as he put it (but it may well have been simply a question of economics). One physician told him bluntly that he was not welcome, and so he moved on to a large psychiatric institution in another state. This happened in 1937, and only several years later was he able to establish himself in private practice. The hostility of the American medical profession toward the influx of foreign colleagues became more acute as the thirties gave way to the forties and physicians flocked here from Europe in increasing numbers. After the United States entered the war, "spy scares" were added to the woes of European-born medical doctors: there was, for instance, an episode related in the report of the National Committee for the Resettlement of Foreign Physicians in which a doctor was accused of dispensing a slow-acting poison in his pills. But spy scares were not limited to physicians: in the war years anyone with a thick accent could become the target of similar accusations.

Still other aspects of American medical practice differed from the European. Kurt Goldstein, a most distinguished neurologist and psychopathologist, commented on some of the differences he found in his work at the Institute for Psychiatry of Columbia University in an interview he gave Radio-Bremen in 1958. A striking difference, in his opinion, was that here there were no "chiefs" and doctors were organized into teams in which each had equal rights; consequently, everything depended on the co-operation of the team, and there were advantages and disadvantages for the well-being of the patient; besides, he thought, contacts between patient and doctor were closer in Europe; and he had to fight against the American tendency toward mechanization that would have turned neurology into a branch of surgery. Outside the hospitals and clinics, too, European medical practice and physicians' habits were different from the American. In Germany there were no "downtown offices," German-born physician Martin Gumpert wrote in *First Papers*, and the same held true for other countries. Doctors practiced at home, and the family living room often doubled as the patients' waiting room. Once in this country, the older physicians retained some European habits, according to Franz Baumann, and were more willing, for instance, to go on house calls than were their American colleagues, although younger European doctors soon became more American than the Americans.

Physiologist Piero Foà considered the Americanization of European physicians from a different point of view. He said that as a group the Europeans have not affected American medicine but have been affected by it and have allowed themselves to become completely assimilated. In the first third of this century, American medicine had made enormous strides and by the thirties it was more advanced in many respects than European medicine. The newcomers realized this, perhaps to their surprise, and impressed as they were by the organization of large American hospitals, the efficiency of the laboratories, and the quality of hospital staffs, they adopted the standards and methods of the American medical profession. When they made contributions to American medicine, Foà remarked, they did so as individuals and not as a group. (But some older physicians disagree with Foà.)

In fact, their contributions are numerous and substantial, but here I can only give an idea of some of them, and only within limited areas. Having devoted a chapter to psychoanalysis I will not discuss here the work of psychonanalysts holding a medical degree or of psychiatrists, and, I shall consider later the contributions of Otto Meyerhof, Fritz Lipmann, and Severo Ochoa, all Nobel laureates and medical doctors, who worked in the field of biochemistry. The German-born Otto Loewi is a singular case: although his doctoral degree was in medicine, he devoted himself to physiological chemistry and pharmacology; in 1936, four years before coming to this country, he received a share of the Nobel Prize in medicine for a discovery as notable because it showed the chemical transfer of nerve actions as for the way in which he made it. He had obtained puzzling results from the work he was doing on frog hearts, and as he lay awake one night he had a flash of intuition in which he saw a possible explanation and the experiment that would prove it. He scribbled some notes to himself and promptly fell asleep, but in the morning he could neither decipher his notes nor remember the explanation. Fortunately, intuition struck again the following night, and this time he took no chances. He got up, walked to his laboratory, and performed the experiment. (A rival theory explained the transmission of nerve impulses by electric actions. Other émigrés, the Spanish-born Rafael Lorente de Nó and the Russian-born, German-educated David Nachmansohn, combined the two theories, showing that electric potentials in the nerve are generated by chemical action.)

The some hundred names of physicians in my file are mostly non-psychiatric men and women connected with universities or large research hospitals. There are among them teachers and researchers of high stature. Kurt Goldstein is best known for his work among patients with brain damage: born in Silesia and an alumnus of the University of Breslau, after World War I he directed the first German hospital for brain injuries. Upon his arrival in America in 1934, he joined the faculty of Columbia University and there resumed his studies of the psychological disturbances caused by brain injuries and of ways to alleviate suffering. He came to the conclusion that the only fruitful method was to regard the organism of the patient as a whole, and thus developed the "holistic, organismic approach" to the evaluation of empirical data "in their significance for the total organism's functioning." From Goldstein's studies emerged the concept of behavior as a result of a unified activity of the organism. At the same time these studies advanced understanding of the human personality and showed the remarkable ability of the human organism to adjust, even under conditions as severe as brain damage. Goldstein wrote several books on these findings in German and in English, including the well-known *The Organism*. His interests were wide and he published also in adjoining fields. In 1938–39 he delivered the William James lectures, later published as *Human Nature in the Light of Psychopathology*, and in *Abstract and Concrete Behavior* he discussed mental tests. In other publications he dealt with schizophrenia and with speech defects.

Dermatologist Stephen Rothman was a familiar figure in the halls of Billings Hospital of the University of Chicago, where he could be seen, tall, broad-shouldered, stooping, making his rounds of hospital patients surrounded by younger men; or when he stepped out of his clinic and turned his gaunt face to a waiting patient, speaking to him in a kindly voice and thick Hungarian accent. He came to Chicago in 1938, directly from Budapest where he had begun his medical career, to join the medical faculty of the university and worked at the university until his death. His wisdom and urbane wit are well remembered — to him is attributed the dictum that one can be quite happy on this planet even if one is a dermatologist — but his lasting reputation is as a researcher and a teacher. Rothman's book *Physiology and Biochemistry of the Skin* is a monumental work which made a great impact on its field. Once addressing a graduating class, he spoke of "the good old days in Billings Hospital." He recalled, among other pleasant memories, that in those days there were "no psychiatric social workers, but the psychiatrists themselves had a few closed-fist fights with genuinely crazy patients," and that doctors "never heard any mention of millions or hundreds of thousands or even tens of thousands of dollars. Such astronomical figures occurred only in counting bacteria." Then he became deadly serious and gave the young physicians sound and difficult advice, appealing to their honesty and sense of duty.

Another teacher and researcher born and educated in Hungary is pediatrician Paul György. He taught six years in Heidelberg and two in Cambridge before coming to America in 1935, where he was associated mainly with Western Reserve and the University of Pennsylvania. A strong thread of continuity in György's geographically jolty career was provided by his interest in nutritional research. As early as 1929 he did pioneering work on vitamins that led him later to isolate riboflavin (a member of the B_2 complex), vitamin B_6, and vitamin H (biotin). He conducted several field studies on nutritional problems, especially on liver diseases and their relation to the ecosystems in which they occur. Thus, having observed children in Jamaica with illnesses little known in the United States, he worked among them for six years in the fifties, with a grant from the Josiah Macy, Jr., Foundation, tracing their liver disease to dietary deficiencies and toxic factors, including a toxic substance in a tea brewed from local plants and drunk abundantly by the children. In the sixties he was instrumental in the elimination of liver fluke from villages in Thailand after ascertaining that the disease was caused by fermented fish. His latest interest is in the nutritional value of human milk.

The Polish-born cancerologist Anna Goldfeder undertook research in the physiology and pathology of cancer in Czechoslovakia, worked there and in Vienna, and in 1931 came to America with a two-year fellowship for cancer research at Lenox Hill Hospital in New York City. When the fellowship expired, she worked at several institutions, mostly in New York City, and for her continued research in cancerology she received a $5,000 award from the Damon Runyon Fund for Cancer Research.

In several instances investigations conducted by European émigrés led to substantial advances in American medical practice. Remarkable in this respect is the case of the French-born André Cournand. He arrived in America in 1930, with the degree of doctor of medicine, to continue to study diseases of the chest. Not long afterward, at Columbia, he met the American Dickinson Richards, and the two joined forces to study disorders of the heart and lungs. As they strove to increase the precision of measurements of cardiac and pulmonary function, an old paper published by the German Werner Forssmann came to their attention: in 1929 Forssmann had pushed into his own heart a thin tube containing a fluoroscope and mirror; but his horrified colleagues had prevailed upon him not to repeat the experiment. Cournand and Richards found that the insertion of catheters did not alter significantly the heart and lung function of chimpanzees, and perfected this technique, now called "cardiac catheterization," for use on humans. Attaching precision gauges to the catheters, they pushed into the heart and beyond it, and thus measured the flow of blood and the pressures in the heart and studied heart diseases. Cardiac catheterization earned its three discoverers, Forssmann, Cournand, and Richards, the Nobel Prize in medicine for the year 1956 and, more importantly, enabled physicians to make accurate diagnoses of anatomic defects and improve their understanding of how the heart works in disease.

Before Cournand and Richards devised their technique to probe inside the heart, another émigré physician invented an instrument to look inside the stomach. The German-born Rudolf Schindler, who came to the United States in 1934, had invented first the rigid, then the flexible gastroscope while living in Germany. Here he became at once a leading figure in gastroscopy. He furthered the study and the growth of gastroscopy at the University of Chicago until 1943 and later at institutions in the Los Angeles area. While he was in Chicago he wrote *Gastroscopy*, the basic textbook on the subject;

subsequently he published *Gastritis*, and he is the author of many publications on diseases of the stomach.

A few physicians made interesting excursions into other fields, sometimes related to medicine and sometimes only loosely connected with it. The orthopedic surgeon William Becker qualifies as a humanitarian. He came to America in 1937, and after serving an internship went into private practice in Chicago. In 1938 he became a member of the board of the Chicago branch of Self-Help of Émigrés from Central Europe, Inc. (The parent Self-Help had been founded in 1933 in the East by theologian Paul Tillich and Albert Einstein; social scientist Walter Friedlander and physicist James Franck established the organization in Chicago. The four men were all German-born.) Becker remained in private practice for several years, but then left it and accepted a position in industry in order to have more time for a project he had very much at heart: the construction of homes for the elderly. In 1949 he founded the Self-Help Home for the Aged in Chicago, and before his death in 1963 saw the opening of the first home. Unlike Becker, Martin Gumpert did not give up his private practice in America to follow his avocation. He wrote many books and articles, at first in German — publishing English translations — and later directly in English. His subjects were in large part medical, and among the medical subjects he often chose gerontology, explaining to the elderly how they could keep in good health. In some of his writings he combined medicine and politics, as when he exposed Nazi nutritional methods that were starving the working classes, and in others he left a record of the migration. Gumpert was a friend of Thomas Mann and is said to have served as a model for the character Mai-Sachme in Mann's *Joseph the Provider*. Before the advent of Hitler he had been the founder and director of the Berlin city center for the study of deformities, for he believed that many who had been crippled and deformed could be treated and then employed rather than remain burdens on society.

It was in the course of this work that Gumpert came in touch with many aged persons and turned his attention to gerontology. But then Hitler came to power and Gumpert lost his post. Being unemployed in the next three years, he began to write. His first two books were biographies of physicians and other scientists, later translated as *Hahnemann* and *Trail Blazers of Science*. In 1936 he came to the United States, and having learned enough English to take the examination for a medical license, he established himself in private practice as a dermatologist. He worked at several hospitals in New York City, was a medical adviser to *Time*, and wrote and wrote. "Exile Writers and America," "Immigrants by Conviction," "Value of His Heritage to the Refugee," and "Hitler's Gift to America": these are some of his articles dealing with the cultural migration. (The medical articles are too numerous to be mentioned here, but one title may give an idea of one of Gumpert's main interests: "Live Longer and Like It.") Some of the thoughts he expressed in his book *First Papers*, describing his Americanization, sound like indictments of European-born intellectuals. "Ignorant of the language and of the country, penniless and presumptuous, we arrived . . . ," he wrote, and thus brought to light the very real fact that the majority of harassed Europeans, however learned and intellectual, had not troubled to seek serious information about the United States before emigrating. The Europeans in the migration were difficult arrivals, Gumpert contended, because they were not tillers of the soil or fellers of trees, but men and women still tied "to the tragedy beneath which Europe is collapsing." To them America was "a paradise, harsh, hard to conquer, but free of decadent Europe's viciousness."

IN THE FIELD OF MOLECULAR BIOLOGY

That wise old man, Galileo, opened his discussion of motion in *Two New Sciences* by stating that he was going to "set forth a very new science dealing with a very ancient subject." Something similar may be said of molecular biology: its name became commonplace as recently as the late fifties, but it is concerned with as ancient a problem as the understanding of the basic processes of life. New is the enormous expansion of research at the macromolecular level, which was made possible by the increasingly refined techniques of biological chemistry and by new scientific instruments. Some biochemists claim that molecular biology is nothing but biochemistry practiced without a license, while other authorities regard it as the area where several streams of biological investigation have merged — principally virology, bacteriology, genetics, and biochemistry. If I adopt this second view it is because it provides a pattern for the presentation of the Europeans' work.

When the cultural migration got underway, genetics was more advanced here than in Europe, and the stream of pure genetics remained mostly in native hands. The Europeans distinguished themselves especially in biochemistry and virology. Eminent biochemists had been coming to this country ever since the early twenties. Carl and Gerty Cori, for example, identified the chain of intermediate products of glycogen metabolism; and Karl Landsteiner discovered blood groups. (All three later received the Nobel Prize.) The cultural wave only reinforced the existing trend. Among the émigré biochemists, many specialized in the study of metabolism and the enzymes that catalyze metabolic reactions.

Several years before the Coris undertook their work in this country, Otto Meyerhof in Germany had begun to investigate the generation of energy in muscle tissue and had shown its relation to the transformation of glycogen into lactic acid. In 1922 he received a share of the Nobel Prize in medicine for his discovery of the fixed relationship between consumption of oxygen and the metabolism of lactic acid in muscle. He also worked out the path of anaerobic oxidation of carbon hydrate in yeast, from glucose to the end product, ethyl alcohol. Meyerhof remained in Germany until 1938, and in 1940, after two years in Paris, came to the United States. Although he was known from previous visits and for his classic *Chemical Dynamics of Life Phenomena,* he did not do well in this country. In his American years he was on the staff of the University of Pennsylvania but did not have his own laboratory. In Germany he had trained many brilliant biochemists, but his teaching activities here are almost forgotten, including the special course that for several years he conducted at Woods Hole on recent advances in biochemistry.

Nevertheless, the Meyerhof tradition was continued by those of his German students and young co-workers who came here. The most outstanding is Fritz Lipmann, who first in Germany and then in Denmark studied enzymatic reactions which brought to light the importance of "high energy" phosphate bonds as the currency of free energy in metabolic reactions. In this country he did the work that earned him the Nobel Prize, discovering co-enzyme A; later he studied its structure and more recently he moved on to investigate the mechanism of protein synthesis. Like Meyerhof in Germany, so Lipmann was the teacher of many students who are now scattered over the United States. Another German student of Meyerhof's, Karl Meyer, has been in this country since 1930 and has done important work in the general field of carbohydrate metabolism. In the same general field of metabolism, enzymology, and biochemical energetics falls the early work of Severo

Ochoa (who was born and educated in Spain but spent some time at one of the Kaiser Wilhelm institutes in Berlin while Meyerhof was there); the research of Efraim Racker (born in Poland and educated in Vienna); and that of the Dane Herman Kalckar, an "oscillating" immigrant who was here before the war and during part of it, then came on visits while holding a position at the University of Copenhagen, and only in 1953 made the final break with Europe.

These biochemists did their research *in vitro*, having ground their biological source material, extracted the portions they wanted, and treated them in test tubes. Other workers observed metabolic processes *in vivo*, in the intact organism. In the middle thirties Rudolf Schoenheimer introduced the systematic use of isotopic tracer techniques in the study of metabolism and made the startling discovery that all body constituents are in a dynamic state; that is, he found that many macro-molecular components of animal cells are constantly broken down and resynthesized. Schoenheimer was led to these investigations almost by accident. Originally a pathologist, he turned to biochemistry in the twenties in Germany and joined the faculty of Columbia University shortly after the rise of Hitler. In 1934 he attended a lecture on deuterium by his Columbia colleague Harold Urey, who had discovered this heavy hydrogen isotope two years earlier. Realizing that it could be used to label organic compounds, Schoenheimer arranged to get from Urey a supply of deuterium and the help of one of Urey's assistants, the American chemist David Rittenberg, who was well trained in the handling of deuterium. (Rittenberg became Schoenheimer's collaborator and continued the investigations of metabolism by means of deuterium and heavy nitrogen tracers after Schoenheimer's death.) Physiologist Piero Foà commented in a letter to me on Schoenheimer's concept of the dynamic state of body constituents, asserting that "it created a revolution in biochemistry and physiology the end of which is not in sight." In Foà's opinion, Schoenheimer's findings represent a true turning point, and it is "due to him if the words 'turnover' and 'pool' have become a part of the biologists' daily vocabulary." (Schoenheimer described his investigations and findings in *The Dynamic State of Body Constituents*, published posthumously. It is now hard to find, and biologists who own a copy treat it as a most precious belonging.)

While Schoenheimer was conducting his researches with stable isotopes, other biochemists began taking advantage of the small amounts of radioactive isotopes that by the middle thirties were being made with the cyclotron. In 1935, in Italy, the future émigré biochemist Camillo Artom and physicist Emilio Segrè, in collaboration with others, investigated the metabolism of some lipids by labeling them with radioactive phosphorus produced at Berkeley, California: Ernest Lawrence, the inventor of the cyclotron, used to send Segrè radioactive phosphorus not needed by American experimenters. Those were pioneer times, and lead-shielded containers to ship radioactive materials were not in use. Lawrence mailed his radioisotopes in plain airmail envelopes, and before Segrè opened any letters from California he cautiously examined them with a Geiger counter to learn whether they contained radioactive material. A few years later, the Austrian-born chemist Erwin Chargaff conducted similar experiments with radiophosphorus in this country.

The study of metabolism was carried on in many countries. Enzymes, the catalysts of all metabolic processes, were found to be proteins. The chemistry of proteins progressed and advanced in greater detail an understanding of their structure. The grandfather of protein chemistry was the German-born Max Bergmann, who in Germany was the director of the Kaiser Wilhelm Institute for Fiber Chemistry, and in 1934 came to the Rockefeller Institute. Another distinguished protein chemist, Hans Neurath, came here from Austria and among other activities edited the monumental work *The Proteins*. Among the tools that sped up these advances is the electron microscope, invented in the early thirties. The Russian-born immigrant of the twenties, Vladimir Zworykin, modified it and built a version with which it is possible to see the large protein molecules and discern the complex structure of cell protoplasma.

In the middle forties American bacteriologists and geneticists came to realize that nucleic acids, not protein, are the carriers of instructions for the transmission of inherited characteristics. Some of the work that shed light on the role of the nucleic acids DNA and RNA was done by virologists. Noteworthy from the point of view of the cultural migration were the members of the "phage group" who began assembling in this country in 1940. (The bacteriophage, now commonly called "phage," is a filtrable virus that lives as a parasite on bacteria.) The story of the phage group begins in Europe in the late thirties when the German physicist Max Delbrück and the Italian physician Salvador Luria became interested in problems outside

311

their own fields. In the middle thirties Delbrück was an assistant to Lise Meitner and Otto Hahn at the Kaiser Wilhelm Institute for Chemistry in Berlin. His work must have been tedious, for Meitner and Hahn were patiently repeating over and over a baffling experiment, first performed by Enrico Fermi and his associates in Rome, which required great accuracy and the handling of extremely minute amounts of radioactive substances. Perhaps to offset the monotony of his work, Delbrück joined a discussion group of physicists exploring the possibility of applying quantum mechanics to genetics and then devised a model of the gene that attracted some attention. Delbrück's interest in genetics proved to be lasting. Realizing that America was ahead of Europe in this field, he took advantage of a Rockefeller Foundation fellowship to come to the California Institute of Technology (and thus missed his chance to share in the discovery of uranium fission). In California he was introduced to the bacteriophage as a suitable material for genetic studies.

Salvador Luria took up research on the phage while spending the academic year 1937–38 in Rome. He had received a medical degree from the University of Turin, studied calculus on his own while serving in the Italian army, and intended to learn radiology in his year in Rome. But his Turin school friend, the physicist Ugo Fano, introduced him to Roman physicists and his plans changed. Physicist Franco Rasetti, who is a naturalist at heart, suggested some experiments to prove the particulate nature of the phage, and Luria eagerly took up the suggestion. In 1940, after two years in Paris and more work on the phage, Luria was pushed to our shores by the fall of France. Late that year he met Delbrück in Philadelphia. The two discovered their common interest, decided to collaborate, and so became the nucleus of the phage group. Delbrück was its leader, as a teacher and as an investigator; he insisted that those who worked with him reject vagueness, do quantitative experiments, and express the results as precisely as possible. He and Luria devised methods to control the growth of bacteriophages and count them; studied the relationship between phages and host bacteria; and did a systematic investigation of mutations in phages and bacteria. (Their joint paper of 1943 on the mutations of bacteria hosting phages has been called the starting point of bacterial genetics.) In 1945 Delbrück organized an annual summer phage course at Cold Spring Harbor which was well attended from the beginning, and that same year Erwin Schroedinger, in his exile in Ireland, published *What is Life?* which included a chapter on Delbrück's early model of the gene. It called the attention of physicists to genetics and the hereditary mechanism, which could be studied advantageously in the phage. In the following years the number of phage workers increased rapidly.

Most proselytes were natives, but there were also some émigrés. For a time Luria's friend Ugo Fano was attracted to the phage sphere. In 1945 he and the Yugoslavian-born director of the Cold Spring Harbor Laboratory, Miljslav Demerec (who came here in the twenties), published the results of a systematic study by means of which they had selected the seven phage strains that could best be grown simultaneously in the same host. The ubiquitous Leo Szilard stayed several years with the phage group between two periods of intense political activity. Before revealing his interest in the phage, Szilard had visited Luria's laboratory at the University of Indiana. "Doctor Szilard, I don't know how much to explain," said Luria, embarrassed by the presence of the great nuclear physicist. "I don't know what to assume. . . ." "You may assume," Szilard replied promptly, "infinite ignorance and unlimited intelligence." The ignorance was soon overcome. Among Szilard's contributions to the phage art was the invention of the chemostat, an apparatus in which bacteria can be grown under conditions especially favorable to physiologic and genetic investigations. Szilard was an experimentalist "without hands" and would not have been able to build the chemostat alone. But in the construction and use of it he had the assistance of a younger American-born physical chemist, Aaron Novick, whom he had driven, as he had himself, out of nuclear physics and into phage research. Szilard did more for biology. A constant traveler, he talked to researchers in all parts of the United States and in Europe, reworked their ideas in his extraordinary mind, and disseminated them in a viable, productive form. Thus he inspired some of the recent advances in biology.

As the various streams of molecular biology converged to elucidate the genetic mechanism, progress was spectacular. A great breakthrough came in 1953 when James Watson and Francis Crick proposed a double helix model for the structure of *DNA*. Watson, a former student of Luria's, spent his formative years with the phage group and went to Cambridge to work with Francis Crick for the specific purpose of determining the structure of *DNA*. The double stranded helix model was deduced from the available experimental data of X-ray crystallography, and its key feature, the complementary base pairing of purine and pyrimidine residues on opposite chains, drew support from the work done by Erwin Chargaff a few years earlier. Having broken down the nucleic acid molecules, Chargaff observed a pattern of symmetry in the relative abundance of purine and pyrimidine bases.

The Watson-Crick model opened the possibility of deciphering the instructions for the duplication of genetic material. The first to suggest a possible genetic code was the nuclear physicist George Gamow, whose name appears in this book only slightly less frequently than Szilard's. Although Gamow's code proved unworkable on the whole, its promulgation initiated a chain of steps that led to more likely but, in the end, also incorrect solutions. I am told on good authority that, in the light of recent advances, Gamow's code is now looked upon more favorably than it was some ten years ago. European-born biochemists also had a part in the search for proofs of the postulated genetic mechanisms. In 1955 Severo Ochoa synthesized a long chain of nucleotides that resembled naturally occurring *RNA*. That same year Heinz Fraenkel-Conrat, working with the tobacco mosaic virus, succeeded in separating its outer, protein coat from the inner strand of nucleic acid and put them back together to reconstitute the active virus. More recently, Fraenkel-Conrat has effected small changes or mutations in the chemical structure of the viral nucleic acid and identified the change in amino acid sequence engendered by that mutation in the viral protein. Lipmann has been investigating the mechanism by which amino acids are assembled in specific permutations for protein synthesis. And others (Herbert Anker is one) are trying to take the next step and understand how the genetic instructions are translated into such complex structures as eyes and other organs. But, Anker thinks, the prospects for gaining such understanding are not yet very good.

This presentation inevitably overstresses the part played by European-born scientists in the rise of molecular biology. The story would be at least as exciting and certainly more complete if it were told with an entirely different set of names: Thomas Morgan, Hermann Muller, George Beadle, Edward Tatum, Joshua Lederberg, James Sumner, John Northrop, Wendell Stanley, Linus Pauling, Arthur Kornberg, Alfred Hershey, Seymour Benzer, and many others who do not belong to the cultural migration. But then, I asked myself, is there anything that can be said in general about the role of the European-born in biology? I posed this question to biochemist Herbert Anker of the University of Chicago and received a startling answer. "Yes," he said. "The European-born scientists who have made the greatest impact on American biology are the atomic physicists." They have shown, he explained, that basic science when sufficiently supported can yield extremely valuable practical results. In the postwar years, the American government gave great encouragement and financial support to biological research, and biologists were able to work out their ideas and put their abilities to good use.

Anker's words called to my mind something that chemist Eugene Rabino-witch once said: "The greatest role of the European-born scientists was to change the American concept of science — it used to mean invention; it seemed impossible to convince the congressmen that basic science is impor-tant . . . after the atomic bomb . . . even biological research. . . ." Two scientists held almost the same opinion. And yet I had reservations. "The physicists will appear conceited if I write what you told me," I said to Anker. "But it is true," Anker replied.

XI

➤➤➤-➤➤➤

Social Scientists and Other Scholars

IN PSYCHOLOGICAL WARFARE

During World War II, qualified European-born scientists collaborated in the development of atomic energy, radar, aviation, and other military projects; some economists, political scientists, and government experts were advisers to our government and its agencies; but possibly the largest number of foreign-born in war work took part in psychological warfare. That so many European-born could be employed in sensitive areas in wartime indicates a drastic change of policy since World War I, when similar participation was not allowed and mistrust of the foreign-born prevailed. But in the intervening years "hyphenated Americans" had become dehyphenated, and European birth in itself was no longer a reason to expect disloyalty (though, unfortunately, Americans of Japanese birth or ancestry were treated with suspicion). The intellectual immigrants themselves had considerably influenced the climate of opinion. They were a vocal lot and made America aware of their presence. They convinced cultured and responsible circles that there was a difference between the totalitarian parties and the oppressed populations, that they, the recent immigrants, were loyal to the United States and eager to help defeat the dictators. Consequently, they were judged more often on their merits than on their nationalities and in general were found worthy of confidence.

This does not mean that as soon as our government felt the need for the specialized knowledge of Europe which the newcomers possessed it rushed to enlist their aid. From what I gather, the situation was rather like this: on the one side were the military and the intelligence services badly needing persons with knowledge of the language, customs, policies, and industrial

316

development of the countries against whom we were fighting. On the other side were the recent immigrants, the largest group with this knowledge, ready to put it at the service of our country — ready also, those who were not satisfactorily employed, to obtain a steady job and income. Initially there was virtually no communication between the two groups, a fact that should not be surprising since a good number of the newcomers were, technically, enemy aliens. But the laws of supply and demand inevitably brought about some contact and collaboration. By 1943 the military Psychological Warfare Division; the civilian Office of Strategic Services, controlling most intelligence activities and its propaganda counterpart, the Office of War Information; and several other agencies were hiring recent immigrants. (PWD, OSS, and OWI were the agencies of psychological warfare, or sykewar, as its historian Daniel Lerner called it. Except for OWI, these agencies hired only the foreign-born who had become citizens; by 1943 only the immigrants who had arrived in the United States in 1938 or earlier and those who had served in the United States Army for at least three months could obtain American citizenship. The OWI had no citizenship requirements.)

In recruiting the foreign-born, these agencies may have been assisted by the Roster of Alien Specialized Personnel, compiled well before Pearl Harbor at the suggestion and under the direction of the Italian émigré economist Fausto Pitigliani. It was a list of some 2,250 persons who had responded to a call for alien experts made through the general and foreign-language press. The roster excluded by definition all the foreign-born who had become United States citizens before it was compiled in 1942; on the other hand some of those listed could have become citizens by 1943. I infer from published statistics of principal occupations that over half the persons listed were not, strictly speaking, intellectuals. (A striking feature, certainly of the greatest value for psychological warfare, was that the group as a whole knew thirty-four languages including Esperanto. However, I was not able to ascertain whether the offices hiring personnel for sykewar made use of this roster.)

Some attempts were made to utilize European specialized knowledge even before America entered the war. One notable example was the Research Project of Totalitarian Communication, initiated in April, 1941, by the graduate faculty (University in Exile) of the New School for Social Research. Its object was to develop methods to study enemy propaganda while training American social scientists for work in this field. One of its two senior leaders was the German-born sociologist Hans Speier, an original member of the University in Exile. The other was the recently arrived Viennese psychoanalyst and art historian Ernst Kris, an exceptionally versatile man, fluent in Italian, French, English, and German. Kris had remained in Vienna with the group of analysts around Freud until the *Anschluss* and then followed Freud to London. There he organized the study of enemy broadcasts for the British government; in 1940 he went to Canada to start a similar program. He had been in New York only a few months when he undertook the project with Speier. Of the five junior members on their staff, two were also from Europe, the Viennese psychologist Hans Herma and the German historian Heinz Paechter (whose names were later anglicized to John Herma and Henry Pachter). Before the project was completed, Hans Speier left to become the chief German analyst of the Foreign Broadcast Intelligence Service of the Federal Communication Commission, in charge of preparing regular and special reports on the content and characteristics of German broadcasts. At the end of the war he was called one of the world's leading experts in propaganda techniques.

It was not easy to obtain a job in sykewar, according to George Rohrlich. He came to this country from Austria in 1938 with a recently acquired law degree that would not enable him to practice law here. After supporting himself for a time by designing jewelry, he went back to school. Once in possession of an American degree in political science he applied several times for a position with the government, feeling that his knowledge of Austria and fluency in European languages would be useful. Eventually it was not his application that got him into the Office of Strategic Services but the initiative of another European already working in OSS, who knew him and his abilities and suggested that he be hired. By that time he had become a citizen. "I cannot recall," said Rohrlich, "that immigrants from continental Europe filled more than a handful of office positions of great responsibility. There were undoubtedly various reasons to account for this. Among them — I couldn't help feeling at the time — may have been the fact that our continental behavior and accents must have struck some native Americans as odd. We were funny." (That word, "funny", struck a familiar note in my memory and made me think of a European-born friend who, when something went wrong in his relations with other people in this country, would say "I know why they don't like me. Because I am ugly." Funny, ugly — an expression of their initial feeling of estrangement, of their realization that upon their arrival they stuck out like a sore thumb.)

Rohrlich was right. There was a certain mistrust of recent immigrants in the echelons of psychological warfare, a certain preconception that refugees might be either too attached or too violently opposed to their countries of origin to be objective. Daniel Lerner, commenting on this attitude, wrote that "not a single German refugee held a responsible position (i.e., one in which he habitually made his own decisions)." But he also stated that "The Sykewar tasks simply could not have been accomplished without the use of refugees." (By "Sykewar" capitalized Lerner indicates the operations under direct military control.) Refugees formed the great majority of those who wrote leaflets for distribution in Europe, spoke on the radio, interrogated prisoners of war, and analyzed interviews with prisoners as well as enemy broadcasts and documents. The political scientist Louise Holborn, who was in the research and analysis branch of the OSS, recalled how she participated in the preparation of a handbook for military affairs. She mentioned another example: Germans in the Biographical Records Section compiled a list of names of Germans who had remained in Germany and could be trusted by the Americans. The catalogue would have been of greater use, she remarked, had the invasion of Germany taken place earlier: by the time the Allies reached Germany many of the persons whose names were listed had died in the increasingly harsh conditions of wartime and in the reprisals following the unsuccessful plot against Hitler on July 20, 1944. (Others have taken exception to the usefulness of this project.)

To take part in psychological warfare was a novel experience for the Europeans as well as for many Americans. They were men and women from many different disciplines who left the academic environment, most of them for the first time, in order to be active in politics, and they enjoyed the meeting of the minds, the mingling of different backgrounds. They had one belief in common; they were convinced that they should use their knowledge to combat totalitarian dictatorship. Among the Europeans were men of high calibre such as social scientists Hans Speier, Franz Neumann, Leo Lowenthal, Paul Lazarsfeld, and Max Horkheimer; political scientists John Herz, Otto

Kirchheimer, George Rohrlich, Karl Deutsch, Louise Holborn, and Nathan Leites; art historian Richard Krautheimer; economists Walter Levy (chief of the petroleum section of the OSS), Giorgio Tagliacozzo, and Gerhard Tintner; psychologists Kurt Lewin and John Herma; historians Hajo Holborn and Felix Gilbert; philosopher Herbert Marcuse; and many others. A consultant to the Office of Strategic Services was Robert Kempner, who in 1930, when a counselor to the Prussian Ministry of Interior, had advised the suppression of the Nazi Party and the prosecution of Hitler for high treason. The Office of Strategic Services and the Office of War Information used many writers, among them Leo Lania, Hans Habe, poet Walter Mehring, Joseph Wechsberg (a frequent contributor to the *New Yorker*), and poet André Breton.

The exploits of the Hungarian novelist and journalist Hans Habe excited pride in his countryman, violinist Joseph Szigeti. To Szigeti it seemed a sign of "typical Hungarian adaptability for other languages" that Captain Hans Habe should have become the editor of the first German daily in the occupied Rhineland at the end of World War II, that he should have taken over the supervision of all German-language papers in occupied Germany, and issued a paper in Frankfurt with the help of anti-Nazi former staff members of the *Frankfurter Zeitung*.

Toward the end of the European campaign, the ranks of the European-born in intelligence and propaganda began to thin out. Some felt that they were no longer needed, since victory in Europe was in sight. When Nazi atrocities and the horrors of concentration camps became known, many Germans were so shocked that they shied away from any thought of Germany. But some stayed on to the end of the war and later served in the Military Government abroad, in the State Department, the Central Intelligence Agency, or with the Voice of America and Radio Free Europe. At least one man was still lecturing at the Army School of Psychological Warfare in 1963.

ECONOMISTS

By far the largest group of European-born social scientists in my file are the economists; they are considerably more numerous than the political scientists and sociologists together. European-born economists have been active in most areas of economics and have pioneered in recently opened fields, laying the foundations for new inquiries. To the study of economics they brought a wider vision than existed in America before the wave, if for no other reason than that the Europeans came from countries with many different economic philosophies and policies and had been trained at learning centers that were fountainheads of modern economic thought.

At least eleven economists in my file were born in Russia or the Baltic states; the percentage of Russians and Baltics in economics is about three times as high as in the entire cultural migration. Among them are such distinguished men as Alexander Gerschenkron, Abba Lerner, Wassily Leontief, Jacob Marschak, and Wladimir Woytinsky. Whatever contributions they made as individuals, as a group the Russian- and Baltic-born broadened and deepened the American understanding of Soviet economic theory and practice.

Several émigré economists of different nationalities (including the Russian) were educated, or taught, at the University of Vienna, which had been a lively center of economic thought ever since Carl Menger initiated the Austrian school in the eighties. Early in this century the University of Vienna reckoned among its students the three schoolmates whom I mentioned in the section on Austrians, Emil Lederer, Joseph Schumpeter, and Ludwig von Mises. The most widely known of the three in America is Schumpeter, whose *Capitalism, Socialism, and Democracy* received acclaim. Ludwig von Mises had the longest and most fruitful association with the University of Vienna, where he taught from 1913 to 1938. Lederer, an economic theorist and a man of broad culture and wisdom, served the cause of American learning in the few years in this country before his death by assisting Alvin Johnson in bringing to the United States some of the best European minds in the social sciences and by teaching at the New School. Among other economists who at one time were associated with the University of Vienna are Gottfried Haberler, Alexander Gerschenkron, Fritz Machlup, Oskar Morgenstern, Karl Pribram, and Gerhard Tintner. Haberler, Machlup, and Morgenstern were von Mises' students.

Another well-known center of economic studies was the Institute for World Economics in Kiel, and several economists who came to the United States had taught there for longer or shorter periods, including Gerhard Colm, Walter Levy, Wassily Leontief, Adolph Lowe, Fritz Mann, and Hans Neisser. Upon the advent of fascism, economists and students from many countries of continental Europe flocked to the London School of Economics.

The school was then directed by Sir William Beveridge, who had taken the initiative in organizing assistance to persecuted intelligentsia in Europe. In the middle thirties the London School was one of those institutions of the intellectual world which "at certain historical junctures, through their topographical location and high prestige, seem likewise to be the natural scene of great clashes of thought, so that for a time they enjoy a supernatural activity and seething intensity of life," as G. L. S. Shackle has written. "Driven by adversity or oppression or visiting more normally, brilliant men in a great stream poured into it from all directions, bringing an immense diversity of ideas to be traded and cried up against each other like the wares of merchants at a medieval fair." The economists who crossed this vociferous marketplace as students or teachers before coming to America included Bruno Foà, Raymond Goldsmith, Michael Heilperin, Albert Hirschman, Leonid Hurwicz, Abba Lerner, Karl Niebyl, and Tibor Scitovsky.

It was the tradition of European economists to participate in the political life of their countries. Accordingly, many were advisers to their governments and some filled high positions: Richard Schueller was a foreign minister in Austria, and Joseph Schumpeter was the first Austrian minister of finance after World War I, a position in which he was confronted with the tremendously difficult conditions in Austria after the war and the collapse of the Austro-Hungarian monarchy. Hans Staudinger served as Ministerial-director to the Prussian Ministry of Trade and Industry and Secretary of State for Prussia.

Several economists came to the United States on visits in the twenties and early thirties, but only two of those in my file settled here before 1933: Wassily Leontief and Joseph Schumpeter joined the Harvard faculty, in 1931 and 1932 respectively. The rush to America began after Hitler's ascent to power and wholesale dismissals from German universities. The American institution that over the years arranged appointments for the largest number of European economists is the New School for Social Research through its Graduate Faculty (originally the University in Exile), which Alvin Johnson established for the specific purpose of bringing German social scientists to America. European economists who are or were connected with the New School include Herbert Block, Karl Brandt, Warner Brook, Gerhard Colm, Arthur Feiler, Eduard Heimann, Julius Hirsch, George Katona, Emil

322

Lederer, Fritz Lehmann, Abba Lerner, Adolph Lowe, Jacob Marschak, Franco Modigliani, Hans Neisser, Karl Niebyl, Richard Schueller, Hans Staudinger, and Giorgio Tagliacozzo. Such a record of appointments of Europeans is unmatched, but most large American universities and not a few colleges have had some European-born economists on their faculties.

When the war broke out and government agencies expanded and multiplied, a considerable number of European economists were appointed to government positions. This was a fortunate circumstance for the émigré economists, for there were not enough academic openings to accommodate them, and the late arrivals were at a loss to find ways to support themselves. I was told that when Alexander Gerschenkron came here in 1938 he first had to earn his living as a longshoreman. But the advantage was reciprocal, and the American government profited by hiring economists who knew at first hand details of the economic and industrial structures of countries with which we were at war.

One or more European economists were hired as economic analysts, advisers, consultants, statisticians, or in other capacities by each of the following government agencies or agencies working for the government, and by others which certainly have escaped me: the Office of Strategic Services and Office of War Information operating as branches of psychological warfare; the Board of Economic Warfare and Foreign Economic Administration; the Office of Price Administration; the War Production Board; the Alien Property Custodian; the Bureau of Latin-American Research; the Social Security Research Council and the Social Security Research Board; the Bureau of the Census; the Federal Reserve System; and the departments of State, Commerce, Agriculture, Treasury, Justice, and War. In the immediate postwar years European-born economists were active in tax treaty negotiations with several European countries; in the Allied Commission in occupied countries; the administration of relief through UNRRA; the Office of War Mobilization and Reconversion; the Economic Co-operation Administration; the Institute of Federal Taxes; the Maritime Commission; the International Bank of Reconstruction and Development; and the International Monetary Fund.

Work in wartime and the early postwar period gave the émigrés insight into the machinery of our government. Some, having become experts in special government areas, continued in the same kind of work for the rest of their careers. A good example is Gerhard Colm, an original member of the graduate faculty of the New School of Social Research. In 1939 he left academic life and never returned: he served mostly as a fiscal expert in various branches of the government as well as in the National Planning Association and wrote extensively on American fiscal policy and public finance. Another example is Joseph Z. Schneider, who gave up teaching in 1942 and as an Acting Division Chief of the Board of Economic Warfare made recommendations on the strategic bombing of German industries. After the war he assisted the army in its work of rehabilitation and reconstruction in Austria.

The majority of economists returned to the universities, and it is from the universities, both before and after the war, that they made their major contributions, an outstanding record. "There is not really an area of economic thought or application where they did not make a mark," said Arcadius Kahan, a Polish-born economist who came to America well after the war. "They were not narrowly restricted, and some went into more than one area, contributing significantly to each." A few of these economists did the bulk of their work in Europe or elaborated here concepts that had fully matured before they came to America. Signal examples in this category are Ludwig von Mises and Joseph Schumpeter. A great polemicist shaped in the tradition of the Austrian school, von Mises spent most of his adult European years in Vienna where he established an early reputation as a paladin of free enterprise and an intransigent foe of socialism. Most of his basic views were published long before he settled in America, and although here he continued to write, he did not add essentially to his economic theories.

Schumpeter's European career included statesmanship, as a minister of finance in 1919; business, as the president of a private Austrian bank in the early twenties; and teaching: he taught in Austria, in Germany, and on visits to Columbia and Harvard. His basic book, *Theory of Economic Development,* containing the seeds of his later work, was published in 1912, the same year that saw the publication of von Mises' *The Theory of Money and Credit,* the core of his economic system. At Harvard Schumpeter wrote *Business Cycles* and the widely known *Capitalism, Socialism, and Democracy,* in both of which he elaborated his theory that in the socio-economic capitalist process an "innovator" or creative entrepreneur is the cause of dynamic change and, indirectly, of business cycles. He also wrote the monumental *History of Economic Analysis,* published after his death.

Both von Mises and Schumpeter were opposed to socialism, although Schumpeter was more moderate in his criticism; but other economists in the migration were advocates of socialism. Paul Baran of Stanford University, a Russian-born neo-Marxist, presented the Soviet model and sparked a great deal of controversy and discussion. The Polish-born Oscar Lange also argued on the side of socialism. Abba Lerner of Michigan State advocated and described a mild form of socialism and government control in capitalistic societies. Educated at the London School of Economics, Lerner came under the influence of the great English economist John Maynard Keynes, who was teaching at Cambridge. Lerner's best known books are *The Economics of Control* and *The Economics of Employment*. Some economists, without taking a definite stand, compared the systems of planned and free economy: one of them is the Russian-born Alexander Erlich who has studied, and written about, the economy of east central Europe.

Some émigré economists opened new vistas in economic analysis. Wassily Leontief, who has been at Harvard since his arrival in 1931, created an "input-output" theory of industrial interdependence which Shackle called "the most beautiful and powerful statistical tool of practical economic policy, perhaps, that we possess." "This technique," Leontief himself explained, "reckons with the intermediate sales and purchases — that is the outputs and inputs — that carry goods and services from industry to industry, from manufacturer to distributor and on to their final purchaser in the market. The technique thus ties predictions about the external configuration of the [economic] system to the indirect flows of supply and demand within." Leontief was only twenty-six years old when he came to this country and yet had already completed his studies in Russia and served two years as economic adviser to the Chinese government. Within five years of his arrival he had constructed and published his first input-output tables for the American economic system in the years 1919–29, breaking the system into forty-two sectors (these tables are included in his book *The Structure of American Economy 1919–1929*, published several years later). During the war he served as a consultant to the Department of Labor and applied his system to the problems that would be created by the shift from a wartime economy; in 1947 he supervised a project that resulted in the construction of an input-output table based on two hundred sectors. Other nations beside the United States have adopted this method of economic analysis, in particular the nations of the Common Market, France, Belgium, West Germany, Italy, and Holland.

Leontief's work is in line with a trend that became most conspicuous in postwar economics, the increased use of mathematical tools, both those that had long existed and the newly invented. Mathematics has been used by a few economists at all times, but the tendency intensified after the foundation in 1930 of the Econometric Society, which reckons among its members both econometricians and mathematical economists. (Econometrics is a recent branch of science aiming at advancing economic theory with the help of the rigorous methods of mathematics and statistics.) A man who did much to explain and advance econometrics in this country is the German-born Gerhard Tintner: he has written books and articles on the subject and has applied mathematical methods not only to problems in recently developed economic areas but also to the economy of Austria and, in one study, to the marketing of meat. As an econometrician, Tintner is claimed by both economists and mathematicians, and so is Leonid Hurwicz, who has been mentioned among the Polish mathematicians.

Mathematical economics underwent a true explosion after World War II. The explosion was facilitated by the advent of electronic computers which permitted the handling of a very large quantity of data and the solving of problems of such complexity that they could not have been tackled without them. In this respect, one of the great contributors to modern economics is John Von Neumann, since his ideas made possible the realization of our modern computers. But economics owes more than the computers to Von Neumann: in the middle thirties he constructed a model of proportional growth of a competitive economy which, according to Tjalling Koopmans, was one of two models (the other being Abraham Wald's) that attracted little attention when published but which "have been at the basis of all subsequent developments [in the field of resource allocation], even if these at times took the form of rediscovery of ideas." In the early forties Von Neumann teamed with the distinguished German-born mathematical economist Oskar Morgenstern of Princeton University to apply Von Neumann's theory of games to economics and study the factors that are common to economic situations and games, such as conflicting interests, incomplete information, and the interplay of rational decision and chance. In 1944 Von Neumann and Morgenstern jointly published

Theory of Games and Economic Behavior. The conceptual novelty of their approach stirred the imagination of many economists and produced a vast crop of studies in economics and related fields. The most deeply affected is the field of operations research. Although Morgenstern's name is associated with the name of Von Neumann and the theory of games, he has done much independent work, first in Vienna where he received his graduate training and taught until 1938, and then at Princeton. He has published books on various economic and financial questions.

An important postwar mathematical development (rooted in studies done for the air force during the war) is linear programming, a method designed to solve problems of maximization and minimization in the presence of restraining factors. A typical example is that of the factory which must schedule its production of automobiles, taking into consideration the capacity limits of subsidiary and parts-producing plants. In the development of linear programming and of its generalization, activity analysis, the Dutch-born and Dutch-educated Tjalling Koopmans had an important part. Koopmans (who received degrees in theoretical physics and mathematical statistics) came to America in 1940. He had a long association with the Cowles Commission for Research in Economics, which promotes mathematical studies, and taught at Chicago and Yale. Many of the applications of linear programming to welfare economics, general equilibrium analysis, and theory of economic growth, which constitute activity analysis, are due to him.

Another mathematical economist, Jacob Marschak, was born in Russia, educated in Russia, Germany, and England and is one of the intellectuals who demurred before taking the long step across the ocean: when he lost his teaching position in Heidelberg, in 1933, Alvin Johnson invited him to join the University in Exile, but Marschak gave preference to Oxford. He accepted the invitation at long last in 1939, was several years at the New School, then moved on to Chicago, Yale, and California. A man of broad economic interests, he made important contributions in different areas. As a director of the Cowles Commission from 1943 to 1948, for instance, he was in charge of studies to explore how mathematics could be used in the investigation of economic behavior and later showed how some of the results he obtained could be extended to human behavior and the social sciences. In 1950 he was co-author of *Economic Aspects of Atomic Energy* in which he foresaw that the peaceful uses of atomic energy would not cause an economic revolution.

The modern methods of economics developed in America were introduced in the Socialist world in the course of Oscar Lange's strange career. He came to America in 1936, joined the University of Chicago in 1938, became a United States citizen, and by 1945 had acquired a distinguished reputation as a mathematical economist. He had also become involved with Polish politics. He resumed his Polish citizenship, became a Polish ambassador, first to the United States and then to the United Nations, lost favor with his government and was recalled to Poland in 1949, and in 1955 became acceptable again. From then to his death ten years later he held courses and wrote books and articles in Polish and other languages that helped to educate a generation of Socialist economists and econometricians.

Among other Europeans who made important contributions to economic theory and analysis and wrote profusely are Gottfried Haberler, a visitor in the United States in the late twenties and early thirties who came back in 1936 to settle at Harvard; Fritz Machlup, an outstanding teacher who at Johns Hopkins attracted a lively group of young American economists before moving to Princeton; and William Fellner, who in Hungary had been in business but came here in 1939 to join the University of California and later Yale. The name of Tibor Scitovsky, a Hungarian like Fellner, is tied to welfare economics, although he has also explored other fields.

A number of European economists did pioneer work in a new field that developed after World War II, the economics of underdeveloped countries, analyzed the causes of backwardness, and studied problems of growth and development, suggesting means to improve economy and promote industrialization. Among those who have been concerned with Latin America are the Czechoslovakian-born John Adler; Ragnar Nurkse, who was born in Estonia; Albert Hirschman of Columbia (Varian Fry's "Beamish" of the Marseilles rescue operations); and the Austrian Bert Hoselitz, a director of the Research Center in Economic Development and Cultural Change at the University of Chicago. Their findings were based mainly on direct observations of the republics of El Salvador, Guatemala, and Colombia, and their proposals for improvement of economic conditions were not, in general, in agreement. Thus, while Nurkse advocated a massive effort through investment in many different industries at the same time, Hirschman maintained that the impetus needed to start progress may be provided by a piecemeal attack on economic problems and suggested that efforts be directed at the develop-

ment of specific sectors of the economy which would then encourage investment in other sectors. And Bert Hoselitz, having studied how economic
changes affect the existing social patterns, asserted that economic development
must be associated with, and allow time for, the transformation of patterns
of social behavior which in primitive societies impede the success of programs
based on the experience of advanced countries; in other words, it is unrealistic
to plan western-style industries and western-style employment systems in societies where certain restraining family-imposed standards may be more important than work and productivity.

Some economists searched the past rather than the present for explanations of backwardness and examples of emerging economies. Outstanding
among these studies is Alexander Gerschenkron's *Economic Backwardness in Historical Perspective*, a series of essays on various aspects of industrial growth in Italy (after the *Risorgimento*), in Bulgaria, and in
Czarist and Soviet Russia. Gerschenkron is described by his colleagues as
a great humanist and a product of European education at its best. He is an
eminent student of European countries (his book *Bread and Democracy*
deals with the agrarian question in Germany), and in this country, first at the
University of California and after 1948 at Harvard, he has been among those
Russian-born economists who have done much to explain Soviet economy to
America (from 1949 to 1956 he was the director of economic projects of the
Russian Research Center). In the book on backwardness, Gerschenkron
relates economic changes to the cultural and political history of the countries
he has observed. In the six essays that he devotes to Russia he goes further,
building a picture of Russian intellectual life and even turning literary
critic to analyze several Russian novels (one essay is entirely devoted to
his reflections on Boris Pasternak's *Doctor Zhivago*). In his analysis of Russian novels, Gerschenkron asserts, he did not intend to deal with literary
qualities but was concerned exclusively with the light these novels cast upon
various aspects of everyday life in Soviet Russia. Gerschenkron's essays are
the most cogent and effective for being written in a vivid English that would
stand comparison with the best work of native writers.

This polivalent approach to economic issues earned Gerschenkron a place
among the builders of bridges between economics and several other disciplines. The bridge he built links economics with social and intellectual history
and literature. Another economist who linked economics and history is the

329

German-born Fritz Redlich, who came to this country in 1936, taught at various colleges, worked at various agencies and eventually retired from Harvard. Redlich's main interests lay in economic, entrepreneurial, and financial history; in many articles he investigated the historical role of entrepreneurs and business leaders in European countries and in America, and he wrote such books as *History of American Business Leaders* and *The Molding of American Banking*. Hoselitz, in his turn, links economic science and sociology and history, both through his investigations mentioned above and through his studies of the role of adventurous, socially deviant entrepreneurs in the economic growth of colonial America. Karl Polanyi, in *The Great Transformation* and in subsequent work, explored interrelations between economics, sociology, and anthropology; and the mathematical economists and econometrists demolished barriers and made mathematics an integral part of economics.

Most of the economists I have mentioned were fully trained in Europe, but a few had little knowledge of economics until they arrived in the United States with a degree in some other field from a European university. Bert Hoselitz and Franco Modigliani are both in this class, but Modigliani's case may well be unique, since the economic education that he received in America was decidedly European. Modigliani was only twenty-one years old when he arrived in New York in 1939, with a law degree from the university of Rome. (His dissertation for the law degree concerned economics.) For two years Modigliani supported himself and his young wife by working as the manager of a book center that imported and sold Italian books. (In love with each other and with America, the Modiglianis were willing to give up the comforts to which they were accustomed and to live on little money in an apartment that Mrs. Modigliani called "invisible.")

Franco Modigliani's interest, however, was not in the book trade, and soon he began to attend night classes at the entirely European University in Exile. Max Ascoli, the Italian members of the faculty, assisted Modigliani in obtaining a fellowship. His teachers were Fritz Lehmann and Adolph Lowe from Germany, Russian-born Jacob Marschak, and others. Even before obtaining his doctoral degree in economics, Modigliani embarked on a teaching career: he taught economics and statistics at the New Jersey College for Women and at Bard College, and mathematical economics and econometrics at the New School. After receiving his doctoral degree and spending a few years teaching in New York, he moved to the Cowles Commission in Chicago and to various other universities; and in 1962 he joined MIT. Modigliani, the author of several books and many articles, considers himself a theoretical economist with an econometric orientation, and his major interest is in macroeconomics. His first important article, "Liquidity Preference and the Theory of Interest and Money," impressive to both those who understand it and those who do not, has contributed to the establishment of a bridge between classical economics and the "Keynesian revolution" brought about by the publication of Keynes' *The General Theory of Employment, Interest and Money.* Modigliani wrote his first book, *National Incomes and International Trade,* in collaboration with the German-born Hans Neisser, who came to America from the Institute of World Economy in Kiel in 1933 and in 1943 became a member of the graduate faculty of the New School.

SOCIOLOGISTS

An American sociologist and friend of intellectual émigrés, Edward Shils, describes the state of sociology in the thirties in the first part of his essay "The Calling of Sociology." Some of the points he makes are pertinent to the migration. By the late thirties, Shils asserts, sociology "presented a picture of disarray" both in America and in Europe. "In the United States, there was already in existence a disconnected mass of particular inquiries, with practically nothing in common except their lively curiosity about contemporary America and their aspiration toward observational discipline . . . the coherent sociological standpoint we now know made an occasional muffled appearance [in the work of a few]." Among the few Shils mentions in this connection is the Austrian-born Paul Lazarsfeld. In the thirties American sociology "underwent a marked expansion at its peripheries," and among the factors of this expansion, Shils lists the influx of German and Austrian refugees. He remarks, however, that the seed of German sociology "ripened only when it was transplanted in America," because before the Nazis rose to power German sociology "led a fruitless, solitary, usually neglected, sometimes dimly stormy career. . . . The seed of sociological theory could not grow without being fertilized by empirical research and by the diversification of its objects." And this was attained in America.

Of special interest in explaining the transplantation of German sociology

331

and its acclimation in America is the story of a group of political and social scientists who came to America from the *Institut für Sozialforschung* (Institute for Social Research) in Frankfurt. The institute, as Herbert Marcuse writes, "had set itself the task of elaborating a theoretical conception which was capable of comprehending the economic, political, and cultural institutions of modern society as a specific historical structure from which the prospective trends of development could be derived." It was based on the belief that "a theory of history was the prerequisite for an adequate understanding of social phenomena." Some of its members were Jewish, others were leftists, and most were affected by the laws promulgated by Hitler in his first months in power. They left almost in a body and many came to America in the following years. The *Institut für Sozialforschung* virtually closed its doors in Frankfurt, reopend them briefly in Paris, and in 1934 moved to New York under the sponsorship of Columbia University. The director of the institute in New York was Max Horkheimer, and its members included Otto Kirchheimer, Leo Lowenthal, Herbert Marcuse, Paul Massing, Felix Weil, and Karl Wittfogel. Theodor Adorno, an eminent member of the Frankfurt institute, accepted a position in Princeton with the Radio Research Project but continued his ties with the institute. (Adorno, a sociologist, philosopher, and music-lover, combined his specialties and made several studies of the social and cultural aspects of music.) In 1949 Max Horkheimer returned to Germany to reconstruct the institute, and within the next two years several members followed him to Frankfurt — more than half remained in the United States — and the American period of the institute came to an end. It was a fruitful period in many respects. For the Germans who went back it was an intellectual experience that they would not want to have missed, as Adorno remarked in an interview with Radio-Bremen: the Germans were familiar with a brand of speculative theory often detached and remote from reality; in America they were exposed to the wholesome confrontation of theory with facts. The importance of the Institute for Social Research to American social and political science was threefold. First, its members pursued investigations they had undertaken abroad or initiated new research and soon began to write abundantly in English: among the earliest books that came out of the institute are Herbert Marcuse's *Reason and Revolution: Hegel and the Rise of Social Theory* (1941) and Franz Neumann's well-known study of German totalitarianism, *Behemoth*

(1942). Second, more than half the members did not return to Germany but settled here and had long university careers in which they came in touch with many students: Otto Kirchheimer at the New School for Social Research and later at Columbia; Leo Lowenthal at California; Herbert Marcuse at Columbia, Harvard, Brandeis, and California; Paul Massing at Rutgers; Franz Neumann at Columbia; and Karl Wittfogel at Columbia and the University of Washington at Seattle. They went on writing, each in his own field: Kirchheimer and Neumann in political science; Lowenthal in the sociology of literature; Karl Wittfogel wrote about Chinese society and the history of Chinese institutions; and Marcuse contributed several books: his *One-Dimensional Man* caught the students' imagination for its powerful protest against our technological society, suddenly turning Marcuse into a symbol on European and American campuses. Third, Max Horkheimer had a leading role and several institute members participated in an important project which resulted in the publication of a five-volume series titled "Studies in Prejudice." The sponsoring organization was the American Jewish Committee, which had called the attention of scholars to religious and racial prejudice by convening a conference on this subject. To implement the project, Horkheimer, who in Germany had edited a series on authority and the family, organized the Department of Scientific Research within the American Jewish Committee, planned the series, and served as editor with the American Samuel Flowerman. The series is important not only for the value of each volume but because it represents an early effort to bring together theory and empirical research, sociology and psychology, émigré and native scholars.

Today the best known of the five volumes is Theodor Adorno's *The Authoritarian Personality*, written with the Austrian psychologist Else Frenkel-Brunswik and Americans Daniel Levinson and Nevitt Sanford. Adorno and his collaborators discovered a correlation between certain personality traits and the propensity toward overt prejudice and described the method they used to measure these traits in different sections of the population. The book aroused much discussion and controversy about both methodology and conclusions; interest has been intense and has spurred the writing of critical works. In *Dynamics of Prejudice* the Austrian-born psychoanalyst Bruno Bettelheim and the American sociologist Morris Janowitz studied prejudice among veterans and the impact on prejudice of the war experience (a revised edition appeared in 1964 under the title *Social Change and Preju-*

333

dice). *Anti-Semitism and Emotional Disorder*, by the American Nathan Ackerman and the Austrian-born psychologist Marie Jahoda, is a psycho-analytic study based upon the histories of individuals who had received intensive psychotherapy. *Rehearsal for Destruction*, by the German-born sociologist Paul Massing, is directed at understanding the causes of German anti-Semitism. And in *Prophets of Deceit*, the German-born sociologist Leo Lowenthal and the American Norbert Guterman explore the agitators' techniques of persuasion and the ways in which they manage to transform vague feelings into beliefs and actions.

In the last several decades great strides have been taken in sociological methodology, the devising and refinement of techniques to analyze and measure large quantities of observational data, the building of mathematical models, and, in general, the development of a quantitative approach to the investigation of social issues. The foremost émigré in this field is Paul Lazarsfeld of Columbia. Born in Austria, Lazarsfeld was trained in psychology at the University of Vienna, where he taught psychology for several years. In his Viennese period he made studies in social psychology for the United States government and for American business concerns, and after a visit in 1933, he settled here in 1937 as the director of a radio research program in Princeton. In 1940 he moved to Columbia where from 1950 to 1959 he served as chairman of the sociology department.

Perhaps Lazarsfeld's major contribution is to have set an example in the creation of special institutions for empirical social research and to have given a great impetus to the development of these institutions in America. He established the Bureau of Applied Social Research at Columbia and directed pioneer work to develop sample surveys and to apply socio-psychological concepts and techniques to the study of social phenomena. Lazarsfeld, in collaboration with others, investigated the social psychology of voting behavior in a study of the 1940 and 1948 presidential elections, thus helping to establish on a firm footing the field of political sociology. He has developed a number of techniques, many of them mathematical, which have become standard procedure in the empirical study of social phenomena. By examining the results of observations in search of structure and to determine whether a model might be constructed, Lazarsfeld created what one of his disciples called "methodological self-consciousness." Finally, through his former students and assistants he has provided leadership for most of the major institutes and departments of sociology throughout the country.

The field of social psychology, which is closely related to sociology, was strongly influenced by the work of Kurt Lewin. Lewin was a member of the German Gestalt school of psychology founded by Max Wertheimer with the support of Kurt Koffka and Wolfgang Köhler, all of whom emigrated to the United States and by their presence spurred the assimilation of their ideas into American psychology. Kurt Lewin came to America in 1932, on a visit that Hitler's laws turned into a permanent stay. At Iowa between 1935 and 1945 he was a professor of child psychology and conducted many experiments with children, but his total work is most relevant to the study of social groups and the causes of their unrest. He constructed a system of psychodynamics, borrowing and adapting concepts from the physical sciences and mathematics, especially from field theory, vector analysis, and topology, and used his system to analyze the behavior of individuals within groups. In World War II he and his students made important applications of his theories to the study of morale. He may be regarded as the founder of group dynamics. After his death in 1947, his influence has continued to grow through his students and his books.

Some sociologists are of special interest because, working in different areas of sociology, they have been interpreters of the sociological thought in their countries of origin. To mention only a few, Hans Gerth and Kurt Wolff, both of Brandeis University, have done much toward the acceptance here of the teachings of Max Weber (Gerth) and Georg Simmel (Wolff), some of whose writings they have themselves translated. Albert Salomon, for many years a member of the graduate faculty of the New School, began divulging Weber's thought in a series of articles in *Social Research* in the middle thirties. Nicholas Timasheff, who taught at Fordham University, wrote about Russian sociology before and after the revolution in many works, the best known of which is *The Great Retreat*, an analysis of the sociological and cultural trends that led to the growth and decline of communism in his native Russia. Dinko Tomasic, born and educated in Yugoslavia, eventually settled at the University of Indiana; he presented the sociological issues of Yugoslavia and other Balkan nations and collected a valuable bibliography of sociological works published in those countries. The work of Polish-born Henrik Infield falls into a somewhat related category: before coming to the United States in

1935, Infield spent a few years in Palestine and became interested in the kib-butz and rural sociology; in America he has written books on co-operative living in Palestine, co-operative communities, and made a study of a veter-ans' co-operative land settlement.

Florian Znaniecki may be included among those who made sociological studies of their native countries, although he owes his distinguished reputa-tion to the role he played in the development of social action theory in this country. Znaniecki taught at the university of Poznan until 1939, when he came to the United States. Here he was well-known, having taught at Chi-cago from 1917 to 1919 at the invitation of William I. Thomas, who had met him in Warsaw. Between 1918 and 1920 Znaniecki and Thomas jointly pub-lished a magnum opus, the five-volume study *The Polish Peasant in Europe and in America*. This, Znaniecki's sole book with a decided national conno-tation, is a classic study of the changes that immigrants undergo in the process of Americanization. In the early thirties Znaniecki again came on a visit and lectured at Columbia; he returned in the summer of 1939 and was here when Poland was invaded by Germany. In 1940 he joined the University of Illinois. As the founder of the *Polish Sociological Review* and the Polish Sociological Institute, and through his early work, Znaniecki earns a place among inter-preters of European cultures.

Many other European sociologists and social psychologists in this country have been greatly productive. Franz Neumann remarked that one role of those who were brought up "in the tradition of the great philosophical and historical systems of Europe" has been to add a note of skepticism to the "extraordinary optimism [of Americans] about the potentialities of social science to change the world." In another role, according to Neumann, they have tried to correct American overemphasis on the collection of empirical data, and "to put social science research into a theoretical framework." But in spite of all that Europeans in America have done, American sociology is primarily a native science, a product of America's self-consciousness and self-directed interest as a nation and of her deep preoccupation with social conditions.

Empirical sociology had long asserted itself, and social theory was being independently developed in the United States when Europeans began to arrive. Outstanding teachers of sociology were not lacking. The American

Morris Janowitz estimates that among the influences that molded him as a sociologist only about 15 per cent could be attributed to the foreign-born in America. If émigrés made a considerable contribution, it is because they came to recognize the value of American empirical research, directed their speculations toward problems of contemporary importance, and took advantage of the scientific tools and techniques they found in America.

POLITICAL SCIENTISTS

Political science as such was not a discipline usually taught in European schools, and some few degrees in political affairs were issued by social science or law faculties. (An exception was the School of Politics, founded in 1920 in Berlin, which brought together several related disciplines.) It may thus be surprising to hear that émigré political scientists have made a strong impact in this country. The fact is that, coming from different fields of learning or professional activities, they broadened American political science by the wide range of their outlook. Moreover, practically all members of the Berlin School of Politics came over to this country. Of the thirty-seven political scientists in my file, twenty-four, or over 60 per cent, were trained in Germany, six in Austria, four had a mixed training in two or more countries (Russia, Germany, Austria, Switzerland, and France), and only three were educated elsewhere (one each in Czechoslovakia, Hungary, and Italy). Many were active in German politics before the rise of Hitler and were ousted as a consequence. Not all came directly to the United States; most stopped on the way, the majority in England.

A comment on their role in America comes from the British author Bernard Crick in *The American Science of Politics*. He criticizes bitingly some tendencies of contemporary American political science, mainly scientism (excessive preoccupation with the application to political science of the methods used in the natural sciences), and the dissociation of political science from American politics. Then, in expressing the hope of a change for the better, he writes: "An infusion of émigré and refugee scholars has certainly helped to widen perspectives from the rather narrow field that was an unfortunate consequence of the nativism and realism of Charles Beard. Some of them, in varying degrees, like Francis Lieber of old, in accepting the American way of life, have tried to distinguish the light of universal example from the paths of a unique dispensation." He explains: "I think

337

particularly of Hannah Arendt (though she is firmly outside the profession), C. J. Friedrich, the late Waldemar Gurian, the late Franz Neumann, Sigmund Neumann, Hans Morgenthau, and Leo Strauss — the list is only partial. I do not cite these names as an invidious comparison with native scholars for it is still one of the great glories of American life that America attracts, receives and assimilates such people."

Limited as Crick's list is, it suggests that European-born political scientists may be divided in three classes according to the principal way in which each has "helped widen perspectives," namely, as interpreters of political systems of modern Europe; as opposers of the trend toward the dissociation of political science from politics and commentators on current political issues; and as political philosophers and theorists. Hence I would place Arendt, Gurian, and Franz Neumann in the first group; Morgenthau in the second; Strauss and Sigmund Neumann in the third. (Political philsopher C. J. Friedrich arrived in America in the twenties and is not considered here.) The classification is artificial, and a political scientist may belong to all three groups: analysis of a political system like bolshevism, for example, may advance theory and at the same time bring political science in closer contact with reality. And yet each émigré is best known for achievements characteristic of one of these groups.

Hannah Arendt belongs in the first class as the author of *The Origins of Totalitarianism* (her first book in English) and the controversial *Eichmann in Jerusalem*. For other works she is a social or cultural philosopher. She undertook to write *The Origins of Totalitarianism* in 1945 (it was published in 1951), after the defeat of Germany. This seemed to her the first appropriate moment "to try to tell and to understand what happened . . . still in grief and sorrow . . . but no longer in speechless outrage and impotent horror." She thus produced a broad and erudite study of anti-Semitism and imperialism in Europe in the eighteenth and nineteenth centuries and an analysis of totalitarian ideology at work in Nazi Germany and Communist Russia.

Eichmann in Jerusalem is a report on the trial of Adolf Eichmann which she attended as an observer for the *New Yorker*. Eichmann was abducted from Argentina by Israeli agents and accused of the mass extermination of European Jews; tried and convicted, he was hanged in May, 1962. His trial raised some of the most crucial moral and legal questions of our times, to which individuals have answered according to their judgment and conscience. It was inevitable that many persons should disagree with Hannah Arendt; her articles in the *New Yorker*, the book which sprang from them, and her lectures on the Chicago campus aroused both dissent and defense.

Waldemar Gurian, a big, awkward, lonely man, not fully understood even by his friends, was a Russian Jew by birth, but as a child of nine was taken to Germany by his mother and was converted to Catholicism. Neither this nor his subsequent experiences could sever his intellectual and sentimental ties with Russia. In America, which he reached in 1937 to join the faculty of the University of Notre Dame, he devoted himself to the interpretation of Russia and bolshevism to make Americans aware of the dangers in the Soviet system, writing several books. His most enduring contribution was the founding in 1939 of *The Review of Politics*, of which he was editor until his death, imparting to it the character of a forum for men and women of different faiths and nationalities. Upon its twenty-fifth anniversary, the current editor, M. A. Fitzsimons, described the journal as "the product of the inspiration of a European scholar and of the co-operation of European émigrés and American scholars." In fact, few émigré political scientists have not published an article, an essay, or a review of a book in Gurian's journal. Fitzsimons further remarked that upon the emergence of a fearfully strong Soviet Union the review "searchingly examined the foreign policy of the Soviet Union and its Russian heritage. [Gurian's] studies of Bolshevism had prepared him so well for this and his knowledge of Russian scholars and students of the Soviet Union was so extensive that . . . *The Review* played a leading role in Slavic and Eastern European studies."

Franz Neumann earned a lasting reputation as the author of the classic *Behemoth*, a study of the structure and practice of National Socialism published in 1942. Neumann examined the roots of nazism in German society and the role of economic conditions, achieving an objective and thorough analysis the more remarkable for having been completed while nazism was in power and seemingly victorious. The manuscript "was finished when Germany attacked Russia; the book was set up when Germany. . . . declared war on the United States," as Neumann explains in the preface. Neumann was a most unusual man. Of the members of the Institute for Social Research in New York, his influence on American social and political science has been most important. He did not belong to the institute in Frankfurt, and his main

339

activity in Germany had been as a labor lawyer. In the spring of 1933 he was arrested but succeeded in escaping from Germany and went to London. He studied at the London School of Economics with Harold Laski and conceived the plan for *Behemoth* before moving to the United States in 1936.

Among émigré political scientists, Ernst Fraenkel is a notable example of a "two-way interpreter." A member of the Berlin bar until he came to America in 1938, Fraenkel was an early commentator on totalitarianism and in 1941 published *The Dual State*, an attempt to formulate a theory of dictatorship. In 1953 he returned to Germany and undertook to interpret the American culture to the German people as a professor of the John F. Kennedy Institute of the Free University of Berlin, a member of the German Association for American Study, and an editor of the association yearbook. An additional circumstance in Fraenkel's life widened his perspective of cultures: before returning to Germany he served for several years with the American military government in Korea and taught at the university in Seoul.

Loosely related to the interpreters of European political systems are the experts in foreign relations. Two names come readily to mind, Hans Simons, who is German, and Arnold Wolfers, who is Swiss. They have both been directors of the School for Politics in Berlin, Simons in the late twenties and Wolfers in the early thirties. Simons was also active in German politics before Hitler, served as the governor of Lower Silesia from 1930 to 1932. He became a member of the graduate faculty of the New School in 1935, and from 1950 to 1960 he was also president of the New School. In 1960 Simons became a consultant of the Ford Foundation in the United States and in India. Wolfers was a professor of international relations at Yale from 1933 until 1960, when he joined the Center of Foreign Policy Research of the Johns Hopkins School of Advanced International Studies in Washington, D. C., of which he later became the director.

The class of those who brought political science in contact with the reality of politics in our times is thinly populated by the European-born. In a sense, Louise Holborn belongs in this class: a former professor of comparative government and international relations at several American colleges, she has been chiefly concerned with the very real and still timely problem of international refugees. To the history of the cultural migration she contributed a paper on the German scholars in the United States after 1933, published in the tenth yearbook of the German Association for American Studies. But refugee and

340

migration problems are only partly political. One émigré is sturdily established in the class, Hans Morgenthau, whose career I have mentioned up to his appointment at the University of Kansas City in 1939. In the context of the émigrés' experiences in resettling in this country, the salient event of Morgenthau's stay in Kansas City was his admission to the Missouri bar. Morgenthau had practiced law in Frankfurt between 1927 and 1932, and had also been acting president of the labor law court in Frankfurt. But that was German law, a law so different from the American that most émigré German lawyers preferred to change profession than to be retrained. Morgenthau did get training in American law, but not in the usual way. At the University of Kansas City, he was asked to teach courses in American law and so he learned along with his students. The examination for admission to the bar was very difficult. A student taking an examination in Germany, Morgenthau explained, is always given "time to think," but in Kansas City he felt as if he had no time at all to prepare an answer. At any rate, he did not make much use of his admission to the bar, which he obtained in 1943. He wrote a couple of briefs for one case, but in the same year he went to the University of Chicago, where he also directed the Center for the Study of American Foreign and Military Policy.

As a political theorist, Morgenthau opposes scientism and positivism. "The object of the social sciences is man," he writes in an essay on the state of political science. "To make susceptibility to quantitative measurement the yardstick of the scientific character of the social sciences in general and of political science in particular is to deprive these sciences of that very orientation which is adequate to the understanding of their subject matter." And he argues against an analogy between the social and the natural sciences in his *Scientific Man vs. Power Politics*. To the layman Morgenthau is better known as a commentator on American international and military policies. In many articles, at round tables, and through appearances on radio and television he has been a powerful voice in the affairs of the nation, almost invariably a critical voice. This is in line with Morgenthau's conviction that "a political science which is faithful to its moral commitment of telling the truth about the political world cannot help telling society things it does not want to hear. It must sit in continuous judgment upon political man and political society, measuring their truth . . . by its own." Morgenthau has written several books on international affairs, of which the most successful is *Politics among*

Nations. It has been noted that a streak of pessimism runs through Morgenthau's writings. This is also in line with the role of the political scientist as Morgenthau sees it; no matter how widely known and respected a critical commentator may be, he cannot hope to change the world through his commitment to the truth and bring it close to the ideals he entertains for it.

Émigré political philosophers and theorists are the largest group in my classification and explored the largest variety of subjects. One of the most outstanding philosophers is Leo Strauss, a conservative neo-Platonist who started his scholarly career at the Academy for Jewish Research in Berlin, from 1925 to 1932. In the studies of those years — Jewish philosophy from the twelfth to the eighteenth century, from Maimonides to Moses Mendelssohn — are the origins of Strauss's later politico-philosophical position. German classical education had acquainted him with the thought of Plato and Aristotle, and he met them again in the interpretation of Jewish philosophers. The study of Spinoza drew him to Hobbes and to the quest to reconstruct the development of Hobbes' moral and political ideas. In 1934, after two years in France, Strauss went to England to examine the Hobbes papers and in 1935 published *The Political Philosophy of Hobbes*. Hobbes was an exponent of natural right, and Strauss became its advocate. In the United States, which he reached in 1938, he expounded the philosophy of natural right in articles and in the book *Natural Right and History*, but he prefers the classical theory developed by Plato and Aristotle to its reformulation by Hobbes and his followers. The "victory of modern natural science" has brought about a crisis of natural right, and in our days natural right is rejected by the social sciences and, Strauss implies, by the American people: the writers of the Declaration of Independence believed in the inalienable right with which all men are endowed by their Creator. But, Strauss asks, "Does this nation in its maturity . . . still hold those 'truths to be self-evident'?" At the University of Chicago, which he joined in 1949 after ten years at the New School, Strauss has trained many students and followers, creating a neo-Platonic school of political thought.

Strauss and his disciples have been active and vocal in the revolt against scientism and positivism in political science. They have had an ally in Eric Voegelin, a German-born, Vienna-trained political philosopher. Voegelin taught law at the University of Vienna (until 1936), government at Louisiana State University, political science at the University of Munich, and became a member of the Hoover Institution on War, Revolution, and Peace at Stanford. For his writings and teaching Voegelin has been called one of the most distinguished interpreters of conservative European thought.

The émigrés theorists have made contributions to various areas of political science, mainly to its general theory, comparative government, and the legal aspects of politics and government. General theory was broadened by the thought of several émigrés. John Herz, a professor at City College of New York, is the author of *Political Realism and Political Idealism*; other books place him also in the field of international relations. Karl Deutsch, who was born and educated in Prague, dealt with nationalism, political community, science and the creative spirit, and foreign and world politics. The Russian-born Ossip Flechtheim, who returned to Europe in 1951, wrote extensively on Hegel and theodicy and on other subjects. Heinrich Rommen of Georgetown University is the author of *State in Catholic Thought*. William Ebenstein of Princeton wrote several books on political thought, and his latest is *American Government in the Twentieth Century*. His countryman Peter Drucker, of New York University, dealt mainly with management and the theory of institutions. Fritz Morstein Marx contributed the book *The Administrative State*.

After witnessing the drastic political changes in Europe and becoming acquainted with the American brand of democracy, many European exiles were well prepared for the study of comparative government. Karl Loewenstein is an eminent explorer in this field. Once a practicing lawyer and university lecturer in Munich and for many years a professor at Amherst, he first studied individual governments, the German government under the Nazis, the Brazilian government under Vargas, "Soviet Germany," and the Bonn Republic, and wrote extensively about them. Then he abandoned the country-to-country approach and in *Political Power and the Governmental Process* attempted to build a conceptual framework to which political institutions and the techniques of different political systems could be subordinated. Sigmund Neumann of Wesleyan University concerned himself with political parties, "the lifeline of modern politics," neglected, in his opinion, by contemporary political scientists. To provide substantive findings that would be useful in the formulation of a theory, Neumann became the editor and generous contributor to the volume *Modern Political Parties*. For other books he belongs with the interpreters of political systems. Ferdinand

Hermens, formerly of Notre Dame and later of Cologne, wrote among many other works *Democracy and Proportional Representation* and *Democracy or Anarchism?* And Robert Neumann, author of *European and Comparative Government*, is in a position to observe a state from a perspective unusual to political scientists — as United States ambassador to Afghanistan.

Arnold Brecht, Hans Kelsen, and Otto Kirchheimer are examples of theorists whose thought leans heavily on their legal training. Brecht and Kelsen were eminent jurists and government officials, one in Germany, the other in Austria. Brecht, who began his career as a judge, served the Ministry of Justice and other ministries and in the Reich Chancellery. As a staunch defender of democracy, he brought the fight against the rising reactionary forces as represented by Hindenburg and von Papen to the Constitutional High Court in 1932. Ousted from office, arrested and released by the Nazis, he came to the graduate faculty of the New School upon its opening in 1933. Kelsen, long before coming to America in 1940, had earned a reputation as one of the most eminent jurists of his time. At the start of his academic career in Vienna he created the "pure theory of law," a logical formal analysis of law, and described it in a basic work published in Germany in 1911. At the end of World War I he was the author of the Austrian constitution of 1920, and until 1930 a judge of the Austrian Supreme Constitutional Court and a professor at the University of Vienna. He then left Vienna and for the next ten years taught in Cologne, Geneva, and Prague.

Brecht's German experiences bore copious fruit in America. His first concern upon arrival was to describe the German struggle for democracy and its failure, and in the early forties he wrote *Prelude to Silence* and *Federalism and Regionalism in Germany*. In the following years his political thinking "evolved out of his philosophy of justice, gradually growing from this and other roots into a comprehensive system of thought on the whole range of political questions," according to his student, Morris D. Forkosch. Brecht wrote about relative and absolute justice, liberty, the search for absolutes, and the possible and impossible in political and legal philosophy; he published the scholarly *Political Theory*, a reassessment of political thought in Europe and America. Of Hans Kelsen some of his Austrian friends say that in America he has not done as well as in Europe and is not as highly regarded or widely known. And yet he taught for ten years at the University of California before his retirement in 1952 and has been a most prolific writer. *Law and Peace in International Relations, The Law of the United Nations*, and *Communist Theory of Law* are only a few examples from a list of his books.

Otto Kirchheimer, born over twenty years later than Brecht and Kelsen, was trained in law in Germany but was not of an age to serve European governments before coming to America. In 1943, after several years at the Institute for Social Research in New York, he became an analyst in the Office of Strategic Services, and from 1945 until 1955 an analyst and branch chief in the division of research for Europe of the State Department. In 1955 he joined the New School and later Columbia. A leading authority on political and social uses of law, he is the author of *Political Justice* and *The Use of Legal Procedure for Political Ends*.

TEACHERS OF LAW

The careers of the lawyers, jurists, and teachers of law that I have mentioned were interrupted and altered in the process of immigration. The changes were drastic in some cases, as when Rudolf Flesch became an analyst of the English language, or when Emanuel Winternitz became a musicologist, and relatively minor in the case of those who became political scientists. There were also a few lawyers and teachers of law who were able to proceed in America on the course undertaken in Europe. The lawyers who were retrained and entered law practice do not belong in this study. Those who filled academic posts in America were, in general, specialists in a branch of law which is of interest in this country, comparative, Roman, or international law. Thus Eberhard Bruck and the papyrologist Adolf Berger, one from Germany, the other from Poland, taught Roman law at Harvard (Bruck) and at City College (Berger) as they had done in their homelands.

In Germany, Arthur Nussbaum and Friedrich Kessler (almost a generation younger than Nussbaum) specialized in aspects of international law. Nussbaum taught at Columbia and was the author of books on international and monetary law, and of a history of the law of nations. Kessler has been at Yale, with a nine-year interruption during which he was on the faculty of the University of Chicago. Max Rheinstein, a professor of comparative law, has had an uninterrupted career at Chicago where he became one of the most distinguished members of the faculty. A teacher highly respected and admired by his students, Rheinstein strove to make them acquainted with

German law and the law of other European countries. The French government recently honored him for introducing courses in French public law into the foreign law program of the University of Chicago. He has worked to strengthen cultural relations with Europe, served as a member of the Committee on Reform of German Law of the Allied Control Authority, and participated in the exchange program between the University of Chicago and the University of Frankfurt. The hardships of the beginnings of Rheinstein's American career were tempered by a fortunate circumstance: as a specialist in comparative law, he had been acquainted with Anglo-Saxon law since his student days. The dissertation for his doctoral degree in 1924 was on a particular issue of English law, and a few years later he published *The Structure of Contractual Obligation in Anglo-American Law*. Upoh his arrival in this country he was conversant with American law. Nevertheless, he had to overcome the difficulties of a system of legal education with which he was not acquainted and a legal mentality totally different from the German.

The Czechoslovakian-born Hans Zeisel became an American professor of law in a turn of career unlike most. A doctor of *rerum politicarum* in the thirties in Vienna, he collaborated with Paul Lazarsfeld and Marie Jahoda in the widely appreciated study *The Unemployed of Marienthal*. In the United States he worked with business firms until he was appointed a professor of sociology and law in the Law School of the University of Chicago. He is the author or co-author of several books, among them *The American Jury* in collaboration with Harry Kalven.

HISTORIANS

The older a civilization, the more mature in a scholarly and intellectual sense will be a history of that civilization. The reason is not so much the greater bulk of accumulated record as the longer period in which historians of successive generations can re-evaluate past events and elaborate interpretations from different theoretical perspectives. It is natural that the science of history should have shown greater progress in Europe than in America through the early decades of this century. Several observers of the cultural migration have commented on this point. Helge Pross remarked that to the Americans the War of Independence and the Civil War are not events of the past but living issues; the founding fathers, Washington, Jefferson, and Lincoln are figures of the present; and in this sense (if not in others) America

346

has no history. Gerhard Stourzh, commenting on the German immigration to the United States, indicated two areas in which, in his opinion, the émigré historians made the greatest contribution, because Americans had not yet paid sufficient attention to them: intellectual history and world history. In the past, American historians tended to interpret political events from a socio-economic viewpoint and neglected the role of ideas and of political thought; they also failed to consider the interdependence of internal and foreign politics and the background of world history against which American history has evolved. Hans Rothfels and Hajo Holborn made similar observations. Both stressed that European historians arrived here at a moment most favorable to bring about needed changes in the interpretation of history, when as a result of the economic crisis America, deeply shaken in her optimism, was going through a spiritual process that promoted self-criticism, and when her growing involvement in world affairs caused a greater awareness of the importance of foreign policy in domestic issues.

The role of émigré historians was given ample recognition by John Higham and Leonard Krieger, two of the three authors of the volume *History* in the series of Princeton Studies in American humanistic scholarship. (The third author, Felix Gilbert, is himself an émigré historian.) Higham, who dealt with American historical scholarship in general, wrote: ". . . European dictatorships drove into exile many scholars trained outside the American historiographical tradition and capable therefore of widening its scope and enriching its substance. The émigré professors brought with them a more intimate understanding of cultures than American scholars had viewed from the perspective of the outsider who can observe external forms more readily than their inner spirit . . . ."

Krieger, who is concerned with the study of European history in America, stated: ". . . the immigrant historians from central Europe during the Thirties worked a profound influence upon the general practice of European history in this country . . . these European scholars not only disseminated an intimate knowledge of the European heritage to American students in unprecedented numbers but they themselves represented a selection from European scholarship based on the awareness, drawn from the circumstances of their own careers, of the actual relationships that linked the various activities of man. Their feeling for historical integration was nurtured by the experience of their totalitarian homelands and developed by their intellectual naturalization in America. . . . The European-born historians contributed to [the American historiographical] tradition by connecting what had been separate in it, for the common strength of their historical teaching and writing lay in their merger of the particularity and generality, in their preservation of the irreducible vitality of the one within the generic meaningfulness of the other."

In their discussion, the authors of *History* mentioned the names of many émigré historians. Some are in specialized fields: Stephan Kuttner is a student of medieval sources and writes of canon and Roman law. Higham wrote that "Kuttner's Institute of Canon Law at the Catholic University of America raised medieval church history to an importance it had lacked due to native preoccupation with American church history." Another specialist is Karl Wittfogel, social scientist and historian of Chinese society and institutions.

Hajo Holborn, a towering figure among teachers of European history, studied with Friedrich Meinecke and other exponents of the so-called German school who stressed social and religious rather than political factors, the meaning of events rather than their causes, and who were especially strong in the very areas of history which the German exiles were to find wanting in America. Holborn was greatly influenced by Meinecke and later passed on this influence to his own students. In 1931 he was appointed to a newly founded chair for international relations at the School of Politics in Berlin, a chair created by the Carnegie Foundation. His few American students in Berlin and the Carnegie Foundation were his main connections with America and became important elements in his decision to come here when Hitler dismissed him. He went to Yale in 1934 and in his long career taught a large number of Americans who have become professors of history in American colleges and universities. (Leonard Krieger is one of them.)

As a scholar, Holborn has been concerned chiefly with European history, especially the German: he has written *The Political Collapse of Europe*; a three-volume *History of Modern Germany*; and numerous other publications, many of them about Germany. After working in the Office of Strategic Services and as a consultant to the State Department he also wrote on military subjects and published *American Military Government: Its Policies and Organization.*

Felix Gilbert, who since 1962 has been in the school for historical studies of the Institute for Advanced Study, and Hans Baron, of the Newberry

Library and the University of Chicago, directed their main attention to the Italian Renaissance and its various cultural aspects. While Baron looked at the Renaissance from many angles, sociological, economic, political, humanistic, and literary, Gilbert sought the origins of modern political thought in the writings of such men as Machiavelli and Guicciardini. Later Gilbert transferred his interest in the development of political thought from the Italian Renaissance to the American fight for independence and wrote *To the Farewell Address: Ideas of Early American Foreign Policy*, in which he fused intellectual and diplomatic history and brought to light the existence of foreign concepts in American thought on foreign relations in the colonial period. Dietrich Gerhard, who like Holborn and Gilbert was a pupil of Meinecke, calls himself "a trans-Atlantic professor," because after 1954 he shared his time between Washington University at St. Louis, which he joined in 1936, and German institutions. The commuting almost symbolizes Gerhard's historical activity: his main work is *Alte und neue Welt in vergleichender Geschichtsbetrachtung (The Old and the New World in Comparative Historical Observation).*

Hans Rothfels' main interest was Bismarck, about whom he published articles and accumulated notes but never wrote the comprehensive work he planned. He may have done Germany a greater service with *The German Opposition to Hitler*. Ever since his arrival in the United States in 1940 (he taught at Brown and Chicago), Rothfels devoted himself to the task of proving to the Americans that there was a difference between the German people and the Nazi regime. At the end of the war, feeling that German resistance to Hitler was not sufficiently known here, he lectured on it, and since the lecture was well-received, decided to write the book. It was issued in English in 1948 and translated into German in the following year. Ernst Kantorowicz, of the University of California and later of the Institute for Advanced Study, was an eminent historian of ideas, preoccupied with the spiritual reinterpretation of medieval history; his last great work, strangely titled *The King's Two Bodies*, is a study in medieval political theology.

The historians mentioned so far were all born in Germany or strongly identified with German culture. The authors of *History*, remarking on the émigrés, name only two who were not German: Americo Castro and Gaetano Salvemini. Castro, born in Brazil and educated in Spain, was a professor of Spanish history in Madrid before coming to the United States. Although

349

he taught for many years in this country, at Wisconsin, Texas, and Princeton, he continued to write in Spanish. In his major work, *The Structure of Spanish History*, which has been translated into English, "Castro revealed an endogenous pattern of development that Americans surely would not themselves have perceived," in Higham's words. In Italy, Salvemini had studied the social struggles of Florence in the thirteenth century and of France during the revolution, but after going into exile, first in France, then in America, his chief concern became fascism and the need to unmask it. Although he lectured and wrote on the nature of history and the social sciences, most of his articles and books were meant to fight Fascist propaganda in the United States, to put in the right perspective documents and data released by the Fascists, and to reveal the true essence of the Fascist dictatorship. Among the books published while he lived in America are *Mussolini Diplomate* (in French), *Under the Axe of Fascism, Italian Fascism*, and *What To Do with Italy*.

There were other émigré historians. To the study of the Fascist period of Italian history both Giuseppe Antonio Borgese and Max Ascoli made substantial contributions, although neither is, strictly speaking, a historian. The Italian-born Robert Lopez of Yale, on the other hand, is a medievalist who studied trade in the Mediterranean world and published on the Dark Ages and the birth of Europe. The phenomenon of modern nationalism in different countries was analyzed in numerous articles and books by the Czechoslovakian-born Hans Kohn, a distinguished and fluent writer now regarded as the main authority on his subject. A timely work (in collaboration with Wallace Sokolsky) is *African Nationalism in the Twentieth Century*.

The Austro-Hungarian empire and the states that emerged from its ruin were not neglected. Some basic works on the dual monarchy and the early struggles of independent Hungary were written by the Hungarian Oscar Jászi, who came to America well ahead of the wave, but historians of the wave proper have added their share. Friedrich Engel-Janosi, who taught at Catholic University in Washington, then went back to Vienna, published books and articles about Austria, especially in relation to the Vatican in the nineteenth century. Robert Kann, an Austrian lawyer who was retrained as a historian in this country, analyzed Austrian nationality problems and the factors of integration and disintegration in the Habsburg Empire. The

Czechoslovakian-born Otakar Odložilík has written about the history and the inheritance of his country; and the vicissitudes of Poland were described by the Polish-born Oscar Halecki of Fordham and Columbia.

Émigré historians, like so many émigrés in other disciplines, recognized that they gained much from living in America. Thus Hajo Holborn wrote: "My transformation into an American has given me a broader perspective on all things German. Many political or intellectual issues over which Germans like to feud lose their significance if looked at from a distance. Even more important was my growing inclination to evaluate historical phenomena on a comparative level. Seen in this light many events and ideas of German history assume, I believe, proper proportions." And Dietrich Gerhard, the trans-Atlantic commuter, is convinced that "living and studying in a foreign country is essential to the training of educators, especially historians. . . . To penetrate the traditions of other countries and civilizations opens up new vistas and reflects on the scholar's work. . . . He realizes the relativity of his old outlook and of the institutions with which he has been familiar. . . . At least this has happened to me. . . ."

To these contributions by émigré historians could be added many by European-born individuals outside the profession. As noted in the chapter on writers, many authors broadened knowledge of modern Europe. Franz Neumann's *Behemoth*, Giuseppe Antonio Borgese's *Goliath*, several of André Maurois's writings, Hannah Arendt's *The Origins of Totalitarianism*, and many others belong undoubtedly to history. Countless autobiographies, personal narratives, and subjective interpretations constitute a valuable source of information, and some historical novels may also be of use. The European-born in the wave did not neglect biography, a field of literature in which historians themselves seldom deign to enter but which they consider in their jurisdiction and not to be trespassed upon. Among biographies by amateur historians are *Der Führer* by Konrad Heiden, *Mussolini* (my own), *Thomas Jefferson* by Karl Lehmann, several studies of Baudelaire by Henri Peyre, and the scholarly *Empress Maria Theresa* by Robert Pick.

The patrimony of ancient history was enlarged by classicists like Werner Jaeger, who wrote many books on the culture of ancient Greece, and by orientalists like Gustav von Grunebaum and Leo Oppenheim, who studied Muslim and Mesopotamian civilizations. In specialized fields, Joachim Wach wrote a history of religion; Guido Kisch and Ernst Levy wrote on Jewish and Roman law; Leo Spitzer dealt with the history of literature; Arturo Castiglioni, Ludwig Edelstein, and Henry Sigerist were historians of medicine; Giorgio de Santillana is a historian of early natural science, as was Alexandre Koyré, who returned to France shortly after the war; and Otto Neugebauer is a historian of ancient mathematics.

ORIENTALISTS

A numerically modest but distinguished group is made up of European-born scholars versed in one or more aspects of Eastern culture. Europe has an older and stronger tradition in the field of Oriental studies than has America, and a demand for European Orientalists developed here in the twenties. The Oriental Institute of the University of Chicago, for instance, was established in 1919 and went through its greatest expansion between 1924 and 1930. There was a large new program and not enough Americans to fill the posts. Several Europeans joined the staff of the institute in the twenties: the Italian Assyriologist Edward Chiera; the German archeologist Erich Schmidt; archeologist Pinhas Delougaz from Russia; and Ignace Gelb, who came so late in the twenties that he will be considered with the wave of the thirties.

The early arrivals in the cultural migration and the depression saturated the American market of Orientalists, and those who came to this country in the late thirties and early forties found a scarcity of openings. The Iranian Institute and School for Asiatic Studies (later the Asia Institute) in New York City, under a grant from the Emergency Committee in Aid of Displaced Foreign Scholars, gave positions to a few Europeans; but the situation did not ease appreciably until the postwar boom in education. Thus, when the Austrian-born Leo Oppenheim landed in America as a refugee after the fall of France, he joined the numbers of those who had "to invent their life." His first position was at the New York Public Library, where he prepared a catalogue of Sumerian cuneiform tablets that the library had acquired but that no one had been able to read.

In the middle thirties the European Orientalists seemed to have a better chance of finding openings in Turkey than in America. At least four of those who were eventually to come to the United States were hired by Kemal Pasha in his program to westernize Turkish education: three were German-born, Wolfram Eberhard, Benno Landsberger, and his former student in Germany, Hans Güterbock; the fourth was Hungarian Tibor Halasi-Kun, a latecomer who arrived in Turkey in 1942. These "Turks" were eventually dismissed from their posts in the late forties and arrived in America between 1948 and 1953.

The word Orientalist is frequently used in a broad sense to indicate scholars in a variety of fields, all related to cultural aspects of the Near or Far East. Among the European-born interested in the Near East, the Assyriologists form a larger group than the Egyptologists, and as a consequence of the cultural migration American Assyriology has been in great part in the hands of European-born, while Egyptology has remained, for the most part, in American hands. The Sinologists are the most numerous among the European-born far-eastern scholars. Not all the men and women interested in the Orient are known as Orientalists: those who participate in excavations and handle the digging tools are regarded as archeologists, and those whose main interest is the art of Eastern cultures are classified as art historians. All this is bound to confuse the outsider. My Orientalist friends list Kurt Weitzmann among their colleagues, but my art-historian friends claim him in a louder voice. Ludwig Bachhofer, a native of Germany, taught the history of Asian art at the University of Chicago from 1935 until his retirement several years ago, but he was a member of the art department, not of the Oriental Institute, because the institute is strictly concerned with the Near East and Bachhofer with India and China.

Wolfram Eberhard shifted from Sinology to sociology when he joined the University of California after his years in Turkey; the change was not as drastic as it appears, for Eberhard had always been interested in the sociological aspects of Chinese culture: as a Sinologist he stressed cultural factors, and as a sociologist he drew examples from Chinese societies. His writings include a history of China, a collection of Chinese fairy tales, a study of the social conditions in colony villages in the Punjab, a book on social forces in medieval China, and a study of Chinese cultures and their development entitled *Conquerors and Rulers*. While he was in Turkey, Eberhard published in the Turkish language, and he made good use of the experience gained at that time to return to Turkey after the war to study minstrel tales. On his Turkish travels he crossed the path that Béla Bartók followed in 1937 when he went to Turkey to gather folk music and listen to minstrel songs.

The case of the German-born Karl Wittfogel is similar to Eberhard's but even more striking in that he has made a name in three different fields. The authors of *History* mention Wittfogel among historians for his "most remarkable contributions" to the study of the history of the Far East; the compilers of *Contemporary Sociology* regard his work as sociological and assert that Wittfogel has given the most clearly documented formulation to the theory of "hydraulic society"; and yet the Orientalists will not give him up and call him a Sinologist. His many books and articles deal with the history of Chinese society, Oriental despotism, Chinese institutional history, the problems of Oriental agro-hydraulic society, the conquest societies in Asia, and Chinese and Russian communism. Through his writings, teachings, and travels Wittfogel has been influential in the three fields that claim him.

The Orientalists from Europe made their way to our foremost universities, museums, and centers for Oriental studies. The German Bernard Bothmer was first with the Museum of Fine Arts in Boston, then with the Brooklyn Museum and the Institute of Fine Arts of New York University, and from 1954 to 1956 directed the American Research Center in Egypt. Serge Elisséeff, who was born in Russia and educated in Russia, Germany, and Japan, became a professor of far-eastern languages at Harvard in 1934; he is the author of works on Japan and the Japanese language. The Columbia University faculty included an expert on Turkic culture, Tibor Halasi-Kun; Bernard Geiger, a Polish-born Iranist trained in Vienna and versed in Sanskrit, the Avesta, and middle and modern Iranian languages; an expert in Mesopotamian art, Edith Porada; Karl Menges, who specializes in North Asiatic languages; and Karl Wittfogel, who taught also at the University of Washington in Seattle. Three Orientalists joined the faculty at Yale: the Assyriologist and Hittitologist Albrecht Goetze, author of books on Babylonian omen texts and the Eshnunna; an expert in Arabic and Semitic languages, Franz Rosenthal, who has written extensively on various aspects of Muslim scholarly activities; and an Indo-European philologist, Paul Tedesco. (Goetze and Rosenthal are originally from Germany, Tedesco from Austria.)

Wolf Leslau, who was born in Poland and received his training in Paris, is said to be the only representative in America of the field of Ethiopian studies. Leslau, who joined the University of California at Los Angeles in 1955 after association with the Asia Institute, the New School for Social Research, and Brandeis University, has written extensively on the Ethiopian language and received a medal from Emperor Haile Selassie in recognition of his work. The University of California can claim at least three European-born experts in far-eastern cultures: sociologist Wolfram Eberhard; Diether von den Steinen, born in Germany, curator of the Chinese-Japanese collection, and a scholar in Chinese language, literature, and history; and Otto Maenchen-Helfen, from Austria, who has written about the Huns and the archeology of Central Asia. Franz Michael, who was born in Germany, teaches far-eastern history at the University of Washington in Seattle and is a director of the Far Eastern Institute. And several other institutions are studded with European Orientalists, in particular the Asia Institute.

But the lion's share went to the University of Chicago and its Oriental Institute, where a large number of European scholars continued to arrive over the years. Ignace Gelb, originally from Poland, arrived in 1929 by way of Italy where he had received a doctoral degree and had studied with the Italian specialist in Semitic languages, Giorgio Levi della Vida. (Levi della Vida himself was to become a member of the migration toward the end of the thirties: in 1931, when the Fascist oath was introduced in Italian universities, he was among the few who refused to take it and was dismissed; for a time on the staff of the Vatican Library, he then came to the University of Pennsylvania, and after the war returned to Italy.)

Two Assyriologists from Germany, Arno Poebel and Arnold Walther, joined the staff of the Oriental Institute in 1930. The Dutch archeologist Henri Frankfort and the Danish Assyriologist Thorkild Jacobsen had an early and varied association with the institute: in 1929 Frankfort became the field director of the institute expedition in Iraq; that year, Jacobsen, who had already received a degree from the University of Copenhagen, earned a doctoral degree at the Oriental Institute and, like Frankfort, joined its field expeditions in the Near East. From 1932 to 1938 Frankfort held concurrent positions at the universities of Chicago and Amsterdam, and in 1938 he settled in Chicago to teach archeology and work on the material gathered in Iraq. Jacobsen received his first appointment at the University of Chicago in 1937, when he became a research associate and instructor.

After the arrival of Poebel and Walther in 1930, Frankfort and Jacobsen were the only Europeans to join the Oriental Institute until 1943, and their appointment on a full-time basis was due to their previous connection with the institute. The depression, then the war, halted field activities in the

Near East and cut down sharply the number of new openings at the institute. In 1943 the Austrian Arabist and specialist in Islamic civilization Gustav von Grunebaum, a man of broad humanistic culture, moved to Chicago from the Asia Institute where he had been since his arrival from Vienna in 1938. Four more years were to pass before the Institute invited other Europeans: Leo Oppenheim, who came to Chicago from the Asia Institute in 1947; Benno Landsberger, who came directly from Turkey to Chicago in 1948 when the University of Ankara dismissed its European Orientalists; and Hans Güterbock, who spent a year in Sweden on the way and arrived in 1949.

Working in co-operation with their American colleagues, the Europeans could share in the great achievements of the Oriental Institute and advance knowledge of the ancient Near East. Several participated in field expeditions in the thirties and after the war, helping to uncover ancient sites. Thorkild Jacobsen, for one, during the excavation of 1936–37 in Iraq, devised techniques for tracing ancient canal systems from the adjoining mounds that covered ruined settlements near Baghdad; over twenty years later, in 1957–58, he directed an archeological survey sponsored by the Iraq government to study ancient agricultural methods in southern Mesopotamia as a part of an effort to gain a better understanding of chronic agricultural problems. Ignace Gelb surveyed hieroglyphs and inscriptions in Anatolia and Iraq. As a result of his interest in the Akkadian language of central Mesopotamia, he was placed in charge of research on early Akkadian economy and social organization and investigated the organization of the rural economy.

An appreciable part of the Oriental Institute's imposing body of publications is the work of the European-born. Most émigré Assyriologists at the institute are collaborating in the preparation of the *Assyrian Dictionary*, a monumental project undertaken in the early twenties and later under the charge of Leo Oppenheim. When the twenty-volume dictionary is complete, it will serve to interpret cuneiform inscriptions in dialects that were spoken in different regions at different times. European-born Orientalists have also contributed to the several series of Oriental Institute publications. For these publications they have described cities, temples, and sculptures brought to light in excavations in Iraq (Frankfort and Jacobsen), and have written about the Hittite hieroglyphs of Anatolia (Gelb); they have drawn up lists of kings and dynasties (Jacobsen and Poebel); they have published studies of the Sumerian and Akkadian languages (Poebel and Gelb) and of such ancient civilizations as the Muslim (von Grunebaum) and Assyrian (Oppenheim). In 1966 Leo Oppenheim's *Ancient Mesopotamia* received the Gordon J. Laing Prize, awarded yearly at the University of Chicago to the faculty author whose book is judged to have added the greatest prestige to the list of the University of Chicago Press.

PHILOSOPHERS

The philosophers who came from Europe with the wave represented many currents and schools of thought, but the main European influence on American philosophy was exerted by the group of "logical positivists" or "logical empiricists." Logical positivism was formulated in Vienna in the twenties by the group of scientists and philosophers who came to be known as the Vienna Circle. The circle started as a seminar to study the *Tractatus Logicus-Philosophicus* of the Austrian philosopher Ludwig Wittgenstein and was strongly influenced by Wittgenstein's ideas. Logical positivism soon spread from Vienna to Berlin, Prague, and other European cities. This movement was, in the words of the logical empiricist Joergen Joergensen, "an expression of a need for the clarification of the foundations and meaning of knowledge" and an attempt to make philosophy "scientifically tenable through critical analysis of details rather than to make it universal by vague generalizations and dogmatic construction of systems." It held that true philosophy is a critique of language, that only those sentences are meaningful which are verifiable, and it tried to describe an adequate language common to all sciences.

There are several reasons for the remarkable success of logical positivism in America: its strong anti-metaphysical leanings appealed to those American philosophers who had taken a position against speculative philosophy; at the time it was brought to the United States it was still a young movement — its first program was issued in 1929 — and its representatives were still animated with the zeal of neophytes; thus the campaign to push it was vigorously and effectively continued here; and finally, because of its many ramifications it affected many fields of philosophy and other disciplines, notably linguistics.

The logical positivists who immigrated to the United States include Gustav

Bergmann, Rudolf Carnap, Herbert Feigl, Philipp Frank, Carl Hempel, Hans Reichenbach, and Richard von Mises. The mathematicians Kurt Gödel and Karl Menger were members of the Vienna Circle; and closely associated with the movement were the Poles Heynrik Mehlberg who came to the United States after the war and Alfred Tarski (the logician writing at the boundary between logic and mathematics) and psychologists Kurt Lewin and Wolfgang Köhler.

One of the chief leaders of logical positivism and its most significant representative in America is Rudolf Carnap. He joined the Vienna Circle in 1926, when he was called from Germany to the University of Vienna, and his arrival marked the beginning of the rapid development of positivism. He continued to be one of its most active propounders after he moved from Vienna to Prague in 1931 and to the United States in 1936. (He was first at the University of Chicago and in 1954 moved to the University of California at Los Angeles.) His philosophical production is impressive for its volume and its reach and was already outstanding at the time he left Europe.

Carnap adheres to the basic doctrine of the logical positivists. At first he held that philosophy is the analysis of the logical syntax of language; later he recognized that other analyses are proper and necessary to philosophy: the analysis of semantics, that is, the relations between the signs and what they stand for, and the analysis of the relations of signs to the persons who use them. Carnap's philosophical influence, however, is not limited to analytical linguistic studies. In the foreword to *Philosophy*, a volume in the series of Princeton Studies which looks at American philosophy in the last few decades, Richard Schlatter wrote: ". . . if we exclude the names of immigrant philosophers like Whitehead [who came long before the migration] and Carnap . . . we have had in recent years no giants who are philosophers pure and simple rather than scholars and historians." The authors of *Philosophy* discuss at length Carnap's work from the point of view of his stand against metaphysics (his paper "Empiricism, Semantics, and Ontology" is called "the most mature and subtle statement of the positivists' case against metaphysics") and his work in the theory of knowledge, linguistics, ethics, and the philosophy of science.

Gustav Bergmann, who like Carnap used to belong to the Vienna Circle, settled at Iowa State in 1939. Like other positivists he accepts the linguistic bent of contemporary philosophy and analyzes the properties of what he calls

358

"the ideal language" — the language "which contains all the features, and only the features," in Manley Thompson's words, "which any language must contain in order to provide an adequate representation of the world." But unlike the other positivists, Bergmann asserts that their rigorous linguistic analysis does not need to cast aside metaphysics, and that indeed the positivists are creating a metaphysics of their own although they are not aware of it.

In 1923, when he was only twenty-two years old, Herbert Feigl attended the seminar of Moritz Schlick at the University of Vienna out of which grew logical positivism and is one of the earliest positivists. He is also one of the earliest immigrants in the wave, arriving in America in 1930 with a Rockefeller fellowship to spend a year at Harvard. Instead of returning to Europe he settled here and taught first at Iowa and then at Minnesota where he became director of the Minnesota Center for the Philosophy of Science. In an article with Albert Blumberg, published in 1931, he introduced the term "logical positivism." Although Feigl has discussed questions concerning ethical theory and the theory of knowledge, his main interest and contributions have been in the philosophy of science. He has written on this subject as a contributor to the book *Philosophy*.

The Austrian-born and Austrian-trained physicist Philipp Frank was also an influential philosopher of science. Frank's mature years are divided into two periods of almost equal length, one spent in Czechoslovakia, the other in the United States. In 1912 he became Einstein's successor to the chair of theoretical physics at the German University in Prague and held that position for the next twenty-six years. In 1939 he joined the faculty of Harvard University and lived in Cambridge until his death in 1966. In the years of the Vienna Circle he was an occasional visitor who contributed much to it. In this country he wrote several philosophical books, but he is better known to the American public for his biography *Einstein: His Life and Times*. Published in 1947, while Einstein was still alive, this perceptive study for the most part avoids hero-worship. (Who could write about Einstein and avoid hero-worship, ever since the theory of relativity proved such wonderful food for the popular imagination?) The reconstruction of the cultural world around Einstein and analysis of the circumstances of science that made possible the evolution of Einstein's thought give Frank's biography a place in the history of ideas.

Reichenbach and Hempel belonged to the group of positivists that formed in pre-Hitler Berlin, and Reichenbach is regarded as being especially representative of its thought. In Berlin Reichenbach showed his interest in the broad questions of physics and mathematics and wrote a book on relativity which was much later published in this country as *The Philosophy of Space and Time*. When Hitler rose to power, Reichenbach went to the University of Istanbul. In 1938 he left Turkey for the University of California, Los Angeles. One of his major works, *Experience and Prediction*, was published the same year he came to this country, and so it seems plausible to consider it a product of his Turkish period. He advanced a probability theory of knowledge, rejecting the view that knowledge must be identified with certainty, and wrote on the rise of scientific philosophy and on the philosophy of quantum mechanics. Hempel, a thinker and teacher concerned with the formation of scientific concepts, stopped a few years in Belgium on the way to the United States, where he taught mainly at Yale and Princeton. He is the author of *Fundamentals of Concept Formation in Empirical Science, Philosophy of Natural Science*, and many articles.

The thought of the logical positivists might not have reached the high favor that it enjoys in America without the work of philosophers who became its interpreters to large audiences and fostered its diffusion. The most important disseminator among them was Max Black, a Russian by birth who was educated in England and did not belong to the Vienna Circle, but during his American career (at Illinois and Cornell) he has been one of the principal expositors of the positivist doctrine — he also contributed to the establishment of the study of the philosophy of science in this country. A brilliant teacher noted for his clarity, Black attracted many students to whom he passed on the positivists' ideas. He is the author of numerous books and articles on topics of philosophy, logic, and mathematics.

Logical positivism is not the only area of the philosophical spectrum in which philosophers from Europe have been influential. Their impact was also great in the study of Christian philosophy, for they have stimulated American interest in theology especially by reconciling theology with the cultural and philosophical needs of modern man. The largest group of Christian philosophers of the cultural wave fell in the Catholic camp led by Jacques Maritain, his pupil and friend, Yves Simon, and the German Dietrich von Hildebrand, who was born in Italy; in the Protestant camp the towering figure was Paul Tillich.

It is perhaps no chance that the Protestant-born Maritain, who was converted to Catholicism at the age of twenty-four, became one of the great Catholic thinkers of our age, for a seriously undertaken religious conversion requires a deep examination of the newly accepted faith. In Maritain's case, another circumstance contributed to his formation: shortly before his conversion he had abandoned the study of science out of a disillusionment with scientism and had become a student of philosopher Henri Bergson. By the time Maritain came to this country in 1939 he had already fully evolved into a Catholic philosopher with his own firmly established views.

Except for the years 1946–48, when he was the French ambassador to the Vatican, Maritain remained in America from his arrival in 1939 until his return to France in 1961. His major works in the United States reveal the wide range of his inquiries, which were directed not only to the field of his main interest, metaphysics, but also to art, politics, and history. His books in English range from existential philosophy to aesthetics, from political science to the approaches to God. If in the fifties his most widely known writings were on politics, his main contribution to American thought has been as a Thomist philosopher.

James Collins has written: "The most elusive portion of Maritain's significance is the encouragement which he has given to Thomistical philosophical studies by the example of his own presence and labors. . . . Within the Catholic community itself Maritain's presence in America has made more concrete and feasible the ideal of a Christian layman devoting himself entirely to the work of philosophy, whether as Thomist or not. Maritain's fidelity to that vocation has encouraged laymen to devote their scholarly energy to work in the field of philosophy. . . . Maritain's guidance is particularly important for Thomists who are learning how to think and teach and write under contemporary conditions. His way of philosophizing rests on a complex fidelity both to the philosophical tradition of Aristotle, Augustine, and Aquinas, and to accomplishments and problems of our time." Thomism and the study of times long past did not cause Maritain to lose contact with his contemporaries. He rationally analyzed the soul and attitudes toward faith within the context of human suffering and the historical and religious forces that shaped mankind.

Yves Simon arrived in America in 1938, a year earlier than his teacher Maritain. In Paris Simon and Maritain had worked closely together, not only as philosophers but also, after the outbreak of the civil war in Spain, as individuals who felt the urge to do something to shorten the duration of the Spanish strife, however faint their hope of achieving this aim. In this country Simon taught first at Notre Dame, then at Chicago, and helped to spread Maritain's way of thought in the Middle West. A prolific writer, Simon published a number of books in English.

When the Protestant theologian Paul Tillich came to the United States at the invitation of Reinhold Niebuhr, toward the end of 1933, he spent only three months learning English before beginning to lecture at the Union Theological Seminary in New York. Many articles about him relate the plight of the man who had to take up a new language at the age of forty-seven. But Tillich may have underestimated the number of mature men who went through similar difficulties. At any rate, fate did not choose this experience to single him out but rather the long and exceptionally productive period that it reserved for him in this country.

In the last ten years or so in Berlin, Tillich had been the leader of the religious Christian Socialist Kairos circle. The Christian Socialists hoped to lead the Socialist parties from utopianism to "belief-ful" realism and to save the Christian churches from social and political isolation. So vigorously had Tillich advocated the establishment of relationships between men of religion and Socialists that he was compelled to leave Germany when Hitler came to power. In America he found the life in theological seminars and the active membership of Protestants in the church closer to his ideal than the conditions that had prevailed in the German Protestant world. He could move on as a thinker, and he assigned himself the task of elaborating an existential theology.

He remained at the Union Theological Seminary until 1955, then became a University Professor at Harvard (the title "University Professor" is reserved for a small number of outstanding scholars at Harvard). In 1962 he went to the University of Chicago and finished his life work, the three-volume *Systematic Theology*, based upon "the method of correlation between questions arising out of the human predicament and the answers given in the classical symbols of religion."

The characteristic features of Tillich's work — in the tradition of the great synthesizers — derived from his sensitivity to the interplay of religious faith and other cultural expressions of the human spirit. He incorporated in his theology notions of existentialism and depth psychology and observations on the arts; he gave a new meaning to the term "religious" when he asserted that religious questions are about the "ultimate concern," that is, about being and not-being. The breadth of Tillich's human interest is evident in his books (there are more than twenty) ranging over the whole field of man's cultural and religious experience. It is evident also in the diversity of the journals on whose editorial boards he served: *Daedalus, Pastoral Psychology,* and *Existential Inquiries.* The originality and scope of his theological constructions placed him in the foremost position in American Protestant thought. To him, and to the American brothers Richard and Reinhold Niebuhr, more than to anyone else, is owed the revival of American interest in Christian thought.

All the examples I have given so far are European-born philosophers who had a long career in the United States and did a considerable part of their work in this country. One older émigré already famous in Europe had a different role, adding prestige to our culture by his very presence. Ernst Cassirer was sixty-seven years old when he came to this country in 1941. His reputation had steadily been growing in Europe since the turn of the century and the publication of his early works in the theory of scientific knowledge. His thought had completed its full course in Europe: it had evolved from an insistence upon the concept of measurability as the basis of scientific knowledge to the recognition of the role of symbolic forms in cognitive processes and had consequently explored applications of his theory of symbolism to linguistics, aesthetics, and mythology.

It was not easy to accommodate in our academic system a man of such status, who had already passed the retirement age of most American universities. Yale invited him for two years and managed to keep him an additional year. Then he had to leave New Haven and accept a position — again temporary — at Columbia. Cassirer had hoped that his Yale colleagues would not let him go. (But the university had made clear to him that in view of his age the appointment would not be prolonged.) Perhaps his attitude was an instance of what Hutchins called "refugee psychology."

Cassirer died in New York in 1945. He wrote a single original work in this country: *Myth of the State* (he also wrote, directly in English, a condensation of the German *Philosophie der symbolischen Formen*, entitled *An Essay on Man*). And yet American philosophy still feels the impact of his presence.

Lengthy as this survey of achievement may appear to be, I have neglected many fields in which intellectuals from Europe have been prominent. On the side of the scholars, my most serious omission may well be classical and medieval philology, where Werner Jaeger and Erich Auerbach were dominant figures and others were outstanding. In the sciences I touched upon fewer areas than I left out, and did not have a chance to introduce men of great stature like the human geneticist Curt Stern, or Konrad Bloch who was trained as a chemical engineer in Germany and in this country took up biochemistry so successfully that in 1964 he received a share of the Nobel Prize. Not having dealt with physicists in general but only with those who developed atomic energy, I did not mention Otto Stern, who as a teacher in Germany inspired a generation of experimental physicists, both European and American, and after coming to the United States was awarded the 1943 Nobel Prize in physics for work in the molecular and nuclear fields. But perhaps my greatest sin is not to have dealt with psychology under its own heading, for European psychologists have flocked to America by the score. A systematic discussion of émigré psychologists is available. At the symposium on the German emigration to the United States held in Frankfurt in 1964, Albert Wellek delivered an exhaustive speech on the psychologists in the migration, published in the tenth volume of *Jahrbuch für Amerikastudien*. Wellek's discussion is limited to the psychologists who emigrated from German-language countries, but in effect the limitation is minor, for there are few émigré psychologists who were not trained in Germany or Austria. I shall note in passing only two eminent husband and wife teams from Austria: Egon Brunswik and Else Frenkel-Brunswik and Karl and Charlotte Bühler.

XII

꙳꙳꙳꙳꙳꙳꙳꙳꙳꙳꙳꙳꙳꙳꙳꙳꙳꙳꙳꙳꙳꙳꙳꙳

Notes Toward an Evaluation

YOUNGER EUROPEAN-BORN INTELLECTUALS

Any attempt to evaluate the full impact of the intellectual wave will require consideration of factors not examined in this study: the influence of the foreign-born who were not fully educated adults upon arrival; of émigrés' wives; and of the British. With the wave came a large number of persons who were too young at the time to hold the equivalent of a college degree but had been molded to a great extent by the cultural forces of their country of origin. It is impractical to define formally this group and indicate its age limits, because the exposure to American schools counteracted the foreign background of the young immigrants to degrees not always determined by age. In fact, some of the oldest in this group, especially if they were separated from their families in America, made a deliberate effort to remove any trace of their foreignness and became "more American than Americans." On the other hand, some of those who were too young to have been affected by the environment in their homeland developed European traits after coming here, under the influence of family traditions and habits and of family ties with Europe.

At any rate, those who were small children when their families brought them here may not have been on the American intellectual scene long enough, on the average, to have affected it much. But many among those who at the time of their arrival were of high school or college age are now well known. By the end of the sixties, the most influential was undoubtedly President Nixon's assistant for national security affairs, Henry Kissinger, an educator and foreign policy analyst who was fifteen years old when he came to America from Germany. A rapid scanning of my own friends and acquaintances reveals many others who are prominent in intellectual fields. The Viennese-born nuclear physicist Frederic de Hoffmann is one of them. In 1938, at the age of fourteen, he escaped from Prague against the advice of his more optimistic relatives; and when events proved him right, his self-assurance received a boost and did not lessen with the passing of the years. In 1941 he reached the United States, studied a few years at Harvard, and then joined the wartime atomic project at Los Alamos where he competed with older and no less self-assured physicists in the production of bright ideas. In 1939 he became the president of General Atomic Division of General Dynamics Corporation and then continued his ascent in the atomic industry.

Like de Hoffmann, Martin Deutsch is a nuclear physicist and a wartime worker in the Los Alamos project. He was not overshadowed by his famous parents, psychoanalysts Helene and Felix Deutsch, but established his own reputation in physics and is a member of the faculty of M.I.T. Next door, at Harvard, is the German-born Gerald Holton, a distinguished professor of physics and historian of science. Peter Gay, who was eighteen when he came from Berlin in 1941, taught at Columbia and then moved to Yale; he is the winner of a National Book Award for his *Enlightenment: An Interpretation*.

Physicist Wolfgang Panofsky, Erwin's son, who can work three times as hard as any native, is a professor at Stanford and has served on advisory or consultative bodies to two presidents (Johnson and Nixon). Two "young" European-born are on the faculty of the University of California: the biochemist Gunther Stent from Germany, an active member of the "phage group" and, through the books he has written and edited, its record-keeping priest; and the highly regarded physicist Frederick Reif, who was born in Austria and studied in France and the United States. The Italian-born mathematician Guido Weiss, son of psychoanalyst Edoardo Weiss, is teaching at Washington University in St. Louis. And Elisabeth Mann Borgese, to whose career I have alluded, also belongs among the "young" intellectuals.

A longer list would be tedious. The essential fact is that the intellectual wave brought with it a large group of young men and women who now stand high on the American intellectual scene. In the give-and-take between European and American cultural patrimonies, the taking was on the average greater and the giving smaller than in the case of the older group. Yet, whether intentionally or not, they have become a strong link between the two cultures. The memory or curiosity about events and persons in their background kept them alert to what happened in Europe; visitors from their homelands sought them out in America and for the sake of the visitors they became interpreters of American ways. They did the same when they went back to visit their homelands. (For example, a thirteen-year-old boy on a visit to Italy entered into a long discussion with a somewhat older Italian boy on the relative merits of the American and Italian constitutions.) And so they sowed seeds of international understanding.

THE WIVES OF INTELLECTUALS

Women were well represented in the cultural wave. Many have had long, satisfactory careers in the United States and attained recognition in their professions. The names of some appear in these pages and many more can be found in biographical directories and the membership lists of professional associations. There is, however, another group of women whose intellectual output is more difficult to evaluate, though the indications are that it is not negligible. They are women who came to this country as the wives of European intellectuals and remained very much in their husbands' shadow but at some time or other have engaged in intellectual occupations.

Many wives became productive in response to the American environment rather than by plan. From the moment they set foot in this country these middle-class European women were aware of the vitality of their American counterparts and vowed to take them as models. They began by mastering household tasks that might not have been required of them in Europe — cooking, scrubbing floors, and .painting walls; then, following the example of American wives and mothers, they joined community organizations, the League of Women Voters, and study groups. Eventually they were led into activities of their own: they had learned the word "achievement" and resolved to have achievements to their credit. A few went back to school and obtained degrees, others took up occupations that did not require a formal education. A few random examples may give an idea of the range of the wives' activities.

Lilla Fano, physicist Ugo's wife, first raised two daughters, then taught mathematics for many years in Washington, experimenting on methods that she herself devised; now she is on the faculty of the elementary school of the University of Chicago. Mici (Augusta Maria) Teller, the wife of Edward Teller, is manager of the Bay Area pilot plan of the Fannie and John Hertz

Engineering Scholarship Foundation. Gretel Lowinsky, wife of musicologist Edward Lowinsky, taught the violin and viola at Black Mountain College and played with several orchestras, and later she prepared to teach young children in a program related to Head Start. Frida Kahn wrote *Generation in Turmoil*, which gives a vivid picture of her Russian childhood and her experiences as a refugee. She was married to pianist Erich Itor Kahn, founder of the Alberneri Trio and recipient of the Coolidge Medal for eminent service to chamber music. Lilli (Mrs. A. Leo) Oppenheim is an artist and has had several exhibits of her work. A description of Else (Mrs. Hans) Staudinger's efforts as founder of the American Council for Émigrés in the Professions was printed in the *Congressional Record* in 1964 at the request of Senator Jacob Javits; she was honored for "thirty years of dedicated selfless service in salvaging the lives and talents of refugee scholars, scientists and other professional people who have sought refuge in this country. . . . These men and women represent human resources that are of inestimable value to the strength of our Nation." The condensation of an article by M. T. Bloom that followed described in greater detail what it called "Else Staudinger's $100 million gift to Uncle Sam": the rehabilitation of over 3,000 unemployed intellectuals undertaken by her organization since 1945. The sum represents the savings of the estimated cost of educating 3,000 persons from elementary school through graduate school.

BRITISH INFLUENCE

In size and quality the British immigration was far from negligible; however, several reasons were against its inclusion in this study. The immigration to the United States from Great Britain and the immigration from continental Europe were so intrinsically different that they could hardly be treated together. The circumstances under which they took place were dissimilar: the interval between the two wars was for Europe a period of political unrest and revolution characterized by the rise of dictators, but for England it was a time of seeming stability. The two main causes of emigration from continental Europe were the political-racial persecutions and the scarcity of academic and other openings for the cultured class. The emigration from England was largely due to individuals' preference and the causes prevailing in peaceful times. For British intellectuals never suffered persecution or mass dismissals and had much less difficulty than continental Europeans in finding employment. Colleges and universities in Great Britain could accommodate the majority of scholars and scientists, and flourishing British industries were eager to take advantage of the overflow of scientists. (The consequences of this situation for the war were especially striking in science. The Scandinavian countries, Holland, and other nations had lost to emigration many scientists who recognized the difficulties of a career at home; the dictators had forced out of Europe hosts of other scientists. But Great Britain had kept her scientific talent and could take a leading part in the development of radar and atomic energy.)

The two immigrations differ also in that the British did not have to learn a new language when they came to the United States and were tied to the new country by the strong bonds of tradition. The sameness of language and the memory of a common background made the decision to leave and the resettlement much easier for the British than for continental Europeans. Thus the forces of selection were not as strong for the British as for the Europeans. As a result, the British immigration brought to America men and women of distinction; but it was not in the same relation to the size and cultural stature of Great Britain as the immigrations from Germany, Austria, or Hungary were to their mother countries. Paradoxically, the British influence on American culture has been strong, and a good part of it has been exerted by the immigrants from continental Europe who stopped in England before coming to the United States.

Examples have been frequent throughout these pages. Russians and Hungarians went to England in the twenties and even earlier; some political refugees from Mussolini's Italy settled there in the years following the establishment of a dictatorship in 1925, and political exiles from other dictator-dominated countries joined them; once Hitler was in power, British colleges and universities, often prodded by the Academic Assistance Council, opened their doors to displaced scholars and scientists and to students who could not pursue their studies at home; the London School of Economics attracted foreign economists and social scientists; artists, physicians, and psychoanalysts chose England as their place of exile. From this huge crowd many eventually came to America, the older intellectually enriched and the younger molded by their experiences in Great Britain.

369

EUROPEAN DEPLETION

While the cultural wave was bringing European talent to America, it was putting an equivalent drain on Europe. In many countries, universities and other institutions of learning lost their best teachers and theaters and concert halls their best musicians; outstanding artists emigrated; and governments were deprived of some of their foremost advisers. When the United States emerged from the war as a leading western nation, the stature of its culture appeared the higher for being measured against the European depletion. Thus the depletion should be taken into account in any attempt to evaluate the impact of the intellectual wave on America.

One of the most obvious losses that Europe suffered was the exodus of scientists. In World War II science and technology played an unprecedented role. "To a certain extent," Maurice Davie wrote in *Refugees in America*, "the war became a struggle between opposing scientists. . . . it weakened the enemy and strengthened the Allied to assist the migration from enemy territory of anti-Nazi and anti-Fascist leaders in the natural sciences and technologies." To stress this point, most early accounts of the refugee movement tell the story of the German chemist and Nobel Prize winner Fritz Haber. His services to Germany in World War I had been exceptional: he had invented a method to synthesize ammonia which insured Germany an adequate supply of nitric acid, the basic material of explosives, and had directed German chemical warfare. The Nazi racial laws made him decide to leave Germany, and he died in 1934 on his way into exile.

Dramatic as Haber's case is, it could not be of great practical importance, for he had reached a ripe age and it is unlikely that he would have continued to be productive. The emigrating scientists of great fame, the bulk of whose scientific contributions was behind them, deprived their countries of prestige and aroused moral indignation against their European oppressors, but in general did not detract from their countries' war effort or add much to ours. The greatest practical loss was of the younger scientists, not yet famous or altogether unknown to the public, who were endowed with energy and talent — men like John Von Neumann, Hans Bethe, Edward Teller, Emilio Segrè, Felix Bloch, Leo Szilard, Eugene Wigner, and scores of others. (The same is true of other classes of intellectuals in the migration: the older added prestige to America, the younger took a place among the builders of American culture.)

Not all countries were equally depleted of scientists, nor did the depletion come to them at the same time. Hungary was one of the earliest and worst hit. Hungarian scientists began to emigrate at the end of World War I, often driven by Horthy's anti-Semitism, for they were almost all Jews. By the late twenties the Hungarian government, aware of the scientific drain, made some effort to recall the expatriates. The Hungarian Minister of Education went to Berlin where many young Hungarian scientists were studying or teaching, called a conference, and exhorted them to return. There was an opening at the University of Szeged, he said, and they should apply for it. But no one did. What little scientific and technical brainpower was left in Hungary was stifled by heavy bureaucracy. It is an idle but fascinating speculation to imagine what Hungary might have been like if Szilard, Teller, Theodore von Karman, Von Neumann, Wigner, and other brilliant scientists had not departed.

It cannot be said that Germany and Italy lost all of their scientists. Many distinguished physicists, chemists, and, especially in Italy, mathematicians stayed on and did outstanding work. But I remember the disconsolate remarks made at the end of the war by Edoardo Amaldi, a pioneer nuclear physicist who had remained in Italy and, like other Italian scientists, had done excellent research during the war: he thought that in the years since Fermi, Rasetti, Rossi, Segrè, and others had left, American nuclear physics had made such a huge jump forward and Italy was in such bad economic shape that Italian physics could never hope to catch up. This dejection must have been shared by other scientists in other European countries, for a few years after the war Isador Rabi of Columbia University (born in Poland but brought to this country in infancy) suggested that European governments pool their resources and build a large center of nuclear research for common use. This is the origin of CERN, the European organization for nuclear research, one of the most remarkable and successful examples of postwar international collaboration in science.

The drain of natural scientists may well have been the most important material loss that Europe suffered as the result of the emigration, but the intellectual impoverishment had drastic consequences in other areas. European psychoanalysis, for instance, never fully recovered from the blows it received in the thirties. One cannot stress too much that psychoanalysis was the creation of the Austrian Freud and that those who helped in its development also lived in Austria. It spread to other European countries, then began to lose members to emigration, and by the end of the thirties it had been wiped out of Europe by Nazi policies. Since the war many European psychoanalytic societies have been reorganized, but they have not regained their original vigor and the great analysts who once formed their membership have not returned to them. In some countries, Hungary among them, psychoanalysis has not revived.

Many celebrated European cultural centers disappeared or lost reputations of long standing. The Vienna Circle is no more. It influenced the thought of many mathematicians, scientists and science historians, linguists, and philosophers who were later driven out of Austria and scattered, many of them reaching the United States. The great Institute of Mathematics of the University of Göttingen bred men like Richard Courant who expressed regret for its virtual extinction. Almost all staff members of the Berlin School of Politics emigrated to America, and the Institut für Sozial Forschung of Frankfurt am Main also lost to the United States a large part of its faculty. The leaders of Gestalt psychology migrated to the United States, including the founder, Max Wertheimer, and his supporters Wolfgang Köhler and Kurt Koffka.

I could go on. The important fact is that depletion of Europe enhanced the effect upon America of the intellectual wave. One result was the change in direction of the flow of students immediately after the war: because many of the best teachers had left Europe and a good number were now in America, many students from all over the world began coming to the United States. It is true that they were drawn here both by the quality of our teaching and by the many American fellowships and grants made available to foreign students. Nevertheless, the teachers from Europe were important attractions. At the end of the war, for example, the young Chinese student Chen Ning Yang came to the United States to study with Wigner or Fermi. (When he arrived, both were still involved in wartime projects, and no one would reveal their whereabouts; so Yang thought that he had come halfway around the world to no purpose.) When Fermi reappeared on the academic scene (sooner than did Wigner), Yang went to study with him. The result was one more Nobel Prize for America: in 1957 Yang and his countryman Tsung Dao Lee shared the prize for disproving the principle of parity.

The intellectual depletion in Europe also affected non-academic fields.

372

Legions of writers from many countries found their way to America. In the forties, the German-born Martin Gumpert, a perceptive observer of the cultural migration, noted that America was the only country where literature thrived. For many years the European literary scene was further impoverished by the appreciable number of suicides that had taken place under the Nazis. Some great literary exiles did not return to their homelands — not Thomas Mann, who spent his last years in Switzerland, not Franz Werfel or Lion Feuchtwanger, who died in the United States, not Stefan Zweig, who committed suicide in Brazil.

As for European arts and music, they too were impoverished. Throughout the forties the Paris school was virtually non-existent, for its artists had come to America, and some never returned to Europe. The Bauhaus, which had been a center of inspiration to the world, was not re-established. Germany and Austria lost most of their great musicians, and the chamber music for which they had been famous was sapped of its vitality. The eyes of the world turned away from the great capitals of Europe and remained fixed elsewhere, often on America, until Europe began to recover and a new generation grew to deserve attention.

EUROPEAN-BORN INTELLECTUALS AS TEACHERS

If future historians wish to evaluate the cultural migration, they will find an ample record of its material achievements: books, works of art, musical compositions and recorded musical performances, patents of inventions, and papers describing contributions to discoveries in many fields. But there is some danger that they may overlook or underestimate the one feature of the migration which seems to me the greatest single cause of its impact on American culture: a stunningly high proportion of the European intellectuals were teachers or took up teaching in this country; artists, musicians, and writers found almost as many niches in our schools as did scholars and scientists.

Teachers can be extremely influential. They come in touch with large numbers of young men and women when these are still malleable, capable of hero worship, and likely to acquire the mental habits of others. And the teachers' influence is not limited to the young people they teach. Some of their students will go into teaching careers and through the methods they have learned and the mental attitudes they have acquired will spread the influence of their teachers and protract it in time. In the case of European teachers, their strong personalities, mannerisms, and habits of mind draw attention and increase the probability of unconscious imitation by the students. There is the example of Leo Strauss, who created a neo-Platonic school of political thought at Chicago. His disciples have espoused his views to such an extent that in university circles they are called "Straussites." They must have adopted more than his views, for I once heard the remark about a young American political scientist that "He is Leo Strauss when he teaches."

Even though other émigré teachers may not have seen their traits so clearly duplicated in their students, the sum total of European influences is very great. Professors teaching in graduate schools led many students to the doctoral degree and an academic career. College teachers and the few who taught in high schools affected to various degrees much vaster numbers of young persons, and in some cases their enthusiasm and dedication to their discipline inspired students to enter their teachers' fields. Testimonials of appreciation by the students themselves are not lacking: to honor some émigré teachers on special occasions, reaching the age of retirement or the completion of decades of teaching, students prepared volumes similar to the European *Festschriften*; and many teachers have been voted the best of their schools (Fermi, when he taught a college course, and Stephen Rothman, are examples at the University of Chicago). Conrad Pirani, at the University of Illinois, was awarded a "Golden Apple" for excellence in teaching by the Sophomore class in 1958 — one of two honors of which he is most proud (the other is his service as president of the Chicago Pathological Society in 1965–66). Undoubtedly a great many émigré teachers received similar honors from their students.

Finally, any attempt to evaluate the influence of the émigré teachers must take into account that some Europeans have been teaching in this country for well over thirty years — I would say over thirty-five years, had not so many spent time away from the classrooms during the war. In this time the flow of students has been immense. The result of this continued European influence in American schools has been a tendency toward the Europeanization of American culture. By their choice of subjects to be studied and problems to be solved, by the questions they raised and the use of methods

374

acquired in their homelands, the émigré teachers have introduced European approaches and traditions.

This Europeanization of our culture is not a new phenomenon; there has always been cultural exchange with Europe. American students who went to European universities for their higher education became imbued with European culture and upon their return were ready to pass it on. But they were only a few: only the privileged could spend a full year or more in Europe. The cultural wave brought the teachers of Europe within the reach of practically any student, in the large eastern and western universities as well as in smaller midwestern and southern colleges. Most Europeans were willing to go anywhere, and the committees assisting them were determined to "scatter them far and wide," as Abraham Flexner put it. (Some Americans now outstanding in their fields have expressed gratitude for the opportunity they had of studying with noted European teachers here in America without traveling to Europe.)

The Europeanization of science, according to some scientists, has resulted in a shift of emphasis from the practical to the theoretical, from invention to the search for basic knowledge regardless of immediately practical value. A similar trend toward pure knowledge is seen in other fields: the humanities have acquired greater prominence, philosophy has expanded, and the teaching of other disciplines has become more theoretically oriented. While these changes cannot be attributed exclusively to European teachers, it is true that most of these teachers did push in this direction in the schools in which they taught.

The influence of Europeans on education in America may prove to be only a return of an earlier stream of influence moving in the opposite direction. In his book *Thomas Jefferson, American Humanist*, the émigré archeologist Karl Lehmann mentioned the similarity of Jefferson's educational plans to the system chartered a generation later by Wilhelm von Humboldt and introduced, with minor adaptations, in most European countries. Lehmann also uncovered a possible channel of influence between Jefferson and von Humboldt through von Humboldt's brother Alexander, who corresponded with Jefferson and owned and knew his *Notes on Virginia* containing his educational ideas. Lehmann's observation opens a fascinating new horizon to historians of the migration and to historians of ideas.

375

NEW INTERNATIONAL CULTURAL RELATIONS

When transatlantic communications were resumed at the end of the war, it became apparent that cultural supremacy had shifted, temporarily at least, from Europe to America. The brightness of the American scene and the poor conditions in most European countries suspended for a time the flow to Europe of American students. They saw no point in traveling to depleted European universities when they could obtain excellent training at home. In contrast, European students were eager to spend some time here. And science students were more than eager; it was essential to them to see what had been done in America during the war. To many European students the choice of a teacher in this country was not important, but others, especially in the older age group, had definite preferences and wished to work with a particular man. The choice fell not infrequently, but by no means always, on the European-born, for not all ties had been cut between the teachers who had emigrated and the younger men who had remained at home. There were often strong bonds due to personal acquaintance or to a teacher's continuing reputation in his homeland. On their part, the émigré teachers in America, well acquainted with colleagues and fields of learning in their countries of origin, could easily secure information about applicants or encourage worthy students to come here. In this and other ways they helped to maintain high standards in the flow of European students to this country.

In America, European students came under the influence of our culture and took home much that they had absorbed. Before the war, the equalizing process had been stimulated by the cultural migration and its Europeanizing effect upon American culture. The differences between cultures decreased once the postwar exchanges gained momentum. The re-emigration to Europe also worked toward a leveling of cultural standards. The leveling is now proceeding at a pace so rapid that it foreshadows the emergence of a common culture for the Western world.

The flow of students is now in both directions; young Americans assisted by fellowships and grants go abroad in larger numbers than ever, and the European exchange student has become a permanent feature of the American scene. Cultural exchanges of many kinds are sponsored by most nations. International cultural events ranging from music festivals to scientific meetings are increasingly popular, to the point of becoming unmanageable in size. The many cultural exchanges are at the same time indications and causes of the emergence of a unified Western culture.

RE-EMIGRATION

Any comprehensive analysis of the cultural migration will have to take into account re-emigration from the United States to Europe and its effect upon the European scene. The indications are that the phenomenon was of considerable magnitude and importance and that it may be worth special study; but here I offer only general considerations.

The earliest group of returnees was made up of statesmen, political leaders, and others who hoped to assist in the reconstruction of their countries. They were not numerous. For one reason, most governments-in-exile had chosen England as their temporary home and there they rallied their exponents. (Thus Eduard Beneš went to London to lead the Czech government-in-exile after teaching for a year at the University of Chicago; he had come to America after his resignation as president of Czechoslovakia in protest of the Munich agreement of 1938.) For another reason, not all the statesmen who spent the war years in America wished to return to their countries, and several political figures once in the limelight preferred to remain in America, grateful for relative obscurity. Such was the case of Heinrich Bruening, former chancellor of the German Reich and leader of the German Catholic party, who after his resignation in 1932 spent months in the seclusion of a German cloister and a few years in England, then came to the United States in 1938 as a professor of public administration at Harvard. Nor did former premier of France, Camille Chautemps, return to political life; nor did Henri de Kerillis of the French Chamber of Deputies, or Hermann Rauschning, who had been president of the Danzig Senate in 1936.

The first politicians to leave the United States followed our troups to the beachheads of Europe and Africa — the Italians, in the wake of the Anzio landing; the French, months after General Charles de Gaulle made his unexpected appearance in Algiers in 1940 and by his firm stand as the leader and defender of France aroused the patriotic feeling of Frenchmen everywhere. I have already commented on the return of Count Carlo Sforza, Alberto Tarchiani, and other Italians and their role in liberated Italy. The

French did not have a Sforza in the United States: French committees of liberation and similar resistance organizations were scattered over three continents, Africa, Europe, and America. The French exiles in the United States who favored de Gaulle sent physicist Francis Perrin as their representative to the consultive assembly in Algiers, and Perrin left Columbia University where he had been teaching since the fall of France. When the assembly followed the victorious de Gaulle into Paris, Perrin was with them; later he resumed his academic career and in 1951 became the head of the French atomic energy commission. Camille Chautemps reported to de Gaulle in Africa, but no suitable position could be found for him, and he returned to America. Captain André Maurois — as he was referred to in the press of those days — served a few months in de Gaulle's army but soon returned to his teaching post at the University of Kansas.

After the surrender of Germany, several exiled politicians went home. The strongest group was that of the Social Democrats, and among them Max Brauer is an interesting example: in 1946 he resumed his position of mayor of Hamburg after a forced interruption that had lasted thirteen years. He spent ten of these years in America where he felt out of place; he gave a few lectures, but otherwise he was supported by labor organizations. Paul Hertz, another Social Democrat, was appointed to a post in the municipal government of Berlin; Rudolf Katz became a judge; and others went back to an active political career in Germany.

These were the political men, or the men moved by political reasons; but as soon as it became possible to travel freely, other intellectuals began to re-emigrate. Though the celebrities were not lacking among them, the majority were little-known: men and women who had not been in this country long enough to build a reputation here, were not listed in biographical directories, and did not leave an easily traceable record of their stay. Nationals of different countries showed varying degrees of desire to go home. The French were in general anxious to return to France and re-emigrated in large numbers, giving grounds to the mistaken belief that they all went back. The French do not like to live outside France, and the French in the cultural migration had no special reasons to remain in America once Germany was defeated, for they held no grievances against their people or most of their leaders. The Germans, on the other hand, had been the victims of their own countrymen, and some nursed resentment.

When the news of German concentration camps and extermination policies became known, many exiles felt estranged irrevocably and refused to have anything more to do with Germany. Even the more tolerant, those who entertained hopes for Germany, realized that it would not be easy to build a bridge "over thirteen years of German night." (These were words used by Kurt Grossmann, an authority on Jewish questions, in reply to a circular letter which the writer Hermann Kesten sent to German-born émigrés, asking them why they did not return to Germany. The answers were published in the volume *Ich lebe nicht in den Bundesrepublik* [I do not live in the Federal Republic], edited by Kesten.) It is true, however, that some Germans had not changed in their affection for their homeland and had not become adjusted to America, as the example of Arnold Bergsträsser has shown. But the return of persons like Bergsträsser was slowed by postwar conditions and a scarcity of satisfactory academic openings in Germany. The re-emigration of Germans to Germany was small in the forties, but some Germans returned to settle in other European countries.

The sentiments of the Italians for Italy should have been between the sentiments of the French for France and those of the Germans for Germany: Italian exiles had indeed suffered at the hands of their countrymen, but on the whole the behavior of the Italian Fascists had been much more moderate than that of the Nazis. In practice, the Italian émigrés did not blame the Italian population for the crimes of the Fascists and their love of Italy was deeper than the wounds received. And yet the majority of the Italians I know remained in the United States; they liked it here. To the re-emigration of the forties the Italians contributed a few intellectuals in the older age group as art historian Lionello Venturi; some physicians; members of families that the war had divided; and a small number of discontented persons.

Nationals of Austria, Russia, and the satellite countries were prevented from going home in the early postwar period by political conditions in those countries and American restrictions on travel. To the re-emigration of the forties they contributed only the few who settled in western European states.

Apart from the considerations of nationality, one occupational group contributed more than others to the early re-emigration: the writers. They were very numerous, if the little known are counted with the celebrities; they were not well adjusted to America; the majority had come as refugees, with no intention of making their homes here; and many had not managed to

379

solve the problems of the foreign language and the translation and publication of their works. They went back in large numbers as soon as they could. Even before the end of the war, the Psychological Warfare Division had brought to Europe many European-born writers, and while most returned to America, some remained in Europe, as did Alfred Döblin. A true exodus began after the war with the departure of Sigrid Undset, Maurice Maeterlinck, André Maurois, Jules Romains, Emil Ludwig, Bertolt Brecht, and Fritz von Unruh, among others.

The advent of the McCarthy era in America and greatly improved economic conditions in Europe in the early fifties gave a new impetus to re-emigration. Many of Hitler's political opponents in Germany and other countries were leftists of one sort or another. They had found a tolerant refuge in the United States, but as the Communist scare swept the nation, they felt ill at ease and sought a less partisan climate in Europe. Western Europe was undergoing its amazingly rapid recovery, and some countries, particularly West Germany, were able to offer alluring positions to the teachers displaced in Fascist times. The wave of the early fifties took Thomas Mann to a home in Switzerland; Ulrich Middledorf to the German Institute for Art History in Florence; and Theodor Adorno, Arnold Bergsträsser, Ernst Fraenkel, Max Horkheimer, Hans Rothfels, and Otto von Simson to permanent positions at German universities. In the late fifties and in the sixties the re-emigration consisted mainly of older persons who returned upon reaching retirement age.

The emeriti undoubtedly belong to the re-emigration and have contributed to its effect on Europe, but from the point of view of the cultural migration they must be reckoned among those who stayed. The teacher who gave to America his productive years and only after reaching retirement age went home to conclude his life where it began was much like his American colleague who retired to a state other than the one where he had made his living. Artists, musicians, and writers who went home in their old age also must be regarded as "stayers-on."

The individual action of the many who have returned to their countries was an important factor in postwar cultural relations. Because they were well acquainted with both America and their countries of origin, they were especially suited to explain America to their countrymen as they had explained their lands to the Americans. In general they have effectively performed

380

this role as two-way interpreters through discussions with friends, lectures, teaching, and the publication of articles and books. They did so honestly and sincerely because their double insight was usually accompanied by a double affection. In few expatriates had the grief and bitterness over their nation's political and moral crimes extinguished completely an original love, and few were the homegoers who had not developed some attachment for the country that had given them asylum, however difficult their experiences might have been.

The cultural impact of the re-emigration, however, cannot be dissociated from the impact exerted by the much larger numbers of European-born who returned to Europe on visits. The earliest influences on European education date back to the time of the Allied military occupation, when émigrés served on committees to analyze and revise European educational programs. Later, émigrés participated in exchange programs: in one of the earliest, Max Rheinstein, Paul Weiss, Hans Morgenthau, and several other professors from the University of Chicago gave lectures and courses at the University of Frankfurt. Others participated in less formal activities, as when André Maurois in France pursued his studies of American history and published a history of America, doing much to promote good relations between France and the United States. The summer school of theoretical physics in Les Houches, France, and the summer school of experimental physics in Varenna, Italy, invited many physicists originally from Europe, among them Enrico Fermi, Bruno Rossi, Emilio Segrè, Victor Weisskopf, Eugene Wigner, and Hans Bethe. Victor Weisskopf held an influential position in Europe for several years as the director of CERN. And examples might continue ad infinitum.

The results of American influence are most evident in West Germany, where it seems to have been greater than in other countries. (This may be true, but German cultural affairs often appear magnified by the fact that the Germans more than other Europeans are given to self-analysis and record-keeping and they alone have contributed substantially to the history of the cultural migration.) Several centers for the study of American culture sprang up in West Germany in the fifties. One is the Deutsche Gesellschaft für Amerikastudien (German Association for Studies of America) which publishes a yearbook of American studies (*Jahrbuch für Amerikastudien*). In 1964, to celebrate the tenth anniversary of the yearbook, the association sponsored a symposium in Frankfurt on the emigration to the United States of German-speaking intellectuals; the addresses were published in the tenth volume of the yearbook. Two of the participants were still living in the United States, political scientist Louise Holborn and philosopher-sociologist Herbert Marcuse. One of the editors of the yearbook was Ernst Fraenkel, once an exile in America, and another was Dietrich Gerhard. Fraenkel has been appointed to a chair at the recently established John F. Kennedy Institute of the Free University of Berlin, an institute engaged in the study of all aspects of American culture. One of those who planned the institute was Arnold Bergsträsser, who returned to Germany from Chicago in 1951 and until his death in 1964 gave himself to promoting the study center.

It may be interesting at this point to let two returning Europeans, Ulrich Middledorf and Dietrich Gerhard, speak for themselves and show some of the ways in which émigrés are ambassadors of good will. In 1963, when the German Institute for Art History in Florence dedicated a new building, the board of directors of the American College Art Association sent a message to the director of the German institute, Ulrich Middledorf. The message recalled "with affection and pride" Middledorf's career in the United States, and asserted that many members of the American association had benefited from the hospitality of the institute in Florence and the generous help provided by Middledorf and his staff. In his reply Middledorf wrote: "I remember with great warmth my friends and associates, my colleagues and pupils in the United States . . . the many institutions with whom I was connected, and always shall be, by the ties of common work and interests. If in my present position I can be useful to them in return for all kindness which I have received . . . I shall be happy."

In an article for a student magazine Dietrich Gerhard explained how in 1954 he was offered the newly established professorship in American civilization at the University of Cologne, and how the offer resulted in his commuting between St. Louis and Cologne and, later, between St. Louis and Göttingen. The compensation has not been financial, he wrote, but rather the constant stimulus. "The university reform which is taking place belatedly in Germany profits from increased contacts with this country. . . . I am not inclined to overestimate the results of a dozen years of academic work like my own. The study of the United States is still far from integrated into the education of young Germans. . . . Important is a full recognition of the role of the United States and its institutions and society in the development of our modern world. My own presentation has been focused on these problems . . . . It has been my good fortune for years to have been associated with the work of the Fulbright Commission in Germany and of the Conference Board in Washington as well as with the U. S. Information Service. Thanks to these contacts, I have been able not only to arouse a greater interest in the United States in students and young teachers and scholars, but also to help them go abroad."

ANOTHER WAVE?

Observers of the cultural migration of the thirties believe that nothing similar has taken place in the history of humanity since the fifteenth century, when the learned men of the dying Byzantine empire, fleeing from the barbarian invasion, sowed seeds of the old Hellenistic culture in European centers. As for America, never before had she seen the arrival of such a cultured multitude within so short a period of time. The wave that reached these shores before Pearl Harbor was unique in American history. But in the future will it remain a unique event?

European intellectuals are still migrating to America. Students arrive from Europe in ever-increasing numbers, and some stay on. Visiting professors temporarily join American faculties, and some stay on. Scientists come to see our great national laboratories, and some stay on. Organizations like the American Council for Émigrés in the Professions still assist intellectuals to settle here. Are we then witnessing another cultural wave, or shall we witness one in the foreseeable future?

I think not. I am strongly inclined to believe that within the time for which predictions may have any sense there will be no cultural migration comparable in importance with the migration of the thirties. My reason for saying so is not based on an evaluation of future American prosperity or the ability to assimilate intellectuals or of the probability that another blow as vicious as that of fascism may be dealt the intelligentsia of continental Europe. I am drawn to my conclusion by my observations of the great changes that have taken place since the thirties in the American intellectual climate and in the means of communication the world over.

Migration from Europe occurred at a time when America was still young as a culture. Although in some areas she had overtaken Europe, on the whole she looked deferentially upon European culture with its rich heritage. The leaders of American education welcomed the migration and treated the exiles with an unprecedented generosity. The growing demand for education in America justified the generosity: culture, once concentrated in certain areas and reserved for the wealthy, was rapidly expanding, a larger proportion of the school population was seeking a college education, and more teachers were needed than American schools could produce. The picture was complicated by the depression which limited the means for cultural expansion but at the same time brought about a reappraisal of values, a shift of interest from the strictly utilitarian. These special features of the American scene not only facilitated the migration from Europe but gave the Europeans a recognition and prestige that fostered achievement. As many of the European-born noted, in the United States they accomplished more than they might have done in their homelands. Another migration would not find the same advantageous circumstances: cultural America now regards Europe as an equal, at most, and since college education is widely offered, in the future the expansion of education is likely to be gradual.

The fantastic transformation of communications is an even more cogent reason for venturing to predict that the phenomenon of the cultural migration will not be repeated. The wave of the thirties coincided in time with the last period of relatively slow travel, before the airplane took over as a popular transcontinental and transatlantic means of movement. Pan American Airlines initiated its first transatlantic passenger flights in 1939, and before World War II civilian air traffic was insignificant in comparison with surface transportation. European intellectuals may have taken an occasional flight within their countries to experience the new sensation, but certainly they were not in the habit of flying. As intercontinental travelers, they lived in a world that did not move faster than transatlantic navigation. They visited America by boat, the few who did, and their visits were likely to last several months, a summer session, or a full academic year. Truly international meetings involving persons from different continents were rare and memorable events, attended only by the elite.

When Europeans decided to come here to settle, the decision had its own finality. True, a few continued to commute between Europe and America for several years before settling here; but the parcels of time spent at each place were usually of the order of six months, and moreover the instances of commuting were so rare that they do not modify this description. Any displacement across the ocean was a serious affair, to be seriously pondered. The war further severed communication between Europe and America. It also suppressed any lingering regrets about emigration in the most nostalgic of European hearts. From the American point of view, the war froze both the assets and liabilities, both the advantages and the disadvantages of the cultural wave. Americans had to face the fact that, in general, the Europeans were here to stay.

It is not to be ruled out entirely that history might repeat itself and that in spite of the changed cultural climate another large immigration might take place, followed by another war. But our prophets depict any future war as frightfully destructive, and it is not likely that during such a cataclysm Europeans who might have the chance to emigrate to this country would continue to pursue their intellectual activities as did the majority of their predecessors in the last war.

Apart from changed wartime conditions, changed communications would deprive a future cultural migration of much of its significance. In the jet age in which we can go to Paris for lunch and be back for dinner, it matters little where the individual makes his home. The cross-fertilization of ideas between the continents is achieved less by settlers from distant lands than by airplane travelers with return tickets in their pockets. They go to meetings by the thousands and hop from Paris to Chicago or Tokyo with greater ease and less mental preparation than were required to go from Paris to London thirty years ago.

In the foreseeable future, faster means of transportation will toss about the sowers of cultural seeds as particles in Brownian motion. At the same time, the increased use of communication media across continents — telephones, television, communication satellites, and inventions yet to come — will further reduce the importance of one's physical presence at any particular point on the earth. The meeting of minds will be a continuous event, subject only to the picking up of a receiver, the pushing of a button, or the boarding of a helicopter at one's door. And for those in need of a change, there may be cultural events on the moon. In any case, cultural phenomena will assume different patterns than they have had in the past. The learned men moving from Byzantium to Italy, or from Göttingen to America, will no longer be the principal instruments of cultural diffusion abroad.

ONLY IN AMERICA

The favorable conditions existing in the United States while the migration was in progress, including the deferential attitude toward European culture and the great expansion in education, are not sufficient to explain the success achieved by European intellectuals. They have accomplished more in America than they might have in their homelands — and they say so themselves. A fully satisfactory explanation of this phenomenon may never be given but some clues are to be found in the very nature of America. No other country could have accommodated such a vast migration or supported it, no other country was large enough and had the willingness and means. But if this is evident, it is not clear how America could assimilate, so rapidly, so many foreign-born who were not "tillers of the soil" and provide the stimulation that developed their intellectual capacity to the full. Undoubtedly their resettlement was facilitated by the fact that America had seen the arrival of wave after wave of immigrants and was used to them; but this fact was double-edged and had caused immigration restrictions after World War I and the xenophobia that existed in many quarters in the thirties.

Other circumstances helped the newcomers upon arrival. It seems almost trite to say that freedom of thought and freedom from fear are essential conditions for productive exercise of the mind and to recall that the many who came to America from totalitarian countries had been deprived of these freedoms for periods that in some instances were of two decades (the youngest in the cultural wave had forgotten the taste of life in a democracy). But the factor of the greatest practical value, one that gave countless Europeans the chance to resume their intellectual careers in this country, may well have been the flexibility of American institutions of higher learning. A small minority of Europeans was obliged to resettle in non-intellectual occupations; but without the flexibility of American institutions the proportion would have been much higher. In contrast to the rigid European systems, American colleges and universities could select the teachers they wanted, appoint foreigners, and create new posts if funds were available. Throughout the thirties, foreigners were indeed appointed and many positions were created for them. American generosity provided the funds. After the war, in the increased demand for education, more foreigners obtained appointments in American schools and more positions were created, but no longer was there need for the citizens' generosity: educational programs were either self-supporting or received government grants. This same flexibility existed in art and music schools, in hospitals and clinics and other institutions; all were able to make room for the arriving intellectuals.

Inside the American cultural world the Europeans met with a greater open-mindedness and fairness than most had known in Europe. Americans were in general inclined to judge men and ideas on their intrinsic worth and did not oppose foreign influence. They were willing to collaborate with Europeans or fight them as equals in clashes of opinions that had little to do with place of birth. The relations among colleagues and between teachers and students were much closer than in Europe and promoted a constant exchange of ideas. The exchange of ideas always heightens productivity, and it heightened the productivity of the newcomers. Wartime experience worked in the same direction. The government displayed an unprecedented trust in the foreign-born, hiring scores of them for work in psychological warfare, in the atomic project, and in other positions of responsibility. The trust engendered loyalty in its recipients and gave them an even greater incentive to join the common cause, the defeat of the totalitarian regimes, and do their absolute best in the war effort.

War work brought together, in close and fruitful collaboration, men and women of many different nationalities and backgrounds, Americans and Europeans, the learned in various fields, the military, and industrialists. These contacts and others of a similar nature in the postwar years favored and sped up the process of establishing human relations and exchanging views conducive to achievement that had begun when the Europeans entered the cultural world of America. It is my contention that through the years in America the Europeans gained a substantial advantage over the Americans: they absorbed a second culture and acquired a second background. Not only did familiarity with two civilizations widen their vision and deepen their wisdom, but it also enabled them to take leading roles in international cultural relations in the postwar years. To the enrichment of the Europeans' cultural patrimony another factor contributed: encounters with other Europeans of different nationalities on American soil. In their early years in the United States, European intellectuals tended to seek each other out regardless of their nationality, as if being a European constituted a bond between them — a bond they had not felt while in Europe. The encounters were usually extraordinarily stimulating: to an Italian in the process of assimilating American culture a friendship with a Hungarian or a Pole offered the possibility of exploring one more culture and *forma mentis* and of gaining an additional element for comparison. The wartime atomic project at Los Alamos proved beyond doubt that the meeting of men from different countries and of different education can be extremely rewarding.

To these considerations, which fall mostly in the realm of the spirit and the intellect, a much more prosaic remark must be added: the success of the Europeans was greatly enhanced by the seldom-failing availability of "a little money." Money made its appearance whenever needed, in small amounts but nonetheless miraculously in depression times, in lavish amounts when the government undertook to support education and research on a large scale. And great achievements were made possible by American money wisely spent.

A more refined analysis of the cultural migration from Europe and its activities in America would most certainly reveal additional interesting facts, but I doubt that it would affect the basic conclusions. The intellectual immigration wave of the thirties and early forties was a phenomenon of great magnitude, new in the history of the United States and unlikely to be repeated in the foreseeable future. It is not conceivable that it might have happened in any country but America, for only America could support such a large number of intellectual émigrés and only through American generosity and friendliness, in the particular cultural climate of America, could they accomplish as much as they did. In making room for countless Europeans and saving many whose lives were threatened, America proved once more a land of opportunity and a haven to which the persecuted of the world might continue to look with confidence. America did not ask a price for her services, but has been repaid in full from the intellectual migration in a currency compounded of prestige, knowledge, and a general enrichment of culture.

REFERENCE NOTES

➤➤➤-➤➤➤

GENERAL

The literature dealing specifically with the intellectual migration is scant and almost entirely concerned with émigrés from Germany and German-speaking countries. Material for this study was collected from disparate sources, the files of newspapers, journals, and magazines, the files of the Press Relations Office of the University of Chicago, biographical reference works, autobiographies, biographies, and books on many subjects. Equally important as the published material were correspondence and conversations with émigrés and American experts in various fields of knowledge, many of whose names appear in the text. The names of persons who gave me substantial assistance and are not identified in the text appear in the notes that follow.

The Cultural Migration: The European Scholar in America, edited by Rex W. Crawford (University of Pennsylvania Press, 1953), contains the text of five lectures by émigrés Franz L. Neumann, Henri Peyre, Erwin Panofsky, Wolfgang Köhler, and Paul Tillich, all German-educated except the French-born Peyre. Donald P. Kent's *The Refugee Intellectual: The Americanization of the Immigrants of 1933–1941* (Columbia University Press, 1953) is limited to a sample group of Germans and Austrians in the professions, and since the data were collected from the files of refugee agencies, the study misses the important, self-sufficient group that did not seek organized assistance; the bibliography is very good. *Refugees in America: Report of the Committee for the Study of Recent Immigration from Europe*, by Maurice R. Davie *et al.* (Harper, 1947), although not exclusively about intellectuals, has been the most valuable and useful work for my study. Next to Davie's the most informative book is *The Rescue of Science and Learning: The Story of the Emergency Committee in Aid of Displaced Foreign Scholars*, by Stephen Duggan and Betty Drury (Viking, 1952). Harold Fields' *The Refugees in the United States* (Oxford University Press, 1938) includes information about the earliest stages of the migration.

The most helpful works in German were *Deutsche Exil-Literatur 1933–1945,*

Eine Bio-Bibliographie, by Wilhelm Sternfeld and Eva Tiedmann (Verlag Lambert Schneider, 1962); Radio Bremen, *Auszug des Geistes: Berichte über eine Sendereihe* (Verlag Heye, 1962), in which is published a series of interviews with Germans in the migration; *Ich lebe nicht in der Bundesrepublik,* of which Hermann Kesten is the editor (List Verlag, 1964); volumes 10 and 11 of *Jahrbuch für Amerikastudien,* parts of which are devoted to the German emigration to the United States and to the publication of an extensive bibliography of its scholarly production; and Helge Pross's slim *Die deutsche akademische Emigration nach den Vereinigten Staaten 1933–1941* (Duncker & Humblot, 1955).

Two distinguished works were published after the first edition of this book. *The Intellectual Migration: Europe and America 1930–1960,* edited by Donald Fleming and Bernard Bailyn (Harvard University Press, 1969), is a collection of essays, many of them written by European-born intellectuals, that does not aim at exhaustive coverage. Kurt R. Grossmann's *Emigration: Die Geschichte der Hitler-Flüchtlinge 1933–1945* (Europäische Verlagsanstalt, 1969) is an ambitious analysis of the whole phenomenon of which only parts concern directly the immigration to the United States.

CHAPTER I

THE GREAT WAVE

The story of the Forty-eighters is brilliantly told by Carl Wittke in *Refugees of the Revolution: The German Forty-eighters in America* (University of Pennsylvania Press, 1952); and *The Americanization of Carl Schurz,* by Chester Verne Easum (University of Chicago Press, 1929), focuses on an important aspect of that migration. Biographies have been written of many men and women who came from Europe almost a century later, and of the most famous there is a wealth to choose from. I used several for this chapter. Sibyl Moholy-Nagy wrote *Moholy-Nagy: Experiment in Totality* (Harper, 1950). W. A. Willibrand published *Ernst Toller: Product of Two Revolutions* (Co-operative Books, 1941). Halsey Stevens' *The Life and Music of Béla Bartók* (Oxford University Press, 1953), from which I've taken the quotations on p. 8, is an excellent definitive biography of the composer, but some of his human traits appear more vividly in Agatha Fasset's *The Naked Face of Genius: Béla Bartók's American Years* (Houghton Mifflin, 1958). Samuel Chotzinoff tells amusing episodes in *Toscanini: An Intimate Portrait* (Knopf, 1956), quoted on p. 9; however, I gathered information about Toscanini from many other sources, including Italian and American newspapers of the time. Franz Alexander's *The Western Mind in Transition; An Eyewitness Story* (Random House, 1960), is only partly autobiographical; while containing the essential facts of his life it is largely about psychoanalysis. Several autobiographical works record the émigrés' early experiences and impressions in America, among them Erna Barschak, *My American Adventure* (Ives Washburn, 1945); Martin Gumpert, *First Papers* (Duell, Sloan & Pierce, 1941); Erika and Klaus Mann, *Escape to Life*

(Houghton Mifflin, 1939); Hans Natonek, *In Search of Myself* (Putnam, 1944); and Maria Augusta Trapp, *The Story of the Trapp Family Singers* (Lippincott, 1949; Image Books edition, 1957). Letters of émigrés in academic positions and of heads of colleges and universities who employed them, published in *The Rescue of Science and Learning*, bring out the flavor of the time and shed light on the difficulties that sometimes arose on the campus. The quotations on p. 5 are from a letter to me from Robert M. Hutchins. In keeping the migration's files I was assisted by Miss Alice Weiner.

CHAPTER II

THE AMERICAN BACKGROUND

Several works out of a vast literature were especially helpful in exploring the background of the National Origin Act and its consequences. Maldwyn Allen Jones, *American Immigration* (University of Chicago Press, 1960), covering the years from 1607 to 1959, is an excellent guide. The best and most informative work about the trends and events that led to passage of the 1924 Act is John Higham's *Strangers in the Land: Patterns of American Nativism 1860–1925* (Rutgers University Press, 1955). The 41-volume *Reports of the United States Immigration Commission* (Government Printing Office, 1911) is a mine of information on the "new" immigration and contemporary economic conditions but strongly tinged with restrictionist sentiment. For a thorough evaluation of these reports see "Old Immigrants and New" in Oscar Handlin's *Race and Nationality in American Life* (Little, Brown, 1957).

The eugenic views at the turn of the century were given vivid and seemingly scientific expression in Madison Grant's *The Passing of the Great Race; or The Racial Basis of European History* (Scribner's, 1916). These views are mirrored in Kenneth Roberts' far from objective *Why Europe Leaves Home* (Bobbs-Merrill, 1922), "a true account of the reasons which cause central Europeans to overrun America . . . ," according to Roberts. (The quotations on p. 23 are from the first three articles of this book, except for one sentence that is taken directly from the *Saturday Evening Post*.) American legislation before and after the passage of the 1924 Act is published in U. S. Department of Labor, Immigration and Naturalization Service, *Immigration Laws: Immigration Rules and Regulations* (Government Printing Office, 1937); the quotations on p. 24 are from this book. Interpretation of immigration legislation and comments on its application can be found in J. P. Shalloo's "United States Immigration Policy, 1882–1948," (quoted on p. 25) in D. E. Lee and G. McReynolds (eds.), *Essays in History and International Relations in Honor of George Hubbard Blakeslee* (Clark University, 1949), and Robert A. Divine, *American Immigration Policy 1924–1952* (Yale University Press, 1957). The last quotation on p. 25 is from *The New York Times*, July 2, 1926.

Useful statistical immigration-emigration tables and an extensive bibliography are published in Francis J. Brown and Joseph S. Roucek (eds.), *One America: The*

History, Contributions, and Present Problems of Our Racial and National Minorities (Prentice-Hall, 1945). The periodical *Interpreter Releases* should be consulted in any study of immigration and emigration: published by the American Council for Nationalities Service, it is "an information service on immigration and related problems" and speaks for the U. S. Immigration and Naturalization Service.

Frederick Lewis Allen's *Only Yesterday: An Informal History of the Nineteen-Twenties* (Harper, 1931) and his *Since Yesterday: The Nineteen-Thirties in America* (Blue Ribbon Books, 1943) shed light on many aspects of American life often by-passed by formal histories; in particular, I am indebted to these works for vivid accounts of the social unrest after World War I and of the Depression. One personal story, among many others, Hans Natonek's, *In Search of Myself*, exemplifies the émigré's difficulties during the Depression.

CHAPTER III

THE INTELLECTUAL IN HIS EUROPEAN HABITAT

Conversations with members of the migration, some of whose names appear in the text, and autobiographical works were important sources in reconstructing the European background. I also had the assistance of Mrs. Louis Gottschalk and Dr. Gregor Wentzel. Most autobiographies used for other chapters had something to contribute; here I drew heavily from a few. The most important is *The World of Yesterday* (Cassell, 1953), by Stefan Zweig, who offers information on several countries. So does another cosmopolitan European, Arthur Koestler, in his *Arrow in the Blue: An Autobiography* (Collins, with Hamish Hamilton, 1952); his chapter "A Bunch of Cosy Cannibals" is a vivid picture of student life in Vienna. Germany is well covered: Bruno Walter, in *Theme and Variations: An Autobiography* (Hamish Hamilton 1947), comments on the rise of nazism and the German intellectuals' reaction to it. *The Two Germanys*, by Kurt von Stutterheim (Sidwick & Jackson, 1939), gives a pro-Nazi view. Franz Schoenberner's two autobiographical volumes, *Confessions of an European Intellectual* (Macmillan, 1946) and *The Inside Story of an Outsider* (Macmillan, 1949), and Hermann Ullstein's *The House of Ullstein* (Simon & Schuster, 1943) describe the world of book and magazine publishers before and during the Hitler era. Also valuable is Klaus Mann, *The Turning Point: Thirty Five Years in This Century* (L. B. Fischer, 1942), which focuses on writers. Although not an autobiography, Philipp Frank's *Einstein: His Life and Times* (Knopf, 1947) belongs here as describing an academic environment of which the author was a part.

Autobiographies containing information on Austria include, among others, Artur Schnabel, *My Life and Music* (St. Martin, 1963) and Prince Hubertus zu Loewenstein's two volumes, *Conquest of the Past* (Houghton Mifflin, 1938) and *On Borrowed Peace* (Doubleday, Doran, 1942). For Hungary, Franz Alexander's *Western Mind in Transition* and Joseph Szigeti's *With Strings Attached* (Cassell, 1949) are usefully supplemented by Paul Ignotus' "The Hungary of Michael

Polanyi," in *The Logic of Personal Knowledge: Essays Presented to Michael Polanyi on his Seventieth Birthday, 11 March 1961* (Routledge & Kegan Paul, 1961) as well as the opening pages of Ignotus' autobiographical *Political Prisoner* (Routledge and Kegan Paul, 1959); and by S. N. Behrman's profile of Ferenc Molnár in the *New Yorker* May 21-June 8, 1946. Leopold Infeld draws a picture of Jewish life in Poland in his *Quest: The Evolution of a Scientist* (Doubleday, Doran, 1941), while Alexander Granach describes the village life of poor Galician Jews in *There Goes an Actor* (Doubleday, Doran, 1945). Different segments of the Russian middle and upper classes are described in Frida Kahn, *Generation in Turmoil* (Channel Press, 1960); Vladimir Nabokov, *Speak Memory* (Grosset & Dunlap, 1951; original title *Conclusive Evidence*); W. S. Woytinsky, *Stormy Passage: A Personal History through Two Russian Revolutions to Democracy and Freedom, 1905-1960* (Vanguard, 1961); and Gregory P. Tschebatarioff, *Russia My Native Land* (McGraw-Hill, 1964), an account of Imperial Russia and the Russian Civil War seen through the eyes of a former officer in the Don Cossacks.

Much information was drawn from works other than autobiographical. The structure and administrative setup of German universities is described in Abraham Flexner, *Universities, American, English, German* (Oxford University Press, 1930); the philosophical trends that determined the development of German universities and the reaction of scholars to the rise of Nazism are analyzed by Frederic Lilge in *The Abuse of Learning: The Failure of the German University* (MacMillan, 1948); Edward Y. Hartshorne, *The German Universities and National Socialism* (Allen & Unwin, 1937) is a scholarly and detailed study of the subject, from which I quoted Rust's words on p. 51; and Philipp E. A. Lenard, *Deutsche Physik* (J. F. Lehmann, 1936), 5 vols, evinces typical Nazi anti-Semitism. Allan Bullock's *Hitler: A Study in Tyranny* (Harper, 1952) and William L. Shirer's *The Rise and Fall of the Third Reich: A History of Nazi Germany* (Simon & Schuster, 1960), both excellent for the German historical background, disregard entirely intellectuals and the intellectual life — Shirer's book, however, includes a useful bibliography. Hans Kohn's *The Mind of Germany: The Education of a Nation* (Scribner, 1960) attempts to explain the alienation of Germany from western Europe.

Richard Pipes (ed.), *The Russian Intelligentsia* (Columbia University Press, 1961) is essential to an understanding of intellectual trends in Russia at the turn of the century and their connections with the Russian Revolution. Good companions to this work are several parts of Alexander Gerschenkron's *Economic Backwardness in Historical Perspective: A Book of Essays* (Belknap Press, 1962). Luigi Salvatorelli and Giovanni Mira, *Storia dell'Italia nel periodo fascista* (Einaudi, 1956) is the best history of Fascist Italy. Other works helpful for the Italian background are Carlo Sforza's *Contemporary Italy: Its Intellectual and Moral Origins* (Muller, 1941) and Giuseppe Antonio Borgese's *Goliath: The March of Fascism* (Viking, 1937).

For the Hungarian historical background I am indebted to several works: Owen Rutter, *Regent of Hungary: The Authorized Life of Admiral Nicholas Horthy* (Rich and Cowan, n.d.); Oscar Jaszi's *Revolution and Counter-Revolu-*

tion in Hungary (King, 1924) and his *The Dissolution of the Habsburg Monarchy* (University of Chicago Press, 1929), a difficult but rewarding and extremely informative book; C. A. Macartney, *Hungary: A Short History* (Aldine, 1962); and Arpad Szelpal, *Les 133 jours de Béla Kun* (Librarie Arthème Fayard, 1959). Szilard's opinion, quoted on pp. 57–58, is from Alice Kimball Smith's article, "Elusive Dr. Szilard," in *Harper's Magazine*, July, 1960.

CHAPTER IV

THE ROADS TO AMERICA

The main published sources about the struggle in Europe to save the intellectual victims of fascism are *A Defence of Free Learning*, by Lord Beveridge (Oxford University Press, 1959), quoted on p. 63, and *The Rescue and Achievement of Refugee Scholars: The Story of Displaced Scholars and Scientists 1933–1952*, by Norman Bentwich (Martinus Nijhoff, 1953), from which come the quotations on pp. 62–64 and Philipp Schwartz's words on p. 70. Early aspects of the problem are treated in Bentwich's *The Refugees from Germany, April 1933 to December 1935* (Allen and Unwin, 1936); and a useful addition is "Leo Szilard: A Memoir," by Edward Shils (in *Encounter*, December, 1964), based on a tape made by Szilard himself, is quoted on p. 64.

Very little published material is available about the émigrés in Turkey: the origin of the venture is briefly related in Beveridge's and Bentwich's works, and the text of an interview with a former German refugee in Turkey is published in *Auszug des Geistes. The New Turks, Pioneers of the Republic, 1920–1950*, by Eleanor Bisbee (University of Pennsylvania Press, 1951) may be consulted for historical perspective. For most of the information about émigré activities in Turkey I am indebted to Dr. and Mrs. Hans Güterbock, to Dr. Suzanne Schulze, and to Philipp Schwartz' manuscript memoirs. James McDonald's sentence on p. 71 is quoted from *The Refugees from Germany*.

The story of the Institute for Advanced Study is told in *I Remember: The Autobiography of Abraham Flexner* (Simon & Schuster, 1940), chapters 27 and 28; that of the University in Exile by Alvin Johnson in *Pioneer's Progress: An Autobiography* (Viking, 1952), chapter 31, from which sentences are quoted on pp. 74 and 75; and Duggan and Drury report on the activities of the Emergency Committee in Aid of Displaced Foreign Scholars in their *The Rescue of Science and Learning*. Davie's *Refugees in America* includes essential information on most phases of American assistance to refugees. On p. 78 Walter Cook's words are from Erwin Panofsky's "The History of Art" in *The Cultural Migration*, and his statement is drawn from *The Rescue of Science and Learning*.

The four-page publication of the Committee for Catholic Refugees from Germany, *Refugee Immigration Facts and Figures*, includes some useful statistics. The history of the National Refugee Service was written by Lyman Cromwell White in *300,000 New Americans* (Harper, 1957). The report of the National

Committee for Resettlement of Foreign Physicians (in *Journal of the American Medical Association*, November 29, 1941) and Alfred Cohn's "Exiled Physicians in the United States" (in *American Scholar*, Summer, 1943) contain interesting and basic data. Fragmentary information on several activities in America on behalf of displaced intellectuals was gathered also from Robert Maynard Hutchins' files deposited in Harper Memorial Library of the University of Chicago.

In Surrender on Demand (Random House, 1945), quoted on pp. 88 and 89, Varian Fry brilliantly reports on the adventurous operations he directed in France to save the lives of intellectuals caught in the French debacle. *Thirty Years of the International Rescue Committee (1933–1966)* (International Rescue Committee, n.d.) is the history of the agency that sent Fry overseas. Mention of Fry's work and additional details are found in H. J. Greenwall, *When France Fell* (Allen Wingate, 1958) and in many personal accounts of émigrés whom Fry helped, among others in Hans Sahl's *The Few and the Many* (Harcourt, Brace, and World, 1962), and Natonek's *In Search of Myself*. The conditions in French concentration camps are described in Lion Feuchtwanger's *The Devil in France: My Encounter with Him in the Summer of 1940* (Viking, 1941); in Leo Lania's *The Darkest Hour* (Houghton Mifflin, 1941); and in Hamilton Basso's profile of Jean Wahl in *The New Yorker*, May 12, 1945; but the most scathing indictment is by a Frenchman, Joseph Weill, in his *Contribution à l'histoire des camps d'internement dans l'Anti-France* (Éditions du Centre, 1946). For the application of immigration legislation during this period see *Interpreter Releases* (the quotation on p. 87 is from the issue of December 20, 1940) and Divine's *American Immigration Policies 1924–1952*.

I am grateful to the late Varian Fry and to Mrs. Helmut Hirsch and Dr. and Mrs. A. Leo Oppenheim for their willingness to recall their experiences for my sake: but for the Oppenheims I would not have heard of the *311ᵉ Compagnie de Travailleurs Étrangers*.

CHAPTER V

IN AMERICA

Conversations with Drs. William H. McNeill and S. William Halperin yielded information used here and in other chapters. The quotation on p. 97 is from Darius Milhaud, *Notes without Music* (Knopf, 1953). "New Coeducational College in North Carolina" in *School and Society*, September 2, 1933, explains the origins and policies of Black Mountain College. Announcements and other literature issued by the college were useful sources for its years in operation, but of greatest help were the recollections of Dr. and Mrs. Edward Lowinsky and Drs. Fritz and Anna Moellenhoff.

The comments of Richard Courant, Paul Tillich, and Arnold Bergsträsser on America are drawn from Radio Bremen, *Auszug des Geistes*; Hans Sahl's remark on p. 102 is from *Ich lebe nicht in der Bundesrepublik*. Biographical data about Dr. Frank Auerbach were obtained through the courtesy of Miss Harriet L. Glenney, Visa Office, Department of State. I learned much about German intellectuals from the late Dr. Helena Gamer who was for many years the chairman of the Department of Germanic Languages and Literatures at the University of Chicago. By frequently reminiscing, Drs. Gerhart and Maria Piers contributed a considerable amount of material on the Austrians. The origins and development of the Vienna Circle are authoritatively discussed in "The Development of Logical Empiricism" by Joergen Joergensen in *The International Encyclopedia of Unified Science*, vol. 2, No. 9 (University of Chicago Press, 1951).

S. N. Behrman's profile of Ferenc Molnár in the *New Yorker* proved useful once more. Information about the Polanyi family was generously furnished by Dr. Michael Polanyi and other members and friends of the family; additional particulars were obtained from "Karl Polanyi, 1886–1964," by Paul Bohannan and George Dalton, in *American Anthropologist*, December, 1965. Any inaccuracies or misinterpretations are on my own.

A vivid picture of the Italian political exiles' activities emerges from the files of *Nazioni Unite, The United Nations: Weekly of the Mazzini Society*, (1942–1946). Valuable information is found also in Gaetano Salvemini, *Memorie di un fuoruscito* (Feltrinelli, 1960); Luigi Sturzo, *La mia battaglia da New York* (Garzanti, 1949); and Carlo Sforza, *L'Italia alle soglie dell'Europa* (Rizzoli 1947), from which are drawn the quotations on p. 120. Max Ascoli added interesting details in a letter to me. For a historical frame of reference see the detailed *Mussolini's Enemies: The Anti-Fascist Resistance in Italy* by Charles F. Delzell (University of Princeton Press, 1961). The quotation on p. 122 is from "Perspective" by J. H. Plumb in *Saturday Review*, December 31, 1966. Henri Peyre commented on his early career in "The Study of Literature" in *The Cultural Migration*, from which are the words quoted on p. 125. Camille Chautemps' *Cahiers secrets de l'armistice* (Plon, 1963) is of special interest as the autobiographical and apologetic work of a statesman. Drs. George Gamow and Roman Jakobson related episodes of their lives in letters to me; and some of Dr. Jakobson's adventures are told by Toni Cassirer in the Italian-language *Ernst Cassirer in America* (Edizioni di Filosofia, 1955).

CHAPTER VI

EUROPEAN PSYCHOANALYSTS ON THE AMERICAN SCENE

The body of writings about psychoanalysis is immense, but the historical literature is limited and does not treat of émigré analysts as such. I could not have written this chapter without the assistance of many persons. I am greatly indebted to Dr. George H. Pollock who gave me the benefit of his advice and criticism on the entire chapter. A long letter to me dictated by Dr. Franz Alexander a few days before his death has provided invaluable guidelines. Dr. Karl Menninger arranged a meeting at which I interviewed him and other members of the Topeka Psychoanalytic Society. I had instructive conversations with Miss Helen Ross, the late Miss Harriet Ray, Drs. Fritz and Anna Moellenhoff, Gerhart and Maria Piers, Therese Benedek, William C. Offenkrantz, Heinz Kohut, and others. I called often on Mr. Glenn Miller, librarian of the Chicago Institute for Psychoanalysis, who was most helpful.

The reader who wishes to orient himself in psychoanalytic theory has many works to choose from: *Basic Theory of Psychoanalysis*, by Robert Waelder (International Universities Press, 1960), is concise, clear, and authoritative. An idea of psychoanalytic techniques may be gained from Theodor Reik's *Listening with the Third Ear* (Farrar Straus, 1948), a very readable book in which the author relates his own experiences. For a presentation of dissenting opinions see *Schools of Psychoanalytic Thought* by Ruth L. Munroe (Holt, Rinehart & Winston, 1955).

Among the several sources frequently used in the preparation of this chapter, Ernest Jones' three-volume *The Life and Work of Sigmund Freud* (Basic Books, 1953–57) is not only the fundamental work on the master by a close associate but also a gold mine of information about the European period of psychoanalysis. Jones' chronicle of the events after the rise of Hitler is particularly relevant to my study. *A History of Psychoanalysis in America*, by the American pioneer analyst Clarence P. Obendorf (Grune and Stratton, 1953) is a standard text on the subject. *Psychoanalytic Pioneers*, edited by Franz Alexander, Samuel Eisenstein, and Martin Grotjahn (Basic Books, 1966) is a most enjoyable collection of sketches, not all equally informative, by authors who were associated with the men and women about whom they write. *Psychoanalytic Education in the United States*, by Bertram D. Lewin and Helen Ross (Norton, 1960), a scholarly, exhaustive treatment of the topic, contains a great deal of historical material. A search of the files of the *International Journal of Psychoanalysis, Journal of the American Psychoanalytic Association, Psychoanalytic Quarterly*, and similar publications is very rewarding to the painstaking investigator.

Jerome M. Schneck, *A History of Psychiatry* (Charles C. Thomas, 1960), and Gregory Zilboorg and J. K. Hall (eds.), *One Hundred Years of American Psychiatry* (Columbia University Press, 1944), are pertinent to this study insofar as they illustrate the psychiatric background. Some sources for the history of American psychoanalysis may be termed "regional," among them *Fruition of an Idea: 50 Years of Psychoanalysis in New York*, edited by Martin Wangh (International Universities Press, 1962); Franz Alexander and Helen Ross (eds.), *20 Years of Psychoanalysis: A Symposium in Celebration of the 20th Anniversary of the Chicago Institute for Psychoanalysis* (Norton, 1953); and Ives Hendrick, *The Birth of an Institute: Twenty-Fifth Anniversary of the Boston Psychoanalytic Institute* (Bond Wheelwright, 1961). Henry M. Brosin's words, quoted on p. 141, are from his discussion of "The Impact of Psychoanalysis on Training in Psychiatry" in *20 Years of Psychoanalysis;* and the following quotation is from "Psychoanalysis and the American Scene," by L. S. Kubie, in *Fruition of an Idea*. A measure of the early impact of psychoanalysis on American culture is obtained from the November, 1939, issue of the *American Journal of Sociology* which is devoted to Freud.

For American trends at the turn of the century that later interacted with psychoanalysis I found useful, among many possible sources, the articles on mental hygiene by Bernard Glueck (with an extensive bibliography), child psychology by Arnold Gesell, child guidance by Bernard Glueck, social work, by Philip Klein, and training for social work by Mary Clarke Burnett, all in the *Encyclopedia of the Social Sciences*, edited by Edwin R. A. Seligman and Alvin Johnson; the chapter "History of Child Development" in Elizabeth B. Hurlock, *Child Development* (McGraw-Hill, first edition 1947, omitted in the third and fourth editions); Clifford W. Beers' *A Mind that Found Itself: An Autobiography*, by the founder of the mental hygiene movement (7th ed.; Doubleday, Doran, 1948, containing supplements by C. E. A. Winslow and L. E. Woodward); Robert H. Bremner *From the Depths: The Discovery of Poverty in the United States* (New York University Press, 1956), illustrating the channeling of humanitarian and missionary impulses into social work; and R. Freeman Butts, *A Cultural History of Education: Reassessing Our Educational Traditions* (McGraw-Hill, 1950).

An account by one of the Americans who in the twenties were trained by Freud in Vienna is "Freud: The Man I Knew, the Scientist, and His Influence," by Abram Kardiner in Benjamin Nelson (ed.), *Freud and the 20th Century* (Meridian, 1957). Information about psychoanalytic lectures at the New School for Social Research is from Alvin Johnson's *Pioneer's Progress* and from a letter from Alvin Johnson to me.

The story of the assistance to European analysts on pp. 148–50 is based on a letter that Dr. Bertram D. Lewin wrote me and on the unpublished report of the Emergency Committee to the American Psychoanalytic Association, which I was able to consult through the courtesy of Drs. George H. Pollock and Bettina Warburg. The story of assistance given by the Menninger Clinic was pieced together from conversations with Dr. Karl Menninger and other analysts.

I leaned heavily on *Psychoanalytic Pioneers* for biographical material on Alexander, Rado, Sachs, Horney, Fenichel, and Reik. The quotation on p. 153 is from this book. For Rado see also *Fruition of an Idea*. For Sachs see his partly autobiographical *Freud: Master and Friend* (Harvard University Press, 1944) and *Birth of an Institute*. For Alexander, his *Western Mind in Transition; 20 Years of Psychoanalysis; Franz Alexander, M.D.* (Chicago Institute for Psychoanalysis, 1964), containing papers delivered at memorial meetings; and "Memorial Tribute: Franz Alexander, 1891–1964," by George H. Pollock, in *Archives of General Psychiatry*, Vol. XI, 1964.

Data about the establishment of institutes and societies may be found in the *Bulletin* section of the *International Journal of Psychoanalysis*, and in the journals and *Roster* of the American Psychoanalytic Association. Psychiatric needs in World War II are cogently presented in *Psychiatry in a Troubled World* (Macmillan, 1948), by William C. Menninger, at the time of its writing the chief consultant in neuropsychiatry to the Surgeon General of the Army; in Appendix D are published figures from the Office of the Surgeon General, Medical Statistics Division. Karl A. Menninger's quotation on p. 161 is from "The Contribution of Psychoanalysis to American Psychiatry" in his *A Psychiatrist's World* (Viking, 1959).

The main sources for the controversy on lay analysts and training standards are Jones' "Lay Analysis" in *The Life and Work of Sigmund Freud; Psychoana-*

lytic Education in the United States quoted on p. 161. George H. Pollock's "Historical Perspectives in the Selection of Candidates for Psychoanalytic Training" in the *Psychoanalytic Quarterly*, Vol. XXX, 1961; and Franz Alexander's "Psychoanalytic Education for Practice" in *The Scope of Psychoanalysis 1921–1961: Selected Papers of Franz Alexander* (Basic Books, 1961), quoted on p. 163. Alexander's words on pp. 165–66 are from his "The Psychosomatic Approach in Medical Therapy," also included in *The Scope of Psychoanalysis;* and Brock Brower's sentence is quoted from his "Psychotherapy in America — The Contemporary Scene" in Charles J. Rolo (ed.), *Psychiatry in American Life* (Little, Brown, 1963). Lionel Trilling's words on p. 166 are drawn from H. M. Ruitenbek (ed.), *Psychoanalysis and Literature* (Dutton, 1964). See also Lionel Trilling's *Freud and the Crisis of Our Culture* (Beacon Press, 1955).

CHAPTER VII

EUROPEAN-BORN ATOMIC SCIENTISTS

Information about the early times of theoretical physics and physicists was gathered from conversations and correspondence with Drs. Hans A. Bethe, Felix Bloch, George Gamow, Dolores B. Hawthorne, I. I. Rabi, Robert G. Sachs, Edward Teller, Eugene P. Wigner, and the late Samuel K. Allison. I am indebted to Dr. Merle A. Tuve for reports and additional details about the series of Washington Conferences on Theoretical Physics. The episode about Gamow and Bukharin is drawn from *The Legacy of Hiroshima*, by Edward Teller with Allen Brown (Doubleday, 1962). Leo Szilard's letter, quoted on pp. 182–83 and the story of Fermi's meeting with the Navy are published in Lewis L. Strauss, *Men and Decisions* (Doubleday, 1962).

The most extensive source for the events from the discovery of fission to the creation of the U. S. Atomic Energy Commission is *The New World, 1939–1946*, by Richard G. Hewlett and Oscar E. Anderson, Jr. (Pennsylvania State University Press, 1962). The basic work on wartime atomic developments is still the so-called Smyth Report: Henry D. Smyth, *Atomic Energy for Military Purposes* (Princeton University Press, 1945). General Leslie R. Groves' *Now It Can Be Told: The Story of the Manhattan Project* (Harper, 1962) is an honest account of the military aspects of the project and the author's often controversial decisions. (Quotations attributed to Groves are from this book.) *Atomic Quest: A Personal Narrative*, by Arthur Holly Compton (Oxford University Press, 1956), is an informative, somewhat one-sided story feelingly told. Dr. Herbert L. Anderson's recollections during many conversations added vivid details. President Roosevelt words on p. 184 are quoted from *The New World*; for the episode of Einstein's letter and other anecdotes see also my *Atoms in the Family* (University of Chicago Press, 1954). Information about implosion is drawn from *The New World* and a conversation with Dr. Hans Bethe. The comments made by German scientists, p. 198, are from *Now It Can Be Told*.

Alice Kimball Smith, *A Peril and a Hope: The Scientist's Movement in America 1945–1947* (University of Chicago Press, 1965), is the definitive history of what has come to be known as "the movement of atomic scientists"; it has been extensively used pp. 198–206. Samuel A. Goudsmit's *Alsos* (Henry Schuman, 1947), is a full report on that mission. For one scientist's feelings about the decision to use the bomb see the chapter "Choice" in *Atomic Quest*. Details about Eugene Rabinowitch's role as editor of the *Bulletin of Atomic Scientists* were provided by Ruth Adams and Eunice Rosen, his collaborators at the *Bulletin*.

Two important sources for the controversial issue about thermonuclear weapons are *The Legacy of Hiroshima*, from which I quoted Teller's words on p. 206, and United States Atomic Energy Commission, *In the Matter of J. Robert Oppenheimer*: Transcript of Hearing before Personnel Security Board, Washington, D. C., April 12, 1954, through May 6, 1954 (Government Printing Office, 1954). Additional material was gathered from *Men and Decisions* and from conversations with Dr. Stan, Ulam and others. Dr. Hans Bethe contributed information about scientists in government positions.

CHAPTER VIII

IN THE WORLD OF ART

In preparing the sections about musicians I was fortunate to have the generous assistance of Drs. Edward Lowinsky and Gerhard Herz. In particular, by greatly strengthening my early draft on musicologists Dr. Lowinsky set a pattern for surveys in other fields. Among the available biographical reference works on musicians the most scholarly and accurate is *Baker's Biographical Dictionary of Musicians* (5th edition, 1958); also helpful are *Grove's Dictionary of Music and Musicians*, David Ewen's *Composers of Today*, and *Jews in Music: From the Age of Enlightenment to the Present* (Philosophical Library, 1959), by Artur Holde, himself a member of the migration.

For the pre-migration American scene see Wittke's cited *Refugees of the Revolution* and the lively *Music in American Life*, by Jacques Barzun (Doubleday, 1956). Sources for Toscanini include Chotzinoff's *Toscanini: An Intimate Portrait* and the files of Italian and American newspapers; see also Samuel Antek and Robert Hupka, *This Was Toscanini* (Vanguard, 1963). For Bruno Walter see his *Theme and Variations* listed in the notes for chap. 3. I drew much information on conductors from John H. Mueller's excellent *The American Symphony Orchestra: A Social History of Musical Taste* (Indiana University Press, 1951). See also David Ewen, *Dictators of the Baton* (Alliance, 1943).

There are many biographies and autobiographies of composers. Halsey Stevens' *The Life and Music of Béla Bartók* was mentioned earlier. Darius Milhaud's entertaining autobiography *Notes sans musique* is available in English under the title *Notes without Music* (Knopf, 1953); a second edition of the French original (R. Julliard, 1963) contains an additional chapter which brings the composer's life story into the early sixties; if not otherwise indicated, quotations of Milhaud's words are from the English version. Paul Hindemith wrote *A Composer's World: Horizons and Limitations* (Harvard University Press, 1952) from which are drawn his words. Igor Stravinsky's *Chronicle of My Life* (Gollancz, 1936) is disappointing and ends early in time, but biographies have been issued in several countries: a recent volume is Eric Walter White's *Stravinsky: The Composer and His Work* (University of California Press, 1966). Many episodes of Stravinsky's collaboration with the choreographer George Balanchine are amusingly told by Bernard Taper in *Balanchine* (Harper & Row, 1960) quoted on p. 223. Other biographies of composers include Glenn Gould. *Arnold Schoenberg: A Perspective* (University of Cincinnati, 1964), and Miloš Šafránek, *Bohuslav Martinu: His Life and Works* (Allan Wingate, 1962).

Records of instrumentalists' lives include the previously cited *With Strings Attached*, by Joseph Szigeti, and *My Life and Music*, by Artur Schnabel. The most exhaustive treatment of musicologists will be found in *Musicology*, by Frank Llewellyn Harrison, Mantle Hood, and Claude V. Palisca (Prentice-Hall, 1963), a volume in the series "Princeton Studies: Humanistic Scholarship in America." An excellent introduction is provided by Manfred F. Bukofzer, *The Place of Musicology in American Institutions of Higher Learning* (Liberal Arts Press, 1957). Data on Winternitz are from "Winternitz: Notes on a Well-Tempered Curator," by James Dalihas, in *Metropolitan Museum Bulletin* (Summer, 1967).

For the sections on artists and art historians I received invaluable guidance from Dr. Joshua C. Taylor; a long conversation with Martyl Langsdorf was very enlightening; Dr. Horst W. Janson read and criticized my draft. I am greatly indebted to them. Among the published sources, Russell Lynes, *The Tastemakers* (Harper, 1949), provides a background to the present scene. General works on architecture include Ian McCallum's *Architecture USA* (Reinhold, 1959), from which I've taken the quotation on p. 234; John Burchard and Albert Bush-Brown, *The Architecture of America: A Social and Cultural History* (Little, Brown, 1961); and *Architecture and the Esthetics of Plenty*, by James Marston Fitch (Columbia University Press, 1961) from which Gropius' words on pp. 235–36 are quoted. Several books on individual architects are available: Sigfried Giedion's authoritative *Walter Gropius: Work and Teamwork* (Reinhold, 1954); *Ludwig Mies van der Rohe*, by Arthur Drexler (Braziller, 1960), and the informal but greatly informative *Mies van der Rohe: Architecture and Structure*, by Peter Blake (Penguin Books, 1960); *Marcel Breuer: Buildings and Projects, 1921–1961* (Thames and Hudson, 1962), a collection of photographs with captions and with an introduction by Cranston Jones; and Arnold Whittick's *Erich Mendelsohn* (Dodge, 1956).

Gropius' sentences quoted on p. 241 are from "Walter Gropius on the Occasion of His Seventieth Birthday Celebrated at the Illinois Institute of Technology," in *Arts and Architecture*, June, 1953. Episodes of Breuer's life are drawn mostly from books about Gropius and Mies. For the Bauhaus see also Herbert Bayer, *Bauhaus 1919–1928* (Museum of Modern Art, 1938; second printing, C. T. Branford, 1952); and for the New Bauhaus and the Institute of Design in Chicago see the cited *Moholy-Nagy: Experiment in Totality*, by Sibyl Moholy-Nagy.

Of the many existing books on painting and sculpture the most pertinent to the migration are Sidney Janis' *Abstract and Surrealist Art in America* (Reynal & Hitchcock, 1944), from which I quote on p. 242, a work now outdated but recreating the atmosphere of the period; Frederick S. Wight's *Milestones of American Painting* (Chanticleer Press, 1949); *Revolution and Tradition in Modern American Art*, by John I. H. Baur (Harvard University Press, 1951), quoted on pp. 244 and 245, and the more recent and equally valuable *American Art of Our Century*, by Lloyd Goodrich and John I. H. Baur (Praeger, 1961); William Harvey Pierson and Martha Davidson, *Arts in the United States: A Pictorial Survey* (McGraw-Hill, 1960); and Jean Selz's *Modern Sculpture: Origins and Evolution* (Braziller, 1963), which includes biographical sketches. The sentences by Robert Goldwater on p. 247 are from his "Reflections on the New York School" in *Quadrum* No. 8, (1960); and the following quotation is from "An Interview with Robert Motherwell" in *Artforum*, "The New York School," September, 1965.

Biographical material on individual artists is not lacking, and I used especially the following: *Lyonel Feininger — Marsden Hartley* (Museum of Modern Art, 1944), which includes essays on Feininger by Alois Schardt and Alfred H. Barr, Jr., and excerpts from Feininger's letters; Walter Erben's *Marc Chagall* (Praeger, 1957): Marcel Duchamp's profile by C. Tomkins in the *New Yorker*, February 6, 1965; Salvador Dali's *The Secret Life of Salvador Dali* (Dial, 1942); *A Little Yes and a Big No: The Autobiography of George Grosz* (Dial, 1946), the source of Grosz's quotation on p. 244; and *Bernard Reder*, by John I. H. Baur, research by Rosalind Irvine (Praeger, 1961).

The quotation on pp. 247–48 is from *Art and Archeology* by James S. Ackerman and Rhys Carpenter (Prentice-Hall, 1963), in the series "Princeton Studies: Humanistic Scholarship in America"; this is a basic work on the subject. For art historians I found useful several articles in the *Encyclopedia of the World of Art* of which, however, only a few volumes had been published at the time I was doing the research for this chapter. See also Erwin Panofsky's already mentioned "The History of Art" in *The Cultural Migration*.

CHAPTER IX

IN THE WORLD OF BOOKS AND MAGAZINES

Biographical reference sources for writers include *Contemporary Authors; Twentieth Century Authors* and its First Supplement; and the already mentioned *Deutsche Exil-Literatur 1933–1945*. *The Reader's Adviser* (10th edition, 1964) is also useful. In wartime, when foreign literature was scarce, *Books Abroad*, "a quarterly devoted to comments on foreign books," turned its attention to émigré writers, and Marc Chadourne's and Alfred Werner's words on p. 261 are from "Symposium on Transplanted Writers" in the Autumn, 1942, issue.

Walter Sorell wrote "English Language is No Sanctuary" in *Saturday Review*, August 25, 1945. Alfred Kazin's comments on *Doctor Faustus*, quoted on p. 264, are from the *New York Herald Tribune Weekly Book Review*, October 31, 1948. For Thomas and Heinrich Mann see the mentioned works, Klaus Mann, *The Turning Point*, and Erika and Klaus Mann, *Escape to Life*. See also, *Thomas Mann*, by James Martin Lindsay (Blackwell, 1954), and John Connop Thirlwall's *In Another Language: A Record of the Thirty-Year Relationship between Thomas Mann and His English Translator Helen Tracy Lowe-Porter* (Knopf, 1966). Thomas Mann's words on pp. 263 and 265 are from his *The Story of a Novel* (Knopf, 1961). For André Maurois see his *Memoires*, Vol. 2, *Les années de travail* (Éditions de la Maison française, 1942) and his *From My Journal* (Harper, 1948); and Jacques Suffels *André Maurois: Portrait-dialogue* (Flammarion, 1963). The quotation on p. 268 is from *Saturday Review*, January 15, 1966.

Sources for the book publishers were their letters to me; the files of *Publisher's Weekly* — on p. 273 I quoted from the July 7, 1945, issue; Charles A. Madison's *Book Publishing in America* (McGraw-Hill, 1966); and Robert Edgar Cazden, *The Free German and Free Austrian Press and Booktrade in the United States 1933–1950 in the Context of German-American History*, a dissertation, Graduate Library School, University of Chicago, September, 1965, which is also valuable for its discussion of publishers of German-language periodicals. The first quotation on p. 273 is from *Unter Fremden Himmeln: Ein Abriss der deutschen Literatur im Exil 1933–1947* by Franz G. Weiskopf (Dietz Verlag, 1947).

The European background of Schocken Books, Inc., is drawn from "Salman Schocken, His Economic and Zionist Activities," by Siegfried Moses in *Yearbook V of the Leo Baeck Institute* (1960) and from *Rechenschaft über vierzig Jahre Verlagsarbeit 1925–1965: Ein Almanach* (Verlag Lambert Schneider). The story of Kurt Wolff and Pantheon Books, Inc., is reconstructed from information supplied by Mrs. Helen Wolff; the article "Pantheon Books Expands on First Anniversary" in *Publisher's Weekly*, April 8, 1944; and Kurt Wolff, *Autoren, Bücher, Abenteur: Betrachtungen und Erinnerungen eines Verlegers* (Verlag Klaus Wagenbach, 1965).

CHAPTER X

MORE NATURAL SCIENTISTS

I am indebted to Drs. Stan Ulam, Antoni Zygmund, and John G. Thompson and to Mr. Philip Marcus for information on mathematicians; and to Dr. Ulam for reading the draft. Among the works used for this section are *The Development of Mathematics* by E. T. Bell (McGraw-Hill, 1940) and James R. Newman (ed.), the three-volume *The World of Mathematics* (Simon & Schuster, 1956). The quotation on p. 291 is from Freeman Dyson's Obituary of Herman Weyl in *Nature*, March 10, 1956. The New York University publication *Courant Institute of Mathematical Science 1966–1967* contains the history of that institute and other relevant facts. Information on the founding of *Mathematical Reviews* was furnished by Dr. Otto Neugebauer and supplemented by material published in issues of the *Bulletin of the American Mathematical Society* of the time (1939).

For the Montecarlo method see "Fermi Invention Rediscovered at LASL" in *The Atom*, October, 1966.

For the section on astronomers I had the invaluable assistance of Dr. S. Chandrasekhar. Published sources include Pontificia Accademia delle Scienze, Rome, *Stellar Populations* (Proceedings of the Conference sponsored by Pontificia Accademia delle Scienze and the Vatican Observatory, May 20–28, 1957 [Interscience, 1958]), including an address by Pope Pius XII; George Gamow's *Matter, Earth, and Sky* (Prentice-Hall, 1958) from which is drawn the quotation on p. 301; and "The Astronomers" in *Great American Scientists: America's Rise to the Forefront of World Science* by the editors of *Fortune* (Prentice-Hall, 1960).

I talked with several physicians, among them Drs. Franz Baumann, Piero Foà, who also read the draft and gave me valuable suggestions, Conrad L. Pirani, and Robert J. Hasterlik. The quotation on p. 308 is from the preface to Kurt Goldstein's *The Organism: A Holistic Approach to Biology Derived from Pathological Data in Man* (Beacon Press, 1963; first American edition, American Book Co., 1939). Rothman's address, "Good Old Days in Billings Hospital," delivered on June 10, 1959, was published in the *Bulletin* of the Alumni Association, School of Medicine, University of Chicago, Autumn, 1959. Information on Dr. Paul György's work is from the *Josiah Macy Jr. Foundation 1930–1955: A Review of Activities* (1955) and from direct communication to me.

I received briefings in biochemistry from Drs. Samuel B. Weiss and Herbert S. Anker; Dr Gunther S. Stent gave me advice and criticized an early draft. Published sources include George and Muriel Beadle, *The Language of Life* (Doubleday, 1966); *The Dynamic State of Body Constituents*, by Rudolf Schoenheimer (Harvard University Press, 1942); Gunther S. Stent's *Molecular Biology of Bacterial Viruses* (W. H. Freeman, 1963); and, most pertinent to this study, *Phage and the Origins of Molecular Biology*, edited by John Cairns, Gunther S. Stent, and James D. Watson (Cold Spring Harbor Laboratory of Quantitative Biology, 1966), a collection of essays published on the occasion of the sixtieth birthday of Max Delbrück.

CHAPTER XI

SOCIAL SCIENTISTS AND OTHER SCHOLARS

Information on psychological warfare was gathered mostly in conversations with Drs. Morris Janowitz, Nathan Leites, and George Rohrlich, who also read the draft, and from a letter from Dr. Fausto Pitigliani. The only published work that came to my attention containing substantial information on the émigrés role is Daniel Lerner's *Sykewar: Psychological Warfare Against Germany, D-Day to VE-Day* (George W. Stewart, Publisher, 1949), from which come the quotations on p. 323. *Psychological Warfare*, by Paul M. A. Linebarger (Combat Forces Press, 1954), may be used as a frame of reference. The story of the "Roster of Alien Specialized Personnel" is told in *They Can Aid America: Survey of Alien Specialized Personnel*, a thirteen-page publication of the National Refugee Service, Inc., 1943. For the

Research Project of Totalitarian Communication see Ernst Kris and Hans Speier, *German Radio Propaganda* (Oxford University Press, 1944). The quotation on p. 324 is from the previously cited *With Strings Attached*, by Joseph Szigeti.

In preparing the section on economists I had the assistance of Dr. Arcadius Kahan, who gave me invaluable help, Dr. Franco Modigliani, and Dr. Zvi Greiliches. Names of émigré economists were suggested also by Dr. Gregg H. Lewis and Dr. Albert Rees. *Main Currents in Modern Economics — Economic Thought Since 1870*, by Ben B. Seligman (Free Press, 1962) discusses the work of many émigrés. The quotations on p. 326 and p. 329 are from G.L.S. Shackle's brilliant *The Nature of Economic Thought* (Cambridge University Press, 1966); and Wassily W. Leontief's words, also on p. 329, are from "Structure of the United States Economy" in *Scientific American*, April 1965. The quotation on p. 330 is from Tjalling Koopmans, *Three Essays on the State of Economic Science* (McGraw Hill, 1957).

I gathered material about sociologists in conversations with Drs. Morris Janowitz, Daniel Bell, and Peter H. Rossi. Edward Shils' sentences on pp. 336–37 are quoted from his "The Calling of Sociology" in *The Theories of Society*, edited by Talcott Parsons and others (Free Press 1961); this two-volume work contains some useful material about a few émigré sociologists. A book relevant to the migration is *Contemporary Sociology*, edited by Joseph S. Roucek (Philosophical Library, 1958). The quotation on p. 337 is from Herbert Marcuse's preface to *The Democratic and the Authoritarian State*, by Franz Neumann. For Florian Znaniecki's contributions see Roscoe C. Hinkle, Jr., and Gisela J. Hinkle, *The Development of Modern Sociology: Its Nature and Growth in the United States* (Random House, 1954). Franz Neumann's remarks are from his "The Social Sciences" in the cited *The Cultural Migration*.

I am grateful to Dr. Hans J. Morgenthau for information on several political scientists. The quotation on pp. 343–44 is from Bernard Crick's *The American Science of Politics: Its Origins and Conditions* (University of Californa Press, 1964). Hannah Arendt's words are from the preface to her *The Origin of Totalitarianism* (Harcourt-Brace, 1951). M. A. Fitzsimons' sentences are from his "Profile of a Crisis: The Review of Politics 1939–1963" in *The Review of Politics*, October, 1963. Franz Neumann's words on p. 346 are quoted from his *Behemoth* (Gollancz, 1942); Hans J. Morgenthau's opinions are from "Reflections on the State of Political Science" in *The Review of Politics*, October, 1955; and the sentences on p. 349 are from the preface to Leo Strauss' *Natural Right and History* (University of Chicago Press, 1949). The quotation on p. 351 is from *The Political Philosophy of Arnold Brecht*, essays edited by Morris D. Forkosch (Exposition Press, 1954).

A basic source for the historians is *History*, by John Higham with Leonard Krieger and Felix Gilbert (Prentice-Hall, 1965), a volume in "Princeton Studies: Humanistic Scholarship in America." I quoted from this work abundantly on p. 354. Gerhardt Stourzh's comments were published in vol. 10 of *Jahrbuch für Amerikastudien*. Hajo Holborn's sentences on p. 358 are from the preface to his *A History of Modern Germany* (Knopf, 1959), and I quoted Dietrich Gerhard from his "Reflections of a Trans-Atlantic Professor" in *Washington University Magazine*, Fall, 1966.

I am indebted to Drs. A. Leo Oppenheim and John A. Wilson for information on Orientalists. The main source for the philosophers is the volume *Philosophy* by Roderick Chisolm, Manley Thomson, and Herbert Feigl (Prentice-Hall, 1964), in "Princeton Studies: Humanistic Scholarship in America," from which I quoted on pp. 365–66. For the Vienna Circle see also "The Development of Logical Empiricism" in *The Encyclopedia of Unified Science* (listed in the notes to chap. 5). The quotation on p. 369 is from James Collins' "Maritain's Impact on Thomism in America," in Joseph E. Evans (ed.), *Jacques Maritain* (Sheed and Ward, 1963). For Ernst Cassirer see also *Ernst Cassirer in America* by his wife Toni.

CHAPTER XII

NOTES TOWARD AN EVALUATION

This chapter requires very few notes. The quotation on p. 376 is from the *Congressional Record*, September 3, 1964. I discussed British influences with Dr. Cyril Stanley Smith. In mentioning the intellectual depletion in Hungary, I used information from Dr. Eugene P. Wigner. The letters to and from Dr. Ulrich Middledorf (p. 391) were published in "German Institute for Art History in Florence" in *Art Journal*, Winter, 1964. And in quoting Dr. Dietrich Gerhard, also on p. 391, I drew again from his article "Reflections of a Trans-Atlantic Professor," mentioned earlier.

INDEX OF PERSONS

The names of members of the migration are followed by biographical data: profession, country of origin, and year of birth. The year of death of members deceased before the autumn of 1970 is indicated whenever it was possible to ascertain it.

Abraham, Karl, 153–54

Abravanel, Maurice (Musical director. Greece, 1903), 135, 221

Ackerman, James S., 247, 250, 252, 402

Ackerman, Nathan, 334

Adams, Ruth, 400

Adams, Walter, 63

Adler, John H. (Economist. Czechoslovakia, 1912), 328

Adler, Kurt (Conductor. Czechoslovakia, 1907), 108, 130

Adler, Kurt Herbert (Conductor. Austria, 1905), 107–8

Adorno, Theodor W. (Social scientist. Germany, 1903–1969), 262, 332–333, 380

Agnon, Shmuel Joseph Halevi, 275

Aichhorn, August, 169

Albers, Anni (Artist, textile designer. Germany, 1899), 97–98

Albers, Josef (Painter. Germany, 1888), 97–99, 238, 242, 246

Albrand, Martha (Writer. Germany, 1914), 268

Alexander, Bernard 10, 55

Alexander, Franz (Psychoanalyst. Hungary, 1891–1964), 9–10, 55, 112, 145, 152–56, 158–59, 163–66, 169, 172, 390, 392, 397–99

Alexander, James W., 287

Allen, Frederick Lewis, 392

Allison, Samuel King, 399

Alphonso XIII, 40

Amaldi, Edoardo, 371

Anderson, Herbert L., 187, 399

Anderson, Oscar E., 399

Anker, Herbert S. (Biochemist, Germany, 1912), 314–15, 404

Antek, Samuel, 400

Apel, Willi (Musicologist. Germany, 1893), 229, 231–32

Aquinas, Thomas, 361

Aragon, Louis, 267

Arendt, Hannah (Political scientist. Germany, 1906), 268, 275, 338, 351, 405

Aristotle, 342, 361

Arnheim, Rudolf (Psychologist, writer. Germany, 1904), 268

Arni, Anna Maria, 269

Artin, Emil (Mathematician. Austria, 1898–1963), 287

Artom, Camillo (Biochemist. Italy, 1893), 96, 122, 311
Ascoli, Max (Writer, editor. Italy, 1898), 75, 118–20, 255, 281–82, 330, 350, 396
Auden, Wystan Hugh, 223, 263
Auerbach, Erich (Philologist, humanist. Germany 1892–1957), 364
Auerbach, Frank (Government official. Germany, 1910–1964), 103, 395
Auger, Pierre V. (Physicist. France, 1899), 123
Augustine, St., 361

Baade, Walter (Astronomer. Germany, 1893–1960), 296–98
Bacher, Robert F., 197
Bachhofer, Ludwig (Art Historian, Orientalist. Germany, 1894), 250, 252, 353
Baer, Reinhold (Mathematician. Germany, 1902), 289–90
Bailyn, Bernard, 390
Balabanoff, Angelica (Political figure, writer. Russia, ?–1964), 255–56
Balanchine, George, 223, 401
Bamberger, Louis, 73
Banach, S., 286
Baran, Paul (Economist. Russia, 1910–1964), 129, 325
Baron, Hans (Historian. Germany, 1900), 348
Barr, Alfred H. Jr., 86, 402
Barschak, Erna (Psychologist, writer. Germany, 1898–1961) 258, 390
Barth, Thomas F. W. (Geologist. Norway, 1899), 134
Bartók, Béla (Composer. Hungary, 1881–1945), 7–8, 54, 57, 108, 112, 115, 221–23, 353
Barzun, Jacques, 217, 400
Basso, Hamilton, 395
Baum, Vicki (Writer. Austria, 1896–1960), 268, 270

Baumann, Franz (Dermatologist. Germany, 1896), 301–3, 404
Baur, John I.H., 244–45, 402
Bayer, Herbert Wilhelm (Architect. Austria, 1900), 238, 242, 280, 401
Beadle, George Wells, 314, 404
Beadle, Muriel, 404
Beard, Charles, 337
Beck, Paul (Metallurgist. Hungary, 1908), 56, 58
Becker, William (Orthopedist, humanitarian. Germany 1896–1963), 307
Beer-Hoffmann, Richard (Poet, dramatist. Austria, 1866–1945), 108, 281
Beers, Clifford W., 398
Behrens, Peter, 234
Behrman, Samuel Nathaniel, 393, 396
Bell, Daniel, 405
Bell, Eric Temple, 403
Benedek, Therese F. (Psychoanalyst. Hungary, 1892), 112, 153, 156, 158, 164, 166, 170–71, 397
Beneš, Edward, 37, 377
Benesch, Otto (Art historian, museum curator. Austria, 1896–1964), 250
Bentwich, Norman, 62, 64, 394
Benzer, Seymour, 314
Berenson, Bernard, 345, 252
Berger, Adolf (Professor of law. Poland, 1882–1962), 345
Bergler, Edmund (Psychoanalyst. Austria, 1899), 167
Bergman, Stefan (Mathematician. Poland, 1903), 285, 293
Bergmann, Gustav (Philosopher. Austria, 1906), 358–59
Bergmann, Max (Chemist. Germany, 1886–1944), 311
Bergmann, Peter Gabriel (Mathematician. Germany, 1915), 98
Bergson, Henri, 361
Bergsträsser, Arnold (Political scientist. Germany, 1896–1964), 102–3, 250, 379–80, 395

Berliner, Bernhard (Psychoanalyst. Germany, 1895), 159

Berman, Eugene (Painter. Russia, 1899), 127, 244, 246, 279

Bermann-Fischer, Gottfried (Book publisher. Germany, 1897), 272

Bernfeld, Siegfried (Psychoanalyst. Poland, 1892–1953), 147, 153, 159

Bernheimer, Richard (Art Historian. Germany, 1907–1958), 249

Bers, Lipman (Mathematician. Latvia, 1914), 127, 289, 292

Bethe, Hans Albrecht (Physicist. France, 1906), vii, 174–76, 178–79, 182, 188–89, 191, 195–96, 203–6, 208, 211–12, 288, 299, 370, 381, 399–400

Bettelheim, Bruno (Psychologist, psychoanalyst. Austria, 1903), 168–71, 257, 333

Beveridge, William H., 62–64, 322, 394

Bier, Justus (Art Historian. Germany, 1899), 249

Bingham, Harry, 87

Biot, Maurice (Physicist. Belgium, 1905), 134

Birnbaum, William Z. (Mathematician. Poland, 1903), 284, 292

Bisbee, Eleanor, 394

Bismarck, Otto von, 349

Black, Max (Philosopher. Russia, 1909), 127, 360

Blake, Peter, 401

Bloch, Ernst (Social scientist. Germany, 1885), 271

Bloch, Felix (Physicist. Switzerland, 1905), 65, 133, 175–76, 178–80, 191, 195, 203, 370, 399

Bloch, Konrad E. (Biochemist. Germany, 1912), 364

Bloch, Robert G., 302

Block, Herbert (Economist. Germany, 1903), 322

Bloom, M. T., 368

Blumberg, Albert, 359

Bobrovnikoff, Nicholas Theodore, 295

Bochner, Salomon (Mathematician. Poland, 1899), 130, 286, 289

Bodky, Erwin (Harpsichordist. Germany, 1896–1958), 98–99, 227

Böhm-Bawerk, Eugen, 107

Bohannan, Paul, 396

Bohn, Frank, 88, 91

Bohr, Niels H. D. (Physicist. Denmark, 1885–1962), 15, 132–33, 175–78, 182, 185–86, 195–96, 199, 201

Bok, Bart (Astronomer. Holland, 1906), 296–97

Bonaparte, Marie, 146

Borel, Émile, 288

Borgese, Elisabeth Mann, 264, 366

Borgese, Giuseppe Antonio (Writer, professor of literature. Italy, 1882–1952), 103, 116–19, 120, 255, 265–66, 350–51, 393

Born, Max, 67, 72

Born, Wolfgang (Art historian. Germany, 1894–1941), 253

Bornstein, Berta (Psychoanalyst. Poland, 1899), 171

Bothmer, Bernard V. (Egyptologist. Germany, 1912), 354

Brandl, Rudolph, 280

Brandt, Karl (Agricultural economist. Germany, 1899), 322

Brauer, Alfred (Mathematician. Germany, 1894), 289, 292

Brauer, Max (Politician. Germany, 1887), 378

Brauer, Richard Dagobert (Mathematician. Germany, 1901), 289

Brecht, Arnold (Political scientist. Germany, 1884), 256, 344

Brecht, Bertolt (Playwright. Germany, 1898–1956), 271, 380

Breisach, Paul (Conductor. Austria, 1896–1952), 107

Bremner, Robert H., 397

Breton, André (Poet. France, 1896–1966), 123, 243, 266, 320

Breuer, Marcel (Architect. Hungary, 1902), 112, 235–38, 401
Brill, Abraham, 148
Brillouin, Léon N. (Physicist. France, 1889–1969), 124
Broch, Hermann (Writer. Austria, 1886–1956), 265, 279
Brook, Warner F. (Economist. Germany, 1880–1945), 322
Brosin, Henry W., 141, 165, 397
Brouwer, Dirk, 295
Brower, Brock, 166, 399
Brown, Allen, 399
Brown, Francis J., 391
Bruck, Eberhard F. (Professor of law. Germany, 1877–1960), 345
Bruckner, Ferdinand (Writer. Austria, 1891–1958), 271
Bruening, Heinrich A. (Statesman. Germany, 1885–1970), 377
Brunswik, Egon (Psychologist. Austria, 1903–1955), 374
Bühler, Charlotte (Psychologist. Germany, 1893), 364
Bühler, Karl (Psychologist. Germany, 1879–1963), 364
Bukharin, N. I., 181, 399
Bukofzer, Manfred F. (Musicologist. Germany, 1910–1955), 229, 231–32, 401
Bullock, Allan, 393
Burks, Arthur Walter, 288
Burchard, John, 401
Burnett, Mary Clark, 398
Busch, Adolf (Violinist. Germany, 1891–1952), 226, 228
Bush, Vannevar, 184, 288
Bush-Brown, Albert, 401
Butts, Freeman R., 398
Buxbaum, Edith (Psychoanalyst. Austria, 1902), 171
Byrnes, James F., 201

Cairns, John, 404
Capone, Alphonse, 30–31

Carmona, Antonio Oscar de Fragoso, 40
Carnap, Rudolf (Philosopher. Germany, 1891–1970), 107, 358
Carpenter, Rhys, 402
Caspari, Fritz (Historian. Switzerland, 1914), 102
Cassirer, Ernst (Philosopher. Germany, 1874–1945), 128, 363, 406
Cassirer, Toni, 128, 396, 406
Castelnuovo-Tedesco, Mario (Composer. Italy, 1885–1968), 117, 122, 221, 225
Castiglioni, Arturo (Historian of medicine. Italy, 1874–1952), 122, 352
Castro, Americo (Historian. Brazil, 1885), 349–50
Cazden, Robert Edgar, 403
Chadourne, Marc (Writer. France, 1895), 259–60, 402
Chagall, Marc (Painter. Russia, 1887), 86, 123, 126–27, 233, 242, 247, 278
Chamberlain, Owen, 186
Chandrasekhar, Subrahmanyan, 182, 296, 298, 404
Chargaff, Erwin (Biochemist. Austria, 1905), 311, 314
Charles I, 36, 47
Chautemps, Camille (Statesman. France, 1885–1963), 125, 377–78, 396.
Chermayeff, Serge (Architect. Russia, 1900), 127, 239–40
Chevalley, Claude S. (Mathematician. South Africa, 1909), 287, 289
Chiera, Edward, 352
Chisolm, Roderick M., 405
Chotzinoff, Samuel, 9, 390, 400
Churchill, Winston Leonard Spencer, 199, 201
Cianca, Alberto (Political figure. Italy, 1884–1966), 118
Ciano, Galeazzo, 8
Clausen, Jens (Botanist. Denmark, 1891), 134
Cohen, Elsa, 98

Cohen, Frederic (Conductor, opera director. Germany, 1904–1967), 98–99

Cohen, Gustave (Philologist. France, 1877–1958), 75

Cohn, Alfred E., 80–81, 395

Collins, James, 361, 406

Colm, Gerhard (Economist. Germany, 1897–1968), 321–323

Compton, Arthur Holly, 190, 192–94, 198, 201–2, 399

Conrad, Joseph, 258, 268

Cook, Walter William Spencer, 78, 248, 394

Cori, Carl F., 309

Cori, Gerty T., 309

Courant, Richard (Mathematician. Poland, 1888), 67, 72, 100, 130, 286, 291, 372, 395

Cournand, André F. (Physiologist. France, 1895), 124, 305

Crawford, Rex W., 389

Crick, Bernard, 337–38, 405

Crick, Francis H. C., 313

Critchfield, Charles Louis, 206

Croce, Benedetto, 49

Dali, Salvador (Painter. Spain, 1904), 134, 243, 402

Dalihas, James, 401

Dallin, David J. (Writer. Russia, 1889–1962), 256

Dalton, George, 396

Dam, C. P. Hendrik (Biochemist. Denmark, 1895), 133

David, Hans Theodor (Musicologist. Germany, 1902–1967), 229, 230

Davidson, Martha, 402

Davie, Maurice R., 11–12, 15–17, 61, 79, 81, 215, 233, 258, 285, 370, 389

De Benedetti, Sergio (Physicist. Italy, 1912), 121

de Bosis, Lauro, 117

Debye, Peter (Chemist. Holland, 1884–1966), 133

de Creeft, José (Sculptor. Spain, 1884), 98, 134, 244–45

Defauw, Richard Desiré (Conductor. Belgium, 1895–1960), 134

de Gaulle, Charles André Joseph Marie, 75–76, 123, 377–78

de Graaff, Frances (Professor of Russian literature. Holland, 1904), 98

Dehn, Max (Mathematician. Germany, 1878–?), 98

de Hoffmann, Frederic, 366

de Kerillis, Henri (Politician, writer. France 1889–1958), 377

Dekker, Maurits (Book publisher. Holland, 1899), 273–75

de Kooning, Willem, 98–99

Delbrück, Max (Biophysicist. Germany, 1906), 311–13, 404

Delougaz, Pinhas, 352

Delzell, Charles F., 396

Demerec, Miljslav, 313

Deri, Frances (Psychoanalyst. Austria, 1888), 159

de Rothschild, Baronesse Edouard, 90

de Santillana, Giorgio D. (Science historian. Italy, 1902), 120, 352

de Saussure, Raymond (Psychoanalyst. Switzerland, 1894), 134

Dessauer, Friedrich, 68–69

de Tolnay, Charles Erich (Art historian. Hungary, 1899), 113, 249, 252

Deutsch, Felix (Psychoanalyst. Austria, 1884–1964), 146, 157, 165, 366

Deutsch, Helene (Psychoanalyst. Poland, 1884), 146–47, 152, 157, 170, 366

Deutsch, Karl W. (Political scientist. Czechoslovakia, 1912), 320, 343

Deutsch, Martin, 146, 366

Devereux, George (Anthropologist, psychoanalyst. Hungary, 1908), 167

d'Harnoncourt, René (Art historian. Austria, 1901–1968), 251

Dick, Marcel (Violinist. Hungary, 1898), 98

411

Dieke, Gerhard H., 181–82
Dies, Martin, 27
di Lampedusa, Giuseppe, 279
Divine, Robert A., 25, 391, 395
Doeblin, Alfred (Writer. Germany, 1887–1957), 271, 380
Dollfuss, Engelbert, 40
Donati, Enrico (Painter. Italy, 1909), 244–45
Donnan, Frederick George, 66, 179
Dorati, Antal (Conductor. Hungary, 1906), 112, 220, 224
Dostoevski, Fëdor Mikhailovich, 154
Draper, Ruth, 117
Drexler, Arthur, 401
Drucker, Peter F., (Management consultant, educator. Austria, 1909), 343
Drury, Betty, 77, 389, 394
Duchamp, Marcel (Painter. France, 1887–1968), 124, 242, 246
Duggan, Stephen, 76–78, 389, 394
Duncan, Isadora, 58
Duncker, Karl, 7
Dunning, John R., 187
Dyson, Freeman J., 289, 403

Easum, Chester Verne, 390
Ebenstein, William (Political Scientist. Austria, 1910), 343
Eberhard, Wolfram (Sociologist, Sinologist. Germany, 1909), 352–53, 355
Ebert, Carl (Opera director. Germany, 1887), 67
Eckert, J. P., 288
Edelstein, Ludwig (Classical philologist, historian of medicine. Germany, 1902–1965), 352
Eichmann, Adolf, 338
Eilenberg, Samuel (Mathematician Poland, 1913), 39, 130, 285
Einaudi, Mario (Political scientist. Italy, 1904), 120
Einstein, Albert (Physicist. Germany, 1879–1955), 4, 30, 52, 73, 83, 104–5, 184, 205, 256, 281, 287–89, 307, 359, 399
Einstein, Alfred (Musicologist. Germany, 1880–1952), 98, 229–32
Eisenhower, Dwight David, 169
Eisenstein, Samuel, 397
Eissler, Kurt (Psychoanalyst. Austria, 1908), 167
Eitingon, Max, 153–54
Ekstein, Hans (Physicist. Russia, 1908), 90
Ekstein, Rudolf (Psychoanalyst. Austria, 1912), 161, 170–72
Eliasberg, George J. (Writer. Austria, 1906), 257
Elisséeff, Serge (Far-eastern languages expert. Russia, 1889), 354
Engel-Janosi, Friedrich (Historian. Austria, 1893), 350
Engels, Friedrich, 52
Enoch, Kurt (Publisher. Germany, 1895), 279
Erben, Walter, 402
Erdös, Paul (Mathematician. Hungary, 1913), 112, 285, 289–90
Erikson, Erik Homburg (Psychoanalyst. Germany, 1902), 162, 166, 169, 171
Erlich, Alexander (Economist. Russia, 1912), 129, 325
Ernst, Max (Painter. Germany, 1891), 86, 91, 243, 246
Ettinghausen, Richard (Museum curator, art historian. Germany, 1906), 249
Eucharren, Matta, 243
Evans, Joseph E., 406
Everett, Cornelius, 209
Ewen, David, 400

Fajans, Kasimir (Physical chemist. Poland, 1887), 130
Fankhauser, Gerhard (Biologist, Switzerland, 1901), 132
Fano, Lilla, 367

Fano, Ugo (Physicist. Italy, 1912), 121, 312–13, 367

Fassett, Agatha, 390

Federn, Paul (Psychoanalyst. Austria, 1872–1950), 106, 157–58

Feigl, Herbert (Philosopher. Austria, 1902), 107, 358–59, 405

Feiler, Arthur (Economist. Germany, 1879–1942), 72, 321

Feininger, Lyonel (Painter. United States, 1871–1956), 98, 238, 242

Feller, William (Mathematician. Yugoslavia, 1906–1970), 134, 287, 293

Fellner, William (Economist. Hungary, 1905), 112, 328

Fenichel, Otto (Psychoanalyst. Austria, 1898–1946), 147, 153, 157, 159, 398

Ferand, Ernest Thomas (Musicologist. Hungary, 1887), 112, 229, 232

Ferenczi, Sándor, 142, 144, 153–54

Fermi, Enrico (Physicist. Italy, 1901–1954), 4, 7, 27, 83, 121, 175–76, 182–83, 186–90, 192–98, 201–2, 204, 206–7, 211, 214, 295, 297, 312 206–7, 211, 214, 295, 297, 312, 371–72, 374, 381, 399

Feuchtwanger, Lion (Writer. Germany, 1884–1958), 86–87, 89, 258, 265, 271, 281, 373, 395

Fields, Harold, 389

Fitch, James Marston, 234, 401

Fitzsimons, Matthew Anthony, 339, 405

Flechtheim, Ossip K. (Political scientist. Russia, 1909), 343

Fleming, Donald, 390

Flesch, Rudolf (Writer. Austria, 1911), 109–10, 345

Flexner, Abraham, 73–74, 249, 289, 375, 393

Flowerman, Samuel, 333

Foà, Bruno (Economist. Italy, 1905), 322

Foà, Piero (Physiologist. Italy, 1911), 122, 303, 310, 404

Ford, Henry, 22–23

Forkosch, Morris D., 344, 405

Forssmann, Werner, 306

Fraenkel, Ernst (Political scientist. Germany, 1898), 80, 256, 340, 380, 382

Fraenkel-Conrat, Heinz (Biochemist. Germany, 1910), 314

Franck, James (Chemist. Germany, 1882–1964), 67, 72, 181, 192, 200–202, 205, 307

Franco, Francisco Bahamonde, 40, 119

Frank, Anna, 86

Frank, Bruno (Writer. Germany, 1887–1945) 218

Frank, Karl B. (Paul Hagen) Political writer. Germany, 1893), 86, 256

Frank, Leonhard (Writer. Germany, 1882–1961), 262

Frank, Philipp G. (Physicist, philosopher. Austria, 1884–1966), 107, 357–59, 392

Frankfort, Henri (Archeologist. Holland, 1877–1954), 133, 355–56

Frankl, Paul (Art historian. Czechoslovakia, 1878–1962), 249

Freccia, Massimo (Conductor. Italy, 1906), 117, 220

Frenkel-Brunswik, Else (Psychologist. Austria, 1908–1958), 333, 364

Freud, Anna, 161, 168, 171

Freud, Sigmund, 52, 106, 139–40, 142–47, 152, 154–55, 157, 161–62, 164, 166, 168, 170, 172, 243, 271, 371, 397–98

Freundlich, Edwin, 69–70

Friedlaender, Walter (Art historian. Germany, 1873–1966), 248, 252, 275

Friedlander, Walter A. (Social scientist. Germany, 1891), 307

Friedrich, Carl Joachim, 343

Friedrichs, Kurt Otto (Mathematician. Germany, 1901), 291

Fromm, Erich (Writer, psychoanalyst. Germany, 1900), 158, 164–65, 168, 254

Fromm-Reichmann, Frieda (Psycho-analyst. Germany, 1889–1957), 158, 170
Frost, E. B., 296
Fry, Varian, 85–92, 124, 263, 328, 395
Fubini, Eugene G. (Electronic engineer. Italy, 1913), 121–22, 211
Fubini, Guido (Mathematician. Italy, 1879–1943), 289
Fuchs, Klaus, 192, 209
Fuld, Mrs. Felix, 73

Galilei, Galileo, 273, 297, 300
Gamer, Helena M., 396
Gamow, George (Physicist. Russia, 1904), 126, 176–79, 181–82, 206, 298–99, 313, 396, 399, 404
Gaposchkin, Sergei I. (Astronomer. Russia, 1898), 127, 296
Gardner, Trevor, 212
Gay, Peter, viii, 366
Geiger, Bernard (Iranist. Poland, 1881–1964), 354
Geiringer, Karl (Musicologist. Austria, 1899), 107, 229, 231
Gelb, Ignace Jay (Assyriologist. Poland, 1907), 352, 355–57
Geleerd, Elizabeth Rosette (Psychoanalyst. Holland, 1909–1969), 133, 171
Gentile, Giovanni, 49
George, Manfred (Magazine publisher. Germany, 1893–1965), 280–82
Gerhard, Dietrich (Historian. Germany, 1896), 349, 351, 382, 405–06
Gero, Alexander (Chemist, Hungary, 1907), 90
Gerschenkron, Alexander (Economist. Russia, 1904), 127, 256, 321, 323, 329, 393
Gerth, Hans H. (Sociologist. Germany, 1908), 335
Gesell, Arnold Lucius, 398
Giedion, Sigfried, 401
Gilbert, Felix (Historian. Germany, 1905), 320, 347–49, 405

Ginsberg, Marie, 62
Glarner, Fritz (Artist. Switzerland, 1899), 134, 242
Glatzer, Nahum Norbert (Historian. Austria, 1903), 275
Glenney, Harriet L., 395
Glueck, Bernard, 397–98
Gobetti, Piero, 48
Goebbels, Josef, 62, 85–86
Gödel, Kurt (Mathematician. Czechoslovakia, 1906), 107, 132, 286, 289, 358
Goethe, Johann Wolfgang von, 103, 166–67
Goetze, Albrecht (Assyriologist. Germany, 1897), 354
Goldfeder, Anna (Cancer researcher. Poland, 1897), 306
Goldsmith, Hyman, 205
Goldsmith, Raymond William (Economist. Belgium, 1904), 134, 322
Goldstein, Kurt (Neurologist. Poland, 1878–1965), 130, 275, 303–04, 404
Goldwater, Robert, 246, 402
Golschmann, Vladimir (Conductor. France, 1893), 220
Gombosi, Otto (Musicologist. Hungary, 1902–1955), 112, 229, 232
Gombrich, Ernst, 37
Gomori, George (Physician. Hungary, 1904–1957), 113
Goodrich, Lloyd, 402
Gottschalk, Fruma, 392
Goudsmit, Samuel A., 175, 186, 199–200, 205, 400
Gould, Alan J., 110
Gould, Glenn, 401
Graf, Oskar Maria (Writer. Germany, 1894–1967), 265, 271
Granach, Alexander (Actor, writer. Austria, 1890), 393
Grant, Madison, 22, 24, 48, 391
Graudan, Nikolai (Cellist. Russia, 1891–1964), 98, 227
Greenewalt, Crawford H., 194

Greenwall, H. J., 395
Greiliches, Zvi, 405
Grodzins, Ruth, vii
Gropius, Walter (Architect. Germany, 1883–1969), 98, 234–241, 401
Grosse, Aristid V. (Chemist. Russia, 1905), 186
Grossmann, Kurt R. (Writer. Germany, 1897), 379, 390
Grosz, George (Painter. Germany, 1893–1959), 244, 246, 277, 402
Grotjahn, Martin (Psychoanalyst. Germany, 1904), 397
Groves, Leslie, L., 192–93, 195–96, 198–99, 399
Gruen, Victor (Architect. Austria, 1903), 237
Güterbock, Frances Hellman, 68, 70, 394
Güterbock, Hans (Hittitologist. Germany, 1908), 67–70, 352, 356, 394
Guicciardini, Francesco, 349
Gumpert, Martin (Physician, writer. Germany, 1897—1955), 258, 262, 303, 307–8, 373, 390
Gunn, Ross, 183–84
Gurian, Waldemar (Political scientist. Russia, 1902–1954), 127, 256, 338–39
Guterman, Norbert, 334
György, Paul (Pediatrician. Hungary, 1893), 305, 404

Haagen-Smit, Arie Jan (Biochemist. Holland, 1900), 133–34
Habe, Hans (Jean Bekessy) (Writer. Hungary, 1911), 267–68, 280, 320
Haber, Fritz, 370
Haberler, Gottfried (Economist. Austria, 1900), 107, 321, 328
Hacker, Frederick Jean (Psychoanalyst Austria, 1914), 159
Hadamard, Jacques (Mathematician. France, 1865–1963), 30, 123

Haenel, Irene (Psychoanalyst. Germany, ?–1941), 159
Hahn, Otto, 175, 312
Haile Selassie, 355
Halasi-Kun, Tibor (Professor of Turkic studies. Hungary, 1914), 352, 354
Halasz, Nicholas (Writer, Hungary, 1895), 266
Halecki, Oscar (Historian. Austria, 1891), 351
Hall, G. Stanley, 142
Hall, J. K., 397
Halle, Hiram, 75
Halperin, S. William, 395
Handlin, Oscar, 391
Hanfmann, George M. A. (Art historian. Russia, 1911), 250
Harris, Margaret, vii
Harrison, Frank Llewellyn, 401
Hartmann, Heinz (Psychoanalyst. Austria, 1894–1970), 106, 157, 169
Hartshorne, Edward Yarnell, 393
Hasterlik, Robert J., 404
Hawthorne, Dolores B., 399
Hayes, Africa, 99
Hayes, Roland, 99
Healy, William, 169
Heiden, Konrad (Writer. Germany, 1901–1966), 86–87, 256, 351
Hegel, Georg Wilhelm Friederich, 343
Heilperin, Michael Angelo (Economist. Poland, 1909), 322
Heimann, Eduard (Economist. Germany, 1889–1967), 322
Heisenberg, Werner, 198
Heitler, Walter, 72
Held, Julius S. (Art historian. Germany, 1905), 248
Hempel, Carl Gustav (Philosopher. Germany, 1903), 358–60
Hendrick, Ives, 154, 397
Herma, John L. (Psychology. Austria, 1911), 318, 320
Herman, Woody, 223

415

Hermens, Ferdinand (Political scientist. Germany, 1906), 344
Hershey, Alfred, 314
Hertz, Paul (Socialist leader. Germany, 1888–1961), 378
Hertzmann, Erich (Musicologist. Germany, 1902–1963), 229
Herz, Gerhard (Musicologist. Germany, 1911), 227–29, 400
Herz, John H. (Political scientist. Germany, 1908), 319, 343
Herzberg, Gerhard, 296
Herzfeld, Ernst Emil (Archeologist. Germany, 1879–1948), 73
Herzfeld, Karl Ferdinand, 181–82, 186
Herzefelde, Wieland (Sociologist. Switzerland, 1896), 271
Herzog, George, 230
Hess, Victor Francis (Physicist. Austria. 1883–1964), 108–9
Hewlett, Richard G., 399
Higham, John, 347–49, 391, 405
Hilberry, Norman, 192
Hilferding, Rudolf, 89, 107
Hindenburg, Paul von, 344
Hindemith, Paul (Composer. Germany, 1895–1963), 67, 221–24, 229, 401
Hinkle, Gisela J., 405
Hinkle, Roscoe C., Jr., 405
Hirsch, Mrs. Helmut, 88, 395
Hirsch, Julius (Economist. Germany, 1882–1961), 322
Hirschman, Albert O. (Economist. Germany, 1915), 88, 322, 328
Hitler, Adolf, 6, 17, 22, 28, 40, 44, 49–52, 60, 62, 66, 74, 78, 84, 86, 94, 95, 98, 106, 112, 128–29, 142, 146, 158, 183–85, 192, 218, 237, 248, 257, 307, 320, 337, 349, 380
Hitschmann, Edward (Psychoanalyst. Austria, 1871–1950), 157, 166
Hobbes, Thomas, 342
Hofmann, Hans (Painter. Germany, 1880–1966), 241, 246
Holborn, Annemarie, vii, 222

Holborn, Hajo (Historian. Germany, 1902–1969), 320, 347–49, 351, 405
Holborn, Louise (Political scientist. Germany, 1898), 319–20, 340, 382
Holde, Artur (Music editor, writer. Germany, 1885–1962), 400
Holton, Gerald, 366
Hood, Mantle, 401
Hoover, Herbert Clark, 25
Horkheimer, Max (Social scientist. Germany, 1895), 168, 319, 332–33, 380
Horner, Imre (Physician. Hungary, 1901), 54, 57, 113
Horney, Karen (Psychoanalyst. Germany, 1885–1953), 153, 156, 158, 160, 168, 171, 397
Horowitz, Vladimir (Pianist. Russia, 1904), 129, 226
Horthy de Nagybanya, Nicholas, 10, 21, 40, 47–48, 51, 111, 145, 379
Hoselitz, Bert F. (Economist. Austria, 1913), 328–330
Hostovsky, Egon (Writer. Czechoslovakia, 1908), 131
Huelsenbeck, Richard (Psychiatrist, writer. Germany, 1892), 277
Hupka, Robert, 400
Hurewicz, Witold (Mathematician. Poland, 1904–1956), 284, 289–90
Hurlock, Elizabeth B., 398
Hurwicz, Leonid (Econometrician. Russia, 1917), 129, 285, 322, 326
Hutchins, Robert Maynard, 5, 72, 76, 155, 296, 363, 391
Huth, Hans (Art historian, curator. Germany, 1892), 251

Ignotus, Hugo (Writer. Hungary, 1872–1949), 38
Ignotus, Paul, 38, 392–93
Infeld, Leopold (Physicist. Poland, 1898–1968), 39, 41, 257, 393
Infield, Henrik F. (Sociologist. Poland, 1901), 335–36
Irvine, Rosalind, 402

Iturbi, José (Pianist, conductor. Spain, 1895–1969), 134, 220

Jacchia, Luigi (Astronomer. Italy, 1910), 122, 296–97
Jacobsen, Thorkild (Assyriologist. Denmark, 1904), 134, 355–57
Jacobson, Edith (Psychoanalyst. Germany, 1897), 158
Jacoby, Kurt (Book publisher. Germany, 1892), 274
Jaeger, Werner W. (Classic philologist. Germany, 1888–1961), 351, 364
Jahoda, Marie (Psychologist. Austria, 1907), 334, 346
Jakobson, Roman (Linguist, literary historian. Russia, 1898), 127–28, 396
Jalowetz, Heinrich (Conductor. Czechoslovakia, 1883–1946), 98
Jalowetz, Johanna, 98
Janis, Sidney, 242, 402
Janowitz, Morris, 168, 333, 337, 404–05
Janson, Horst W. (Art historian. Russia, 1913), 249, 252, 401
Jászi, Oscar, 47, 350, 393
Javits, Jacob K., 368
Jedrzejewicz, Waclaw (Slavist. Russia, 1893), 126
Jefferson, Thomas, 248, 346, 375
Jeffries, Zay, 201
Jekels, Ludwig (Psychoanalyst. Austria, 1897–1954), 157
Joergensen, Joergen, 357, 396
John, Fritz (Mathematician. Germany, 1910), 292
Johnson, Alvin, 29, 74–76, 78, 85, 100, 107, 123, 145, 321–22, 327, 394, 398
Johnson, Walter (Book publisher from Germany), 274
Jolles, Otto J. M. (Germanist. Germany, 1911), 102
Jones, Cranston, 401
Jones, Ernest, 146–48, 154, 161, 397–98
Jones, Maldwyn Allen, 391

Jonniaux, Alfred (Painter from Belgium), 134
Joseph II, 56
Jung, Carl Gustav, 142

Kac, Mark (Mathematician. Poland, 1914), 39, 130, 284
Kafka, Franz, 275–76
Kahan, Arcadius, 324, 405
Kahler, Erich G. (Author, expert in German literature. Czechoslovakia, 1885–1970), 98, 132
Kahn, Erich Itor (Pianist. Germany, 1905–1956), 89, 368
Kahn, Frida, 368, 393
Kalckar, Herman M. (Physiologist, biochemist. Denmark, 1908), 310
Kallen, Horace Meyer, 75
Kallman, Chester, 223
Kalven, Harry, Jr., 345
Kamenev, Leo Borisovich, 43
Kamm, Bernhard (Psychoanalyst, Czechoslovakia, 1899), 132, 159
Kanitz, Ernst (Composer. Austria, 1894), 96
Kann, Robert (Historian. Austria, 1906), 106, 350
Kantorowicz, Ernst Hartwig (Historian. Poland, 1895–1963), 130, 349
Kapteyn, Jacobus C., 295
Kardiner, Abram, 398
Katona, George (Economist. Hungary, 1901), 112, 322
Katz, Rudolf (Socialist leader. Germany, 1895–1961), 378
Katzenellenbogen, Adolf (Art historian. Germany, 1901–1964), 249
Kauder, Hugo (Composer, Czechoslovakia, 1888), 98
Kazin, Alfred, 262, 402
Kelemen, Pál (Archeologist, art historian. Hungary, 1894), 253
Keller, Helen Adams, 52
Kelsen, Hans (Jurist, professor of law. Czechoslovakia, 1881), 72, 132, 344

Kempner, Robert Max Wassilli (Jurist, political scientist. Germany, 1899), 256, 320

Kennedy, John Fitzgerald, 131, 267, 340

Kent, Donald P., 389

Kepes, Gyorgy (Painter, designer. Hungary, 1906), 112, 239–40

Kerenski, Aleksandr Feodorovich, 86–87

Kessler, Friedrich (Professor of law. Germany, 1901), 345

Kesten, Hermann (Writer. Germany, 1900), 86, 379, 390

Keynes, John Maynard, 325

Kieve, Rudolph (Psychiatrist. Germany, 1911), 96

King, L. D. Percival, 295

Kingdon, Frank, 85

Kinkeldey, Otto, 228–29

Kirchheimer, Otto (Social scientist. Germany, 1905–1965), 320, 332–33, 344–45

Kisch, Guido (Law historian. Czechoslovakia, 1889), 351

Kissinger, Henry Alfred, 365

Kistiakowsky, George Bogdan, 126, 196–98, 211

Klein, Philip, 397

Klemperer, Otto (Conductor. Germany, 1885), 220

Koehler, Wilhelm (Art historian. Estonia, 1884–1959), 250

Köhler, Wolfgang (Psychologist. Estonia, 1887–1967), 126–27, 345, 358, 372, 389

Koerner, Henry (Painter. Austria, 1915), 245

Koestler, Arthur, 53, 392

Koffka, Kurt, 345, 372

Kohn, Hans (Historian. Czechoslovakia, 1891), 132, 350, 393

Kohut, Heinz (Psychoanalyst. Austria, 1913), 158, 167, 172, 397

Kokeritz, K. A. Helge (Professor of English. Sweden, 1902–1964), 134

Kolin, Alexander (Biophysicist. Russia, 1910), 127

Koopmans, Tjalling (Economist. Holland, 1910), 133, 326–27, 405

Kopal, Zdeněk (Astronomer. Czechoslovakia, 1914), 132, 297

Koppell, H. G. (Book publisher from Germany), 272

Kornberg, Arthur, 314

Korngold, Erich Wolfgang (Composer. Austria, 1897–1957), 107, 108

Korngold, Julius (Music critic. Austria, 1861–1945), 108

Korsching, Horst, 198

Kossuth, Lajos (Louis), 55

Kotschnig, Walter Maria (Government official, writer. Austria, 1901), 71

Koussevitzsky, Serge, 126

Koyré, Alexander (Science historian. Russia (1912–1964), 127, 352

Kramer, Paul (Psychoanalyst. Latvia, 1908), 127

Krautheimer, Richard (Art historian. Germany, 1897), 249, 252, 320

Krenek, Ernst (Composer, musicologist. Austria, 1900), 98, 107, 222, 229, 262

Krieger, Leonard, 347–48, 405

Kris, Ernst (Psychoanalyst. Austria, 1900–1957), 106, 158, 161, 167, 169, 318, 405

Kubie, Lawrence S., 141, 148, 165, 397

Kuiper, Gerard (Astronomer. Holland, 1905), 133, 199, 296, 298

Kun, Béla, 10, 40, 47, 111, 145

Kunswald, Ernst, 216

Kuttner, Stephan George (Historian of canon law. Germany, 1907), 348

Lanczos, Cornelius (Mathematician. Hungary, 1893), 112, 285

Land, Gustav (Astronomer. Germany, 1880–1959), 297

Landowska, Wanda (Harpsichordist. Poland, 1879–1959), 130, 226–27

Landsberger, Benno (Assyriologist. Germany, 1890–1968), 352

Landshoff, Fritz H. (Book publisher from Germany), 262, 272

Landsteiner, Karl, 309

Lang, Paul Henry, 113, 229

Lange, Oscar (Economist, Poland, 1904–1965), 325, 328

Langsdorf, Martyl, 401

Lania, Leo (Hermann Lazar) (Writer. Russia, 1896–1961), 258, 268, 320, 395

Laski, Harold, 340

Lattes, Raffaele (Pathologist. Italy, 1910), 122

Lawrence, Ernest Orlando, 185, 202, 204, 311

Lazarsfeld, Paul Felix (Sociologist. Austria, 1901), 319, 331, 334, 345

LeCorbeiller, Philippe (Educator. France, 1891), 125

Le Corbusier, 234

Lederberg, Joshua, 314

Lederer, Emil (Economist. Austria, 1882–1939), 74–75, 107, 321–22

Lee, D. E., 391

Lee, Tsung Dao, 372

Léger, Fernand (Painter. France, 1881–1955), 97, 123, 233, 242, 246–47

Lehmann, Fritz (Economist. Germany, 1901), 323, 330

Lehmann, Karl (Archeologist. Germany, 1894–1960), 248, 351, 375

Leichtentritt, Hugo (Musicologist. Poland, 1874–1951), 130, 229

Leinsdorf, Erich (Conductor. Austria, 1912), 107, 220

Leites, Nathan (Political scientist. Russia, 1912), 320, 404

Lenard, Philipp E. A., 393

Lenin, Nicolai, 39, 40, 43–44, 256

Leonhardt, Hans Leo (Lawyer, writer. Germany, 1901), 256–57

Leontief, Wassily W. (Economist. Russia, 1906), 129, 321–22, 325, 405

Lerner, Abba (Economist. Russia, 1903), 126–27, 321–23, 325

Lerner, Daniel, 317, 319

Leser, Paul W. (Anthropologist. Germany, 1889), 98

Leslau, Wolf (Ethiopian scholar. Poland, 1906), 354

Levi-Civita, Tullio, 292

Levi della Vida, Giorgio (Semitist. Italy, 1886–1967), 355

Levinson, Daniel, 393

Lévi-Strauss, Claude (Archeologist. Belgium, 1908), 123–24, 134

Levy, Ernst (Law historian. Germany, 1881), 351

Levy, Walter J. (Economist, oil consultant. Germany, 1911), 320–21

Lewin, Bertram D., 148–49, 397–98

Lewin, Kurt (Psychologist. Germany, 1890–1947), 320, 335, 358

Lewis, Gregg H., 405

Lewy, Ernst (Psychoanalyst. Germany, 1891), 159

Lewy, Hans (Mathematician. Germany, 1904), 286

Lieber, Francis, 337

Liepe, Wolfgang (Germanist. Germany, 1888–1962), 103

Lilge, Frederic, 393

Lincoln, Abraham, 4, 346

Lindbergh, Anne Spencer Morrow, 279

Lindsay, Martin James, 403

Linebarger, Paul M. A., 404

Lipchitz, Jacques (Sculptor. Poland, 1891), 86, 130, 244–46

Lipinsky de Orlov, Lino Sigismond (Painter. Italy, 1908), 117

Lipmann, Fritz (Biochemist. Germany, 1899), 303, 309, 314

Lodge, Henry Cabot, 20

Loewenstein, Hubertus Friedrich zu (Writer, diplomat. Austria, 1906), 82, 392

Loewenstein, Karl (Political scientist. Germany, 1891), 343

Loewenstein, Rudolph M. (Psychoanalyst. Poland, 1898), 169
Loewi, Otto (Physiologist, pharmacologist. Germany, 1873–1961), 281, 303
Loewner, Charles (Mathematician. Czechoslovakia, 1893–1968), 132, 293
London, Fritz Wolfgang (Physicist. Germany, 1900–1954), 72
Lopatnikoff, Nicolai (Composer. Russia, 1903), 222
Lopez, Robert Sabatino (Historian. Italy, 1910), 350
López-Rey, José (Art historian. Spain, 1905), 249
Lorand, Sandor, 144
Lorant, Stefan (Writer. Hungary, 1901), 266, 268
Lorente de Nó, Rafael (Physiologist. Spain, 1902), 134, 304
Lossky, Andrew (Historian. Russia, 1917), 127
Lowe, Adolph (Economist. Germany, 1893), 321, 323, 330
Lowenthal, Leo (Sociologist. Germany, 1900), 319, 332–34
Lowinsky, Edward E. (Musicologist. Germany, 1908), vii, 97–99, 229, 232, 368, 395, 400
Lowinsky, Gretel, 98, 368
Ludwig, Emil (Writer. Germany, 1881–1948), 50, 266, 272, 281, 380
Luebke, Heinrich, 76
Luisada, Aldo (Cardiologist. Italy, 1901), 122
Luria, Salvador E. (Virologist. Italy, 1912), 122, 311–13
Luther, Martin, 166
Lynes, Russell, 401

Macartney, C. A., 394
Machiavelli, Niccolò, 349
Machlup, Fritz (Economist. Austria, 1902), 321, 23

Madison, Charles A., 403
Maenchen-Helfen, Otto J. (Art historian. Austria, 1894), 250, 355
Maeterlinck, Maurice (Writer. Belgium, 1862–1949), 133, 264–65, 380
Mahler, Fritz (Conductor. Austria, 1903), 221
Mahler, Gustav, 218, 221
Mahler, Margaret Schoenberger (Psychoanalyst. Hungary, 1897), 171
Maimonides, 342
Malche, Albert, 66
Malinowski, Bronislaw (Anthropologist. Poland, 1884–1942), 130
Malko, Nicolai (Conductor. Russia, 1883–1961), 129, 220
Mandelbrojt, Szolem (Mathematician. Poland, 1899), 129
Mann, Erika (Writer, German, 1905–1969), 258, 261, 263–64, 390, 403
Mann, Fritz Karl (Economist. Germany, 1883), 321
Mann, Golo (Historian. Germany, 1909), 85–86, 88, 260, 264
Mann, Heinrich (Writer. Germany, 1872–1950), 86–88, 262–63, 271, 276, 403
Mann, Klaus (Writer. Germany, 1906–1949), 258, 260, 263–64, 390, 403
Mann, Michael, 264
Mann, Monika, 264
Mann, Thomas (Writer. Germany, 1875–1955), 16, 52, 85–87, 104, 166–67, 218, 258, 261–66, 270, 307, 373, 380, 403
Marcus, Philip, 403
Marcuse, Herbert (Philosopher. Germany, 1898), 320, 332–33, 382, 405
Margo, Boris (Artist. Russia, 1902), 241
Maritain, Jacques (Philosopher. France, 1882), 125, 279, 360–61
Marschak, Jakob (Economist. Russia, 1899), 127, 321–23, 327, 330
Martinu, Bohuslav (Composer. Czecho-

slovakia, 1890–1959), 131, 222, 224–25

Marx, Karl Heinrich, 52

Masaryk, Tomás Garrigue, 37

Masereel, Frans, 278

Massing, Paul (Sociologist. Germany, 1902), 256, 268, 332–34

Masson, André (Painter. France, 1896), 123, 233, 243, 246

Mauchly, James William, 288

Maurois, André (Writer. France, 1885–1967), 97, 123, 256, 266–67; 351 378, 380–81, 403

Mayer, Joseph E., 203–4

Mayer, Maria Goeppert (Physicist. Poland, 1906), 129, 181, 203–4

Mazzini, Giuseppe, 119

McCallum, Ian Robert More, 233, 236, 401

McCloy, John Jay, 131

McDonald, James G., 71, 394

McKinley, William, 19

McNeill, William H., 395

McReynolds, G., 391

Mehlberg, Heynrik, 358

Mehring, Walter (Poet, writer. Germany, 1896), 266, 277, 320

Meinicke, Friedrich, 348–49

Meitner, Lise, 175, 312

Mendelsohn, Erich (Architect. Germany, 1887–1953), 237–38, 275

Mendelssohn, Moses, 342

Menger, Carl, 107, 321

Menger, Karl (Mathematician. Austria, 1902), viii, 107, 288, 294, 358

Menges, Karl (North Asiatic linguist. Germany, 1908), 354

Menkes, Sigmund Josef (Painter. Poland, 1896), 130

Menninger, Charles Frederick, 150

Menninger, Karl Augustus, 145, 150–51, 159, 160, 396, 398

Menninger, William Claire, 150–51, 159, 398

Meyer, Karl (Biochemist. Germany, 1899), 309

Meyer-Baer, Kathi (Musicologist, 1892), 232

Meyerhof, Otto (Biochemist, Germany, 1884–1951), 303, 309–10

Michael, Franz (Sinologist, political scientist. Germany, 1907), 355

Middledorf, Ulrich A. (Art historian. Germany, 1901), 102, 249–50, 380, 382, 406

Mies van der Rohe, Ludwig (Architect. Germany, 1886–1969), 233–36, 238, 240

Milhaud, Darius (Composer. France, 1892), 97, 125, 221–22, 224, 244, 395, 400

Miller, Glenn, 397

Milstein, Nathan (Violinist. Russia, 1904), 129, 226

Minkowski, Rudolph Leo B. (Astronomer. France, 1895), 296, 298

Mintz, Harry (Painter. Poland, 1909), 130

Mira, Giovanni, 393

Mirkine-Guetzévitch, Boris (Professor of law. Russia, 1892–1955), 127

Mirski, Michael (Economist, Slavist. Russia, 1904), 256

Mitrany, David, 135

Mitropoulos, Dimitri (Conductor. Greece, 1896–1960), 135, 220

Modigliani, Franco (Economist. Italy, 1918), 122, 323, 330–31, 405

Moellenhoff, Anna (Psychotherapist. Germany, 1893), 97–98, 495–96

Moellenhoff, Fritz (Psychoanalyst. Germany, 1891), 98–99, 154, 159, 495–96

Moholy-Nagy, László (Painter, designer. Hungary, 1895–1946), 6–7, 112, 115, 238–40, 242, 280

Moholy-Nagy, Sibyl (Historian of architecture from Germany), 7, 115, 239, 390, 401

Molnár, Ferenc (Playwright. Hungary, 1878–1952), 112, 393, 396
Mondrian, Piet (Painter, designer. Holland, 1872–1944), 133, 242, 246–47
Monteux, Pierre (Conductor. France, 1875–1964), 125, 219, 221
Morgan, Thomas Hunt, 314
Morgenstern, Oskar (Economist. Germany, 1902), 321, 326–27
Morgenthau, Hans Joachim (Political scientist. Germany, 1904), 28–29, 338, 341–42, 381, 405
Morgenthau, Irma T., vii 28–29, 280
Morstein Marx, Fritz (Political scientist. Germany, 1900–1969), 343
Moses, Siegfried, 403
Motherwell, Robert, 246–47, 402
Muck, Karl, 216
Mueller, John Henry, 219, 400
Muensterberger, Warner, 167
Muller, Hermann J., 314
Munroe, Ruth L., 397
Murrow, Edward R., 77
Mussolini, Benito, 6, 8–9, 21, 25, 40, 48–51, 118, 121, 184, 186, 218, 255–56
Mustafa Kemal Atatürk, 66, 70, 352

Nabokov, Vladimir (Writer, poet. Russia, 1899), 35, 44, 127, 268–70, 393
Nachmansohn, David (Neurologist. Russia, 1907), 127, 304
Nathan, Hans (Musicologist. Germany, 1910), 229, 230
Nathan, Otto (Economist, Germany, 1893), 257
Natoli, Aurelio (Political figure. Italy, 1888), 119
Natonek, Hans (Writer. Czechoslovakia, 1802–1963), 31, 89, 131, 258, 260, 268, 391–92, 395
Neddermeyer, Seth, 197
Neisser, Hans Philip (Economist. Germany, 1895), 321, 323, 331
Nelson, Benjamin, 398
Nervi, Pier Luigi, 237

Nettl, Paul (Musicologist. Czechoslovakia, 1889), 131, 229
Neugebauer, Otto (Historian of mathematics. Austria, 1899), 286, 292–93, 352, 403
Neumann, Alfred (Writer. Germany, 1895–1952), 262
Neumann, Franz L. (Leopold Franz) (Social scientist. Poland. 1900–1954), 100, 256, 319, 332–3, 336, 338–39, 351, 358, 389, 405
Neumann, Robert (Political scientist. Austria, 1916), 344
Neumann, Sigmund (Political scientist. Germany, 1904–1962), 338, 343
Neumeyer, Alfred (Art historian. Germany, 1901), 250, 253
Neurath, Hans (Biochemist. Austria, 1909), 311
Newman, James R., 286, 403
Neyman, Jerzy (Mathematician. Rumania, 1894), 135, 384
Nicholas I, 295
Niebuhr, H. Richard, 363
Niebur, Reinhold, 362–63
Niebyl, Karl H. (Economist. Czechoslovakia, 1906), 98, 322–23
Noether, Emmy (Mathematician. Germany, ?–1935), 286
Northrop, John Howard, 314
Novick, Aaron, 313
Nunberg, Hermann (Psychoanalyst. Poland, 1884), 157
Nurkse, Ragnar (Economist. Estonia, 1907–1959), 129, 328
Nussbaum, Arthur (Professor of law. Germany, 1877–1964), 345

Obendorf, Clarence P., 397
Ochoa, Severo (Biochemist. Spain 1905), 133, 303, 310, 314
Odložilíc, Otakar (Historian. Czechoslovakia, 1899), 132, 351
Offenkrantz, William C., 397
Oppenheim, Adolf Leo (Assyriologist.

Austria, 1904), 90, 351–52, 356–57, 395, 405

Oppenheim, Lilli, 368, 395

Oppenheimer, J. Robert, 191, 195, 198, 202, 204, 206–8, 210, 213

Ozenfant, Amedée Julien (Painter. France, 1886–1966), 98, 242, 246

Pacciardi, Randolfo (Political leader. Italy, 1899), 118

Pachter, Henry (Historian. Germany, 1907), 318

Palisca, Claude V., 401

Palyi, Melchior (Economist. Hungary, 1892–1970), 72

Panofsky, Dora (Art historian. Germany, ?–1965), 247, 271

Panofsky, Erwin J. (Art historian. Germany, 1892–1968), 73, 78, 247, 249, 251–53, 277, 366, 388, 394, 402

Panofsky, Wolfgang K. H., 366

Parsons, Talcott, 405

Pascal, Blaise, 288

Pasternak, Boris, 279, 329

Pauli, Wolfgang (Physicist. Austria, 1900–1958), 108–9

Pauling, Linus Carl, 314

Pegram, George B., 187

Perrin, Francis Henri (Physicist. France, 1901), 123, 377

Pessl, Yella (Harpsichordist. Austria), 98, 227

Pétain, Henri Philippe, 82, 85, 125

Peterson, Frederick, 139

Peyre, Henri Maurice (Professor of comparative literature. France, 1901), 125, 351, 389, 396

Piatigorsky, Gregor (Cellist. Russia, 1903), 129, 227

Pichler, J. Franz, 114

Pick, Robert (Writer. Austria, 1898), 268, 351

Piers, Gerhart (Psychoanalyst. Austria, 1908), vii, 156, 158, 396–97

Piers, Maria (Psychoanalyst. Austria, 1911), vii, 37, 158, 171, 396–97

Pierson, William Harvey, 402

Pikler, Julius, 58

Pilsudski, Jósef, 40

Pinthus, Kurt (Critic, historian of literature and the theater. Germany, 1886), 276

Pipes, Richard, 43, 393

Pirani, Conrad L. (Pathologist. Italy, 1914), 301, 374, 404

Pitigliani, Fausto R. (Political scientist. Italy, 1904), 317, 404

Pius XII, 404

Placzek, George (Physicist. Czechoslovakia, 1905–1955), 132, 205, 208

Plamenac, Dragan (Musicologist. Yugoslavia, 1895), 134, 229, 232

Plato, 342

Plaut, Richard (Writer. Germany, 1911), 268

Plumb, John Harold, 123, 396

Poebel, Arno (Assyriologist. Germany, 1881–1958), 355–57

Poggioli, Renato (Philologist. Italy, 1907–1963), 116–117

Pol, Heinz (Writer. Germany, 1901), 256

Polanyi, Cecilia, 113

Polanyi, Karl (Social scientist. Austria, 1881–1963), 58, 112–14, 330

Polyani, Michael, 113, 393, 396

Pollock, George H., vii, 396, 398–99

Polya, George (Mathematician. Hungary, 1887), 112, 285, 294

Porada, Edith (Art historian. Austria, 1912), 354

Praeger, Frederick Amos (Book publisher. Austria, 1915), 275–76

Prager, William (Applied mathematician. Germany, 1903), 286, 293

Přibram, Karl (Economist. Czechoslovakia, 1877), 132, 321

Primo de Rivera, Miguel, 40

Pringsheim, Peter (Physicist. Germany, 1881–1963), 89

Proskauer, Eric S. (Book publisher, Germany, 1901), 273–74

Pross, Helge, 346, 390

Purcell, Edward Mills, 178

Pushkin, Alexander, 269

Rabi, Isidor Isaac, 207, 371, 399

Rabinowitch, Eugene (Chemist, biologist. Russia, 1901), 66, 127, 200–201, 205–6, 315, 400

Racker, Efraim (Biochemist. Poland, 1913), 310

Racz, Andre (Painter, engraver. Rumania, 1916), 134

Rademacher, Hans (Mathematician. Germany, 1892–1969), 289

Rado, Sandor (Psychoanalyst. Hungary, 1890), 112, 145, 147, 152–53, 163, 398

Rado, Tibor (Mathematician. Hungary, 1895–1965), 112, 285

Randers, Gunnar (Astronomer. Norway, 1914), 296

Rank, Beata (Psychoanalyst. Poland, 1897–1967), 147

Rank, Otto (Psychoanalyst. Austria, 1884–1939), 144, 154, 157

Rapaport, David (Psychologist. Hungary, 1911–1960), 161

Rappard, professor, 63

Rasetti, Franco (Physicist. Italy, 1901), 121, 313, 371

Rauschning, Hermann (Statesman, writer. Germany, 1887), 256, 272, 377

Ray, Harriet, 396

Reder, Bernard (Sculptor. Rumania, 1897–1963), 134, 244–46

Redl, Fritz (Psychoanalyst. Austria, 1902), 169–71

Redlich, Fritz (Economist. Germany, 1892), 330

Rees, Albert, 405

Reich, Annie (Psychoanalyst. Austria, 1902), 147

Reich, John (Stage director. Austria, 1906), 108

Reich, Wilhelm (Psychoanalyst. Austria, 1897–1957), 147

Reichenbach, Hans (Philosopher of science. Germany, 1891–1953), 358–60

Reif, Frederick, 366

Reik, Theodor (Psychoanalyst. Austria, 1888–1969), 147, 153, 157, 160–61, 164–66, 397–98

Reinhardt, Max (Stage director. Austria, 1873–1943), 108, 262

Remarque, Erich Maria (Writer. Germany, 1898–1970), 53, 266, 270

Rewald, John (Art historian. Germany, 1912), 250

Rheinstein, Max (Professor of law. Germany, 1899), 345–46, 380

Richards, Dickinson W., 306

Richter, Anders, vii

Richter, Werner (Philosopher. Germany, 1888–1960), 102

Riesman, David, 86, 168

Riess, Curt (Writer. Germany, 1902), 257

Rilke, Rainer Maria, 294

Rittenberg, David, 310

Robbins, Herbert Ellis, 292

Roberts, Kenneth, 23–24, 48, 391

Rockfeller, Nelson Aldrich, 115

Róheim, Géza (Psychoanalyst. Hungary, 1891–1953), 112, 115, 161, 167

Rohrlich, George F. (Social scientist. Austria, 1914), 318–20, 404

Rolo, Charles J., 399

Romains, Jules (Writer. France, 1885), 123, 256, 266, 380

Rommen, Heinrich A. (Political scientist. Germany, 1897), 343

Roosevelt, Anna Eleanor, 87, 92

Roosevelt, Franklin Delano, 27–28, 30,

87, 92, 120, 125, 184, 188, 199–201, 262, 266

Roosevelt, Theodore, 21

Rosen, Eunice, 400

Rosenberg, Alfred, 44

Rosenberg, Hans (Astronomer. Germany, 1879–1940), 296

Rosenberg, Jakob (Art curator. Germany, 1893), 250

Rosenstock-Huessy, Eugen (Philosopher. Germany, 1888), 102

Rosenthal, Franz (Arabist, Semitist. Germany, 1914), 354

Ross, Helen, 396–97

Rosselli, Carlo, 48, 118

Rosselli, Nello, 48

Rossi, Bruno (Physicist. Italy, 1905), 121, 195, 197, 371, 381

Rossi, Peter H., 405

Rothfels, Hans (Historian. Germany, 1891), 102, 347, 349, 380

Rothman, Stephen (Dermatologist. Hungary, 1894–1963), 113, 304–5, 374, 404

Roucek, Joseph S., 391, 405

Rubinstein, Artur (Pianist. Poland, 1889), 226

Rubinstein, Boris B., 171

Ruitenbek, Hendrik M., 399

Ruml, Beardsley, 76

Rust, Bernard, 51–52

Rutherford, Ernest, 63, 177

Rutter, Owen, 393

Sacco, Nicola, 30

Sachs, Alexander, 184

Sachs, Curt (Musicologist. Germany, 1881–1959), 229–32

Sachs, Hanns (Psychoanalyst. Austria, 1881–1947), 106, 153–55, 157, 161–62, 398

Sachs, Robert G., 180, 399

Šafránek, Miloš, 401

Sahl, Hans (Writer. Germany, 1902), 92, 102, 258, 395

Salazar, Antonio de Olivera, 40

Salerno, Luigi, 252

Salmony, Alfred (Art historian. Germany, 1892–1958), 248, 250, 252

Salomon, Albert (Sociologist. Germany, 1891–1966), 335

Salvadori, Mario Giorgio (Professor of engineering. Italy, 1907), 122

Salvatorelli, Luigi, 393

Salvemini, Gaetano (Historian. Italy, 1873–1957), 117–19, 120, 255, 349–50, 396

Sandage, Allan R., 297

Sanford, Nevitt, 333

Sarnoff, David, 9

Schabert, Kyril, 277

Schardt, Alois, 402

Scharl, Josef (Artist. Germany, 1896–1954), 278

Schein, Hilde, 65, 130

Schein, Marcel (Physicist. Czechoslovakia, 1902–1960), 65, 113, 130

Schick, George (Conductor. Czechoslovakia, 1908), 131

Schiffrin, Alexander (Max Werner) (Writer. Russia, 1901–1953), 127

Schiffrin, Jacques (Book publisher. Russia, ?–1950), 127, 277–78

Schilder, Paul, 144

Schilt, Jan, 295

Schindler, Rudolf (Gastroenterologist. Germany, 1888–1968), 306

Schlatter, Richard, 358

Schlick, Moritz, 359

Schmidt, Erich Friedrich, 352

Schnabel, Artur (Pianist. Austria, 1882–1951), 107, 226, 392, 401

Schneck, Jerome M., 397

Schneider, Joseph Z. (Economist. Czechoslovakia, 1897), 132, 324

Schocken, Salman, 275

Schocken, Theodore (Book publisher. Germany, 1914), 275

Schoenberg, Arnold (Composer. Austria, 1874–1951), 107, 222–23, 262

Schoenberger, Guido (Art historian. Germany, 1891), 248
Schoenberner, Franz (Writer. Germany, 1892–1970), 258, 268, 392
Schoenheimer, Rudolf (Biochemist. Germany, 1898–1941), 7, 310, 404
Schrade, Leo (Musicologist. Germany, 1903), 229, 231–32
Schroedinger, Erwin, 312
Schueller, Richard (Economist, Czechoslovakia, 1870), 322–23
Schultz, H. Stefan (Germanist. Germany, 1905), 102
Schulze, Oskar, 69–70
Schulze, Suzanne (Social scientist. Germany, 1898), 69–70, 170, 394
Schumpeter, Joseph Alois (Economist. Czechoslovakia. 1883–1950), 107, 130, 132, 321–22, 324–25
Schurz, Carl, 4
Schuster, Alexander (Cellist. Russia, 1888), 129
Schuyler, Garrett L., 183
Schwartz, Philipp (Pathologist. Hungary, 1894), viii, 62, 66, 69–70, 394
Schwarzschild, Karl, 297
Schwarzschild, Martin (Astronomer. Germany, 1912), 297–98
Scitovsky, Tibor (Economist. Hungary, 1910), 112, 322, 328
Seaborg, Glenn T., 204
Seitz, Frederick, 29
Segrè Emilio (Physicist. Italy, 1905), 121, 186, 191, 195, 203, 311, 370–71, 381
Seligman, Ben B., 405
Seligman, Edwin R. A., 74, 398
Seligmann, Kurt (Painter. Switzerland, 1900–1962), 134, 243, 246, 279
Selz, Jean, 402
Serkin, Irene Busch, 226
Serkin, Rudolf (Pianist. Czechoslovakia, 1903), 131, 226
Sert, José Luis (Architect. Spain, 1902), 98, 134, 240

Sforza, Count Carlo (Statesman. Italy, 1873–1952), 49, 118–20, 255, 377, 393, 396
Shackle, George Lennox Sharman, 322, 325, 405
Shalloo, Jeremiah Patrick, 25, 391
Shapley, Harlow, 78
Shils, Edward A., 331, 394, 405
Shirer, William Lawrence, 393
Siegel, Carl Ludwig (Mathematician. Germany, 1896), 289
Sierpiński, Waclaw, 284
Sigerist, Henry Ernest (Historian of medicine. France, 1891–1957), 352
Sikorsky, Igor I., 126
Simmel, Ernst (Psychoanalyst. Germany, 1882–1947), 147, 153, 158–59
Simmel, Georg, 335
Simon, Yves (Philosopher. France, 1903–1961), 125, 360, 362
Simons, Hans (Political scientist. Germany, 1893), 281, 340
Simpson, Esther, 63–64
Sinclair, Upton, 52
Singer, Kurt (Writer. Austria, 1911), 257
Smith, Alfred Emanuel, 27
Smith, Alice Kimball, viii, 58, 199, 394, 408
Smith, Bradford, 114
Smith, Cyril Stanley, 196, 406
Smith, Captain John, 114
Smith, Lloyd P., 179
Smyth, Henry De Wolf, 196, 399
Sohn, Louis (Professor of law. Poland, 1914), 130–31
Sokolsky, Wallace, 350
Sorell, Walter, 258, 402
Speier, Hans (Sociologist. Germany, 1905), 318–19, 405
Spinoza, Benedictus de, 342
Spitz, René Arpad (Psychoanalyst. Austria, 1887), 152, 171

Spitzer, Leo (Philologist. Austria, 1887–1960), 352

Stalin, Joseph Vissarionovich, 39–40, 44, 46, 126, 329

Stanley, Wendell Meredith, 314

Staub, Hans (Physicist. Switzerland, 1908), 134, 195

Staudinger, Else, 368

Staudinger, Hans (Economist. Germany, 1889), vii, 322–23

Stechow, Wolfgang (Art historian. Germany, 1896), 251

Steinberg, Saul (Cartoonist. Rumania, 1914), 134–35

Steinberg, William (Conductor. Germany, 1899), 220, 224

Steiner-Prag, Hugo (Book designer and illustrator, educator. Czechoslovakia, 1880–1945), 131

Steinhaus, Hugo, 284

Stent, Gunther S., 366, 404

Sterba, Editha (Psychoanalyst. Hungary, 1897), 159, 166, 279

Sterba, Richard (Psychoanalyst. Austria. 1896), 159, 166, 279

Stern, Curt (Geneticist. Germany, 1902), 364

Stern, Otto (Physicist. Germany, 1888–1969), 364

Sternberg, Fritz (Writer. Germany, 1895–1963), 256

Sternfeld, Wilhelm, 390

Stevens, Halsey, 222, 390, 400

Stimson, Henry L., 202

Stoker, James J., 291

Stolper, Gustav (Economist. Austria, 1888–1947), 257

Stourzh, Gerhard, 347

Stowkowski, Leopold, 108

Strand, K. Aa. (Astronomer. Denmark, 1907), 134, 296

Strassmann, Fritz, 175

Straus, Erwin Walter (Psychiatrist. Germany, 1891), 98–99

Strauss, Leo (Political scientist. Germany, 1899), 275, 338, 342, 374, 415

Strauss, Lewis L., 182–84, 212, 399

Stravinsky, Igor (Composer. Russia, 1882), 127, 221–23, 401

Striker, Laura Polanyi (Historian. Hungary, 1882–1959), 114

Stromgren, Bengt Georg Daniel, 182, 296

Struve, Friedrich Georg Wilhelm, 295

Struve, Otto, 295–96, 299

Stücklen, Hildegard (Physicist. Germany, 1891–1963), 96

Sturzo, Luigi (Catholic priest, political leader. Italy, 1871–1959), 49, 118, 396

Stutzman, Frances, vii

Suffels, Jacques, 403

Sumner, James, 314

Swarzenski, George (Art historian. Germany, 1876–1957), 251

Swarzenski, Hanns (Art historian. Germany, 1903), 249, 251

Swing, Raymond Gram, 85

Swings, Pol (Astrophysicist. Belgium, 1906), 296, 298

Szasz, Otto (Mathematician. Hungary, 1884–1952), 112, 285

Szegö, Gabor (Mathematician. Hungary, 1895), 112, 285

Szekely, D. K., 54–55

Szell, George (Conductor. Hungary, 1897–1970), 131, 219–20, 225

Szelpal, Arpad, 394

Szent-Györgyi, Albert, 57

Szigeti, Joseph (Violinist. Hungary, 1892), 58, 112, 226, 320, 392, 401 405

Szilard, Leo (Physicist. Hungary, 1898–1964), 58, 63–64, 66, 111, 115, 175, 182–85, 189–90, 192–93, 195, 198, 200–201, 205, 313–14, 370–71, 394

Szyk, Arthur (Cartoonist. Poland, 1894–1951), 130

Tagliacozzo, Giorgio (Economist. Italy, 1909), 320, 323

Tamarkin, Jacob David, 292–93

Tanguy, Yves (Painter. France, 1900–1955), 125, 243, 246

Taper, Bernard, 223, 401

Tarchiani, Alberto (Political figure, journalist. Italy, 1885–1964), 49, 118, 377

Tarski, Alfred (Mathematician. Poland, 1902), 130, 285, 289–90, 358

Tatum, Edward L., 314

Taylor, Joshua C., 401

Tedesco, Paul M. (Philologist, Orientalist. Austria, 1898), 354

Teller, Edward (Physicist. Hungary, 1908), 53–54, 66, 111, 115, 176, 179–83, 185, 191, 195, 197, 204–12, 214, 299, 367, 371, 399–400

Teller, Mici (Augusta Maria), 367

Thirlwall, John Connop, 403

Thomas, Dylan, 223

Thomas, William I., 336

Thompson, Dorothy, 85

Thompson, John G., 403

Thompson, Manley H., Jr., 359, 406

Tiedmann, Eva, 390

Tillich, Paul (Theologian. Germany, 1886–1965), 16, 101, 254, 262, 281, 307, 361–63, 389, 395

Timasheff, Nicholas S. (Sociologist. Russia, 1886–1970), 335

Tintner, Gerhard (Econometrician. Germany, 1907), 320–21, 326

Tischler, Hans (Musicologist. Austria, 1915), 107, 229

Toch, Ernst (Composer. Austria, 1887–1964), 107, 222, 224, 262

Toller, Ernst (Writer. Germany, 1893–1939), 7, 277

Tomasic, Dinko Anthony (Sociologist. Yugoslovia, 1902), 134, 335

Tomkins, Calvin, 402

Toscanini, Arturo (Conductor. Italy, 1867–1957), 8–9, 83, 117, 120, 217–18, 390, 400

Trapp, Maria Augusta (Singer, writer. Austria, 1905), 391

Trilling, Lionel, 166, 399

Trotsky, Lev Davidovich, 43

Truman, Harry S., 200, 209

Tschebatarioff, Gregory P. (Professor of civil engineering. Russia, 1899), 393

Tucci, Niccolò (Writer. Italy, 1908), 255, 268

Tuve, Merle A., 181, 399

Uhlenbeck, George Eugene, 186

Ulam, Stanislaw Marcin (Mathematician. Poland, 1909), vii, 29–30, 39, 130, 195, 209–10, 284–87, 289–90, 294–95, 400, 403

Ullstein, Hermann (Book publisher, writer. Germany, 1875–1943), 258, 392

Undset, Sigrid (Writer. Denmark, 1882–1949), 264–65, 380

Ungar, Frederick (Book publisher. Austria, 1898), 273

Urey, Harold C., 185–86, 310

Vajna, George (Book publisher. Hungary, 1889–1968), 272–73

Vajna, Ladislas, 273

Valtin, Jan (Writer. Germany, 1905–1951), 257, 270, 272

van de Kamp, Peter, 295

Vanzetti, Bartolomeo, 30

Veblen, Oswald, 287

Venturi, Lionello (Art historian. Italy, 1885–1961), 252, 379

Victor, Emmanuel III, 40

Viertel, Berthold (Writer. Austria, 1895–1953), 271

Voegelin, Eric (Political scientist. Germany, 1901), 342–43

von Böhm-Bawerk, Eugen, 107

von den Steinen, Diether (Far Eastern expert. Germany, 1903), 355

von Faber du Faur, Curt (Germanicist, book collector. Germany, 1890–1966), 277

von Grunebaum, Gustav (Islamist, Arabist. Austria, 1909), 351, 356–57

von Hildebrand, Dietrich (Philosopher. Italy, 1889), 361

von Humboldt, Alexander, 375

von Humboldt, Karl Wilhelm, 37, 375

von Karman, Theodore (Aeronautical engineer. Hungary, 1881–1963), 47, 111, 115, 211, 371

von Mises, Ludwig (Economist. Austria, 1881), 107, 294, 321, 324–25

von Mises, Richard (Mathematician. Austria, 1883–1953), 293, 358

Von Neumann, John (Mathematician. Hungary, 1903–1957), 9–10, 39, 47, 54, 83, 111, 115, 121, 182, 195–97, 204, 207–13, 285, 286–89, 294, 326–27, 370–71

von Ossietzky, Karl, 281

von Papen, Franz, 344

von Simson, Otto (Art historian. Germany, 1912), 102, 250, 252, 279, 380

von Stutterheim, Kurt, 392

von Suttner, Bertha, 52

von Unruh, Fritz (Poet, writer. Germany, 1885), 266, 277, 281, 380

Vyssotsky, Alexander N., 295

Wach, Joachim (Historian of religion. Germany, 1898–1955), 351

Waelder, Robert (Psychoanalyst. Austria, 1900–1967), 106, 157, 161, 164, 397

Waelder-Hall, Jenny (Psychoanalyst. Austria, 1898), 171

Wagner, Martin (Architect. Germany, 1885–1957), 240

Wahl, Jean (Philosopher. France, 1888), 90, 395

Wald, Abraham (Statistician. Rumania, 1902–1950), 135, 294, 326

Waldinger, Ernst (Poet, writer. Austria, 1896), 268, 271

Walter, Bruno (Conductor. Germany, 1876–1962), 218, 262, 392, 400

Walther, Arnold (Assyriologist. Germany, 1880–1938), 355

Wangh, Martin (Psychoanalyst. Germany, 1911), 397

Warburg, Bettina, 148, 398

Warton, Henry, 114

Wasow, Wolfgang (Mathematician. Switzerland, 1909), 292

Watson, James Dewey, 313, 404

Weber, Max, 335

Wechsberg, Joseph (Writer. Czechoslovakia, 1907), 268, 320

Weigert, Edith V. (Psychoanalyst. Germany, 1894), 147, 158

Weigert, Hans W. (Jurist. Germany, 1902), 256

Weigl, Karl (Composer. Austria, 1881–1949), 108, 222

Weil, André (Mathematician. France, 1906), 289

Weil, Felix (Social scientist. Argentina, 1898), 332

Weill, Joseph, 89–90, 395

Weill, Kurt (Composer. Germany, 1900–1950), 225

Weinberger, Martin (Art historian. Germany, 1893–1965), 248

Weiner, Alice, 391

Weinryb, Bernard (Economist, historian. Poland, 1901), 130

Weiskopf, Franz Carl (Writer. Czechoslovakia, 1900–1955), 131, 271, 403

Weiss, Edoardo (Psychoanalyst. Italy, 1889), 158, 366

Weiss, Guido, 366

Weiss, Paul Alfred (Biologist. Austria, 1898), 109, 380

Weiss, Samuel B., 404

Weisskopf, Victor Frederick (Physicist.

Austria, 1908), 176, 179–80, 195, 197, 205–6, 208, 381

Weitzmann, Kurt (Archeologist, art historian. Germany, 1904), 249, 253, 353

Welleck, Albert, 364

Welleck, René (Historian of literary criticism. Austria, 1903), 131–32

Welles, Bella Fromm (Writer. Germany, 1900), 268

Welles, Sumner, 125

Wentzel, Anne, vii

Wentzel, Gregor, 392

Werfel, Alma Mahler Gropius, 88, 218

Werfel, Franz (Writer. Czechoslovakia, 1890–1945), 86–88, 131, 218, 262, 265, 270, 276, 281, 373

Werner, Alfred (Writer, literary critic. Austria, 1911), 260, 268, 402

Werner, Eric (Musicologist. Austria, 1901), 229, 231

Wertheimer, Max (Psychologist. Germany, 1880–1943), 345, 372

Weybright, Victor, 279

Weyl, Hermann (Mathematician. Germany, 1885–1955), 286–89

Wheeler, John Archibald, 185

White, Eric Walter, 401

White, Lyman Cromwell, 394

Whitehead, Alfred North, 365

Whitman, Walt, 224

Whittick, Arnold, 401

Wight, Frederick S., 402

Wigner, Eugene Paul (Physicist. Hungary, 1902), vii, 9–10, 29, 53–54, 64, 111, 115, 176–77, 179, 183–85, 190, 192–93, 195, 198, 203–4, 211, 370–72, 381, 399, 406

Wildt, Rupert (Astronomer. Germany, 1905), 297

Willibrand, William Anthony, 390

Wilson, John A., 406

Wilson, Woodrow, 21, 267

Windholz, Emanuel (Psychoanalyst. Czechoslovakia, 1903), 132, 159

Wineman, David, 169

Winslow, Charles Edward Amory, 398

Winternitz, Emanuel (Musicologist. Austria, 1898), 108, 231–32, 345, 401

Wintner, Aurel (Mathematician. Austria, 1903–1958), 289

Wittels, Fritz, 144

Wittfogel, Karl (Sinologist, social scientist. Germany, 1896), 332–33, 342, 348, 353–54

Wittgenstein, Ludwig, 357

Wittke, Carl, 390, 400

Wittlin, Jósef (Writer. Poland, 1896), 130

Wolf, František (Mathematician. Czechoslovakia, 1904), 132

Wolfers, Arnold (Political scientist. Switzerland, 1892), 134, 340

Wolff, Helen, 277, 279, 403

Wolff, Kurt (Book publisher. Germany, 1889–1963), 276–79, 403

Wolff, Kurt H. (Sociologist. Germany, 1912), 335

Wolpe, Stefan (Composer. Germany, 1902), 98

Woodward, L. E., 398

Woytinsky, Wladimir S. (Economist. Russia, 1885–1960), 127, 321, 393

Wright, Frank Lloyd, 234, 237

Wundheiler, Alexander (Mathematician. Poland, 1902–1957), 285

Yakobson, Sergius (Slavist. Russia, 1901), 127

Yang, Chen Ning, 372

Zachariasen, William (Physicist. Norway, 1906), 60, 134

Zadkine, Ossip (Sculptor. Russia, 1890), 98, 127, 244

Zariski, Oscar, 126

Zehrfuss, Bernard, 237

Zeisel, Eva (Art designer. Hungary, 1906), 114

Zeisel, Hans (Social scientist. Czechoslovakia, 1905), 132, 345

Zerbe, Karl (Painter. Germany, 1903), 244, 246

Zilborg, Gregory, 397

Zinoviev, Grigory Eseevich, 43

Zita, 36

Znaniecki, Florian Witold (Sociologist. Poland, 1882–1958), 336, 405

Zuckmayer, Carl (Writer. Germany, 1896), 277

Zweig, Stefan (Writer. Austria, 1881–1942), 7, 36, 39, 41, 53, 108, 257, 266, 270, 373, 392

Zworykin, Vladimir Kosma, 126, 311

Zygmund, Antoni (Mathematician. Poland, 1900), 39, 130, 284–85, 297, 403